ward

Town

With every good wish!

John Roden

13/7/99

John Roden was an engineer with the English Electric Company Ltd., Bradford, before training as a teacher at St. John's College, York. He taught at York Minster Song School and York College of Further Education before spending four years as a teacher of African history and as Head of Religious Education at Sefula Secondary School in Western Zambia. During his time there he was the chief English collaborator for the English-Lozi Dictionary. On his return from Africa he trained for the Anglican Ministry at Ripon Hall, Oxford. He has served as a curate in Saltburn-by-the-Sea, as Senior Chaplain at St. Peter's School, York, Head of Religious Education at Batley Boys' Grammar School, and as a Diocesan Youth Officer. The author is currently the Senior Chaplain of the Selby Coalfield Industrial Chaplaincy and part-time priest-in-charge of a small parish near York. He is married, with two children.

South African Church Railway Mission.

OCTOBER, 1905.

THANKSGIVINGS AND INTERCESSIONS.

Thanksgiving is offered—

For the opening of the great bridge across the Zambesi, and all that it stands for in the extension of the Kingdom of Christ in Central Africa.

For the rapid development of the work among the women and girls, and for the removal of some of the Nursing difficulties.

That our prayers for more workers have again been answered in the Rev. H. A. Lewis's offer of himself for the work.

Prayer is asked—

That a priest may respond to the call of the Rhodesia Railways.

That a lady may offer herself for work among the women and girls.

For the Rev. Douglas Ellison, that his enforced rest may be blessed to his recovery.

For Mr. Hale in his lonely and arduous work in Rhodesia.

Northward from Cape Town

THE ANGLICAN CHURCH RAILWAY MISSION IN SOUTHERN AFRICA 1885 - 1980

John Roden

Senior Chaplain, Selby Coalfield Industrial Chaplaincy
Priest-in-charge, Appleton Roebuck with Acaster Selby, York

Foreword by the Archbishop of York

Sacram Publishing

SEMPER ALIQUID NOVI EX AFRICA

First published in 1999
by Sacram Publishing
The Vicarage, Main Street,
Appleton Roebuck
York, Y023 7DG

Cover image: Colour options, Technology House, 47-49 Lawrence Street, York, YO10 3BU

British Library Cataloguing-in-Publication Data
A catalogue record for this book is available from the British Library

ISBN 0 9535775 0 3

Printed by Quacks the Printers,
Jackson House, 7 Grape Lane, Petergate, York YO1 2HU

Contents

To the late Emily Procter with thanks and love

and to all who served on the Anglican Railway Mission
in the countries of southern Africa

Foreword

by Dr David Hope, Archbishop of York

Fifty or more years ago, 'Geography' for a small boy at school was still very much the 'story of Empire' - in which Africa still had about it all the mystery of the 'dark continent', scarce fully explored. Though the schoolroom maps were fairly sketchy, somehow the snaking lines of the railways still managed to convey a feeling of the unstoppable march of discovery and progress.

All that sense of adventure and excitement is rekindled for me in the story of the Church's mission to those who pioneered that great surge forward. It captures the heady elation of those early days when progress was measured, not in miles, but in degrees of latitude; and when the sheer scale of the enterprise drew in thousands upon thousands of native and immigrant workers. It was to those workers - and to their isolated and lonely families - that, in the 1880s, the South African Church Railway Mission set itself "To minister along the railway lines to people of any creed or colour living far from any place of worship."

It was a ministry which, it has to be said, involved not only ordained clergymen but also some quite formidable 'women workers', such as the legendary Maude (Aggie) Agg-Large and the frankly amazing Mary Attlee. It was a ministry which demanded the most enormous effort and dedication - so much so, that virtually every missionary returned home completely exhausted by the end of their 3 year contract.

With his great interest in railways, his experience in Africa and with his early training as an engineer, John Roden is exceptionally well placed to tell this epic story. It is a story of courage, devotion and good humour which is all the more immediate through its being told very largely in the words of the missionaries themselves.

Towards the end of its 90 years of existence - with the great days of construction long gone, the maintenance staff dramatically reduced and with much of the Mission's work being absorbed by the dioceses - it became clear that SACRM had had its day. But what a day it had been! And what a story it has made!

+ David Ebor:

List of Plates

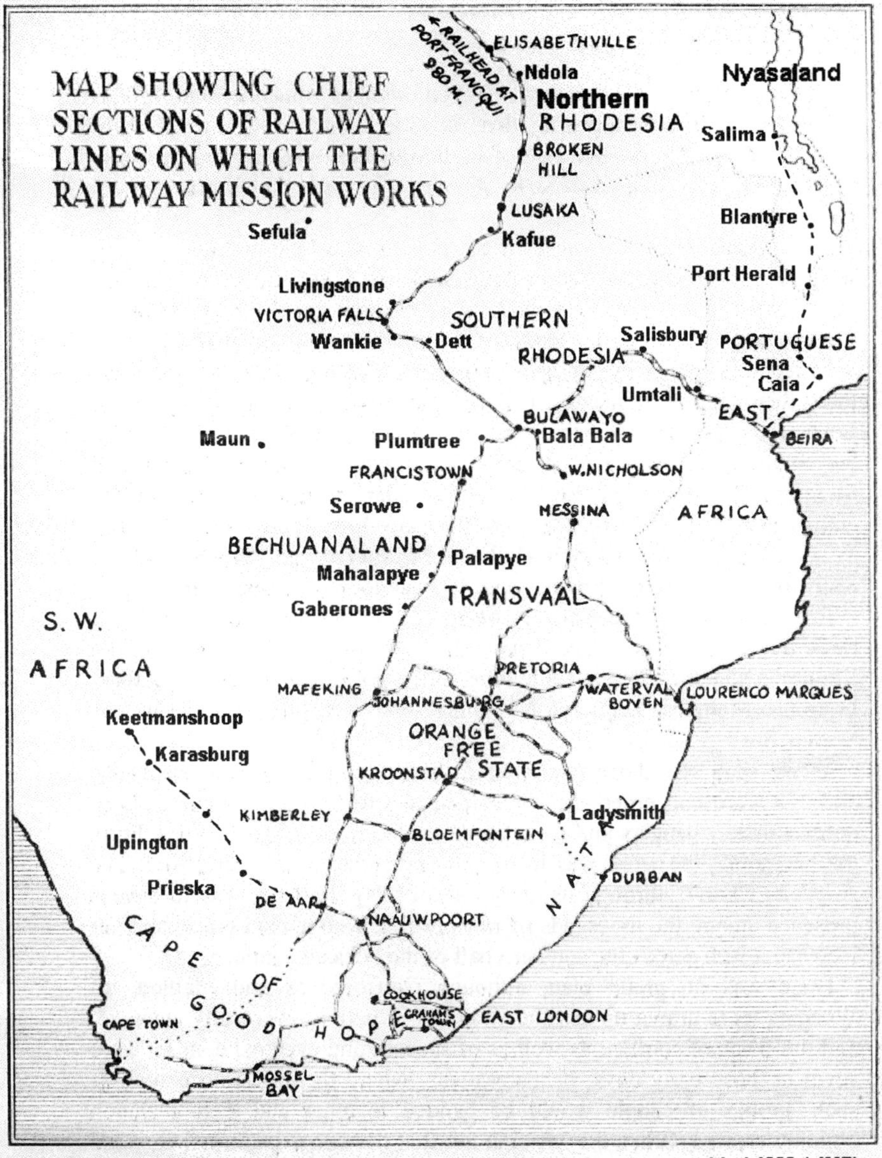

(From 'God's Highwaymen', 1938 edition) **(Names in lower case added 1999 / JMR)**

The scale of this map is about 200 miles to the inch

Preface

The very idea of a Railway Mission sounds romantic and full of adventure. It is not surprising that the South African Church Railway Mission (SACRM) entitled one of its information leaflets, *The Romance of Train Travel in Southern Africa,* and its first book, *God's Highwaymen.*

I am fascinated by Railways, by the people who built and ran them, as well as by the engines and rolling stock used and the signalling and maintenance that make them work. It is intriguing to look at nineteenth century maps of central and southern Africa and be able to work out when the map was drawn by noting where the various railways had reached, their then current railheads. I lived and worked for a few years in Barotseland (Western Zambia) which, although devoid of railway lines, had supplied thousands of African (Lozi) workers for the railways of Southern Rhodesia. My love of Africa and African history and my enthusiasm for Missions stem from that period. My first occupation was as an engineer. The Church Railway Mission brings together Africa, Railways, Missions and Engineering, so I cannot but be enthusiastic!

The 'highway' of the Railway Mission was the hundreds of miles of track that ran up from Cape Town, through much of South Africa, into Rhodesia and the Congo, with other lines going eastwards to Durban, Lourenco Marques, Beira and Nyasaland, and westwards to Luderitz and Walvis Bay.

As we shall see, those who started the Railway Mission in the 1880s and 90s were concerned that something had to be done for the isolated people, mainly gangers and their families, who lived along the lines. From the beginning, the work was to be pastoral rather than evangelistic. The Anglican Church, through its clergy and its lay workers, was to have a presence among the thousands of railway folk who spread out in an ever increasing web across the southern half of the African continent.

There was no grand plan, although Constitutions and Methods of Working were drawn up as time went on. A pattern eventually emerged, and the seeds of conflict, as well as of success and eventual demise, were sown in those early days. In many areas, where there was no church as such, groups of people would be banded together and then a church building erected. When the Mission felt that the congregation could stand alone it would ask the particular diocese to incorporate it into its normal parochial/diocesan structure. Sometimes the bishop had insufficient clergy to do this, or the place was just too isolated. The Railway Missioners thus became the equivalent of mendicant friars and 'hedge priests'.

The work of the missioners, as they moved along hundreds of miles in any one week, brought them up against racial prejudice. It also made them painfully aware of the need for pastoral care of the indigenous population, particularly those who were employed by the Railways.

Robert Selby Taylor, former Archbishop of Cape Town, in his Preface to *Mission Unaccomplished,* wrote,

> The Provinces of South and Central Africa owe a great debt to the Railway Mission. For 85 years [95] the priests and lay workers of the Mission travelled on foot, or bicycle, or sometimes more luxuriously in a Railway caboose along the line of rail, ministering to isolated individuals or tiny congregations. Thanks to this faithful ministry, many individuals had their faith in God strengthened and tiny congregations are now flourishing parishes.

The Railway Mission played an important and sometimes central part in the formative years of the Anglican Church in the countries in which it served. No history of southern and central Africa between 1890 and 1980 can afford to ignore SACRM's pioneering role, or the reflections of the men and women as they moved up with the construction trains laying the new railways, or their dealings with Railway and Church officials, or their observations of the inhuman way that some Whites treated the Africans.

Yet, the work and the role of this Mission has been largely ignored. Hinchliff, in his invaluable *The Anglican Church in South Africa* has two pages on what he refers to as an 'experiment', and Lewis and Edwards make some references in their *Historical Records of the CPSA.* Apart from extremely brief comments in a handful of other historical accounts, that is almost, but not quite, the limit of generally accessible knowledge. Two books have been written about the Railway Mission, *God's Highwaymen,* written by the sister of the founder and published in 1930, and *Mission Unaccomplished,* 'concocted' (to quote its author, Tony Grain) in 1985. The first has been unavailable in most libraries for over fifty years, and the second was privately printed and mainly distributed to former missioners and supporters. The sole academic appearance of any of SACRM's history is in Pirie's articles, chiefly his 'Railway ganging in southern Africa' (1993), where he dips into the 'treasure trove' of the 'Blue Quarterly' magazines. The present book, based on my doctoral thesis (1995), will, I hope, correct what I see as an injustice, and bring to light before it is too late the written and spoken and visual records of the men and women who served with the South African Church Railway Mission over its ninety-five years.

This has been an urgent task. Some of the former missioners interviewed by Grain in 1985 have since died. My main informant, Michael Fidgin, died shortly before I completed the initial MA thesis. At least six others have died during the writing of this book. Those still living, numbered under fifteen, are mainly in their seventies, eighties or nineties. It has been essential to collect the written or oral memories of all those still able to give these, both as primary material for this work and for preservation in archives for future students and historians. The letters, documents, reports, photographs and films given by the former chaplains and women workers have added to the available knowledge and form a marvellous record of the Railway Mission.

When the 'Railway Mission of Rhodesia and Botswana' ended in 1980 its records and archives, other than those held by individuals or already deposited within southern Africa, were handed for safe keeping to the USPG in London. That Society, in turn, eventually passed these over to the Rhodes House Library, Oxford, though I suspect that some documents remain 'lost' and unlabelled in a back room in USPG's current headquarters. Along with the Committee Minutes and Accounts and boxes of letters in Rhodes House Library, also are the bound volumes of the Railway Mission's *Quarterly*. Between 1904 and 1964 over two hundred magazines were issued and, along with the magazines published earlier by the Grahamstown Diocesan Railway Mission and those articles printed between 1965 and 1980 in *Partners,* these form the major primary printed source of information.

In 1993, accompanied by my family, I spent five weeks in southern Africa researching and collecting material for this work. The journey proved traumatic and heartbreaking (in Zambia), rewarding and exciting (in Zimbabwe), and fascinating, challenging and unnerving (in a South Africa approaching its first democratic elections). The archives in the Anglican Cathedral in Bulawayo and in the city's Railway Museum yielded invaluable information on the Mission's work in the former Southern Rhodesia. The extremely well-catalogued and preserved collection in the Railway Museum was, unfortunately, extremely difficult to access, and one would wish that the bulk of the material (including Registers) be preserved in the archives of the Anglican Church or in the National Archives in Harare.

Plumtree School has an interesting collection of letters and documents relating to the School's founding by the Railway Mission. Grahamstown, as befits the city which gave birth to this particular itinerant work, houses in its Cory Library a fascinating collection of correspondence and Minutes of the early decades of the Railway Mission's life. Visiting Johannesburg not only gave me the opportunity of obtaining considerable material from the CPSA archives in WITS Library, but of meeting Gordon Pirie, whose work on transport and mission geography is essential for anyone writing about any aspect of southern African railway history.

One main aim of the visit was to travel on the railway lines that the missioners had been on and to see the various small stations and sidings that they visited. Eighty hours and over 3000 miles of rail travel - from Victoria Falls to Bulawayo and Plumtree and on to Johannesburg, to Port Elizabeth and then Cape Town back to Johannesburg - sounds like a lengthy journey. Yet it pales into insignificance in comparison with the Railway Mission workers and their travels. However, it did give a real picture of the vast distances, the isolation of small stations, the importance, even today, of the rail network. The scenes, so vividly described by the missioners in the pages of the 'Blue Quarterly', are in many cases little changed and came vividly to life.

No amount of reading could replace seeing and experiencing the Mission's own chapel in the Victoria Falls Hotel, or walking over the Falls bridge, carefully chronicled by Herbert Hale ninety years previously as it was being constructed, or wandering through the preserved Railway Mission coach in Bulawayo Railway Museum, or walking along the track at Grahamstown station just one hundred years after Simeon had handed over his work there to Ellison. The twenty-five hours on the 'Trans-Karoo' was much as all the missioners described their first train journey in southern Africa, save that we were hauled by electric traction rather than the recently discarded Beyer-Garratts. Such steam as is still in operation was passed during the night, and the family forbade me to climb down from the bunk and open the blinds!

Phimister (like Pirie, one of the essential writers on the railway history of southern Africa), in his 'Essay Review' on the history of Zimbabwe's railways, wrote that 'the most striking characteristic of the few general railway histories which have been published is precisely what they leave out ... vast regions of labour history are completely lost to scholarly view.' I am aware that much has been left out of this work. A complete study of the collection of SACRM's *Light for the Line* magazines, only available in archives in South Africa, or the discovery of the 'lost' London Committee Minutes of the period from 1908 to 1938 are but two examples of areas which would furnish different information. But I do believe that the basic story of this Anglican Railway Mission has been revealed through the sources as outlined above. I have attempted, wherever possible, to let the witnesses tell their own story. It was particularly gratifying to meet one of the few African priests who worked on the Mission and to have his 'memoirs', along with those of some of his Zimbabwean colleagues. Similarly, to meet and record former employees of the Rhodesia Railways, and to meet and correspond with a few people whose families had been ministered to by SACRM, was not only a bonus, but went some way to give a balanced account of the influence and work of this unique Mission.

Acknowledgements

I wish to thank the Gilchrist Educational Trust, the Lady Elizabeth Hastings' Non-Educational Charity and the Tranquility House Trust for help in financing my field-trip to southern Africa in 1993, and the West Riding Charitable Society and York Diocese for help towards University fees during the research.

My initial interest in Africa comes from my late brother, Bill, and in mission history from time spent in the company of the Rev. Etienne Berger and his colleagues in the former Paris Missionary Society, along with my fellow teachers at Sefula Secondary School, Mongu, Zambia.

I have been fortunate in having York University and its Centre for Southern African Studies almost on my doorstep. I am especially indebted to Landeg White, the Director of the Centre and my supervisor, for all his insights and suggestions. My appreciation is coupled with sadness, for the submission of the D.Phil thesis coincided with the regrettable closing of the Centre for Southern African Studies.

Many former Railway Missioners, here and overseas, have given me invaluable help, with letters or photographs or by agreeing to be interviewed. I thank Harold Crane, Basil French, Richard Holderness, Richard Hughes, John Mhlabi, Hugh Palmer, Willie Sigeca, Stephen Skemp, Sister Mary Stella CSP, with the late Dennis Charlton, Leslie Millins and Constance Piers, and the relatives of Maude Agg-Large. In particular I appreciate the considerable help given by Stephen Easter and Earle Hawkes, and the late Michael Fidgin, Peter Garnett, Monica James and Fred Naylor. I am deeply indebted to Lavinia Fidgin for giving me all the archive material, including the SACRM films, that had belonged to her husband, and for her warm hospitality.

The family of the pioneer missioner, Herbert Hale, have been unfailingly generous, helpful and understanding. I appreciate their trust in letting me have the many original 'HH' photographs, along with the volume of Hale's letters from southern Africa and his typed autobiographical books. I am especially indebted to Herbert Hale's daughters, Mrs. Frances Folliott and Lady Ursula Redwood.

Without Tony Grain's book, much of the history of the Railway Mission would have been lost. I thank him for his work and for a great amount of material and information, including addresses, all of which has made my task the easier. Many other people in this country have contributed information or expertise, or have helped in bringing this work to a completion, namely: Vin Arthey, Antony Baxter, Norman Botham, Bishop Paul Burrough, David Candler, Peter Cole, Mrs. J.E. Ellison, Mrs. Franklin, Vic Harding, David Littley, Jon Lunn, Dick Nyenhuis, Gordon

Pirie, Miss Plumtre, Mrs. Rusbridger, John Strouts, Murray Thompson and Wilf Wareham. Olive Granger, former Secretary of the Transvaal, Zimbabwe and Botswana Association (TZABA) has been a mine of information about former missioners and I am grateful to her for all her help. The letters from Bishop Robert Mercer, in Canada, enabled me to look more critically at many of the questions raised in the closing years of the Railway Mission, and I appreciate his initiative.

The staff of Rhodes House Library, Oxford, have continually gone out of their way to assist and have allowed me to search through their archives. Similarly, I wish to thank the staffs of the Cory Library in Grahamstown, the CPSA Archives in the University of the Witwatersrand, the Anglican Church Archives in Bulawayo Cathedral, and the Railway Archives in Bulawayo Railway Museum.

Very many people gave help and assistance in 1993 during the time spent in southern Africa. I am very grateful to John Adams, Michael Berning, Louis Bolze, Alex and Beryl Crosby, Mrs. D.E. Leavey, Ken Lyell, Bishop Theophilus Naledi, Bill and Sybil Richards, Denys and Margaret Whitehead, and the staff of Plumtree School, especially Jeff and Gwen Calvert and Felix and Harold Westwood. Monica Waddy was exceptionally hospitable and has been instrumental in obtaining archive material against almost insuperable odds. Many others (black and white) along the way appeared at just the right moment to effect various rescues. To single out Doris Shiels is not to lessen the thanks to others. It was good and propitious that our friend Marlene Wilkinson was with us for the most fraught part of the journey.

As Archbishop of York, Dr. John Habgood generously allowed me time for the research, recommended me for grants for the African trip and took an active interest in the work. I am extremely appreciative of all his help. I thank too the former Bishop of Selby (Clifford Barker), the Archdeacon of York (George Austin) and the Director of Training for York Diocese (Michael Searle) for their recommendations and help towards grants. Thanks are also due to the Church Council of Appleton Roebuck with Acaster Selby for their understanding, and to Canon Ron Metcalfe for his encouragement and interest. I am deeply grateful to Daniel Kilbert, former colleague at Sefula, Zambia, for all his support and practical help.

I cannot thank enough my wife, Sheila, and our children, Alan and Elizabeth, who have shared in much of this journey, at times paying a greater price than I would have wished, yet who have shown remarkable forbearance and have given much practical help and encouragement.

My final thanks to the present Archbishop of York, Dr. David Hope, for reading the whole text and for his very generous and enthusiastic Foreword.

John Roden May 1999

Abbreviations and Definitions

BSA Co	British South Africa Company ('The Chartered Company')
CAR	Central Africa Railway
CESA	Church of England in South Africa
CFK	Chemin de fer du Katanga (Katanga Railway)
CFM	Caminhos de Ferro Mocambique (Mocambique Railway)
CGR	Cape Government Railways
CMS	Church Missionary Society
CNA	Colonial Nursing Association (later, Overseas Nursing Association)
COV	Children of the Veld
CPSA	Church of the Province of South Africa
CR	Community of the Resurrection
CSAR	Central South African Railways
CTC	Centralised Train Control
DRC	Dutch Reformed Church
Garratt	= Beyer-Garratt articulated locomotive
GDRM	Grahamstown Diocesan Railway Mission
GFS	Girls' Friendly Society
GM	(Railway) General Manager
LL	'Light for the Line' (See Bibliography)
LMS	London Missionary Society
Lozi	= The maLozi peoples of Western Zambia (Barotseland)
Mail	= Express train conveying passenger stock only
Mandated Territory	= South West Africa (Namibia)
Metropolitan	= Provincial archbishop or primate
Mixed	= Train conveying a mixed load of goods vans and passenger coaches
NWR	North West Rhodesia
Offices	= Services of Matins, Evensong, etc.
OFS	Orange Free State
PEA	Portuguese East Africa (Mocambique)
Permanent Way	= Ballast, sleepers and track
Province	= Group of dioceses under an Archbishop
PWI	Permanent Way Inspector
QP	'Quarterly Paper' (See Bibliography)
RHL	Rhodes House Library (Oxford)
RM	Railway Mission
RMR&B	Railway Mission of Rhodesia & Botswana
R&NRM	Rhodesia and Nyasaland Railway Mission
R-N RCR	Rhodesia & Nyasaland Royal Commission Report (Bledisloe Report)
RR	Rhodesia Railways
SACRM	South African Church Railway Mission
SAR	South African Railways
SSE	Sena Sugar Estate
TZR	Trans-Zambesia Railway
UCZ	United Church of Zambia
UMCA	Universities' Mission to Central Africa
(U)SPG	(United) Society for the Propagation of the Gospel (in Foreign Parts)
WITS	University of the Witwatersrand
WNLA('WENELA')	Witwatersrand Native Labour Association

1. Introduction

'the country is rising into civilisation' (Bishop Gray, of Cape Town, 1848)

You are out upon the Highways,
  Gallant plunderers for the Lord,
Down the lone, untrodden by-ways,
  With the Spirit as your sword.

Capture souls upon the Highways
  Through the long day's dust and heat;
At life's even ride you sky-ways,
  Lay your booty at His Feet.[1]

Thus was the reader introduced to *God's Highwaymen*, the first official history (to 1930) of the South African Church Railway Mission. In his seminal *Politics and Christianity in Malawi*, John McCracken approaches mission work somewhat differently:

> All missions in the 1890s recognised that the prime task of religious conversion could not be achieved without the introduction of at least a modicum of Western education; all that were Protestant shared Henry Venn's ideal of a self-governing, self-supporting native church. Where they differed most markedly was on the type of society they wished to create and on the means at their disposal for carrying those wishes into effect.[2]

The Anglican Railway Mission, as we shall see, was different from other missions in southern Africa, yet without their history and existence this story would not be there for the telling. A brief reminder of Christian activity in that part of the continent will prepare us for our journey.

In 1560 the Jesuit priest, Father Goncalo da Silveira, landed at Sofala on the Mozambique coast. Moving inland, and then up the Zambezi to Sena, Silveira baptised many African chiefs and their people and endeavoured to 'restore a moral tone' among the Portuguese. On March 16, 1561, at Zumbo/Zumbi (600 miles from the mouth of the Zambezi) the pioneer was killed in his sleep on the order of the king, the 'Monomotapa', who had been advised by local Muslims that Silveira was a spy. Thus ended the first Christian mission in southern Africa. It was to be over 200 years later that the Roman Catholics started systematic mission work (at the Cape), with Bishop Ricards' establishment in 1879 of a Trappist centre at Dunbrody, near Port Elizabeth. This was transferred in 1882 to become the great centre of Mariannhill.

Silveira and the 16th century Jesuits apart, missionary work in southern Africa can be said to have started in 1737 when the Moravian, George Schmidt, arrived at the Cape and began his work among the Khoi ('Hottentots') at Baviaans Kloof (Genadendal). Although the Dutch authorities forced the work to be abandoned, other Moravian missionaries re-started at Genadendal in 1792, still seven years before the next group, the London Missionary Society (LMS), arrived on the scene. The Moravians had a profound and formative influence on almost all the Protestant missionaries and Societies, a fact not always acknowledged.

Dr. Johannes Theodorus Van der Kemp, arguably the 'most exceptionally gifted, significant and controversial figure in the history of Dutch missionary activity', was the Convenor and one of the founders, in 1797, of the Netherlands Missionary Society. This was but two years after the interdenominational London Missionary Society was founded as one result of the Evangelical Revival in England. Van der Kemp heard of the LMS via Moravian friends and he offered himself to the Directors of the Society 'if it be the will of God' to be sent by them 'to the heathen'. He was subsequently appointed a Director of the LMS and, with three colleagues, arrived in the Cape Colony on April 1st 1799 in order to start a 'mission among the kaffirs'. The work soon centred on the Khoi and the settlement and refuge of Bethelsdorp. For the LMS the later work of Moffatt and Livingstone became known internationally and inspired future generations of missionaries and supporters of missions. However, Van der Kemp was the real founder of the LMS work, and John Philip (his successor) the outstanding mission leader of the first half of the nineteenth century and the central figure who linked almost all the Protestant Missionary Societies in southern Africa.

The early nineteenth century saw the arrival of the Wesleyan Methodists and the (Presbyterian) Glasgow Missionary Society (later the United Free Church of Scotland). Lovedale, the famous educational centre, was founded by the Presbyterians in 1824 at Incehra Stream (the Institution itself opened in 1841 at a different site). By the mid 1830s the Paris Evangelical Missionary Society, the Rhenish and the Berlin Missionary Societies and the American Board of Mission had all sent their pioneers and started work in southern Africa, all with advice from Dr. Philip.

Anglicans as such arrived at the Cape in 1795, with the advent of the first British Governor, garrison and chaplains. Captain Allen Gardiner (RN) started missionary work among Dingaan's Zulu in 1835 and was influential in the Church Missionary Society's sending of Francis Owen in 1837. CMS work ceased in South Africa with Owen's departure in 1841. It was only with the arrival in 1848 of Robert Gray, the first Bishop of Cape Town, that Anglican missionary work started in any real sense. Gray insisted on missions to non-Europeans, and in this was assisted by SPG - the Society for the Propagation of the Gospel (in Foreign Parts).

The last half of the nineteenth century saw the arrival in South Africa of six various missionary groups from Scandinavia, along with the Primitive Methodists, American Free Methodists and the Salvation Army. Although Baptists had arrived at the Cape with the 1820 settlers, it was only in 1892 that the South African Baptist Missionary Society was founded. The year saw also the formal beginning of the (Anglican) Railway Mission in Grahamstown Diocese, the forerunner of the South African Church Railway Mission. Just over one hundred years had passed since 1792, when the pioneering Moravians had started their work in earnest. 1892 was, in many ways, the year in which the pioneering establishment of missions came to an end and a new chapter opened in the history of the Christian churches and their work with peoples of different races.

'Christian instruction ... and ... the temporal happiness and usefulness of the [London Missionary] Society with respect to the country at large ..' was one of the strategies laid down by Van der Kemp in 1801 for the work among the Khoi. However, LMS policies changed over the period in question, often as a result of altered circumstances rather than from carefully formulated plans. The different Societies, though often sharing a common aim of 'converting the heathen' and 'bringing light into darkness', varied considerably in the practicalities of their work and in their involvement with the 'politics' of southern Africa. The individual missionaries inevitably faced a conflict or even collision between the theology and liturgy that they brought with them and the expectations of the local culture and chiefs. These conflicts and tensions produced changes in mission policies and in the workers themselves. For some Missionary Societies their history was one of clashes between settler groups and themselves; for others it was one of initial hostility to local customs. Particular European Societies found themselves in areas where their nation was not the colonising power; others worked almost hand in glove with their compatriot colonisers. Some set up Missionary Settlements where Africans were encouraged to live and work - seen as oases of 'christian civilisation', whereas others wandered over large areas evangelising small groups.

In looking at the 'historical geography of missions in nineteenth century Africa', Pirie pointed out that

> the place of origin of missions and their particular denomination imbued them with more or less distinctive philosophies of conversion and affected their relations with the government of the day in southern Africa. ... [Also] different countries of origin, philosophies

and resources were reflected in the different successes of missions in the subcontinent.

Certainly there was a great variety and distinctiveness of missionary experience and practice. The missionaries 'endured loneliness, squalor, hunger, disease, and not least, frustrations and disappointment. Theirs was no monolithic intrusion and their work was neither innocuous nor passive.' Yet, the words 'variety' and 'distinctive' are perhaps not strong enough. Although, as stated above, the different Societies shared many common aims, they nevertheless embodied completely different ways of looking at the world, particularly the African world, and they experienced different types of moral frontier as they sought to put their mission vision into practice.

The beliefs and practices of the Moravians, for example, were in many ways diametrically opposite to those of the Anglicans (although each could admire some aspects of the others' work). Unlike hierarchical Anglicanism, the Moravian mission (as the Baptists) stressed the priesthood of all believers. Yet, whereas this democratic and pietistic belief was accepted by the brethren in Europe, the Moravians were somewhat chagrined - if not outraged - when their African converts took them at their word and proclaimed their independent churches! The Trappists, who moved from Dunbrody to Mariannhill (noted above), as contemplative Cistercians were bound to a life of solitude and silence. The founding of what became the largest Cistercian monastery in the world obliged them to turn to educational and mission work, both of which were incompatible with their contemplative calling. They could hardly have been more ill-equipped for the work.

The well-educated and practical Huguenots of the Paris Missionary Society, who pioneered Christian evangelism in Lesotho, were able to accept Africans as equals (and be accepted by them) in a way that few Anglican colonial missionaries were ever able to. The London Missionary Society, perhaps because it was more interdenominational than most other such Societies, had a changing pattern of theological beliefs, largely dependent on the Director or senior missionary 'in the field' at the time. Whereas Philip passionately believed in the political and social implications of the Christian gospel, Moffat and many others distrusted this involvement and believed that they were in Africa 'simply' to convert 'the heathen'.

The Moravian, the London (LMS), the Paris (PEMS) and the Anglican SPG were each distinctive in their own way. Yet, all of their work was quite different from the work of the Railway Mission, serving to emphasise its uniqueness. The Societies presented Christianity in particular cultural packaging. This could be threatening and always involved change. The Railway Mission was never threatening to those it served, although fellow Anglicans who were diocesan or parish clergy (and whose hierarchical and localised structure was openly breached by the itinerant missioners), or settlers whose racist views were being challenged, certainly felt threatened. However, they were on the sidelines of the Railway Mission's work, for its unique remit was with the railway workers and their families. The Mission was equipped, as no other Church or Missionary Society was, to serve the needs of its constituency.

Ranger noted that

> Very little developed as the missionaries planned or hoped or feared. ...historians of the Christian Movement in Africa have to read between the lines of missionary records, passing by apparent but illusory triumphs in order to locate real but unperceived successes.[3]

The Railway Mission of the Anglican Church in southern Africa was, as we shall note in the chapters which follow, not 'just another mission'. Whereas every mission was distinct, the Railway Mission was unique. Although (obviously) Anglican, it often sat lightly on its denominational tag. Called a 'mission', it did not set out to convert or proselytise. Its constituents did belong, on the whole, to one group, but not one based on language or tribe or nation-state or even colour, but one that shared a common culture - a railway culture, within a 'railway state', a 'tribalistic grouping of men [and families] with a ritualistic adherence to territory, myth, symbolism and insignia ..'

The Church Railway Mission - from its tentative beginnings in Grahamstown in 1885, as the first century of European mission work in southern Africa came to an end; through its 'days of glory', as it served almost the whole railway system south of the 12th parallel; to its difficult ending, as the new Zimbabwe was born - was the 'travelling church', the 'church between the churches', the itinerant mission. Unlike other missions, it defined its sphere not in miles or in areas but rather in 'degrees of latitude and longitude', as Herbert Hale noted in his 1905 diary. Following Ranger, we shall 'read between the lines' of the records of this particular mission, as well as frequently quoting 'the lines' themselves - a treasure trove that has lain unread and little known. I believe, too, that we shall also 'locate real but unperceived successes' .

The Missioners

As our story of 'Anglicanism on the move' gets under way, once we have looked at the railways themselves and their workers, there will be little time to stop and ask questions such as 'what sort of person went to the Railway Mission?', or 'why did they go?', or 'was it the railways that 'grabbed' them?'. Some of these questions will be answered concerning the pioneer missioners and the African workers in the chapters outlining their work. For the rest, the vast majority of railway missioners, we have the direct words of fourteen, who may represent them all. Their letters to the author and to other earlier recipients happen, by good fortune, to cover every single decade of the life of this Mission.

Lawrence Skey [1898-1903, 1905-12] was the

> youngest of a family of 17. His father was the vicar of Weare in Somerset where the family lived in considerable poverty. Laurie (as he was called) worked for a time as a clerk on the London Underground. He then went to S.A. [South Africa] and later joined the Railway Mission as a layman. After a time he was ordained at Grahamstown. ... For much of the Great War he served as a chaplain to the S.A. forces in East Africa ...[4]

Norah Short, herself a missioner for most of the 1920s, in writing about Laurie Skey, ended her letter by stating, 'wherever I travelled in Southern Africa ... I met men ... who had known and loved him.'

We shall meet **Herbert Hale** [1903-6] many times in this story, not least because of the detailed record of his work outlined in letters to his sister, as well as his autobiographical *Pilgrimage of an ordinary Padre*. One of his surviving children, Lady Ursula Redwood, after explaining how Herbert's father had refused the inheritance of a Brewery and Inn, because of the 'appalling drunkenness which developed amongst the poorer folk in Victorian days', went on to note:

> (My grandfather) ... took his family off to New Zealand, bought virgin land and with his two boys tried to make a go of it. He failed because the farming slump then hit New Zealand. They came home with little money.[5]

After a time in Brighton, Herbert Hale obtained a post as clerk in a sports outfitters in London. He continued to be closely involved in Church activities. He learned shorthand but became increasingly frustrated with his 'cul-de-sac and futureless existence', as he put it.

> One morning there arrived a letter from my sister which changed the whole course of my life and all its prospects. It announced that my Grandfather had expressed a wish to do something for me. ... Dared I suggest that I would like to be ordained? ... A letter was written and the answer was awaited with fear and trembling. It came - and said my Grandfather was willing.[6]

After initial reservations over finance, Hale was allowed to prepare for ordination by first obtaining a degree at University, rather than via Theological College. He was accepted at S.Edmund Hall, Oxford, where he obtained a Third Class Honours in Theology. He later wrote:

> I could not feel that Oxford was in any immediate sense a preparation for Holy Orders ... the Church did nothing in those days to get into close and intimate touch at the Universities with men who were proposing to take Holy Orders. ... It will show, I think, how deeply I felt the need of a more spiritual approach to ordination that I decided to go to a Theological College, and that I borrowed £200 from my grandfather's Trust estate to do so ...
>
> I decided upon Lichfield Theological College, largely because they were prepared to give me an Exhibition towards the cost.

He went to Lichfield in 1894 and was made Deacon in Southwell Cathedral on Trinity Sunday, 1895. A curacy at S. Peter's, Mansfield, followed, as he 'stood on the threshold of [his] life's work'. It was at Mansfield that he became interested in 'Lantern work', becoming 'one of the pioneers in Notts of the use of Acetylene as the illuminant.' This, coupled with his photography skills, was to prove a boon on the Railway Mission. In Autumn 1898 Herbert Hale went to be in charge of the new Mission Church of S.Saviour's, Wilmington, Hull. This was followed by a brief interval before becoming the senior curate in Bakewell. His *Pilgrimage* continues:

> Sometime in the spring of 1903, I received, all unexpectedly, a letter which was to change the whole course of my life. It was from Mr Douglas Ellison, the Founder and Head of the now well-known South African Church Railway Mission. He heard of me accidentally ... My youngest Lieutenant in the Church Lads Brigade at Mansfield, Moxon by name, was the connecting link. His brother was a curate in a Hammersmith Parish, the Vicar of which had just volunteered for the Railway Mission. He was asked, "Could he find another man?" and passed the question on to his Curate. His curate mentioned it to his young brother, and he thought of m ....

I never sought work abroad. But the call came and I was bound to decide. ... I saw Douglas Ellison, and learnt what the work was; I consulted F.A. Rogers, who had worked on the Mission as a layman, was just ordained, and was afterwards Head of the Mission (1911-14); and I also saw Lawrence Hands, then at S. Saviour's, Eastbourne, who was just going out to the Mission himself, and is today (1932) its Head. Then I crossed the Rubicon. I could not promise more than three years. My father was 77, and my sister would be awkwardly placed in my absence, if anything happened to him ...

I said "goodbye" to my father and sister at Ross-on-Wye, wondering most of all whether I should see the face of my father any more. At Southampton, I boarded the Union Castle Company's "Kinfauns Castle", towards the middle of October 1903. The voyage was quite uneventful ...[7]

Ralph Seacombe [1916-18] was another missioner who wrote home frequently. After his death from influenza in 1918 his letters were gathered together, edited and had a Preface added by the then Bishop of Southwark, who had been the vicar in Portsea when Seacombe was curate. It is unclear whether or not 'Cyril Southwark' also wrote the introduction to the letters:

> From the beginning he had a desire to take Holy Orders, but when the time came to leave school he gave up the idea on account of a very bad stammer, and decided to join the Army. ... a friend happened to ask him if he had ever thought of treating stammering as a sin. The idea appealed to him and he decided to try "giving it up for Lent", with the result that, by Easter, his stammer was reduced to an occasional catch in his breath! Having overcome the one obstacle between himself and the priesthood, he gave up the idea of the Army and went to Keble College, Oxford. From thence, after three years, he went to Cuddesdon Theological College in 1911.[8]

Ordination and Portsea, including prison work, followed. He held that,

> any able-bodied priest should, if possible, do a term of service in the Mission Field abroad and in 1910 he put his name down for three years with the South African Church Railway Mission. He hoped, on his return ..., to be married and to obtain a prison chaplaincy.

At the end of December 1945 **Maude Agg-Large** [1929-45, 1951-2] received a 'Secret and Personal' letter from the Governor of Southern Rhodesia, informing her that she was to receive the M.B.E. in the New Year's Honours List. A separate letter from an official in Government House, Salisbury, informed her that this was for 'the wonderful work which you have done for our good friends up and down the Line.'[9] Agg-Large was the only missioner to be so honoured. In 1980 'Aggie' wrote:

> Gladys Raikes [1923-9], a worker on the Grahamstown Section was a friend who first told me of the work she was doing on the Railway Mission, this resulted in my applying to join in 1929.[10]

Maude Agg-Large had trained as a school teacher and had been actively involved with the Guide movement before she went out to Africa.

Howard Bostock [1931-2] served in the Railway Mission as a layman, prior to his return to England. He wrote:

> I always consider myself extremely fortunate for having been accepted for service for such a short time. Harry Ellison, who had followed my Father as a Curate in Yorkshire, most kindly asked Lawrence Hands to have me. B.K.Cunningham liked us to have some overseas or Business experience before entering Westcott House, and I have always been most glad to have had that glimpse of S.Africa.[11]

Almost all the chaplains went out to Africa from England. One of the few exceptions was **Richard Holderness** [1932-4]. In retirement at the Borradaile Trust, Marondera, Zimbabwe, he wrote in 1985 of his life before and during his missioner years:

> ... though we all knew of the Railway Mission in Rhodesia and Maude Agg-Large was a legend, I had never imagined that it might concern me, so when I met Lawrence Hands while he was visiting Bishop Paget, it was quite a new idea that I might join it.
>
> I had just completed three years at Rhodes University in Grahamstown where I had done a B.A. in Law, intending to join my father's firm, Scanlen & Holderness. At Rhodes I had met the Oxford Group and committed my life to Jesus Christ, and begun to hear the call to be a priest, which was a strange thing, for we thought clergy came from England. In fact I was the first white Rhodesian to be ordained.

I had been discussing the idea with the Bishop when Fr Hands appeared and said, "I am needing a layman in the Orange Free State." Paget said something like this: "First rate. You take the job, and if you can stick it out for a year I'll see that the Diocese pays for your training." It is interesting that my mother told me later that at my baptism she had prayed that I would be a priest. .. my father's father, Harry Holderness, was vicar (or rector?) of a little town called Adlingfleet near Goole ... So I set off for Bloemfontein in 1932 ...

... Lionel Borradaile Bell .. was Rector of Plumtree and our school chaplain while I was at school there, 1924-28. His life was the first to make me think of ordination. ... we knew of our school's start as a Railway Mission work, and I knew Edgar Lloyd [co-founder of Plumtree School], and belonged to Lloyd House. Bishop Gaul also came to visit us. Strange that I never connected these facts in my mind before.[12]

In 1934 Richard Holderness left the Mission to begin his theological training at St.Paul's, Grahamstown, prior to working as a deacon in Gwelo, Rhodesia, and being ordained in December 1936.

Ray White [1934-8, 1947-60] came onto the Railway Mission scene as Richard Holderness bowed out. In 1980 he started to write an account of the Mission's history, although that task was then taken up by Tony Grain, followed by the author. In his account, Ray White wrote of how he 'came into the picture':

I had come into the reality of Christian living through All-Hallows -by-the-Tower and Toc H and while I was working in the shipping office of the renowned hosiery and general material firm of J.C.R.Morley ... I had come into touch, through 'Tubby' Clayton and George Moore, with Tom Savage ....

Tom and I lost touch with each other for several years and then, when I had been ordained and was just finishing my curacy at St. John's, Carlton Hill - the officially recognised slum parish of Brighton - I had a letter from him in 1934 saying that the priest who had succeeded him as Railway Missioner in 1931, Maurice Clack, was leaving his old section on the Eastern Transvaal after his three year tour of duty and Tom [RM 1928-31; afterwards Bishop of Zululand] was very keen that the tradition of keeping the teaching of Toc H and scouting should be kept going - so would I volunteer.

..... It was all a bit complicated as I had just fallen madly in love with Lilah Nicholson. Lilah had founded and built the first Rachel

MacMillan Nursery School outside London and had done so in St. John's parish.

However, I had still got nearly two years of my five year vow of celibacy to go, so we decided it was right that I should accept. So at the beginning of November 1934, I sailed for South Africa ...[13]

White returned in December 1937, was offered by George Bell, Bishop of Chichester, the parish of Fairwarp on Ashdown Forest, married Lilah in 1938, served in the army during the Second World War and then returned to Fairwarp:

Then during 1947 Maurice Lancaster, then Head of the Railway Mission, came and succeeded in talking us to going back and doing another spell, with Lilah being signed on as a Lady worker .

They stayed on the mission until 1960, Ray being acting-Head and then, from 1952, the Head of the Railway Mission.

Roy Sinker [1935-8] achieved some notoriety by having the 'effrontery to stop an express at a pretty little dorp', as we shall later discover. In his 1984 account of his time with the Railway Mission he wrote:

Most small boys in the age of the steam train were fascinated by trains. When this fascination is later combined with a vocation to the ordained ministry of the Church, service on the South African Church Railway Mission is the obvious solution. After three years as an Assistant Curate in the Diocese of Carlisle I was accepted for service in the Karroo district between Grahamstown and Port Elizabeth in the Cape Province.[14]

Here, then, was one missioner who had indeed been 'grabbed' by the lure of railways.

Stephen Skemp [1939-42] first heard of the Railway Mission 'in the early 30s' when he was a student at Cuddesdon Theological College, Oxford:

Arthur Hobson [various 'tours' between 1916 and 55] came and told us about the Mission and, although I didn't know it at the time, he must have hooked me. Because - after ordination, and 4+ years as curate of a suburban parish in the diocese of London, it was of the Mission that I thought first of all when I felt it was time to move on to "pastures new". And so it proved to be, in more ways than one, the romance of my life.

First, I fell in love on the "Warwick Castle", and later on proposed and was accepted in the shabby backyard of Johannesburg Station. And then, after travelling on to Rhodesia, 600 miles away from my fiancée, I found a parallel romance in the very nature of my work on the S.A.C.R.M ...[15]

During the 95 years of the Railway Mission there were about twenty couples who either met on the Mission and then got married or who were already married before starting their work as chaplains or women workers. Stephen Skemp must hold the Mission record for the shortest time taken to become engaged after arrival in Africa!

Michael Fidgin [1952-5] served his title [first post as assistant curate after ordination] under Canon Albert Eaton at Leicester. Eaton had been a Church Army worker in the Kimberley mine fields and had then trained for the ordained ministry in Grahamstown.

One thing that Canon Eaton said was that all Priests ought to do a spell in the Mission Field to complete their knowledge of the Church world wide; so, after his two and a half years [at S.Peter's, Leicester] Michael was more or less "sent" out to do a spell on the Railway Mission. He was based at Waterval Boven as Missioner to Eastern Transvaal ...[16]

Lavinia Fidgin (nee Roberts) [1954-5] was sent to work with Michael Fidgin at Waterval Boven. She had trained as a Parish Worker at Ranyard House, London, prior to working in the 'pleasant parish' of South Harrow.

After four and a half years there I decided to see what a poorer parish was like and went to Bethnal Green, East End London, with all the problems of post -war London - masses of Peabody flats and bombed roads undeveloped. Most social workers lived in "settlements" which were Church or College residents. I went to one sponsored by Cheltenham Ladies College ... So, lots of single ladies .. got together at nights to recall their experiences. While there - 3 years - Maude Agg-Large returned from Rhodesia and took up residence while she worked in S.P.G. House, Westminster. So at night over tea/coffee she recalled her life out there especially during the War. I think I must have asked lots of questions and showed great interest. One day some time later on she told me that Ray White, Head of the Mission, would be in London and would I like to come to the Office and meet him. I did so and he told me that I was just the person needed out there - used to working with Mothers and families and the right age, 27, to cope with travelling distances. I don't think it was 'Railways' that got me as much as it sounded an interesting type of work and a needy one. So off I went.[17]

Stephen Easter [1953-6], when he was preparing for ordination, was not exactly encouraged to think about working overseas. His bishop suggested that 'the home front' was much more important. In one of his very many informative letters to the author Stephen Easter states:

> The challenge really came from the 'Tait Mission' (Canterbury), [led by] Thomas Savage (SACRM 1928-31), whose sense of urgency and profound sincerity stirred a vocation to spend some time in the mission field. Doctors and nurses in the U.M.C.A had a salary of £7 per month; the Bush Brotherhood in Australia had a five year contract, so I suppose the Railway Mission seemed a good compromise.[18]

Harold Crane [1963-9] was one of the very few (white) Railway chaplains who joined the Mission in Africa itself. He had, however, moved to Rhodesia earlier. He was born in Long Eaton, Derbyshire, and went out to Rhodesia with his parents and sister in 1929 when he was just turned seven. His father, having served some years as a fireman on the L.M.S. railway in Britain, had joined the Rhodesia Railways. In a private letter Harold Crane wrote:

> My first contact with the SACRM was at Inyazura in the Eastern Districts of Rhodesia ... - a railway re-crewing depot, where my late father was an engine driver (one of the best!).
>
> I was a teenager and Miss Maude Agg-Large, a truly grand and untiring Railway Missioner, used to visit the community from time to time, holding confirmation classes (though I was not in them then), caring about the families; and what drew us youngsters was that she had a paraffin-fuelled 'magic lantern' and gave talks and showed slides of the Holy Land in the old wood and iron Railway Institute there.
>
> Truly a saintly lady. ... In my time on the line I had coach 872 marshalled behind the locomotive or, on the Botswana line, behind the relief crew's caboose (same in Zambia with coach 859) ...[19]

After serving with the RAF back in England during the second world war Harold Crane followed in his father's footsteps by joining Rhodesia Railways, in 1947, as a station Foreman. Once again he had 'the visits of the Railway Missioner [which] were always a joy to us.' He later became the Railway Mission's 'own ordinand', having been 'adopted', as he put it, by the London Committee. Harold Crane joined the Mission, as Missioner/Secretary, in 1963 and 'had the opportunity of re-visiting or passing through all the places [he] used to live at and many more besides.'[20]

Earle and Ruth Hawkes [1976-7], after a fascinating and shared ministry in various and often remote parts of Canada, came to England to live in retirement. They had no sooner settled than a clergy neighbour brought them the *Church of England Newspaper*, which had in it an advert that was to give them yet more challenges:

WOULD YOU LIKE A CHANGE FROM PAROCHIAL WORK AND AN OPPORTUNITY TO TRAVEL?
As **CHAPLAIN** with the **RAILWAY MISSION** of **RHODESIA** and **BOTSWANA**, you could find a stimulating and challenging sphere of work.

THE RAILWAY MISSION has a long history dating back to Cecil Rhodes' 'Cape to Cairo' Railway and down the years there have been Railway Missioners working from the Cape to the Congo. The need now is for an Anglican priest with wide experience, flexible and adaptable, preferably married but free of other family ties, who would minister along the Railway Lines to people of any creed or colour living far from any place of worship. The period of service is in the first place for three years, and given the fitness required for a fair amount of travelling this would be an interesting and worthwhile ministry for the last years before retirement. The present Chaplain and his wife are leaving solely because of age.

Please reply to the Hon.Sec., The Railway Mission, T.R.A.B.A, Office, 15 Tufton Street, London SW1P 3QB

At the time sanctions were in force against Rhodesia, in the hope of weakening the Ian Smith government. Special permission had had to be given by the Secretary of State in the Colonial Office for the advert to be placed. When Ruth Hawkes drew her husband's attention to the advert his reply was, 'Do you want to have us both killed?'[21] They did, however, decide to apply. After meeting various past missioners, including the eighty two year old Maude Agg-Large who wanted to go with them, the Hawkes left Southampton for Cape Town in the RMS *Edinburgh Castle* on March 5, 1976, the last missioners in the Railway Mission's then ninety years to take the leisurely sea journey to Africa. Only George and Gertrude Deacon [1977-80] were to follow them - but they were to fly out and to brave the last three years of the Mission's life at the height of the armed struggle for majority rule and independence in Southern Rhodesia.

Clearly, it was rather the feeling that time spent on the 'mission field' was a good and proper thing to do, and having this particular Mission recommended or mentioned by others, that were the chief factors in helping most of our representative sample join the Railway Mission. Only in a few cases was it the 'lure of the Railways' that 'grabbed' them. But their unique ministry was to the Railways and their workers, to whom we now turn.

---

1 from *God's Highwaymen*, 1930, vi
2 McCracken, 1977, 176
3 Ranger, 1994, 275
4 N.Short, letter to A.Grain, 1985
5 Lady U. Redwood, letter to author, 29.10.1995
6 *Pilgrimage of an ordinary Padre*, H.Hale, pt I, 1932, 158/9
7 *Pilgrimage of an ordinary Padre*, H.Hale, pt I, 1932, 159f
8 Seacombe Letters, X1441/1, f10. RHL
9 M.Agg-Large papers / JMR
10 M Agg-Large, letter to A.Grain, 1980
11 Canon H.Bostock, letter to A.Grain, 17.6.1985
12 R.Holderness, letter to author, 1.4.1995
13 R.White, *Memoirs, 1980,* 1-2
14 R.Sinker, letter to A.Grain, 1984
15 S.R.Skemp, letter to author, 3.2.1992
16 Lavinia Fidgin, letter to author 17.3.1999
17 Lavinia Fidgin, letter to author 17.3.1999
18 S. Easter, letter to author, 13.3.1999
19 H. Crane to JMR 17.11.1994
20 H. Crane to Railway Mission London Office, 14.11.1961
21 E.Hawkes, *The Wonder of Divine Influence* (Autobiography), 1995, 97

2. Railways and their workers

- servants of the 'Cape to Cairo'

Each bolt, each nut, each metal bar
Could tell a story - grim but true -
And where the gangers' houses are
Maybe are ghosts of dead men too -
Ghosts of men who worked and knew
The fever-swamp, the sickening jar
That came when life was rusted through
Upon the lonely B.M.R.[1]

Beira, the 'disputed gateway to Central Africa', gave its name to the 'lonely B.M.R.' - the Beira and Mashonaland Railway, but its entry onto the railway scene came some thirty years after that of another port, Durban, nine-hundred coast-hugging miles to the south. The first railway to run in southern Africa was the 2-mile line between Durban and the Custom House at Durban Point, opened for traffic on June 26th, 1860. Railway construction as such had started in the previous year when the first sod was cut on the 45-mile line between Cape Town and Wellington. However, this line was not fully opened until 1863. With the discovery of diamonds in 1867 near Hopetown and in 1870/1 in what was to become Kimberley, railway construction quickly expanded. By 1884 the Cape Government had started buying privately built railways and converting them from the standard 4 ft. 8 1/2 in. gauge to the 'cape' 3ft. 6 in. Pietermaritzburg was reached (from Durban) and the Cape Town and Port Elizabeth lines met at De Aar in that year.

In October 1889 the British South Africa Company was incorporated and Cecil Rhodes started on the 'Cape to Cairo', beginning with the line from Kimberley to Vryburg, carried out by the Cape Government. The main ports of Durban, Cape Town, Port Elizabeth and East London were all keen to have rail connections with Johannesburg once gold had been discovered in the area, although there were many other factors involved in the race for railways. By 1896, when a full service was introduced between Pretoria and Durban, all the ports had been connected.

In Portuguese East Africa, as a result of the Anglo-Portuguese Treaty in 1891, a concession had been granted to Rhodes to build a railway from Beira to Umtali, including the right to use the port of Beira and the Pungwe river. In 1898 the first train entered Umtali from Beira on a 2 ft. gauge line. The Salisbury to Umtali route opened in May 1899, and then, so that through running could be possible between Salisbury and the coast, the eastern arm was widened to 3 ft. 6 in.

The line from the Cape had reached Vryburg, in the then British Bechuanaland, in 1890 and Mafeking in 1893. George Pauling had the contract from Rhodes to build the 500-mile section north of Mafeking. The work was started at the end of 1895, the first train entering Bulawayo, 70 miles over the Rhodesian border, on November 4th, 1897. By June 1899 the section to the north of Bulawayo had been started towards Wankie and the Victoria Falls. To the east, the line was being laid from Salisbury westwards through Gwelo (June 1902), reaching Bulawayo in October 1902, and making possible a rail journey from Cape Town to Beira. The following year large railway construction works were started in Johannesburg. These were manned by Europeans, as Africans were deemed necessary for the ever-increasing work in the mines.

The immediate goal of the Victoria Falls was reached (from Wankie) in April 1904, and opened to the public two months later While the bridge over the Falls was being completed, the line north of Livingstone was well under way, reaching Kalomo, 94 miles from the Falls, in May 1905. The track moved ever northwards to the lure of the mineral deposits of Broken Hill [Kabwe], which became the Railhead by January 1906. The surveying of the route to Bwana M'Kubwa, on the Congo border 116 miles to the north, was then started. The line reached there on December 11th, 1909 when, 'without interruption, the railway was continued into Belgian territory as far as Elizabethville. .. which was reached in 1910 ..' By 1913 the railway was at Kambove and, by 1916, at T'schilonga, with Bukama on the Upper Congo connected a little later.

As the railway was reaching Elizabethville in 1910 the Union of South Africa came into being. 'This paved the way to the combination of the Cape, Natal, Transvaal and Orange Free State railways ... the beginning of South African Railways and Harbours.' However, the Cape and Natal railways (in the former British colonies) continued to work somewhat separate from the other (Afrikaner) railways, which had come together as Central South African Railways. It took another Act, in 1916, to bring all the railways in southern Africa together.

In South-West Africa (Namibia) Keetmanshoop and Windhoek were linked by rail in March 1912, the line from Luderitz having reached Keetmanshoop in 1908, and the (then) branch line from Seeheim (near Keetmanshoop) to Kalkfontein (later called Karasburg) in 1909. At the beginning of the First World War this branch line was rapidly connected (at Kalkfontein) to the South African railway system.

Most of the main-line system in South Africa and the Rhodesias was completed by 1916. Branch lines continued to be laid right up to the 1950s. Bulawayo was linked directly with the port of Lourenco Marques [Maputo] in 1955, after the completion of the line through Malvernia.

In Nyasaland [Malawi] the 'Shire Highlands' Railway, between Port Herald [Nsanje] and Blantyre, was opened in 1908, with the line southwards to Chindio, on the north bank of the Zambezi, completed in 1915. The First World War then held up any further work until the Trans-Zambesia Railway Company built a line connecting Beira with Murraca, on the south bank of the Zambezi, opposite Chindio. The line was opened to traffic in 1922.

In 1935 the Central Africa and Trans-Zambesia Railways were connected by the Lower Zambezi bridge, at Sena.[2] The extension from Blantyre to Salima on Lake Nyasa/Malawi in 1935 brought to an end most of the railway construction in Trans-Zambezia and Nyasaland; and the Rutenga - Beit Bridge line of the 70s (linking Rhodesia directly through Messina to Johannesburg), completed all the trunk line construction in southern Africa.

Kingsley Fairbridge, in his autobiography, relates how he came across the builders of the Mashonaland Railway being laid from Umtali to Salisbury:

> At various points on the survey line were contractors' huts, where great gangs of Kafirs [sic] - ranging from the Mabandawi of the Lakes [Malawi] to ... the men of Matshanga - were digging the cuttings and laying down the embankments of the permanent way... Some of the men had worked on the Beira railway - you knew them by their yellow faces. ...
>
> A lad of thirteen, dressed in knickers and shirt sleeves, I walked on the outskirts of the Empire, where the shouting of men, the ring of hammers on stone, and the thud of picks in the baked earth were always in my ears ... villages of grass and canvass sprang to life amidst the virgin veld ... And so I went ahead on the tide of progress, wondering and observing, and thinking of the thousand homesteads that would some day dot these fields.[3]

Fairbridge's encounter was in 1898/9. A quarter of a century earlier his father - a land surveyor to the Cape government - must have seen similar pioneering activity taking place with the railway-building in the Cape Colony, though with much of the labour being white, rather than black. As construction took on an urgency from 1870 it was necessary to import large numbers of white skilled and semi-skilled workmen from Europe. 'There was no time to wait while labourers in the Cape were trained. Artisnal, let alone specialised railway skills were in limited supply after a decade of relatively low demand.' A major reason for employing white unskilled labour was the Cape Government's failure to procure an adequate black labour-force 'on terms which the Government was willing to offer.' A wage-differential was established, as it was felt that the wages of the black labourers had to be kept 'within bounds', or there would be an outcry from the settler population. When increasing numbers of African workers were employed there was a corresponding attempt to reduce their wages.

Evidence of the condition and extent of unskilled labour used in railway-construction in southern Africa is scanty. Purkiss points out that 'the colonists were not interested in the experience of labour at the work-place or the nature of the contribution which labourers made to the building of the railways, choosing to see railway-building as an achievement of engineering rather than muscle, pick and shovel ..'[4] Such records as are available demonstrate that at the peak of railway construction in the Cape in the late 1870s, up to 9000 Blacks were working alongside 3000 or so Whites. In Rhodesia 'scraps of evidence gleaned from secondary sources show a total [black] labour force of 1,200 employed on the construction of the East Coast route in 1895 growing to over 12,000 by 1902-3.' The Shire Highlands Railway in Nyasaland employed some 10,000 African workers during the 1903-1908 construction.

In his work on the railwaymen of Sekondi-Takoradi (Ghana), Jeffries notes that in the early years of the construction of a railway, 'the principal labour requirement was a large army of unskilled and semi-skilled labourers.' He is right in observing that literature on the political economy of sub-Saharan Africa tends to emphasise the distinction between skilled and unskilled workers, 'portraying the former as a "labour aristocracy" relative to the latter.' He also observes, correctly, that the majority of railway manual workers actually fell in the ranks of the semi-skilled. In South Africa the majority of these semi-skilled workers were imported from Britain.

Between 1873 and 1883 some 22,000 people were shipped from Europe to South Africa under the Cape Government Emigration Service. Purkiss, by looking at the Annual Reports on Immigration (Cape Parliamentary Papers, 1876-1884), gives a useful table of numbers of immigrants, including those for the railway service, year by year. However, analysis of his figures reveals that, of the 1000 emigrants (men, women and children) to the Cape in 1874, some 50 per cent were 'ordered' as navvies and 75 per cent for railways and public works (not all for construction work). The greatest number of railway workers to arrive at the Cape in any one year was in the following year, 1875, when 1170 arrived for railway employment, some two-thirds of the total 1800 immigrants. Over 40 per cent were navvies. By the mid-1880s immigration figures had risen from the 8000 total to just over 14,000, but the railway recruitment fell from

3500 to 588 - just 4 per cent. No orders specifically for navvies were issued after 1877.

The railway employees who were not navvies were mainly 'artisans', ie. quarrymen, masons, miners, carpenters and blacksmiths. As the numbers of railway immigrants declined, the emphasis changed from unskilled and semi-skilled labour to that of the more skilled workers - men to lay and then maintain the track, and men to fire and drive the locomotives. We shall look at these occupations later, but the pioneers were the navvies, those 'gipsies of labour', Patrick MacGill's 'army of scarecrows, ragged, unkempt scarecrows of civilisation.'[5]

Navvies

> The nineteenth century is not only the railway age but also the age of the navvy ...
> ... the railway was made by navvies, not by machines. [6]

This was as true in southern Africa as in Britain and the rest of the world, and, as we have seen above, great numbers of navvies migrated from Europe to make the railways of Africa. Who were these men? What sort of men became navvies? As Coleman, in his all-important *The Railway Navvies*, pointed out, they must not be confused with

> the rabble of steady, common labourers, whom they out-worked, out-drank, out-rioted and despised. A navvy was not a mere labourer, though a labourer might become a navvy. The first navvies came from . .. the fenmen of Lincolnshire who had built the sea walls, and from the gangs who had built roads and canals [canal builders were known as "navigators", hence "navvies"]. Many came from Scotland and Ireland, and from the Dales of Yorkshire and Lancashire.[7]

Patrick MacGill was unique among navvies in writing and having published an autobiographical novel, but his story as one of the 'children of the dead end' - hired at twelve in Strabane, going in a gang to Scotland at fourteen, brutalised, oppressed, and then working as a navvy in Kinlochleven - was far from unique. He articulated the life of an itinerant navvy in a way no one else has done.

The navvies excavated and tunnelled, laboured with pick-axe and shovel, worked and lived together in encampments, and drank and ate 'like a navvy'! 'Some deserted their families; others took wives and children with them on [their] trecks.' The last major railway-use of navvies in Britain was in the building of the Settle to Carlisle railway

(1869-75). Writing in 1965, Coleman did not have the 1871 Census Returns available. That for Hawes, for example, includes 'Navvies' working on the railway in Upper Wensleydale, who were living temporarily in lodgings or huts. The Return shows ninety-six in 'Railway occupation', and, of these, sixteen men had their wives with them and eight had children (one ten year old boy was listed as 'railway labourer' and one eight year old farmer's son as 'railway errand boy'). Ignoring child workers, the men's ages ranged from 14 to 62, with an average of 35. Some of the men came from Ireland and Scotland, many from Devon, Somerset and South Wales, and just a few were local. For his, *The Railway Navvy,* Brooke examined the 1871 Census returns of 38,900 workers, with 26,580 women and children, employed on seventy-nine lines in Britain. Of these, some 5,863 men were present on Census day on the Settle-Carlisle line.

> In 1875 and 1876, as the works came to an end, the men gradually left... [and] they had to go farther to look for work ... Some went out to places like the Sudan, built their railways and then returned, as the navvies of the 1840s had returned from their French and Italian contracts, but most were now emigrating for good. They spread all over the world.[8]

It is not unreasonable to imagine that some of those employed in the Settle-Carlisle construction emigrated to the Cape just in time for the major works starting there. J.W. Miles, a navvy, writing home from South Africa, said, 'It would make you laugh to see the Black Kaffers come to work with hardly any clothes and no boots on [sic].' Pauling, writing about the construction of the Grahamstown railway (opened in 1879), noted, 'Railway construction foremen had by this time been sent to various parts of the new railways under construction, including the Grahamstown railway, so I created a somewhat heterogeneous syndicate, consisting of an Italian, a Scotchman, and an old English navvy... [who] proved a terror.'[9] The 'riotous living' of the navvy was almost par for the course, although Purkiss states,

> One of the purposes of continuing to send for selected groups of English navvies in 1876-77 was to procure navvies "of good character" who could lead gangs of black workers skilfully. The successful ganger could also hope, increasingly after 1876, to become a sub-contractor to the Government engineers or main contractors.[10]

Whilst it is true that some navvies became 'gangers', the two tasks were not the same, and it is confusing and inaccurate to use the names interchangeably. The navvies stand alone, the railways they built 'remain their monument.... their handiwork would be the wonder and admiration of succeeding generations.'

'Traffic', 'locomotive' and 'permanent way'

Even in the early days of southern African railways, the different employees were classed as 'traffic', 'locomotive' or 'permanent way' workers. Railwaymen were the first 'organisation men', and the system of labour control and of a railway 'bailiwick' was imported from Britain.

> Trapped in space and time, railway workers learned how to defend their space. However humble his status, control of his own thinking and of the technology he operated was always in the grasp of the railway worker. Very quickly the engineman was referring to "my engine", the signalman to "my box" and the shunter to "my yard". [There] was created a new form of industrial anthropology, a tribalistic grouping of men based on an elaborate division of labour, a hierarchy of groups and a ritualistic adherence to territory, myth, symbolism and insignia unknown outside the specified boundaries. [11]

By 1870 in Britain there were almost one hundred grades of post on the railways. This was one of the most 'important characteristics of railway service and of railway servants, as the railwaymen alone among industrial workers were called.' Even at the height of railway operation in southern Africa, the number of different posts and grades never approached the British 1870 mark. However, taking the (southern African) railways as a whole, at least forty categories of work and responsibility were created. Within the three main areas of 'traffic', 'locomotive' and 'permanent way', fifteen to twenty separate railway jobs, with their own wage rates, were normal. Most had a more lowly or assistant grade of the particular work, and many had Supervisors or Inspectors overall in charge - particularly over the three 'classes' (ie. a Permanent Way Inspector would be responsible for all the workers in his section, such as gangers, platelayers, and labourers).

Within the category of 'traffic' the chief posts were stationmaster, clerk, ticket collector, guard (passenger and goods), signalman, porter and pumper. Most of these are self-descriptive and well-known and do not need explanation here. Care must be taken with the term 'signalman', however, for in much of southern Africa's railway history there was no signalling in the ordinary sense of the word. Most traffic movements were regulated by train orders (telegraphed ahead) and working at stations was by hand signals and by hand-operated points. Little interlocking of the signals with the points was used in the early days (and in some sections only recently installed, with the introduction of centralised train control). Even the main stations in the Cape and Natal did not begin to (slowly) introduce interlocking until after 1900.

> All this, of course, was directly related to the speed of traffic, and the methods of working unattended crossing places. There the practice of train crews working the points was accepted in view of the scarcity of much of the traffic, and the very slow speeds. Generally speaking signalling on the Natal railways was conducted by hand signal, and until the Boer War there was little or no signalling in the Orange Free State. It was the outbreak of war, and the additional traffic ..., that compelled the introduction of more up-to-date methods.[12]

Where there were some kind of signal boxes in the stations in the pioneering period of railway construction, the men were usually termed signal box attendants, rather than signalmen, as they had no part in the control of train working. A 'pumper' was one railway position basically unknown in Britain, yet common to much of southern Africa. His was the task of maintaining and working the water pump at a railway station or siding. The pump was the means whereby the large water tank could be filled. All the people who lived in the station community, such as railwaymen and their families, storekeepers and police, would obtain their water from the tank, direct or piped. But, seen as more important than that, was the need for water for the steam locomotives that pulled the railway traffic.

A Railway Missioner wrote:

> I leave the "troops" [relaying gangs and their platelayers] at Kafulafuta and walk down to the pumps where I find the Pumper supervising his [pumping] engine. Here is one of the most beautiful little rivers... The visit . . comes to an end with tea and prayers at the Pumper's house, and a goods train takes me back to Walamba where I rejoin the coach.[13]

At least one Missioner found the pumper's work 'heroic':

> I had planned to arrive early at a ganger's cottage to give Communion and leave later in the morning. The train arrived before daylight at about 5 a.m., so there was something over an hour before

> the family was astire. As the train grunted off to Mafeking I noticed a friendly light not far from the siding, and hearing the steady pumping of an engine I went up to investigate. I found the pumper there, who invited me into his pump-house to share the welcome warmth of his boiler fire. He had a deck-chair and an acetylene lamp with him, and stretched out asleep in the firelight were a native boy and several cats. The pumper, I thought, looked dreadfully tired and ill, and I was not surprised when I heard his story. The water at his siding had given out and the plant was now standing idle. Meanwhile he had to leave his cottage and furniture, and move here with his wife and children, and live in a tiny tin hut that had been hurriedly thrown together. He was watering every train that passed up or down from this kind of relief pump, and being kept at it day and night ... And so there he was at his job, watching the engine and watering the trains as they passed, carrying passengers and mails, cattle or dynamite, troops or stores for the north - they all depended on him. I think you will agree that work such as that is really heroic ...[14]

It is only in the last few years, with the virtual demise of steam in southern Africa south of Zimbabwe, that many of the very smallest railway communities have been demolished. The pumpers are no longer needed and the locos and trains no longer need to quench their thirst.

Although there was little differentiation in the wages of (say) pumpers, or gangers, or engine-drivers because of the location of their work (ie, a pumper in a small station was paid only a little less than one in a very large one), this did not apply to Station Masters. Alone in the railway grades, there was great fluidity of rates of pay for these senior men at stations. Pay and status were based primarily on the importance and size of the station, in terms of either operational or traffic movement. The status and pay could change in any one place from year to year, particularly as the railway expanded - which could result in a station becoming more, or less, important.

Throughout the whole of railway history, status, glory and romance have been attached to the work of engine-drivers - often known as 'Kings of the Road' (a claim always disputed by signalmen, who set up the routes for drivers to follow). In the heyday of steam there was usually a seven step sequence to becoming a full passenger express driver, starting from engine-cleaning and shed duties, and via 'Black Ink Fireman' to 'Black Ink Driver'. In the different conditions of southern Africa these steps were not followed exactly, though most first-class drivers climbed a similar - if shorter - ladder to the top. Jeffries, with reference to Ghanaian railway workers, states that enginemen have regarded themselves 'from the earliest days, and largely succeeded in being treated, as a particularly high-status group.' Many of his studies are unique to Ghana and cannot be paralleled with southern Africa, yet his general conclusions regarding skilled work and engine-driving obtain in the south as much as the west of Africa. He notes that some 'skilled' railway workers in Ghana would be classed as 'semi-skilled' internationally, yet

> the railway artisans and enginemen ... are a genuinely skilled group who have undergone many years of training, and who ... take a great deal of pride in their work and abilities ... The strategic importance of the railway engine, together with its technological qualities, tend to imbue those working with it a corresponding sense of their own importance and power... For the engine-driver, or those artisans responsible for keeping it in running order, it reflects strength and glory on themselves. [15]

The ganger, or platelayer, was 'the most neglected man in the [railway] service.' He was the 'outcast of the railway system, drudging on in his dangerous work, exposed to all weathers, receiving in return the scantest pay, and with little prospect of any promotion to a higher and more remunerative grade... hard work, danger and exposure are encountered by him.' British law ensured that no one worked on the main running lines as a platelayer until he had passed his twenty first birthday.

Patrick MacGill informed his readers that they ought not to believe that he started such work 'with the -- [Caledonian] Railway Company' at twenty-two, but when he was only eighteen. He 'told a lie in order to obtain the post.' This lying over age was not unusual, either in the railway system or (later) when men enlisted for war service. In southern Africa there were few restrictions on age, and the annals of Railway Mission history record many funerals of young (under twenty one) gangers and labourers conducted by railway Missioners.

In a 1919 SACRM leaflet (reproduced in 1935/36) the Head of the Railway Mission wrote:

> People who travel on the railways sometimes think of what they owe to the work of the engine-driver and fireman, the signalman and the guard, but they seldom remember the ganger or platelayer, on the thoroughness of whose work the safety of the passengers depends. It is his business to watch the rails in case they split or work loose, to see that the ballast is kept firm, and generally to be responsible for the condition of the permanent way on his particular section.[16]

On the Cape Midland section in the 1890s gangs were responsible for track sections of between 8km and 15km, whereas in Rhodesia this extended to lengths of 16km and in 'German South West' [Namibia] to 24km. Ganging, as with other railway work, was organised on a grading system. Both the Cape and Natal Government Railways classified gangers ('platelayers', in Natal) into three tiers. The (Afrikaner) Central South African Railways (Transvaal and O.F.S) had four grades of ganger. Unification of the railways in 1910 (completed in 1916) saw, in 1913, a total of 1,885 gangers

> employed on the unified.. [railways].., divided into eight grades, ranging from Special Ganger (fifty-nine men) and Second-class Gangers (the biggest grade, with 602 men), to Second Class Sub-gangers (309 men) and Apprentice Gangers (thirty-three men). Gangs were usually led by a white ganger, whose immediate superiors were a Permanent Way Inspector and a District Engineer. These senior staff periodically toured sections of the line, generally with the help of a gangers' trolley. The railway work gangs themselves comprised between five and fourteen men, most of whom were Africans.[17]

At the large railway stations and large junctions the gangers were accommodated in railway camps along with all the other railway personnel. At smaller stations the ganger's house would often be one among a cluster of houses occupied by (say) the station master, storekeeper, hotelier and wheelwright. On the open veldt ganger's cottages were 'more often quite by themselves.' In 1914 a missioner noted that 'at a siding in the [Orange] Free State... there [was] just a ganger's cottage and a cluster of huts for the white labourers. The entire population [was] Dutch, very Dutch.'

> Even in the smallest railway settlements the work hierarchy was reflected in differences between the accommodation given to gangers, sub-gangers and labourers. Married gangers (in 1913 approximately 80 per cent of gangers were married) lived with their families in their own small houses.[18]

These 'small houses' were dismissed in 1930 by H.B. Ellison (Chairman of SACRM) as 'something which few English farmers would pass as a fowl-house; and that was the home of an Englishman, and perhaps an Englishman's wife and children.

Dorothy Ellison noted that 'every ganger's cottage [had] its row of native dwellings, constructed of old sleepers.' Many of the gangers and their families, particularly in the Cape, were mixed race 'Coloureds'. One Railway Missioner contrasted the appearance of their houses to those of the 'poor whites' (Afrikaners):

> I am spending tonight at a "coloured" ganger's cottage. We have many coloured gangers and labourers up here.Their houses are nearly all spotlessly clean, in striking contrast to those of the "poor whites", who yet pride themselves on their superiority as white men ..[19]

In all the reports and letters of the Railway Mission, certainly up to the 1960s, the most frequently used words relating to the people, especially gangers, visited, were 'loneliness' and 'isolation'. This isolation was more apparent the further from Capetown the railway stretched:

> The further North one gets, the fewer become the married gangers. This is accounted for by the prevalence of fever and the loneliness which the wife would have to put up with. There are, for instance, on one stretch no less than five gangers who never see a white man to speak to except the Permanent Way Inspector, who passes through once a week, and the Pay Train, which goes through monthly.[20]

Inevitably, human and social relationships proved difficult and problematical in such isolated and lonely places. Even in South Africa, where gangers were able to have their families with them and where they were likely to see friends or colleagues more frequently than gangers 'up North', life for a ganger and his family was anything but easy. A SACRM Woman Worker, Miss Constance Saunders, in one of her letters, epitomised 'normal' ganger life:

> The other day I was at a siding called Oven. A place very aptly named..! Here there is nothing to be seen except the interminable plains and mountains of the Karroo and, some way off, one solitary farm house ... Now and again a goods train thundered past the spot where the mission coach stood, and the mail [train] to Capetown flashed by, bringing a fleeting breath of the outside world to this desolate spot. About half a mile down the line lay the reason for my visit. A ganger's house, with a group of railway labourers' cottages. The men living in these cottages assist the ganger in his responsible work of keeping in repair the large expanse of line which he tends.... Their work makes it necessary for them to live, with their families, in spots which are lonely in the extreme.

> Here ... the school is twelve miles away. Children of school age are living in a hostel in the nearest town. The available telephone is at the distant farm, and the only way of posting a letter is to give it to a guard on a train ... [The] grouping together of about half-a-dozen families, in such conditions, brings about many a problem of human relationships.[21]

A visitor today sees merely a few piles of bricks and rubble as the Diesel or Electric-hauled train passes what once was a 'siding called Oven.'

Any account of railway ganging life in southern Africa, as, for example, Pirie's vital investigation, has to rely heavily on the reports of the SACRM personnel. Archive Railway material on the life and work of gangers, or indeed of any other railway employees, is virtually non-existent in most areas, other than incomplete lists of names and wages. The Railway Missioners did not set out to write a social history of the 'congregations' they served, yet their observations about 'life and labour along the line .. presented as background to accounts about mission work' had an immediacy and frankness that makes them an invaluable, though not flawless, record of railway ganging.

The recurrent themes of railway navvy literature are hardship and exploitation; those of train and railway working are danger and routine; whereas those of railway ganging are drudgery and isolation.

> The gangers, pumpers and station personnel in the countryside led dreary lives that were on the fringe of society. Their work facilitated the passage of people, commodities and ideas, but in the process they were stranded as bystanders. Modernisation and prosperity surged past. Married railwaymen drew their wives and children into this static, circumscribed and predominantly male dead-end. [22]

The limits of their sections of the permanent way were 'practically the boundaries of the sphere of [their] existence.' We shall see, in a later discussion on the role of SACRM women workers, how the isolation was more keenly felt by the gangers' wives.

Racial division of labour

The term 'outside' was frequently used not only in relation to the large centres and cities hundreds of miles up or down 'the line', but also for anyone who had 'outside', non-railway, employment. The railways in southern Africa 'did, indeed, sometimes resemble a "state within a state", replete with its own laws, language, science and philosophy, and its own social structure.' The 'railway bailiwick' concept is very useful in understanding the work and identity of (white) railwaymen, particularly in South Africa and in Southern Rhodesia, not least in their control of the racial division of labour.

Groups such as gangers and pumpers, classed as semi-skilled whites, were particularly careful about 'division of labour' and 'hierarchy' in order to define their own 'skill' and to keep 'the natives' on a lower-skill level. Management were not averse to suggesting that 'a Black' could quite easily do the job of a pumper or ganger.

The flow of engineers and railway workers from Britain and Europe to southern Africa in the 1860s to 1880s and 1890s eventually became a steady trickle as the countries trained their own workers and as the white population expanded. Before 1907 migrant African workers were employed for unskilled labouring work. The 1906-09 recession, however, led to the various states replacing many Africans by 'poor whites' on line-maintenance and new construction work.

During the 1920s South Africa introduced the 'civilised labour policy' ('civilised' being a euphemism for 'white'). This had the effect of increasing the number of unskilled white railway workers from 6,300 to 12,000 in the period between 1924 and 1932, and halving the number of Africans employed from 35,000 to 17,500 in the same period.

With the rise of Afrikaner nationalism before and during the Second World War, it was argued that African workers were filling places vacated by white railworkers and that therefore the position of Afrikaners on the railways was being threatened 'from below' by 'the Blacks.' The Nationalists set themselves up as 'the lone champions of the unskilled Afrikaner railway employee in his struggle onto or up the ladder.'

In Rhodesia, the Railways recruited at first from Britain. Many, who settled in Rhodesia, themselves then recruited friends and workmates from home. Also, a regular stream of white manual workers, often semi- and unskilled, made their way up from South Africa. 'A large number of men came up to this territory in the vain hope that when the railway extension commenced, there would be an outlet for their labour..'

Statistics show that white railway workers in Rhodesia, between 1907 and 1941, always formed from 7-12 per cent of the European population. Skilled and semi- or unskilled railwaymen, who entered Rhodesia as immigrants, ranged from ninety-nine in 1926, to a peak of 186 in 1928, dropping down to thirty-nine in 1939. It was only in 1936 that more Whites were actually born in Rhodesia (34 per cent) than came in from South Africa (32 per cent).

In 1904, for contrast, 53 per cent were from England and 41 per cent from South Africa. The employment of both black and white railwaymen in Rhodesia will be explored later.

Most white railway workers in South Africa and in Rhodesia had Africans to assist them in their work.

> Master-servant was the primary relationship between white and black worker, not just at work, however, but also in the home, where the white was direct employer. White railway workers, no less than any others of their race, saw life without black domestic servants as inconceivable. [23]

---

1 from Cullen Gouldsbury, 'A Ballad of the B.M.R.', in *Songs Out of Exile.*

2 The best and fullest account of the building of the lower Zambezi bridge is to be found in Landeg White's *Bridging the Zambesi* (1993). The bridge, with 33 main spans, was 2.3 miles long - the longest railway bridge in the world.

3 Fairbridge, 1927, 40/41

4 Purkiss, A.J., 1978, 343

5 MacGill, 1914, 1983, 250

6 Coleman, 1965, 20

7 Coleman, 1965, 24

8 Coleman, 198

9 Pauling, 1926, 1969, 28

10 Purkiss, 17

11 McKenna, 41

12 Knock, 1971, 91

13 USPG 'X' 1441/2, 5, n.d.

14 QP147, 1941, 20

15 Jeffries, 1978, 205/6

16 AB940/WITS/CPSA

17 Pirie, 1993, 66

18 Pirie, 1993, 68

19 QP 103, 1930, 7

20 QP 43, 1914, 13

21 QP 171, 1950, 11

22 Pirie, 1993, 74

23 Lunn, 208/9

3. The Church Railway Mission begins

- 'a good deal of roughing it'

> Do I see the Priest from the Mission? yes, thank God, now and then,
> He's got so much to do, what with distance and hundreds of men;
> The funds are low they tell me, and men are needed so bad,
> It does us good to see them, where companionship's not to be had.'[1]

By 1908, when 'A Low-Veld Ganger' was first penned, and its author could thank God for 'the Priest from the Mission', the work of the railway chaplains had become well-established.

The South African Church Railway Mission (SACRM) can be said to have originated in 1885, shortly after the Rev. Philip Barrington Simeon's arrival in Grahamstown, which had been reached by the railways just two years earlier. The Diocese of Grahamstown, the second oldest in southern Africa, formed the eastern part of Cape Colony and contained an area of 75,000 square miles (roughly 300 miles North to South, and 250 miles East to West). The 1891 Census, just six years after Simeon's arrival, gave the population as 50,000 'English speaking' and 450,000 'other than English speaking.' Robert Gray had been consecrated as (the first) Bishop of Cape Town Diocese in June 1843. His diocese included the Cape Colony, Natal and British Kaffraria, the island of St. Helena, plus the Orange River Sovereignty (whilst it was British territory). Within a year he had started his first Visitation of the vast diocese. He was in 'Graham's Town' from October 9th, 1848, until the 17th and wrote from Bathurst on the 19th:

> This Diocese is really a much more important one than I had any idea of when I was in England. ... It is almost a mystery to me to see what a field there is before us after our long neglect of this Colony ...

Two years later his second Visitation 'took the bishop to Graham's Town.. [where he expressed] his strong conviction that a sub division of the Diocese was the only way by which its needs could be in any way properly supplied ..'[2] Early in 1852 the bishop returned to England to arrange for the division of the diocese, as well as to raise funds and find more priests. Soon he could write,

> The great joy of my mission to England has been accomplished and the Diocese is subdivided ... the Church will now, I think, fix her roots deep in South Africa. Now there are three centres of unity.

His choice of Colenso for Natal was, alas, to be a cause of disunity. Gray was left with a reduced diocese and was to be the Metropolitan-bishop for the whole of British South Africa. In 1883, Bishop Webb of Bloemfontein was translated south to Grahamstown, just thirty years after it had become a separate diocese. Alan Webb was a 'man of silence, immense spiritual power, statesmanship and administrative ability.' Whilst still in Bloemfontein he had established Church work among the gold and diamond mines, 'ministering to those ..diggers who were Anglicans, trying to redeem those of the riff-raff who were only nominally Anglican.'[3]

The few references to Simeon in SACRM literature, such as *God's Highwaymen* and *Mission Unaccomplished,* give 1885 as the year of his arrival. It is clear from official Church archives and from his own 'Reminiscences' (in *Light for the Line,* April 1925) that Simeon - 'one of those originators who appear from time to time in Church history' - arrived in Grahamstown just before Christmas, 1884. He hoped to found a Religious Community, where students would eventually be trained for the ordained Ministry. He bought a house for the purpose, calling it 'St. Paul's Mission House'. Although his own project was eventually abandoned, St. Paul's did become the Diocesan Theological College - a role it still retains, though as a Provincial College under its recent (1993) name of the College of the Transfiguration.

Given Bishop Webb's previous concern for itinerant and new mission work, it is not surprising that he asked Simeon to work as a 'Diocesan Mission Preacher' in order to open up new work 'with special reference to the villages and farms which were scattered over the country far away from any resident Priest, and from all Church privileges [ie, baptisms, weddings, funerals etc.]..'[4] Bishop Webb himself wrote, 'I am very thankful that Fr. Simeon is likely to take root in this Diocese, and St. Paul's Mission House to be a power for good. I trust he will take charge of some districts and railway centres which are without clergy.'

Many of these 'railway centres', such as Cradock, Cookhouse, De Aar, Aliwal North and Naauwpoort, were more like camps than the word 'centre' suggests. De Aar was only just inside the diocese and was later to outstrip Naauwpoort and become the busiest and most famous of all the southern African railway 'crossroads'. It was formerly a lonely collection of sheep farms and narrowly escaped being named 'Von Brandis Junction' and 'Brounger Junction' (its official name). Even in 1896, Naauwpoort - 'the principal railway junction in South Africa ... [with] nearly 1000 inhabitants .. [had] no minister of religion resident but our own', stated a Railway Mission leaflet. Cookhouse, on the Port Elizabeth-Cradock line, was 'the second largest unoccupied [by clergy!] railway camp.' Alicedale was the only camp, in 1898, where there was an actual church building . The camps themselves, though of varying sizes, usually housed a motley collection of gangers, pumpers, train crew, yardmen, construction workers and storekeepers, along with their families.

Simeon's first up-country journey was by train to Tafelberg, some fifty miles from its nearest town, Cradock. In visiting the farmers and their families he became aware of the 'extreme isolation and loneliness of the Railway officials at the small stations and sidings, and of the still more lonely lives of the gangers and second men, whose cottages stood at regular intervals of five to seven miles along the line.'

These comments about isolation and loneliness and the 'womenfolk at the cottages', whom he later mentions, were to become a constant refrain by every missioner who followed Simeon in the next ninety or so years. It was during the course of his journey to Cradock and Tafelberg, and the return to Grahamstown, that Father Simeon (as he was invariably known) formed his plan which he submitted to Bishop Webb. I quote at length from his 'Reminiscences', as this not only appears to be the only full extant account, but also set the basic *modus operandi* for all subsequent railway mission work:

> ...[Bishop Webb] gave a ready consent ... for bringing the Church's ministrations to them [Railway officials, gangers etc]; and I then wrote to the Commissioner of Railways at Capetown, explained my desire to him, and asked to be allowed to make use of the gangers' trollies, as a means of enabling me to make a house to house visitation along the whole Railway, from Grahamstown to Orange River Station, the limit of the Diocese ... He fully granted [the request], extending his permission to the whole of the Railway system and in addition he granted me the right of free travelling by any train whether passenger or goods train; and ... the right of stopping any train, at any point ... whenever needed for the purpose of my ministry, the only exceptions being the two weekly mail expresses. He also issued strict orders to see that the trollies were always at my disposal, and to assist me generally in any way that might be in their power. [5]

Simeon's matter-of-fact account is, however, a quite remarkable statement, the practicalities of which are examined below. Although he was writing in his retirement and looking back some forty years, there is ample evidence that his 'Reminiscences' were accurate. Letters published in the Grahamstown Diocesan Railway Mission *Quarterly* (1890s), and in *Light for the Line,* as well as post-1900 SACRM magazines, all confirm the details given by Simeon. He is referring to the year 1885. As we have seen, it was entirely in character for Bishop Webb to encourage this work; he was a remarkable and far-seeing bishop, willing - more than most - for his clergy to be freed from parochial constraints. The 'Commissioner of Railways at Capetown' that Simeon wrote to was the Hon. F. Schermbrucker. The State had taken control of railways in South Africa from January 1, 1873. The General Manager of the Railways was, of course, always the person in charge of the day to day running of the system and it was to the Manager that the Railway Mission looked for assistance, particularly after the Union in 1910. But in the very early days the parliamentary head of the C.G.R - the Commissioner for Public Works - was the person to approach.

In those days, even in 'new' and pioneering areas for the Anglican Church, it was unthinkable for a priest working in one diocese to undertake any tasks in another. This is still rare, wedded as the Church is to the diocesan and parochial system. Simeon, naturally, made his requests relating to Grahamstown Diocese (only). The Commissioner, however, gave the necessary permissions for the whole of the Cape Railways. More than half of the Cape Colony lay in the Diocese of Cape Town, and the Hopetown to Kimberley route was in the Diocese of Bloemfontein. It was still unusual for a priest to be itinerant within a diocese, let alone outside it. Yet here was the Head of the Railways giving special (and generous) authority to this Anglican clergyman to travel up and down the (then) 1654 miles of railway in the Cape, as opposed to the mere 300 miles or so in the Eastern Province/Grahamstown Diocese. Commissioner Schermbrucker, was not, of course, bound by Anglican constraints and almost certainly did not consider the niceties of diocesan practice when he made his offer.

We must not, however, treat the issue as a matter merely of Anglican habit and structure. Here, right at the very start of a unique ministry, both the bishop and the priest involved were being offered a chance to challenge and change their basic theological understanding of Anglicanism and of evangelism. I believe that Bishop Webb was exactly the right person to make the radical departure necessary. But he was not the Metropolitan. Like other bishops in the Province, he owed his allegiance to the bishop of Cape Town. Within his own diocese he could be, and was, inovative and radical. The physical boundaries of Grahamstown Diocese (as Bloemfontein earlier) had to remain the boundaries of new theological understanding. For Simeon there was no question of moving outside the diocese. Even to travel distances within the boundaries was departure enough from normal practice. But the seeds had been sown; the distinctive feature of the Railway Mission stated at the outset.

This was in many ways a precursor to other challenges to the parochial and diocesan systems and, equally, to the difficulties and tensions that arose. We shall note the frustrations encountered by the missioners in their dealings with the bishops (frequently regarding Confirmations) and with parochial clergy (sensitive to itinerant priests straying on to their 'patch'). Over forty years after the challenge to the system faced by Bishop Webb and Simeon, Bishop Paget of Mashonaland, as we shall discover, was constrained to ask the Archbishop of Cape Town for permission to send consecrated Communion wafers down the River Zambesi. When looking at The Railway Mission's work in education we shall observe how, although the Mission was attempting to have the 'particular accents of Anglicanism' in all its parish manifestations - such as schools, Sunday Schools, Guilds, Scouts and Guides, this was being done (usually) on the move. This was its uniqueness, its challenge to immobile parochialism and to diocesan 'fences'. It was a major shift from centuries of theological and ecclesiastical stagnation.

Douglas Ellison, writing of the time immediately before Simeon started his work, stated: 'The Cape Government authorities, having placed their servants in many cases in almost impossible local circumstances, made no sort of provision for their spiritual needs, beyond the offer of a free railway pass to any chance volunteer ...'[6] This was a period, as Pirie has commented, 'before the establishment of a social welfare division within railway organisations.'

Returning to Simeon's statement (above), we may note that there was no suggestion at that stage of a special carriage, or caboose, being made available. Travelling by goods train normally entailed a journey in an open waggon; yet that was marginally preferable to 'trolleying'. The 'right of stopping any train' was not as exceptional as it may appear. The majority of trains, with the exception of the mail expresses, travelled quite slowly and would normally slow down even more at a siding or crossing point (either to receive permission to proceed on the single track, or to wait for another train to pass). Special stopping of the mail trains was never, officially, sanctioned, although it was known to happen. The Rev. Roy Sinker, writing in 1984 of his time with SACRM between 1935 and 1938, noted:

> I found [on joining] that I had in my possession a first class pass on any train in my section and the authority to stop any goods train at any authorised station or passing place ... I remember one particular night at a small place called Aloes a few miles north of Port Elizabeth, I thought it would be grand to get back to Alicedale around midnight ... the only train going North through the station was the Johannesburg express which would come along at speed in about two hours time.

He then persuaded the station foreman to stop the train which, 'with screeching of brakes and a good deal of swearing in Dutch came to an abrupt halt.' The ticket examiner was 'speechless with rage' when he discovered that the new passenger only wished to go to Alicedale and that he had no ticket. However, he produced his Railway Mission Pass -

> 'What! A pass signed by the General Manager himself. Oh sir, my apologies ... come along with me and I will put you in a first class compartment ... and I will wake you just before the train gets into Alicedale.' He wished to pay tribute to the marvellous work of the Railway Mission over many years in serving the railway workers up and down the rail roads of South Africa ...

Sinker did, however, promise not to repeat the incident.

Simeon's first official railway visiting took place in February 1886. Everywhere he received a 'hearty welcome', stopping at each cottage for a quarter of an hour. 'Prayers were said, sometimes a baby baptised, sometimes in the case of a new-comer two or even three children, for whose baptism they had never before had an opportunity. The majority of the gangers were Church people, though some of course were sectarians and occasionally Roman Catholics...' He soon began to travel the length and breadth of the diocese (though not of the whole Cape system, for the Commissioner's suggestion was still alien to the Anglican mind and structure, as indicated above) taking with him parcels of newspapers and other literature, such as religious Tracts, for those 'sadly cut off from the outer world'; taking Services in a variety of buildings; and showing concern for the 'natives working on the railway under a ganger [who] .. constantly asked him for spelling books, and bought from him Bibles and Prayer Books in Xosa and Dutch.'[7]

Simeon soon so established quarterly visits to various centres and lengths of the line that his mission, with its base at St. Paul's in Grahamstown, became known as 'St. Paul's Railway Mission'. This was its unofficial title before becoming the official 'Grahamstown Diocesan Railway Mission' (GDRM) in 1893/4. The title 'Railway Chaplain' began to be used of Simeon as he continued his solo work. He was joined for a short time, in 1888, by the Rev W.H. Ramsbottom, until the bishop (surprisingly for Webb) 'persuaded' the new helper to move to a parish. This was a foretaste of the not-infrequent offers that were to appear during much of the Railway Mission's history. At some stage he was also joined, briefly, by the Rev. S.C. Freer. The practice of Ramsbottom and Freer 'appears to have been to take a run through the Midland and Graff-Reinet Lines on the trolley, one or other of them, about once a quarter.'

The lone missioner became concerned about the education of the children of railway workers, most of whom had little or no schooling. He persuaded Mother Cecile, Superior of the Sisters of the Resurrection,

Grahamstown, to take gangers' children (girls) as boarders. 'There the "Railways" - twenty five of them - drawn from every corner of the great Diocese, found a .. home and a splendid education.' Dorothy Ellison, in her book *God's Highwaymen,* places the above passage in the section on the work of her brother, Douglas Ellison, who was to succeed Simeon. But it was Simeon who not only pioneered the railway mission work, but who was responsible for the founding of the education of railway children. It is interesting to note that Simeon's crucial account of the beginnings of the railway mission, printed in (the South African) *Light for the Line,* was ignored in the sister publication in England, *SACRM Quarterly Paper,* although it frequently did quote from *Light for the Line.* Similarly, Dorothy Ellison's book ignored the account. 'In Journeyings Often', a booklet featuring missioners' letters, did include a few selected paragraphs from Simeon. In a letter written in 1907 the Rev. H.B. Ellison stated, 'The Mission was started some 16 years ago [=1891] by a single priest [ie. his brother, Douglas Ellison] in the Diocese of Grahamstown.'[8] No one would wish to deny the Ellisons their seminal and magnificent work, that will be detailed later, but Philip Barrington Simeon's record should stand.

In 1891 Simeon wrote an account of his work on the Midland Railway in Cape Colony. He firstly described the different 'classes' of railway employees, as detailed in the previous chapter and realised that the permanent way men were the ones out of reach of parochial clergy. Simeon went on to write:

> I use a trolley, with which each ganger is provided, for the line is single, and a train could not be stopped for me to visit. For over four years I have made quarterly journeys, each day about 32 miles, including visits to 13 families, and in the time have baptised 180 children ... One's welcome is very encouraging.

Trolleying, however, apart from being exposed to the elements, considerably limited the distances that could be covered. Simeon, therefore, 'in the early part of 1891... approached the Commissioner of Railways once more [Sir James Sivewright], with an earnest request that he would grant a small special carriage for the use of the "Railway Chaplain" ... and, again he granted [the] request ..' The Uitenhage railway works were told to build a suitable vehicle, which was subsequently placed at the disposal of Simeon's successor, Douglas Ellison, whose sister again gave him the benefit of an original idea!:

> The Chaplain, boarding a train on the Karoo at midnight, found himself alone with a bearded stranger [The Hon. J. Laing]. They soon

> got yarning together. His companion's comment was: 'Of course you ought to have one' - viz., a coach. Was it mere chance that the speaker proved to be ... Mr. Lang [sic], the new Commissioner of Railways?.. [9]

Simeon himself never either saw nor used the vehicle he had requested. The short-wheel based 'pill-box', "Number 404", was the first of many cabooses that were to feature in the next ninety years. The final (long-wheel based) caboose now rests in Bulawayo Railway Museum as a tribute to the work of the Church Railway Mission.

Simeon realised that 'the Church ought to have a priest who could give his whole time to the railway folk, [for he] could only scratch on the surface ..' Towards the end of 1891 the Rev. Douglas Ellison arrived from England to be the chaplain to Bishop Webb of Grahamstown. Early in 1892 Ellison wrote:

> I believe it as good as settled that I am to succeed Father Simeon in the Railway work when he leaves for England next month. ..it sounds very attractive, a whole fortnight each quarter spent in the open air upon a trolley, visiting all the gangers and stations over 300 miles of line; and also looking in en route at any wayside house within reasonable distance, most of which never see a parson the long year through. I expect it will involve a good deal of roughing it ...[10]

His expectations were more than realised, and the 'trolleying' was to lose much of its attraction in the sixteen years that Douglas Ellison was to be a Railway Missioner and Head of Mission. It is a tribute to Bishop Webb's vision, again, that he released his new chaplain to become the full-time chaplain and Head of the diocese's expanding work with railway people. He had clearly seen the need for the work and was flexible enough in his thinking to promote this departure from traditional Anglicanism.

And so Simeon moved off to become Rector of Fort Beaufort, giving his 'St. Paul's' house to the bishop for itinerating evangelistic work and a theological students' hostel. In his 'Reminiscences' he believed that he had baptised 217 children in his years, 1886-91, as a railway missioner. It is clear from the original Register that he was still baptising children of railway people in 1892. His last entry (April 6, 1892) is numbered 207, one Ben Johannes Burnett, the seven week old son of Peter and Rachel. Peter was a 'second man' on the railways, and the family lived at 'Thorngrove Siding'. [11]

By 1894 Douglas Ellison was writing, in a printed leaflet headed 'Grahamstown Diocesan Railway Mission', of the position of Church work along the Cape Government Railways. He estimated some '2000 white men - English and Dutch - (together with their families), living and working in various capacities along those parts of the Cape Railways ... [which they served].' He stated, '... our chief care is, if possible, to save these white people from falling right back ...' (ie. from Christianity to paganism). This was to be a constant refrain for the greater part of the Railway Mission's life, and a theme frequently taken up by the main speakers at the Annual SACRM Meetings in London, as we shall see when examining the formative years of SACRM from 1903.

Ellison continued, in his leaflet,

> A great mass of Natives, both heathen and Christian, is also ready to our hand; but as things are at present, I am usually obliged, though with feelings of the most genuine regret, to pass by the row of Native huts which adjoin most of the white men's cottages.[12]

The problem of 'passing by' was rarely solved throughout the Mission's life, despite regrets and promises, faced - as it was - with special pleading for ministry to the Whites. Ellison again, in an information leaflet in 1896, stated that the 'Object' of the Mission was,

> to provide spiritual ministrations for a large number of railway people, farmers, store keepers, police, and others, scattered round some 1500 miles of the Cape Government Railways [ie.still only within the diocese of Grahamstown]. It has also begun what, with more men and money, should hereafter be a great work among the thousands of natives, both heathen and Christian, along the Line.[13]

We shall return to the whole question of work by and among black Africans. Suffice to state here that those who tried to minister to the Africans were usually frustrated either by local Whites or by lack of Mission staff (as intimated above) - priority being given to the Whites. Unlike most Missionary Societies, the Railway Mission (under its various names, and as observed earlier) was not concerned primarily with converting Africans to Christianity, or even with ministering to them, but rather with bringing the ministrations of the (Anglican) Church to (mainly white and coloured) Railway employees. Without fulfilling the latter obligation there would have been no free passes or Mission coaches provided.

By 1896 the Grahamstown Diocesan Railway Mission was on a fairly sound footing, with Douglas Ellison helped by one Assistant Chaplain, three Lay Evangelists, a 'Native Catechist', an honorary treasurer and various honorary secretaries of Local Associations such as Colesburg, Graaff-Reinet and Port Elizabeth. The 1897 Annual Statement lists a

Diocesan Grant of £40 along with a Grant of £50 from the S.P.G.[Society for the Propagation of the Gospel; now USPG] Missionary Society in England. Ellison lists seventy two names of children baptised by the Missioners in 1896. At least 21 of these have 'Dutch' names and were therefore less likely to be Anglican. Until the Railway Mission moved out of South Africa in 1957 many Afrikaner families were happy to see the arrival of the Anglican Missioner - not least because their own Predikants were few and far between. In 1896 the 'Monthly Letters' (sent to the UK) and *Light for the Line* (quarterly and for local readership) were started. Douglas Ellison became the first official 'Head' of the Mission, and by the following year the GDRM was able to begin putting money aside for Church buildings at Naauwpoort [Noupoort] and Cookhouse.

The variety of buildings used for worship is indicated in the account given by Mr. Ambrose Leefe, one of the Lay Evangelists, writing in the 1898/9 Year Book of the GDRM:

> It has been my privilege to hold during the past year 117 services. The offerings amounted to £21 0s. 2d. Alicedale is the only camp where there is a church. In Stormberg, Rosmead and Norval's Pont, the other chief camps on the Midland, the services are held in the schoolrooms. This is also the case in 24 other stations. If there is no schoolroom, the waiting room is used. If there is no waiting room, the service is held in somebody's private dwelling. I try to visit at least three cottages each day, and at each one I desire to have a short service ...

In those early Diocese of Grahamstown days of the Railway Mission, 1898/9 stands out as the most important and busy twelve months of its existence. Four more workers had arrived, including the Rev. Frederick Rogers, who was to work on the Mission until 1914, and Laurence (Laurie) Skey who was a layman, an ex railway clerk, who then went on to be ordained and to work on and off for SACRM until 1932, when he became Dean of Salisbury [Harare]. Archdeacon William Gaul, of Kimberley, had moved north to Bulawayo in 1895 (at the invitation of his friend Cecil Rhodes), becoming the second Bishop of Mashonaland, following pioneering Knight-Bruce. By June 1898 Bishop Gaul had given 'temporary' charge of the Bechuanaland Railway line to the Rev. Nelson Fogarty 'with a sphere of work extending from Vryburg to Bulawayo, nearly 600 miles; and later on ... up to the Victoria Falls, another 250 miles..'[14] The bishop had applied to the railway for a special coach as the 'church van' to be put off at any spot along the line. The Railway Mission was therefore at last, by 1898, moving across diocesan boundaries, although it was still officially the Mission of one diocese (Grahamstown), and four years before SACRM came into being. In the space of thirteen years (a short time, by Anglican standards!) the bishops of the Province had come to accept this cross-diocesan itinerant mission, or at least to turn a blind eye to its irregular ministry.

In 1899 a London Committee was formed, with the Rev. John Ellison as Chairman. This Committee continued to operate until 1980/1, with its main task that of recruiting men and women for the Mission work in southern Africa, paying their fares, giving them a clothing allowance, and maintaining or assisting them at their posts. By Christmas, 1899, Douglas Ellison was able to write to England from 'Bishopsbourne Cottage, Grahamstown'. He reported that it had been clear to him for some time that 'a central House ... [was] essential for the healthy development of the Mission ..(and for) the 'permanence and consolidation of the work.' In the 1898/9 GDRM 'Year Book' Ellison wrote:

> I anxiously await the day when a house in Grahamstown for our workers will become practicable. They return to headquarters, as a rule, in urgent need of rest alike for soul and body, and a central Mission House will greatly simplify matters in this as in other directions.

Dr. Cornish, the new bishop, gave the Mission the cottage (which stood in his grounds) 'on exceptionally easy terms.' At last the Railway Mission had a base. Dr. Cornish was one bishop who took a great interest in the work, and would on occasions accompany Ellison in the 'pill-box' coach attached to goods trains, as the chaplain travelled up and down the railway system. Ellison, similarly, often went with the bishop in his mule-drawn Cape-cart as he journeyed through his vast diocese. Not all bishops were to show such interest, nor were relationships between the pioneering missioners and the diocesan hierarchy always as cordial.

A photograph taken in 1899 shows the staff standing inside and outside of the '404' coach. There are seven members shown (Nelson Fogarty and Laurence Skey were busy elsewhere) and this total of nine was not far short of the average number even in SACRM's heyday, when fifteen staff meant a good year. Included in the group is Josiah Ngcambu, the 'native catechist', who had recently left his work as head coal porter to be appointed officially as the Catechist at Naauwpoort. The July 1900 'Monthly Letter' states, '.. Josiah is doing good work among the natives in that [Naauwpoort military] camp, with an average of 60 or 70 at his Sunday services, of which there are usually four, and regular classes for Catechumers [sic] and Confirmation candidates during the week.' Ellison, in subsequent Letters, returns to the question of 'native work', to which we shall also later return.

By 1899 Ellison was already urging the expansion of the Mission, not only in Grahamstown diocese, but northwards. In the July Letter of that year he emphasised to the supporters in England what he conceived to be the special opportunity which lay open before the Mission:

> The immense development of South Africa towards the North - thanks to its gold and its diamonds and its Cecil Rhodes - has been accomplished, these last few years, by a corresponding burst of new life along the entire length of our Cape Railways, which forms not only the base of supply for that new country to the North, but are in a very real sense the main arteries of our young and stirring national life. ...during the seven years and more through which my own connection with South Africa extends, little railway camps or villages have been fairly bursting into existence. These camps, so far as any religious effort is concerned, are practically virgin soil. ... A year or two since there was a good reason for thinking that an English Church had the chance of exercising a permanent influence in the spiritual oversight of these people. Had we been backed up at that time with really adequate and effective assistance, I believe it might have been so. To-day it is far from certain. Other religious bodies have now inaugurated itinerating work, on the [railway] lines of our own Railway Mission ... meanwhile, we must clearly make the most of any advantage we may have gained by being first in the field.[15]

Ellison took care to see that comments such as these did not appear in the (local) *Light for the Line.* It is a truism that different churches cooperated more 'on the mission field' than they did at that time in Europe. Rivalry, however, was never far below the surface - particularly in pioneering work where each group wanted to have first claim. To be fair to the missioners themselves, in practice their first priorities were almost always the needs of the railway workers and their families, rather than gaining converts or members for 'the English Church' (by which they meant 'Anglican').

In 1901 Harry Ellison joined his brother, later becoming Head. 1902 saw the first (and most important) change of official name (classing 'St. Paul's Railway Mission' as unofficial). In his report in 1902 Douglas Ellison stated, at the request of the bishops, '... the work of the Mission will no longer be confined to a single Diocese, but is to be immediately extended into the Dioceses of Bloemfontein and Mashonaland, and possibly throughout the Transvaal.' He went on to announce that the Archbishop of Capetown had provisionally approved the name change to the 'South African Church Railway Mission', an approval which was confirmed at the next Provincial Synod. In the last Letter under the Grahamstown title, Douglas Ellison, in his appeal for funds, stated:

> Our work is, in a sense, unique. So far as my own knowledge goes, there is no other distinctively Railway Mission in our English Church: and that being so, we may well hope to appeal to some few, even where other Missionary Work of a more conventional type has been long established. ... There can be no question as to the greatness of our opportunity, if only the necessary funds are forthcoming to enable us to make the most of it. [16]

Subsequent letters, published under the SACRM title, were never silent on the question of funds, but made a greater appeal for chaplains and lady workers. As the Grahamstown Diocesan Railway Mission bowed out, it was with a Mission Staff of twelve (The Revds Douglas Ellison, Alfred Long, J.W.R. Brocklebank, H. Forshaw, L.D. Richards, Eustace St.C. Hill, H.B. Ellison and Laurie Skey; lay evangelists Kenneth Mather and Reginald Wathen; and 'Native Catechists' Josiah Ngcambu and Benjamin Kaba). There was a London Committee of twelve, under the chairmanship of the Rev. J.H.Ellison, and which included the General Secretary and Treasurer, Miss Elise Astley, and the Editorial Secretary, Mrs W.A. Hewett. A Newspaper Secretary completed the 'home team'. Up and down England twenty two 'Local Representatives' ensured that the work of the Mission was supported in many Dioceses and parishes. In Grahamstown Diocese itself, in the 1899 Year Book there were some fifteen Local Associations listed, over ninety 'General Subscribers' to the work of the Mission, and over one hundred subscribers to Church Building Funds. By 1902 these numbers almost certainly had increased. It was all a very far cry from the solo work of Philip Barrington Simeon, some seventeen years earlier, and an excellent group of staff and supporters to move the Railway Mission into its next important phase.

The move Northwards

In 1902 the Grahamstown Diocesan Railway Mission became the South African Church Railway Mission - a title it retained for the next fifty-five years. The SPG £50 grant was boosted up to £1000; the English 'Blue Quarterly' [equivalent to the South African *Light for the Line*] was started in the following October as a replacement to the Monthly Letter; the first nurse, Nurse Eardley, was appointed [forerunner of many women workers]; and the two year-old Railway School moved from Francistown (just south of the Rhodesian border) a little north to Plumtree, just inside Rhodesia. The first issue of the *Quarterly Paper* reported negotiations with Sir Percy Girouard, Commissioner of the Central South African

Railways. Douglas Ellison requested free Passes to the Missioners [in line with those in the Cape Railways area] Railway Rates for food - 'a blessing enjoyed by all bona-fide Railway men' and the reinstatement of a 'lost' 'Kitchener coach'. He also asked 'as a matter of principle' for financial aid for the Mission from the Government, though realised that none would be forthcoming.

We have noted, above, how the Rev. Nelson Fogarty in 1898 had been given 'temporary charge' of the line to Bulawayo. A letter from Fogarty, dated 'Church House, Bulawayo, 14 September 1897', was printed that year in *Mashonaland,* the quarterly paper of the Mashonaland Mission Association:

> On Thursday I am going off down the line to Palapswie [Palapye], to hold services on the road. We do sadly need a priest to be always on the line. The line will run from here to Mochudi, and we shall have to try and go up and down once a month. The distance will be about 360 miles. It is a terrible thing to think of all the gangers' cottages along this line - miles from any church - children brought up without any religious instruction. There is a great need that a man should be constantly travelling up and down, holding services at every place, and visiting every cottage along the line.

The next issue of *Mashonaland,* February 1898, printed in full a letter from Fogarty to Mrs. Knight-Bruce, the previous bishop's wife. In it he stated:

> After dinner at Francistown I got into the guard's van of a goods train and started off at 7 p.m. for Palapye. The guard was most kind and gave me rugs and made a bed for me on the floor of the van as comfortable as he could. The van was an old one, and one of the doors would not shut, so we had plenty of draught. After a very tedious journey - the shaking was too great to allow of sleep - we arrived at Palapye siding at 7 a.m. on Saturday morning.

Marriage and then chaplaincy in the South African War took Fogarty away from the 'northern line' (and we shall meet him again when looking at South-West Africa) and he was replaced for a time by the Rev. John Hallward. Hallward's successor was the Rev. Herbert Hale, who arrived from England in November 1903. His three years were to be pioneering ones, as he visited the men constructing the lines in the north - up to and then beyond the Victoria Falls. Harry Ellison took charge of the new work in the Transvaal. He realised that most people on 'his' six railway lines were completely outside any parochial boundaries, even where there were places with 6-700 Whites. Fresh townships were growing up which, in their initial stages, would be 'entirely dependent on the Railway Mission.' It was the same year, 1903, that local Committees, such as 'The Loyal Women's Guild' [later 'Victoria League'] started to have collections for the Mission and to distribute papers and magazines along the lines.

As a result of the break up of the military camp and hospital at Naauwpoort, after the Boer war had ended, SACRM bought in 1903/4 some of the many huts that came on to the market - enough for six temporary churches, mainly in the Transvaal, and a house for the catechist, Josiah Ngcambu. SACRM held its first public meeting in 1904, in Johannesburg, and appealed for a permanent Heaquarters. Sir Thomas Price, the General Manager of Central South African Railways, offered every help to the Mission. This included a new coach, '21660', which was longer than the old 'pill-box' and meant that a 'Native boy' could be allocated to the coach when it was in use - for cleaning, cooking and general assistance. Sir Thomas was a Baptist and his warmth and help towards the (Anglican) Railway Mission was continued by almost all of the Railway hierarchy right down the Mission's history. In the days before 'social welfare', the Railway Mission was virtually the only organisation that cared in any real sense for railway workers, a fact that General Managers were not slow to realise.

In 1907 work started in Bloemfontein Diocese (Orange River Colony), with a Mission 'patch' of 300 miles, from Vereeniging, just over the Transvaal border, to Norval's Pont at the start of Cape Colony. To the north, in the Transvaal [Diocese of Pretoria] SACRM was receiving frequent requests to extend its remit to being a 'Veld Mission' also. By 1907/9 the majority of the white labourers and gangers in the Transvaal were already 'Dutch' [=Afrikaner], and of the rest few were Anglican. 'Church people' were mostly settlers on the farms, at a distance from the railway lines, and were usually reached on horseback. SACRM refused to become a Veld Mission, as it existed on free Passes which were conditional on the chaplains visiting railway workers first, and then others who lived near the line.

1907 saw the first house built [at Naauwpoort] for women workers, and the inauguration of the Diocese of North Rhodesia. By then the railway had already reached Broken Hill [Kabwe] and was only two years from crossing the Congo border. The Railway Mission was to play its part in bringing the ministrations of the Church to those northern areas.

The formation of the Union of South Africa in 1910 brought about the unification of the four main Railways - the beginning of 'South African Railways and Harbours'. The Railway Mission had therefore only one company to deal with in South Africa itself. 1910 also saw Plumtree

School coming under Governmental control, although SACRM Chaplains continued their work in the school up to 1920.

By 1912 Railhead had reached 60 miles north-east of Elisabethville, the capital of Katanga. The Rev. Fred Rogers, the Mission's new Head, and Mr. Douglas, the local Chaplain, paid two visits there in 1912 as 'there was no Anglican priest within 800 miles.' In 1916, E.F.Winnington-Ingram reported, 'the British population in the Congo continues to increase, especially as regards Railway work. There are now some 40 or 50 Britishers employed by the C.F.K.[Chemin de Fer du Katange].' The construction of the railway was continually moving northwards. 'As soon as ... the Elisabethville-Kambove section was completed, they were anxious to continue the construction of the section between Kambove-Tshilongo [just north of Tenke] ...'[17]

Winnington-Ingram visited Tshilongo ('Pauling's base') at the end of 1916. He found 'about 12 Britishers, of whom three had their wives with them.' He travelled on the construction trains over the "Plateau", north of Tshilongo, where the gangs had almost linked up with the line going down from Bukama:

> The gangers, wood-cutters, etc., are mostly foreigners - Greek, Italian etc. There are various farms on the "Plateau", cattle, and even traction engines! A few English people are scattered here and there. The "Plateau" was crossed by about 10 [a.m.], and at 12 we reached Railhead [south of Bukama]. Here I found two Britishers, a man and his wife, living in a K.[cattle?] truck, converted into a house, alongside the line, and no one else but Greek store-keepers, and hundreds of natives. I went and sat on the last rail... and sighed for a camera![18]

The inauguration of the Tshilongo-Bukama section was carried out in June 1918, although it was only in 1931 that the section from Tenke, near Tshilongo, to Luao on the Angolan-Belgian frontier, was linked with the Benguela Railway. The extensions north, as well as those east and west, put a great strain on the Head of the Mission as he tried to follow them up. The 'advance guard' had left the Province of South Africa and the church heirs of Bishop Gray of Cape Town far behind.

North Rhodesia, with its northern border 150 miles south of Elisabethville, was in Central Africa, and under the jurisdiction of the Universities' Mission [to Central Africa, UMCA]. The new Diocese of North-East Rhodesia was being formed, taken in part from the Diocese of Likoma, which itself had originally been in the Diocese of Zanzibar. For the Anglican Church, all this part of Africa was headed by the Missionary

Bishops, started with Bishop Mackenzie in 1861. The work continued to be supported by UMCA.

In 1913 the Synod of Pretoria Diocese decided that, for every Railway chaplain working in that diocese, the bishop would provide £50 per year towards his stipend. The Dioceses of Grahamstown and Mashonaland soon followed Pretoria's example. One by one the various dioceses were beginning to take over Railway Mission centres/churches, which had been more or less self-supporting. This was entirely right, in SACRM's view, and left the Mission more free for its pioneering work. In the following year Frederick Rogers gave in his resignation to the Archbishop of Capetown. He had been sixteen years on SACRM's staff and was the last of the 'original' [Grahamstown] staff. The Archbishop, along with the Bishop of Pretoria, wanted to close down the Railway Mission, as will be detailed later. Fortunately, Douglas Ellison and common sense prevailed!

Railway Mission work in Namibia will be outlined when dealing with 'far flung places'. We may note here that, by 1916, some of the South African bishops felt that the Railway Mission should be working in the newly conquered 'German South-West'[Namibia]. Canon Thornely Jones, the new Head, visited the area, which already had 1500 miles of rail. He felt that it was 'not enough to have captured the country; [they had] to hold it.' His concern was with the 'station masters, firemen and gangers who [had] gone up there with their wives and in many cases with their children also.' He believed that they had needs other than being 'housed, clothed and fed', but noted,

> in South West Africa we have not got a Church, we have not got an altar; we have not a stick or stone.... [but] the Bishops have realised that something must be done for the spiritual needs of the white people and also of the natives.[19]

The 'also' appears to be the usual afterthought with respect to work among Africans. The Head found great isolation among the railway workers, with gangers cottages often 15 miles apart and the women going at least 100 miles to shop. The authorities at first were not much in favour of the Railway Mission working in South West Africa, though by 1917 those who attended the SACRM Annual Meeting heard that the Mission was 'asked to send men to open up Church work along the railways [in South-West Africa].. proof that it was understood that the Railway Mission had got the right idea for a bit of country like that ..' The Bishop of Pretoria was persuaded to spare 'one of the Mission's best men, Mr. Esdaile' to open up the work. The new venture, however, was certainly limited to occasional visits.

The Spanish influenza epidemic of 1918, which killed over 5,000 people in Cape Town and 3,500 in Kimberley, resulted in the deaths of two of SACRM's workers - Agnes Burt, an ex-school principal who had joined the Mission because of staff shortages during the War, and Ralphe Seacombe, who was due shortly to leave SACRM after his three year chaplaincy. Both died nursing African victims of the epidemic.

By 1920 the Railway Mission was officially (and rather belatedly) recognised by the Provincial Synod of the South African Church as a Provincial Organisation 'in so far ... as its work was in that province.' Pleas were constantly being made for more men and women, and it was pointed out that two thirds of the money needed for salaries was being raised locally. The role of the Railway Missioners in education and nursing and in general 'women's work' was being increasingly recognised and accepted. All this work will shortly be examined in detail.

Practicalities

Almost from the start of the Railway Mission there developed a set pattern of working, which, with few variations, lasted throughout its life. To read an account of how the Missioners worked - whether that be in a Grahamstown Railway Mission leaflet of 1894, or in a letter written by George Deacon (the very last missioner) in the 1980s - is to be aware of many similarities of practice.

A 'typical' missioner would be issued with a Railway Pass by the authorities, giving him free transport. Through timetables and train schedules he would work out his itinerary and send out letters of advice to various Station Masters to let them know when he hoped to arrive. A label was then put on the Mission coach/caboose giving its next destination, ie. where the missioner wanted it to be shunted off the train. The coach was attached usually to the rear of a goods train and duly shunted off after a journey of anything from two to twelve hours. After his visiting, the chaplain might then label the coach for another destination. There he would pick it up after first having gone on his bike ten or fifteen miles to a ganger's cottage where there was no siding; be given food and a bed for the night at the cottage, or a nearby farm; and then cycle on in the morning to the next siding where he hoped the coach would be waiting. Services would be taken in station waiting rooms or offices, cottages, tin lean-tos, stores or even in the open. Particularly in the earlier days of SACRM, the missioner might have to travel a considerable distance on an engineer's trolley (hand-pumped and then, later, motorised). After perhaps two or three weeks away, a tired missioner would return 'home' to digs or a Railway Mission centre/house for a few days rest. The next month might then be based near the home base, or consist of travelling up and down the lines by ordinary passenger train, visiting the larger railway centres, while another chaplain had the use of the Mission Coach.

The various practicalities of Railway Mission work may be examined by looking at the written accounts - particularly by Herbert Hale [HH] (1903-6), Ralph Seacombe [RS] (1916-18), and Allen Rusbridger [AR] (1932-7).

In his very first letter home (4th November, 1903) to his sister, Herbert Hale writes,

> I have been to the Cape Government Railway people about a pass to Grahamstown, and was shunted from pillar to post in fine style. But I have got passes for myself and my lay companion. Also I have arranged, by a visit to the Rhodesian Railways Office [in Cape Town], to have my luggage sent on to Bulawayo in bond at lowest rates [a useful concession]...

The Passes had to be renewed each year and this could cause problems. In February 1906 Hale writes from Bulawayo, 'I am having a lot of trouble over my railway passes ... I applied for my Pass on the Beira and Mashonaland Railway at the beginning of December. But, in spite of reminders, they have not had the common decency to reply... My Pass on the Cape Railways, from Bulawayo to Mafeking [has not arrived].' He had not, in fact, complied with new regulations. His application had been sent from one person to another, he had to write to the bishop 'as to [his] bona fides', and was then found 'travelling on railway without available pass.' He was left with having to spend 'pounds on pounds' for railway tickets, 'so the business stands and meanwhile [the] work is handicapped.'[20] Two weeks later he was still bemoaning the lack of the Passes, though by March 2nd his Beira and Mashonaland Railway Pass had arrived and so he was able to set off to Wankie and Victoria Falls. After a three months' delay, Herbert Hale received the Cape Railways Pass and so was able to re-commence the work on the Mafeking-Bulawayo section. All the published literature and letters of SACRM give no hint of difficulties with the Railway Authorities, rather the reverse. They are frequently praised for their cooperation and generosity. The private letters of Hale and others do not always give such a rosy picture.

Towards the end of his time on SACRM, Hale met a 'Wesleyan Railway Missioner'. Although welcoming 'any spiritual ministrations along the line', he feared that if 'other religious bodies' began applying for Passes, then the Railway might 'in self-defense .. stop passes altogether.' There is no evidence that his fears were justified.

Ralphe Seacombe was delighted when, in June 1917, the General Manager of South African Railways granted to each of the chaplains 'a 1st Class free Pass annually which will mean ... a much more comfortable journey to Port Alfred in January [for the Annual SACRM Conference and break] and a great saving to the Mission Funds.' [21]

Roy Sinker, who joined the Mission thirty years later, recalled (as noted earlier),

> I found that I had in my possession a first class free pass on any train in my section & the authority to stop any goods train at any authorised station or passing place and authority to attach the Mission Van - a converted four-wheeled guard's van - to most goods trains. [22]

Travelling along Southern Africa's railway lines was never straightforward for the Missioners, even when they had their free Passes. At one extreme it could mean going considerable distances in open trucks (in the early days) or having a, relatively, smooth ride in one of the longer cabooses with bogie-wheels.

On 29th December 1903, Herbert Hale wrote,

> I went [to Deka] by what is called the Construction train; that is the train which takes out material to railhead. You select the truck which promises the most comfortable seat. Often your choice is limited to rails or steel sleepers, and on a roaring hot day you experience the same conditions and feelings as being grilled. My first experience.. [was] a box of rivets for my seat ...

Writing a year later, from Plumtree, he mentions finding a 'pick-up train just starting its slow and weary way to Wankie ... and commenced a miserable 10 hours crawl, with only a packing case to sit on, on board an open truck.'

On some journeys the chaplains had to travel by a variety of trains and coaches. In May, 1906, Hale returned to Bulawayo from a stay in 'B[echuanaland] P[rotectorate]'(Botswana) by "train de luxe" [passenger], then moved on by goods train, found his 'letter of advice' had not reached its destination and so there was no one to meet him at a siding, 'loafed around until 6am, and returned by goods train to Towani.' He then christened the baby of a coloured ganger, heard that there was a 'sub-ganger at the next cottage [who] had a baby to baptise', and so he and the ganger 'started off by trolley with the wind against us, and it was bitterly cold.' Further trolleying, goods train, and "train de luxe" brought Hale back to Kimberley for a connection to Grahamstown!

After the early days of open trucks, the railway authorities often supplied one or more coaches, which were specially adapted for the Railway Mission. At first, these coaches were short 4-wheeled (non-bogie) cabooses, known as 'pill-boxes', which were very bumpy. Nelson Fogarty, again in his letter to Mrs. Knight-Bruce, reported:

> For our work we have applied to the company to give us a special coach, as the church van to be used by the priest who is working the line. With a coach like this we shall be able to have it put off at any spot on the line, and spend a few days with the people. The sidings are about 60 miles apart, so it will mean that we have to do a great deal of walking to visit the Gangers' cottages. I hope to have a library fitted up in the van so as to supply the people with books and papers.

One year later ('Easter Eve, 1899') Fogarty was able to inform readers of *Mashonaland:*

> The coach, which the Cape Government Railways have given for the use of the chaplain, has arrived. It is a very comfortable house indeed, and now the journeys instead of being burdensome, are most delightful. The coach is fitted up with a bed and a lavatory, easy chairs, tables, cooking stove and cupboards, etc. I have had shelves put in on the sides, and on them I have the library books, now about 350 [650 by July]. I have 100 subscribers [129 by July] to the library, and allow each man to take out two books. My object is now to travel every month on the pay train which stops at every cottage on the line, and then I am able to change the book for the gangers. I cannot say how much the library is appreciated by the men ... The papers too, which friends send me from England are most acceptable.[23]

Ralphe Seacombe wrote of a new coach promised, which kept failing to appear, for the Traffic Superintendent and the Engineer kept using it and 'wouldn't give it up!' Eventually he could report; 'Ingram [the Head of SACRM] came down to the Falls on Tuesday and brought 89002 with him: a perfectly delightful Coach ... I am so glad he has got it as he has now done nearly four years in the old Pill Box and latterly has had no headquarters at all.' One week later he was pleased to report [from 'Mission Coach, Figtree'], 'Yes, I have a coach at last! Ingram's discarded Pill Box, but just right for my purpose and most useful here.'

Many of the missioners wrote about the constant jolting they received as the coach was being shunted. Some, although stating that most of the railwaymen appreciated SACRM's work and would do anything for them, mention occasions when drivers deliberately gave the coach an extra bump or two, especially if a bishop was present! The drivers were a very mixed bunch and there must have been some who found the extra shunting involved inconvenient to say the least. Some incidents were purely accidental. Ray White, the last Head of SACRM/first Head of the Rhodesia and Nyasaland Railway Mission, writes in his 'Memoirs',

> I got back to Johannesburg at the end of August [1953] to find to my horror that Lilah [his wife and co-worker] had suffered a compacted fracture of three of her lumbar vertebrae due to being thrown across the caboose when the wheels were slipping on wet rails on a steep incline.

Her pain and injuries stayed with her until she died 25 years later.

The design of the eight-wheeled, two-bogied cabooses changed little over the years. The last Mission coach, now in the Bulawayo Railway Museum, apart from having its corridor on the left hand side, is almost identical to that described and illustrated by Edward Winckley in 1943:

> I am writing this in my new Coach at Addo station. I wish I could adequately describe it to you, as it is a wonderful piece of work, more elaborate than anything I have seen on the railways in England. It will make my work much easier. ... This new [coach] is more than three times the size [of the old four-wheeled caboose]: it is about 42 feet long and 9 feet wide. Here is a plan:

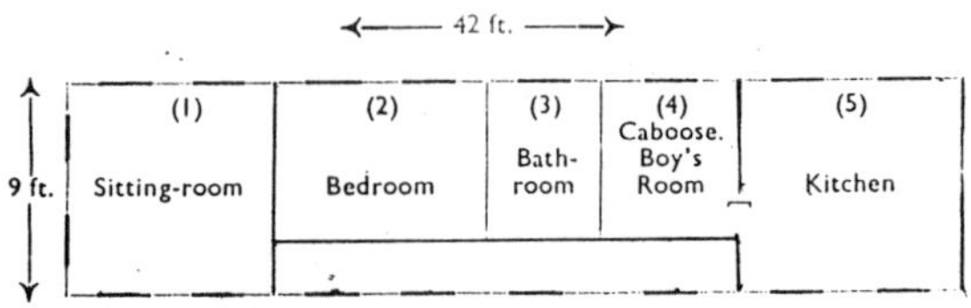

> There are six windows in the sitting-room as marked. Two are at the end, so when the Coach is buttoned on to the end of a train, one can look out along the Line. There is a very comfortable convertable sofa in the sitting-room, a 3 by 5-ft. table, four chairs and a cupboard, with heating apparatus and drinking water supply. The bedroom is beautifully fitted with wash-basin (water laid on), wardrobe, vi-spring mattress bed, etc. The bathroom has hot and cold water and shower, and is nicely painted white. There are two bunks in the

> Caboose boy's room, one with a mattress. The kitchen has a fine deep zinc sink, large refrigerator, coal stove and hot water apparatus large enough for two deep baths. The water tank, under the Coach, holds 2,000 gallons of water and the coal box about half a ton of coal, so I can start on quite a long journey without having to refill water or coal. The Coach runs very smoothly on eight bogey-wheels... It is fully lighted with electricity. ... I hope to have an electric fan soon.[24]

Hale, after commenting bitterly about the attitude of (some) white people to 'the natives', writes, without any sense of irony, a week later,

> At Inyantue, we had arranged to leave the train and trolley into Wankie, 40 miles. A trolley is a miniature four wheeled truck, without springs, and pushed along by 4 or 6 native "boys". A rough kind of box seat is fitted up for the white folk, and the pace you travel at depends on the gradient ... I used this method of travelling in order to get to know the gangers along the line away from the stations. I could only say, "How d'ye do" to them. The Engineer had his business to transact with them, and then we were off .... We were trolleying from 6 in the morning to 4.30 in the afternoon..!

On another occasion Hale mentions all the things that he had to carry with him, even on a trolley, such as a portable altar, canvass carrier with pyjamas, surplice and cassock, as well as his camera and equipment which, fortunately, went with him on most of his journeys. If it was difficult carrying all this equipment on a trolley, it was even worse on a bicycle. At times the chaplains also carried a haversack on their back, containing books for people to borrow.

The 'Mission bicycle' was not universally welcomed on the trains. Some Station Masters wanted the chaplains to book and pay for such an extra item, whereas the Missioners (reasonably) argued that their Passes entitled them to take a bicycle free, at their own risk. Such an altercation was not, of course, hinted at in the 'S.A.Railways & Harbours Magazine' which, in August 1926, reported, 'As a rule the missioner [in Kimberley Diocese] works north and south, chiefly because he often has to rely on a bicycle for the shorter distances and the prevailing wind is from the north.'

Other means of transport, such as motor bikes, cars and lorries, were also used by SACRM. Ray White quotes a letter of Allen Rusbridger, dated 26th October 1979, in which he states, 'I was the first Anglican to visit Maun, on Lake Ngami, 400 miles from the Railway line, a journey which took three days by lorry.' White comments, 'Allen does not record that on that 800 miles of line [De Aar to Shashi, near Francistown] every inch of it had been covered by him on a bicycle so that every ganger and platelayers' cottage was visited as nearly as possible once a year.'[25]

Much of SACRM's work was spent among the 'poor whites' who worked on the railways of southern Africa. Very few had spare rooms or, indeed, food for the Missioners, yet time after time in Diaries and letters and SACRM publications we can read of the generosity of these people. Bedrooms and beds were shared, living rooms or space in stores made available. A typical comment can be that of Seacombe, writing in April 1916 'On the 14 Up, Near Wankie',

> I am stuck for the night in a ganger's cottage, having [just seen] .. my coach go through on a train for which I wasn't ready ...They are very nice coloured people who have been most hospitable and have put me up a nice bed, promising to call me in good time [4.30 am] and see me safely off... in a most uncomfortable Guard's Van ...

The monthly Cash Accounts Lists, at the back of Rusbridger's Diaries, show that he usually paid three shillings for a bed for the night in a hotel. However, quite often, when he stayed at (say) a ganger's cottage, he also entered '3 shillings' for a bed. This suggests that the poorer families were more than happy to receive this extra income. The poverty is noted in his entry for June 20th, 1932:

> Two subgangers at M[oreomabele?] [near Palapye] had not had a Service for two years & about 10 of us crushed into a little hut & had E[vensong] by the light of a guttering oil lamp. Had a fire afterwards which consisted of bringing live embers in on a piece of tin and sticking [it] in the middle of the floor. Too poor to give me food so brought out my own bread & cheese.

Usually the chaplains took their own food ('scoff') with them for the train journeys, sometimes pooling this with guards or other officials. From the earliest days the Mission staff often stayed in small hotels / inns, where no other accommodation was available. At least one Missioner, the Rev. Wilfrid Ellis, wrote about the Mission's 'Debt to the Inns',

> Only those who have worked on the Railway Mission up and down the line can realize how much every mission worker owes to these ubiquitous establishments ... here in Africa you will find an "Hotel" where very often there are only two or three [White] families, or perhaps none at all. There is an "Hotel" at every station of any size, and usually a store connected with it, as likely as not under the same management ... The railway missioner who stops at some very small

township has not much choice as to where his services shall be held. There is, of course, the goods-shed or the waiting room ... there may be a school-room available ... On the other hand, the inn is any man's home ... once inside we are all equal ...There is no one who has a greater sense of propriety than the proprietor of an African inn. He is always glad to have us; he will often put himself out to make things reverent ... [26]

Allen Rusbridger's Diary for 1932 illustrates well the variety of accommodation used by missioners. In the period from mid-January to mid-February, for example, he notes:

> Slept at Stationmaster's..; Stayed at Boarding House - very comfortable ..; Had quarters in [Mahalapye] hotel & evrything spotless ..; Stayed with ganger ..; Went to farm 5 miles out [of Lobatsi]..; Motored to Mr. Crosslingham [near Pitsani] where stayed the night .., Taken to Hotel at [Fourteen] Streams ... Kept awake by mosquitos half the night ..; The S[tation] M[aster] & wife put me up & very decent people [Windsorton Road] ...; Very good Hotel here [Modder River]... Full house at hotel [Palapye Road].

Other nights were spent 'in the train' or at his base in Warrenton. Rusbridger, as other missioners, would have had a copy of the South African Railways *Hotel and Boarding House Guide.* This gave details of every such establishment in all areas served by the SAR and its connections (such places as Beira, Broken Hill, Kafue, Lourenco Marques, and Umtali featured with every expected settlement from Aberdeen Road to Zwartruggens). Hotel fare, distance, altitude and local features were listed, although in my 1921 copy some missioner has pencilled against Amanzimtoti's 'Popular seaside resort. Good bathing' description, "Many fatalities. Extremely dangerous", and against the various Boarding Houses in Durban, "noisy trams"! Daily fares in 1921 ranged on average from 8/6d (42p) to 11/6d (57p). Of all the hundreds of hotels and boarding houses listed, only the Victoria Falls Hotel then had a daily rate of over one pound (£1/1/0 [£1-05]). This, however, was the one hotel where railway missioners had free accommodation.

In the final decades of the Railway Mission's work, with generally improved facilities and higher standards of living of railway workers, accommodation and food no longer posed too many problems.

Stephen Skemp pointed out that the 'long, long journeys by goods train' had to be occupied somehow:

> I evolved a routine programme to pass the time:- Pray & meditate - play patience - read a novel - go to sleep. I can't think how it came up, but years later, at a conference when he was Archbishop of York, Michael Ramsey was fascinated by this programme and seemed to be memorizing it! In a hot climate, plenty of mugs of tea were needed - made with water drawn off the engine boiler. The trouble was, the water was brown before ever I put the tea in.[27]

We have already noted how SACRM Reports and letters enable the modern reader to examine the social and working conditions of 'ordinary' railway employees and their families (in a way that Official Railway statistics cannot). Another SACRM source describes their lives with an immediate and often vivid effect and that is the Registers of Births, Marriages and Deaths that were kept by the Railway Mission in respect of its work 'along the Line.' Michael Berning, of the Cory Library, Grahamstown (Diocesan archives) has pointed out how, through the Registers, individual railway people can be identified and, at times, followed in their 'lonely progress... up and down the line.'

Simeon's note, in the April 1925 *Light for the Line*, of Cape Government policy to use English and Scottish workers is borne out by the Cory Library Baptismal Registers, which show 'the original subjects of mission as white gangers, sub-gangers and similar trades, with English and Scots names predominating.' It must be said, however, that a fair proportion of 'Dutch' names are also listed - a fact which, in itself, adds to the evidence of (unexpected) involvement of English-Anglican clergy with Afrikaner people, even accepting that some Afrikaners were Anglicans. Eventually, as will be observed later, very few English-speaking employees were working on the Railways in South Africa (which led to the ending of the Railway Mission there) and increasing numbers of white Afrikaners and black and coloured Africans were used. Again, this is observed in the Registers with 'black' and 'brown' railway workers being listed - usually in the less-skilled trade of 'labourer' - 'railway native' or 'railway servant' becoming prominent. The 1910 Union of South Africa resulted in the Registers having a column drawn (pencilled-in) to include race. (The first such Marriage to include 'race' was between John Henry Heath, subganger, and Mary Ann Deacon [both 'European'], at Witmos on 21 February, 1910. The next Marriage listed, solemnised at 'the Native church, Cookhouse', was between Booi Gogela and Sarah Magscaka [both 'Native'], on 17 May, 1910.)

The term 'race' had a wide variety of interpretations, and the Registers reveal:

> Kaffers (occasionally), Natives (frequently), Basuto, 'Xosa', Fingo, Tembu and, finally in 1934, Bantu.
>
> OR
>
> European, Dutch, European (British), British (European), European (Dutch), South African (European) and, finally in 1936, White.

The distinction between the various railway jobs and grades is always observed. This is understandable in the Marriage Registers, yet it is also apparent in those for Baptism; ie No.46 (1888) 'Platelayer'; No.149 (1898) 'Ganger'; No.150 (1898) 'subganger'; No.274 (1902) 'Pumper'. The poverty, particularly of the lower-grade workers, may be noted. For example, the Baptism page for 1892 shows two families, one Afrikaner (the Van der Mawes) and one British (the Carters) sharing a cottage - 'No.51, Midland Railway'- and having their children baptised on the same day, one of the Van der Mawes being a sponsor (godparent) for the young Hannah Margaret Carter. Each father was a 'Second man'.

Berning's remark about the 'lonely progress' of families up and down the railway system - a situation frequently commented on by the Railway Missioners - may be illustrated by taking one family, that of Mark Henry and Kate Hornabrook (spelt as 'Honeybrook' in the first two entries, until corrected by Douglas Ellison). When their first child was baptised in 1893 they lived at Cottage no.25 Midland System. Mark Henry was a sub-ganger. Two years later the next child was baptised, and no changes are apparent. The third child arrived in 1902 and by then the family were living at Cottage no.11 Midland System, with Mark Henry listed as a plate-layer; ie. he had been demoted. The fourth child was baptised in Alicedale in 1905, with its father now a (railway) 'coalman-in-charge'. The fifth and sixth children saw their father returned to being a sub-ganger, first at Cold Spring (1909) and lastly at Middelton (1913). Although 36 per cent of the burials for that period were for children under five, and 39 per cent for those under 10, the Railway Mission Burial Registers do not list any Hornabrooks between 1893 and 1913 so we may reasonably assume that they survived and were, relatively, healthy. Not all deaths were noted, however (nor were births) - a similar 'slipping though the net' as obtained in Britain then - and so we cannot be certain of the survival rate of the Hornabrook children (without a detailed examination of many other Marriage and Burial Registers in the Cape).

Typical of the period is the 1901/2 Burial page, where the five people listed were aged 29 years; 3 months; 8 days; 63 years; and 21 days. This was not just typical for southern Africa, or in Railway areas: a Burial page for the same period in Appleton Roebuck (York Diocese) in Britain, reveals five deaths at 2 months; 36 years; 79 years; 13 days; and 1 hour.

The Railway Mission Marriage Registers show, not surprisingly, that many of the brides were quite young (often 16-18), with their signatures rather schoolgirlish, whereas the grooms were usually older (in the 22-27 range). The missioners were not confined to conducting 'standard' Anglican weddings. As with the rest of their ministry, they had to be far more flexible than their parish-based colleagues. Sitting in the Cory Library in August 1993, I held and looked at an entry made exactly eighty-four years previously. Marriage entry no.29, dated 16 August 1909, records a Marriage solemnized at Alicedale, in the Parish of Grahamstown (Albany Division). Percy E Barnes, The Railway Missioner, married Alfred Santi, aged 'about 32'- a 'CGR [Cape Government Railway] fitter's boy' - to Noyeti Tsagele, aged 'about 29'. Rather than 'Condition' being listed as 'bachelor' and 'spinster', it states 'married by native custom'. The Marriage took place in the 'Native (Ethiopian) Church' at Alicedale, with the details also 'Entered in Ethiopian Order register at Alicedale'. The groom wrote his signature with some difficulty, and his bride put her mark ('X') against her name written by Percy Barnes. Both of the African witnesses signed their names. The missioner would have had the 'Native catechist', Samuel Kula, to assist and interpret for him. Perhaps the Witness, one William Kula, was either a relative of his, or the catechist himself - using the Christian name he preferred? Barnes frequently wrote about his various Services in the 'Native churches'. Except at the very end of SACRM's history, none of the African staff were fully ordained clergy, and were therefore unlicensed to solemnize Marriages.

Berning notes that 'fewer than 20 brides had occupations listed by 1940 and most of these were black or brown women who worked as domestic workers, cooks and washerwomen while married to labourers employed by the railways.' The first such entry appears in 1921 (a cook). Clergy in England also rarely entered details of a bride's occupation (the few that had specific work, other than 'housewife') until during and after the Second World War. Appleton Roebuck waited from 1853 to 1926 to have a bride's work listed ('parlour maid') and then another twenty years before the next. Almost all southern African Anglican clergy were trained in England and it is not surprising that they followed similar social conventions and Church practices.

The various Railway Mission Registers held in Bulawayo (with very difficult access) and Harare, in Zimbabwe, are equally important to those in Grahamstown, although their value is more related to the later history of SACRM than to the pioneering days of the late 1890s and early 1900s.

Other Railway Missions

As we have seen earlier, Ellison made reference to other Railway Missions, though maintaining that SACRM was 'first in the field' and was certainly the only Railway Mission of 'the English Church' [ie.Anglican]. I look briefly, below, at 'the others' in southern Africa. It is beyond the scope of this book to examine railway missions in other parts of Africa (such as the work of the 'Church Saloon', provided for the Anglican Church by the Railways of the Sudan) or elsewhere in the world (such as Douglas Ellison's work - after his time in South Africa - in Canada, as part of the Archbishops' Western Canada Fund). The latter enterprise makes a fascinating study in its own right. [28]

Spencer Walton founded the Cape General Mission in 1888, which soon became the interdenominational South Africa General Mission. In 1889 six recruits arrived from England, including Daniel Jackson who was asked to work among railwaymen. The aim of the Mission was evangelistic 'among the Native tribes of South and South-Central Africa', to 'reach out a helping hand to various classes of the community, whether railway men, soldiers, Malays or others.'

At the turn of the century the Woodstock and Salt River Railway Mission, in the Cape peninsula, started its work, soon followed by a Mission in Touws River. These Missions resulted in the forming of the South Africa Railways (SAR) Christian Union in 1918. This body assumed responsibility for any interdenominational Railway Mission work. South African Railways and Harbours recognised the SAR Christian Union as one of the three railway missions [ie along with SACRM and the Dutch Reformed Church] to whom they would grant passes and coaches. The main figure in the history of the SAR Christian Union was James Potter, who left the Caledonian Railway in Scotland in 1891, joined the Natal Government Railways, and then resigned to give his whole time to the evangelical work of the Christian Union among railway people. He continued in the work until his death by accident in 1950, aged 93. Mr Jim Barrow, of Pietermaritzburg, a former employee of South African Railways at Salt River and at Johannesburg, recalls the work of the above (SAR&H Christian Union) Railway Mission, which forms a helpful comparison with the (larger-scale) activities of SACRM:

> When I was about six years of age my father was transferred to De Dooms, and my parents established a Sunday School under the auspices of the Railway Mission in our home. On moving to Hutchinson they continued this activity in the local school building, but on later moving to Fraserburg Road (now Leeu-Gamka) they

switched their attention to the Coloured community. The De Dooms and Hutchinson activities spanned a period of no more than four years. ... There were for many years three Railway Missioners, working in [ie. covering the whole of] the Cape Province and South West Africa, the Transvaal and Orange Free State, and Natal. My association with the Railway Mission was limited to the Cape Province. I do not remember the name of the Missioner in my earliest days, but while we were living at Fraserburg Road a Mr. Robert Thompson ... assumed this position.

The Thompsons were based at Touws River, and I have a recollection that there was an arrangement by which Mr. Thompson had to spend alternate week-ends at Touws River, as there were no other facilities for services conducted in English. Coach No. 8012 was allocated to the Railway Mission ... It was initially a 4-wheeled vehicle, but in the course of time a bogie was fitted at the 'living room' end.

I do not recall how often the Thompsons visited Fraserburg Road, but it was probably not more than five times during our sojourn there. Services were held in the open air over a period of 3 or 4 days, and the magic lantern was a great attraction. We used still to see the Thompsons after moving to Beaufort West, but their visits were few and far between, as there were ample opportunities for worship in the town. I do, however, recall attending an occasional Railway Mission service at the Railway Institute. During the sixteen months when I was on the staff of the Stores Superintendent, Salt River, I used to attend the Sunday afternoon services held at the Mission headquarters, and also a week-night youth meeting. The Railway Mission was strictly non-Denominational and non-Sectarian, which meant that we had a wide spectrum of preachers on Sunday afternoons ...[29]

In about 1903 the Dutch Reformed Church started a Mission to its railway people. Ds. Bennie Pienaar was one of the pioneers, backed by a standing committee of 'De Nederduitse Gereformeerde Kerk in Zuid-Afrika'. An annual appeal to all their congregations was issued for the Mission work.

A much more localised Mission was the Cape Town Railway Mission. This was started in 1892 by a Miss Cleghorn who held (religious) Meetings on Sunday afternoons in the 1st Class Waiting Room on Cape Town Station. Within two years a Reading Room was established for railway workers, and by 1898 there was a Coffee Bar. In 1942 Michael Cleghorn, the founder's brother, had to ask South African Railways and Harbours to take over the work of (at least) the Coffee Bar. He stated,

> The work includes regular religious meetings; the homes of employees are visited whenever possible, and also Railway and Harbour patients in hospitals; the distribution of periodicals and papers to fourteen lighthouses, to three hundred small stations and to twenty P.W.I's for their gangers.[30]

The Administration of the Railways took over the Reading Room and the Coffee Bar. All these 'other' Railway Missions were much smaller in scope and area and man (and woman)-power than the South African Church Railway Mission and those among the English-speaking railway men and families were far more overtly evangelical in outlook.

---

1 from 'A Low-Veld Ganger', in QP 19, 1908, p.1
2 Gray, 1883, p.134/5
3 Hinchliff, 1963, p.157
4 Simeon, 1925, p.6
5 Simeon, 1925, p.6
6 GDRM, 1894, USPG X1441/1
7 Lewis & Edwards, p.295
8 X1441/1 f5, RHL
9 Ellison, 1930, p.19
10 Ellison. 1930, p.13
11 Cory MS 14 886/1
12 X1441/1, RHL, July 30, 1894, p.2
13 X1441/1, RHL, 1896, p.1
14 Vickery, 1981, p.26
15 GDRM, July 1899, Monthly Letter, p.4
16 GDRM, July 1902, Monthly Letter, p.13
17 Varian, 1953, 1973, p.212
18 QP 54, 1917, p.17
19 QP 51, 1916, p.17
20 Hale, HP, 'Letters from South Africa' (1903-1906)
21 Seacombe, R., 'Seacombe Letters' (1916-1918), X1441/1 f10, RHL
22 Sinker, R., 'SACRM Jan.1935-Jan.1938', 1984
23 Vickery, 1981, p.27
24 QP 151, 1943, p.25/6
25 White, 'Memoirs', 1980, p.18
26 QP 91, 1927, p.7/8
27 Skemp, S, letter to author, 3.2.1992
28 In 1977, Earle Hawkes, the last-but-one Railway Missioner, discovered letters and papers in Bulawayo (in a mission chest that had originated in South Africa) relating to the founding of the Railway Mission in Western Canada by Douglas Ellison. Carter's articles on the Canadian Mission Fund [=Archbishops' Western Canada Fund], and its link with Ellison and South Africa, are helpful accounts. (see Bibliography).
29 Barrow, priv.let., 10.6.1995
30 CTRM, 4.2.1942

4. Education

- a story of Anglican innovation

> As the quarterly visits passed by, the question of the education of the children forced itself more and more upon me. Government did what they could by causing a goods train here and there to stop and take them to school and take them home again ... but very few children could be helped in that way.[1]

Mr. Holmes, the English chaplain, opened a private school in Cape Town in 1803, at the start of the occupation of the Cape by the Dutch Batavian government. Four years later another chaplain (though, as it turned out, a clerical impostor) - Dr. Halloran - opened a school in Burg Street, Cape Town, and was appointed principal of the classical school there in 1809. In 1811 the first 'colonial' chaplain was appointed, for civilians. Robert Jones went to the Cape as tutor to the son of the Governor, Sir John Craddock. 'Backed by the governor he started a fund throughout the colony to provide Bibles and free schools for those who could not afford them. His school fund was supported by all classes of people ... and the result was the opening of a free school in Long Street.'[2]

In 1821 the SPG sent the Rev. W. Wright to the Cape in response to the government's offer of £100 a year to a clergyman for 'native or negro' work. He soon started schools and services for 'coloured people'. His schools for English, Dutch, Malays, 'Negroes and Hottentots' became such models of evangelical, educational and social work that, 'when the Royal Commission of Enquiry came out to investigate Somerset's rule, the governor confiscated Wright's school intact and exhibited it as an example of his own work for the under-privileged.'[3]

Bishop Gray, on his arrival at the Cape in 1848, made sure that he had well-educated and impressive priests to help him in his task of revitalising the Anglican work in the colony. Among them were people such as H.M. White and Hopkins Badnall, responsible for setting up a variety of schools for English and Africans, as well as a theological college. Education was obviously of primary importance for the 'new' Church. Educational activities were not confined to the Cape area. Graham's Town (as it was originally named) - the 'city of saints' - was founded in 1812 as a military garrison and, with the arrival of the 1820 British Settlers, grew in importance. By 1836, when it was designated the Eastern Provincial capital, it was the largest centre in southern Africa outside Cape Town. It was to become, and remains, a town famous for its religious institutions, schools, university and museums. On St. Andrew's Day, 1855, the foundation stone was laid of St. Andrew's, a college 'that was intended to carry out Bishop Gray's wish for a school in [Grahamstown] where vocations for Holy Orders might be developed.' Other schools and colleges in the city were soon to spring up, many of which still remain.

It is not surprising that there were specific schools and educational work connected with or run by the South African Church Railway Mission and its forerunner, the Grahamstown Diocesan Railway Mission. We shall note how the Railway Missioners, time and time again, had to adapt to the situations which faced them and adapt their own skills within the situations. They were not always successful in their efforts and did not always understand the need for changes, such as in school curriculum, for example. Yet, when they did look carefully at problems faced, they were willing to be flexible and change the more formal and historic patterns of traditional Anglicanism and become innovative rather than merely adaptive. We shall see this most clearly when looking at Confirmation preparation and general work among children.

School for Railway Girls, St. Peter's Home, Grahamstown

Simeon's concern regarding 'railway children', as noted at the Chapter's beginning, was voiced to Mother Cecile, Superior of the Sisters of the Resurrection, Grahamstown, and 'she agreed to try the experiment of receiving gangers' children as boarders, and she provided schooling for them.'

When Bishop Webb, the new Bishop of Grahamstown, visited England in 1883 he preached one Sunday at St. Peter's Church, Eaton Square, in London. Annie Cecile Ramsbottom Isherwood was so moved by the sermon that, after consultation, she 'offered herself to Bishop Webb' for three years for work in the Diocese of Grahamstown. Back in South Africa the bishop felt that a Religious Community was needed for the work among girls and in education. He asked Cecile Isherwood if she would begin the Community, and in April 1884 the twenty-one year old Cecile was admitted by the bishop as a Novice of the new Community. Property was purchased and became 'St. Peter's Home'; Sister Cecile became the leader of the 'Community of the Resurrection (of our Lord)' [no connection with the (male) 'Community of the Resurrection' (CR), founded later - in 1892 - and based in Mirfield]; and Sisters began to join the Community. By 1886 the chapel had been built and by the following year work had begun in the locality, a Home for Destitute Children founded, St. Peter's School and that of The Good Shepherd both started, along with a Mission at Port Elizabeth. In November 1887 Cecile 'professed' and became 'Mother Cecile'. The only biography of Mother Cecile, compiled 'by a Sister of the Community' in 1930, gives 1893 as the year in which the Boarding School started for 'railway and other children.'[4] However, it is clear from Simeon that the year could have been no later than 1891 (ie, while he was still working as the Railway Missioner). A GDRM leaflet, written by Douglas Ellison in July 1894, states, '..the Sisters ... for the last two or three years [have] been carrying on a Boarding School for Railway Girls ("The Railways" we call them, to distinguish them from their neighbours, the Orphans at St. Peter's Home, Grahamstown).' In the same leaflet Ellison writes:

> ... one word about the question of Education. How in the world do these poor scattered children manage to get their schooling? Well, you will find a school to-day in most of the larger [railway] camps, where an education of sorts is to be obtained, and the cottage children make the most heroic efforts to obtain it ... But .. many of these poor mites cannot contrive to reach a local school ...

It was because of this need that Simeon, followed by Ellison, encouraged the running of the 'School for Railway Girls'. Ellison noted that, in the Home, 'you will find some twenty-five of our railway girls, gathered in from every corner of our vast Diocese ..[with] more at this moment awaiting their earliest chance of admission.' It is in this leaflet/Letter that the first mention is made about education for boys, a need that was only met - as we shall see - five years later.

A very early advertisement for St. Peter's School gave brief details of the education offered:

> The School is under the charge of the Sisters, and competent and certified teachers. The school course includes Divinity, the ordinary English subjects, Dutch, Latin, French, Natural Science, Drawing, Class Singing, Callisthenics [gymnastics] and Needlework. Pupils are prepared for the Elementary and Third Class Teachers' Examinations.[5]

It is not at all clear whether or not the different groups of children educated at St. Peter's Home were taught and treated differently. It is more than likely that they were. One former teacher at Cheltenham Ladies' College described the 'different sets of people' living at the Home. She wrote of the 'blue-robed children [who were] the industrials or Home children. Separate from them [were] the boarders ... again divided into boarders who [were] "railways" and boarders who [were] not "railways".' We may well wonder why Latin, for example, was deemed necessary for these particular children. The Sisters, it would seem, were of a mind set that could not see the necessity to drastically change from the type of education that they themselves had received. There appears to have been an absence of self-examination, of asking themselves what they were doing. It was all somewhat reminiscent of the Anglican education given by UMCA missionaries at Magomero (Malawi) in the 1860s:

> The church and graveyard, the boys' residential school, the singing lessons, the drill, the charitable health work, the refectory, even ... an embryo Mothers' Union - these were signs of their confidence, not simply in their ability to bring Christianity and Civilisation to central Africa but in the particular accents of Anglicanism. In no way was their vision adapted to circumstances.[6]

It seemed that the experiment with the "railways" was a success, at least initially. Mother Cecile herself wrote, in a letter:

> The work with the railways has now largely increased, and seems much appreciated by the men. The Government pays a grant of £6 per annum, and the parents the other £6, and for £12 a year we feed and educate these small people. They are of English artisan class, and come to us mostly quite uneducated - in fact, we only take them when their homes are at least twelve miles from a school ... It is for the benefit of these children that we are trying to convert our loft into a dormitory. [7]

Writing generally in the 1897 GDRM Annual Report (on the work of the Railway Mission), Douglas Ellison - by then also the Chaplain to St. Peter's Home - thought it a pity that more people did not avail themselves of the opportunities offered by the School. However, he does add: 'One hears, I know, many reckless and unreliable statements about the School from time to time; but I would suggest that instead of giving ear to them, you should put the matter to a practical test, and you may be quite sure you will not live to regret it.' None of the extant GDRM leaflets and letters, nor the work on Mother Cecile, spell out or even hint at 'reckless statements' about the School. We may speculate that some of the girls were as unruly as their male counterparts turned out to be at Plumtree School, as we shall note. Perhaps the daughters of gangers, living uncomplicated and 'simple' lives, found the experience of boarding in an Anglican school run by nuns too constraining? The gap between the curriculum offered and the needs of the pupils cannot have helped matters.

Within the 1897 Annual Report appears also a two-page Report on the School itself. We may note that the girls were educated 'with the sanction of the General Manager of Railways and the Educational Department at Capetown' and that the children needed a certificate of health before admission. Free railway passes were to be granted to would-be boarders provided that their parents applied to their heads of Departments. A similar concession applied to children of railway employees travelling to local schools. The Training School run by the Sisters, where girls were taught, in particular, cookery and laundry work, expanded in numbers to the extent that the Orphanage moved out of the premises, as did the Boarding House for railway children. The 'railways' moved to a house in Thompson Street which was promptly named 'Railway House'. The GDRM 1899 Report, in its section on the School, noted that the number of girls had increased slightly during the year. It was honest enough to state:

> We cannot say much for the scholastic attainments of the boarders, no one at present being above Standard III; but as this is the result of living out of reach of day schools, and beginning their school life late, it only shows the need of such a boarding house ... Among the children are two sisters from the Steynsburg Line, two from the Indwe Line and three from Lobatsi Siding in the British Protectorate, these three are motherless. All these children live at long distances from any village or school.

The 'long distances' may have been true in the case of those particular children, but by 1899 the minimum 'distance from a school' rule had been reduced from six miles to three, which suggests that the School was basically willing to take any girl who was not living in an actual railway camp or centre which would already be provided with schools. It is also clear from the various Railway Mission reports that many of the girls were quite young, which brings into question the excuse given for lack of academic achievement. Similar observations were to be made when 'railway boys' were educated in Rhodesia. Most of these children came from poor and often uneducated gangers' families. Perhaps the Oxford-trained Railway missioners expected too much.

The work of the Sisters was not supported by the Church and the Railway Mission just for the sake of education itself, even if that was 'Christian'. There was another motive, never far beneath the surface of all the Anglican endeavours - that of 'white/Christian "civilisation".' At a meeting in London in 1899 or 1900, in support of the Grahamstown Sisters, one speaker 'went on to speak of the supreme importance to the white children of the Sisters' work... [He showed] the real danger of the children of white parents growing up uncared-for in a population ... of coloured people or natives ...' He went on to say: '..there is before the Sisters the great responsibility ... of guarding the future mothers of the European society of South Africa ... Nothing can be graver than the necessity for this work.'[8] To some extent, of course, this was pious rhetoric uttered thousands of miles away from the realities of the lonely lives of children in gangers' families. Through the endeavours of the Church Railway Mission and the efforts of the Sisters in Grahamstown hundreds of girls obtained an education which otherwise they would not have had. Yet Ellison and the Mission did have other motives for 'using' the Sisters. In a GDRM Children's Letter, dated June 1902, Ellison tells his young readers:

> In Capetown too - if you can keep a secret! - I hope to arrange for the bringing out of 50 English girls to S. Africa, children of your own age, about 10 or 12. We are to teach and train them for six years at St. Peter's Home, and then send them all over that far off land - a waste by Nature, and now doubly wasted by the War - as qualified servants and generally useful members of Society.

No mention is made of this 'scheme' in any of the (adult) GDRM quarterly Letters or Reports. By the time that Douglas Ellison returned from England later in 1902 the (Grahamstown Diocesan) Railway Mission was undergoing its transformation into the South African Church Railway Mission (completed the following year) and expanding northwards. Ellison's scheme was a diversion and not something appropriate for a Church Mission whose remit was with railway families.

The expansion of the Railway Mission, with its ending of Grahamstown as centre, saw the ending of any mention of the School for Railway Girls, at St. Peter's Home. The pages of the SACRM Quarterly Magazines and of the Annual Reports are silent on the matter, as is the account of Mother Cecile after this point. SACRM's attention was turned towards its own school for Railway Children. By 1902/3 there were also many more schools being run by the Railway authorities, some of which were helped by the Railway Mission, such as in providing reading books, and there were an increasing number of Government schools. The 'School for Railway Girls' had run for at least twelve years. The Grahamstown Community of the Resurrection, however, did retain for many years their link with the Mission by keeping the Head of SACRM as their chaplain.

Plumtree School

> May I .. emphasize the crying need which exists for a ... Boarding School for Railway *Boys?* In his last letter to me the Bishop writes: "I wish you could induce some ladies, with means of their own, to come here, and begin a work for Orphan and Railway *Boys*, such as they have at the Home for *Girls*. The Railway people are very

> anxious to send down boys to some similar institution.." I would only add that, failing the ladies for whose help the Bishop pleads, a *gentleman* of independent means might, perhaps, do this particular bit of work as well, or even better.[9]

So wrote Douglas Ellison in his first published account of the Railway Mission's work on the Cape Government Railways. The history of Anglicanism, and indeed of Christianity as a whole, is not one of girls' education taking priority over boys. In many ways it is remarkable that the Railway Mission promoted the education of 'Railway Girls' first, but this was chiefly because there were Grahamstown Sisters already engaged in educating girls. The Railway authorities and the Church were, however, more anxious that boys received a good and 'useful' education, even if initially neither were too keen to pay for suitable teachers.

It was only in 1899 that the Railway Mission was able to start its own schools and to ensure that boys as well as girls were catered for, but it was in 'the North' rather than the Cape area. There were no schooling facilities for the children of those who worked for the Cape Government Railways on the section of line between Mafeking and Bulawayo. The Rev. Nelson Fogarty, Railway Missioner on that section, noted the sad state of affairs. At first he took classes on a coach 'dropped off' at various sidings along the line. He was, though, appalled at seeing (white) children literally running wild, and he urged Bishop Gaul to establish permanent schools. Fogarty wrote to the bishop in May 1899: 'I am now very anxious to start schools at Plum Tree, Francistown and Palapye Road. I could get about twelve children at each place ... It is very terrible to think that there are about one hundred and twenty children on the line growing up without any education whatsoever.'[10]

In July 1899 Francistown was chosen as the site of the first distinct school for 'railway children'. It is generally stated that the Railway School was transferred from Francistown to Plumtree, just inside Rhodesia (ie. that there was one such school). However, letters make it clear that for a short time the Railway Mission was responsible for education in both places.

On 21 March, 1902, John Hallward - a SACRM chaplain - wrote:

> The remnants of a school which used to number 20 white children is collected whenever I am here [Francistown] there are only eight now, because so many of the people have left in these bad times. At Plumtree our other centre on the Mafeking-Bulawayo line, we have at present no buildings, but Mr. Wadeson, who is for a short time there in charge of customs, has put his office at Mr. Lloyd's disposal and a school for white children is gradually collecting there ...[11]

Edgar Lloyd was a lay-reader in the Railway Mission. He was ordained in November 1902, just a few days before the first classes began on the present site of Plumtree School. The siding near the border of the then Rhodesia and Bechuanaland was given its name of 'Plumtree' as the railway line was laid in 1897. One reason given for the Church-sponsored (Railway Mission) school being sited at Plumtree was the presence there of a large railway family. Mr Samuel James Smith, the permanent way Inspector, and his wife had nine children and had long been pressing for a school [The tree on the Plumtree School badge has nine red plums!] Three of their children were among the first nine pupils. The diocese was given a grant of land by the B.S.A. Company for the purpose of building permanent school huts and a church. This was soon exchanged for Stands 8 and 9 of Plumtree Trading Lots, adjacent to the railway line and only 200 metres from the buildings at Plumtree siding. In August 1993, as the southward train drew in to Plumtree some three hours after leaving Bulawayo and on the 96th anniversary of the day the line reached there, the first buildings that I saw from the train were the Hall and Chapel of Plumtree School.

Edgar Lloyd was instructed to occupy the new site and begin the construction of five large huts. These cost £40 each, split between the diocese and the Railways. Just over one year later Herbert Hale was to photograph these first school buildings. Three of the original five huts still remain, some ninety years later, though education long since ceased in them. Edgar Lloyd's ordination resulted in the appointment of a lady principal to succeed him at a salary of £15 per month. Miss Ann Musson moved in, with her first nine pupils, on December 1st, 1902. In his regular letter in *Mashonaland* that month Bishop Gaul wrote:

> At Plumtree the furniture of our boarding house for children had arrived, bought in Cape Town by Mrs Gaul, from a fine gift of £100 from the Rhodes Trustees. Six children had arrived too. The splendid huts built by Mr Lloyd and Mr Hallward looked the picture of neatness. Miss Musson's handiwork was everywhere, and with a helpmeet for her in the shape of a lady fellow-worker, I prophecy great things for this school.

A new schoolroom (forty feet by twenty feet) of brick under iron was completed by the following July and an 'iron lean-to chancel was added by the Plumtree congregation so that the building could double as a church.'

The Rev. E.J. Parker took over from Edgar Lloyd as Railway Missioner and set up an administrative Council or Board for the School. This comprised himself, as Chairman, the local doctor, the diocesan accountant, three officials of the Railways and, later, Bishop Gaul. The new Board announced:

> The Bishop and Railway authorities are deeply sensible of the absolute necessity of Education for the children of the Railway employees. These children, without continuous and definite instruction, must certainly in later life be worsted by those who have used their opportunities. Accordingly, this Boarding School has been established as a "Voluntary Public School" under Ordinance No.18 of 1899 for the purpose of supplying a good primary education (secular and religious) at as low a cost as possible. [12]

The same notice stated that the Ordinary Fees ('irrespective of age') were to be £1.l0s [£1.50] per School Quarter, for Education only, and £10.l0s [£10.50] for Board and Education. Of crucial importance to railway families was the added note:

> By Special Arrangements made with the Government of Southern Rhodesia and with the Rhodesia Railway, the amount payable by Railway employees for each child has been reduced to the following:-
> For Education only - - l0s [50p] per School Quarter.
> For Board and Education - £3 l0s [£3.50] per School Quarter

The School Board also managed to persuade the Government to admit liability to educate children of non-railway parents who were unable to meet fees, provided that the 'Inspector of Schools [was] satisfied that without such aid the children would have to grow up in ignorance.' In the early days there must have been very few parents who were required to pay the full fees. Twenty four pupils had enrolled by January 1903, fifteen of whom were boarders.

By August the numbers had increased to forty-four. Bishop Gaul visited the school in order to

> dedicate the Chancel and conduct Evensong; Fr. Parker took advantage of the visit to ask for a "lean-to" for 2 mistresses rooms, a store-room and 2 rainwater tanks, as the staff had now gone up to 3 women. The Bishop returned in December to conduct the first Confirmation at Plumtree (6 candidates on 12th December 1903). [13]

In the previous month (November 1903) the Rev. Parker had written:

> Monday 6th. Up to Bulawayo, another five hours to get building additions to Plumtree School sanctioned. Three new rooms, to be built of strong poles and ant-heap mud, with iron roof. How strange it must sound to you! How familiar to us!..[14]

Herbert Hale arrived in Bulawayo at the beginning of December 1903, to take up his new work as Railway Missioner. His lengthy letters home to his sister, written once or twice every week for the next three years, along with his innumerable superb photographs give a unique picture of the early life and struggles of Plumtree School, as well as the broader commentary on railway construction and life in 'Rhodesia and Bechuanaland' and the work of SACRM.

Thirty of his letters contain detailed references to the School, which he visited mainly at monthly intervals. Two weeks after his arrival in Rhodesia his first visit to Plumtree was 'to be present at a Prize Giving and Sports at the School ... which is very successful. The functions (over which the Bishop presided) were very much like those at home; the youngsters true veldt children, rough, sturdy, and freckled.'[15] Yet, inevitably, there was an enormous gap between his own culture and experience and that of these 'rough, sturdy' railway children. In the following February Hale stayed at Plumtree for a week or so, teaching 'during religious instruction' and at other times and taking the Sunday Services. He stayed at the 'Siding Refreshment Room.. .put up.. [by] the Proprietor... without charge of any kind..' He informed his sister that he would send photographs of the School Cadet Corps (which he duly did, with four excellent photos), the 'product of the noted, some would say notorious, "Bulala" Taylor.'

The first mention of cadets at the School was in connection with the bishop's visit in December 1903, when 'Bulala' Taylor wrote: 'I will have a Church Parade and Cadet Drill when the Bishop comes, just to show him how we are getting on.'[16] Hale's comment on the existence of a cadet corps was, 'Remember, there is always the possibility of a native rising after each harvest time.' New to the country, Herbert Hale was obviously passing on the received wisdom of the Whites, still nervous after the 1896 'Rebellion.' There is no record of the cadet corps ever using their guns in anger, or defence. The Corps was eventually disbanded in 1968, after sixty-five years and many successes.

The missioner at first enjoyed his visits to Plumtree School, a kind of oasis in his itinerant life of unsocial hours and rough travelling. He felt that Plumtree's importance was 'largely due to the Railway School; for apart from that, there [were] not more than a dozen white people in the place.' H.S. Keigwin, assistant Native Commissioner at Tegwani, noted that 'Most of Plumtree is Scotch and Jew.'[17] The 'Scotch' would be the railway workers, with the Stores, as in much of southern Africa at that time, run by Jewish families.

Hale, in common with other early Railway Mission staff, was always keen to find new entrants for the Mission's own school. Not only was this a genuine concern that 'wild young people' should receive some education, but a concern that the Railway School itself should grow and prosper. In September 1904, whilst journeying to Victoria Falls from Wankie, he 'bagged a couple of children for the Plumtree School at Matetsi Station.' One can only assume that their parents were both willing and delighted that their children were 'bagged'! Although the letter conjures up an improbable picture of children literally being brought onto the train and 'dropped off' at Plumtree, Hale was merely enrolling new pupils for the term about to start. A week later he wrote:

> The School is just starting term, and only part of the children have arrived. Their homes are very remote in many cases. Some come from near the Falls [340 railway-miles away], one from the 72 miles "straight" on the Wankie line [between Gwaai Siding and Dett], another hales from close to Mafeking, 400 miles S. They are rough and mostly shockingly backward, but on the whole jolly and amenable. I always enjoy a visit to Plumtree. There is always a welcome.

A few days later, 'On Train to Gwanda', he added: 'I was anxious at Plumtree to see how the new pupils settled down. I was responsible for three of them, and they seemed to be of a superior class to the average.' We may assume that these 'superior class' children were the ones he had 'bagged' at Matetsi Station. Perhaps they were the children of the (better educated) station master, rather than gangers' children?

The following term Herbert Hale found the School 'overflowing with scholars and new officers [and he looked] ... for really good progress .. in every way.' Sadly, things were 'working out badly again' he discovered a few weeks later, as the new teacher, Miss Clara Slinn, the 'Lady Principal', had 'developed a week heart.' By May of that year Hale was obliged to preside over a Council Meeting at the School in order to persuade a Committee 'afraid to do anything but potter and spend driblets on temporary secondhand gangers' cottages' to put up permanent buildings. He felt that the School was 'on the crest of a wave of prosperity ... except in funds' with both teaching and numbers satisfactory. Nevertheless, all was not well. Housekeeping proved a problem, the School being without a trained cook for many months (the Principal had to undertake the duties), and discipline was a constant difficulty. On May 6th 1905, the missioner was obliged to travel to Tsessebe [a pumping station] to sort out a boy's suspension. It was clear to him that many of the parents would not back up the School discipline. He softened his unpleasant task of visiting the Tsessebe parents by also taking a Service for the small community - 'the first they had ever had.'[18]

June that year saw Hale reporting boys running away from School because of clashes over discipline. Even his Confirmation candidates 'were not conspicuous for shining examples.' He had what he termed an 'unpleasant visit' to Plumtree, with its 'spirit of insubordination' and felt that the only course was 'to get a man as Principal of the School, for no woman can possibly keep wild boys of 14-16 in order.' The Council Meeting debated the runaway boys, one of whom turned up 'prov[ing] that he wanted a good thrashing.' Hale no doubt had 'need' rather than 'desire' in mind. They informed the boy's parents about giving him a thrashing, and then decided to 'have another meeting, when . . the whole affair will be thrashed [sic] out.' It is not surprising that the boys caused problems, given their age and background and the fact that, as he admitted, disciplining 'wild boys' was not an easy task for most women.

Herbert Hale, as with most of the Railway Missioners, had had no training in Education (other than his own education), whether that be the running and administration of schools or teaching in them. His introduction to schools had been as a seven year old starting at a Dame school in Troy, near Monmouth, moving to Monmouth Grammar School when he was eight. The school combined both a Classical School and a Commercial School. At twelve, Herbert Hale was higher up the school than any other boy of his age and won the Latin prize. The family moved to New Zealand when he was thirteen and, after their return, he entered St. Edmund Hall, Oxford, as a twenty-three year old, as noted in Chapter 1. When he applied to join the Railway Mission, to work among railway men and their families, Hale little realised that much of his time would be taken up with the problems of a Railway School.

It is interesting to note that the first record of books donated to Plumtree School library is a letter addressed to Herbert Hale. It was sent from the Victoria League, in London, in January 1906:

> To: The Rev.H.P. Hale.
> Dear Sir,
> We have heard from Rev Douglas Ellison that a case of good children's books would be of use towards starting a Library at the Railway School at Plumtree, Rhodesia - we are therefore sending out a case of books via S.S.. [name obscured] ... via Cape Town... with instructions to send it up to you, at Plumtree [via] Mafeking ..[19]

The letter was marked as 'acknowledged 14/4/06' in a hand that appears to be that of Miss Slinn.

Hale's involvement in Plumtree made him realise that it was 'certainly one of the most important and interesting pieces of Church work in Rhodesia from an educational point of view...' He was concerned to get 'a thoroughly keen Churchman, fully qualified as an elementary teacher' to take over from Miss Slinn, and was amazed and annoyed to meet on a train the new Assistant Teacher, Miss Helm. His annoyance came through not being informed of the appointment, though he was a member of the Council, and the fact that Miss Helm was a Congregationalist ('extremely nice and all that, but ... not loyal to the Church or fair to her to ask her to give [Anglican] Church teaching.')

He wrote an angry letter to the bishop, who, it turned out, had known all about the appointment and had promised previously, after the appointment of a Presbyterian Matron, that in future all the staff would be 'Church people'. Again, this was an example of rather narrow parochialism, even if it was based on the early 'failure' at Plumtree.

As the months went by, Hale's letters note 'insubordination' not only by the pupils but also by the staff (to the Principal), of much friction, too little 'pulling together' and continual problems over the discipline of the 14-16 year-old boys. He felt it his duty to back the Principal, aware that the staff worked against her and encouraged the children and Plumtree people to be hostile to him.

At a Council Meeting in November 1905 they 'electrocuted [sic] two of the subordinate officials .. [and he felt that] the Principal [would] have to go next, unless [they could] get harmony.' Matters came to a head and the Committee decided to dismiss the whole staff. Keigwin, the Assistant Native Commissioner noted earlier, wrote to his friend R.W. Hammond, Headmaster of Amsterdam School in the Transvaal, to persuade him to go to Plumtree: 'You would be your own master as beyond the Railway Chaplain who turns up about once a fortnight you have no supervision.'[20]

Hammond was appointed, but Hale was livid that the Council had told the (former) assistant staff that their re-applications would be considered. He resigned from the Council and was immediately asked by the bishop to withdraw his resignation. Hale refused, feeling that to re-employ 'troublemakers' was to invite yet more trouble. His fears were soon realised when one of the former 'malcontents' was re-instated. However, Hammond soon stabilised school affairs and started to build up the community, remaining as Head for thirty years.

By the time Hammond took over, in July 1906, Herbert Hale was in his last four months as Railway Missioner and felt it wise to 'let matters go.' His last visits were more happy occasions and he was able to write to his sister, after his farewell visit to the whole community:

> I had to say goodbye to Plumtree people [Station houses plus School]. I was very sorry to leave them, especially the School. It is getting on an amicable basis and I like the new staff. They gave me a silver cigarette case, with my initials engraved on it. Quite a number of children piped their eyes, when I said good bye to them, and one little missie I left on the platform sobbing her heart out and refusing to be comforted by her mother.[21]

The Railway Chaplains who succeeded Herbert Hale in that part of Mashonaland Diocese continued the visits to Plumtree School, though, with Hammond's appointment bringing stability, none needed to be as involved as Hale had been. James Toy's letter in the SACRM *Quarterly* of January 1909, may be taken as representative of those who followed Hale:

> The Church communicants on the section are few, except at Plumtree, where there is a flourishing school of white children with a fair proportion of communicants among both staff and pupils. The Chaplaincy of this school is, by a long way, the most interesting part of my work, the children are delightful, and the whole school regime is healthy and happy. If I ever want a bit of cheering up and a renewal of the buoyancy of youth, I get it at Plumtree. During the past year, at the Bishop's request, I have endeavoured to visit the school twice a month during term time, instead of once as previously.[22]

Five of the first nine children at Plumtree were girls, and the School continued to be co-educational until the last day of 1913 when, in order to reduce costs, 'the girl boarders passed out of the history of Plumtree School.'

The education of 'Whites only' continued at Plumtree until Rhodesia became Zimbabwe in 1980. Since then the School has happily changed to educating both black and white Zimbabweans (currently 50-50 ratio). The Railway Mission was relieved of its responsibility of running the School in 1910, when it came under Government control. SACRM chaplains, however, continued their work at the School until 1920 and were always welcome to visit, unofficially, until the ending of the Railway Mission in 1980. The School Archives Room continues to give a prominent place to all the correspondence, documents and photographs relating to Plumtree's early Railway Mission days.

African Schools

The Railway Mission was very conscious about the paucity of schooling not only for white children but also for black and coloured. In 1905 Herbert Hale noted: 'A coloured ganger importunes me to find a school to send his daughter to. These coloured people are keenly alive to the advantages of education, but I can only shake my head hopelessly and say, "Non possumus".' The situation remained the same five years later, when James Toy wrote from the 'Mafeking-Bulawayo' Section:

> It would be a great gain to many of the employees here, and a work of charity, if a school could be provided for the children of coloured parents. These are not admitted to any of the existing schools, and no provision of any kind is made for their education. The children are growing up wild and untaught, and the parents themselves are helpless and seriously concerned ... What is wanted is a Boarding establishment similar to Plumtree, at some healthy centre, and for coloured children only. If we were not so poverty-stricken the Church would gladly provide this.[23]

As we shall see, when examining in particular the SACRM work to and by Africans, the Mission often felt frustrated because of the basic racism among many Whites, and the hostility encountered if missioners attempted to treat equally the different races. James Toy and others could bewail lack of money, yet, despite being 'A Mission to all races', it was always clear that Whites took priority. In Rhodesia, with its influx of new (mainly white) settlers, black and coloured Africans were helped only when money and staffing allowed. The situation was different in South Africa, where the Churches had had a relatively long history of educating 'the natives'. At Cookhouse, in the heart of Grahamstown Diocese, SACRM helped to run and finance a 'native school'. Documentary evidence is scarce on this venture. In 1914 Sidney Griggs, a missioner of three-years' standing, wrote:

> ... our School at Cookhouse ... is the only one in connection with the Railway Mission. Unfortunately at the moment we have only one or two of the teachers certificated ... consequently this year the School will cost the Mission more than its wont. There are just 80 children on the books, and last year the School cost the Mission £15. The children are taken up to and including the fifth standard. ... It is from the School that the majority of candidates for Confirmation are drawn ... It can readily be seen that the School forms an important adjunct to work among the natives. ... Readers may wonder what this work

> has got to do with the Railway Mission. It is true that the Railway Mission exists primarily for Britishers, but in this Diocese, with but few exceptions, the priest-in-charge of white work in a place is also held responsible for work among the natives.... It comes about, then, that... the Mission which is in charge of white work at the Railway Camps must also take over the native work ...[24]

One senses that Sydney Griggs was not too happy with the Mission spending £15, that he felt he had to explain carefully why 'native work' was being undertaken, and that the missioner only did such work because of that diocese's policy. He does in fact call the policy 'a thoroughly bad system', though his reasoning was that special qualifications were needed for non-white work.

The Railway authorities, as mentioned earlier, did run some schools for children who were within 'reasonable' travelling distance. The Church Railway Mission gave what help it could, usually in the form of visits by the chaplains, particularly to take Religious Instruction. In *Letters from the Line,* the Quarterly leaflets written specifically for children in England who supported SACRM, the missioners frequently wrote of their visits to the Railway Schools, and of the difficult journeys undertaken by railway children to get to and from the schools. Often the children had to take whatever train happened to come along. Sometimes the return train did not arrive and so the teachers 'had to arrange .. to get over twenty children sheltered for the night.' [25]

Some Railway Schools catered for children who stayed during the week, usually having to fend for themselves, with little or no supervision regarding food or sleeping arrangements. SACRM's most travelled missioner, the Rev. A.C. Hobson, on a slow journey north from Mafeking in 1917, wrote of the School at Shaslir [Shashi ?] that he expected to reach by midnight:

> There is a Railway School [there] for coloured children, and I visit them occasionally to give a Scripture lesson. They mostly come from the gangers' cottages up and down the line, travelling to school by train on a Monday, and staying there till the end of the week. It's a regular picnic school, as the children do their own cooking (such as it is), and have a shakedown in some tin hut or in the schoolroom.[26]

The Railway Mission, in its final period, became involved with one other 'African school' - that of Mbizi, in Zimbabwe. It was founded by one of the few African railway mission priests, the Rev. John Mhlabi, and will be detailed when looking at 'African work'.

Sunday Schools

From the very earliest Grahamstown days the Railway Mission carried on the English Church Sunday School tradition, particularly in the towns and larger centres of the Cape. The Sunday Schools were usually held in the afternoon, with numbers varying, though often around the forty mark. The missioner's role was typically that of encouraging members of the local congregation to teach the children, with themselves calling in whenever possible.

Even in such centres, a weekly Sunday School was not always possible. Miss Ramadge was a Women's Worker for SACRM in the Bloemfontein Diocese. In 1913 she wrote about the Monthly Sunday School held at Viljoensdrift, in the extreme north of the Diocese and of the Orange Free State:

> Viljoen's Drift is our largest Railway Camp in the O.F.S., and has a coal mine - the Cornelia - quite close to it. There are a lot of children both in the Camp and at the mine, and I think the number of names on the school register is 65. Our Sunday School, held on the Sunday of our monthly Service, has ... varied between 40 and 60 [ie. 60 per cent to over 90 per cent of the available children] ...
>
> If there is a Railway Mission Chaplain, he takes the elder boys, including his Boy Scouts, by themselves, and I have the rest of the children in the Court-house ... after a short opening Service the younger children go out with some of the elder girls as their teachers and sit on the grass in the shade looking at Bible pictures and learning what they mean. ... I hope to have a Preparation Class [for girl helpers] once a month in future.

However, away from any centre it was necessary to be even more adaptable and flexible. Fresh from 'the rush of a big London parish', J. Coombs found himself 'being pulled along at the end of a goods train':

> We stopped at a cottage to pick up some four or five children for the school, which was just 30 miles up the line ... I got permission from the guard to allow them to come into our Coach, and so we talked until we reached the next siding, where four boys and two girls got in. Then we began Sunday School although it was a Tuesday morning. We had our hymns, our Lesson from the Bible, our instruction, and then I told them a story or two, and all too soon for them they had to say good-bye. One little boy wanted to know if I would not meet them every day and have Sunday School. [27]

The formalities of the English parochial system could not apply to an itinerant ministry. Opportunities had to be taken as and when they occurred, even if that meant a 'Sunday' School on the move and on a different day - real innovations.

One of the most detailed accounts of 'Veldt Sunday School' work was given by 'A Woman Worker' in Bloemfontein Diocese (almost certainly Miss M.E. Watson) in 1916. She noted that very large part of her time was taken up with this work, which was held on any and every day of the week, though a Sunday was preferred:

> ... each of these regular *Sunday* Sunday Schools is worked on different [railway] lines and under totally different conditions. Sometimes I feel the first requisite for a Railway Mission Worker is adaptability! The largest is held at W_, where there are about eight railway houses and some adjacent farms, furnishing about twenty-five children, nearly all English ...We meet in the Government School, where there is a really good piano and plenty of blackboards; it is seldom that permission can be gained to use the schools on Sunday, but here there is a ... sympathetic committee, and we have plenty of movement and hymn singing, an informal lesson on dogma is followed by a bible story and expression work ...
>
> At M__ the [Sunday] school is held in the waiting room and it is very difficult to establish or maintain any proper atmosphere ... there is continual passing too and fro of passengers and a kaffir, cleaning lamps, sits just outside [sic]. The big boys bring in station seats ... There are about twelve children, ranging from four to twelve and we are having a course of lessons on the Catechism ...
>
> Another place, T_, we have a school in the Court House, again far from ideal; the blackboard hangs just over the prisoner's dock ... The police barracks adjoin, and the police often join us in singing .. There are about ten children there and I have often wondered if it is worth while continuing, but nowhere are the children keener or the school more appreciated ... it is the only school at which any of the pupils arrive in a wheel-barrow! ...
>
> Another Sunday morning is devoted to teaching a single, large family, English, nearly all boys ... the eldest boy is now seventeen and S.M's [Station Master's] clerk, but he takes real pains to come Sunday by Sunday ... If we could only reach the children every Sunday! I consider it quite remarkable the response we get to the monthly teaching; but we have so much ground to cover.
>
> They are mostly sadly ignorant, and we have to try to teach ethics and morality as well as the Christian faith ... One point is proved, that it is possible to carry out the more modern methods of teaching with

> little in the way of appliances and under various conditions ... imagine teaching a child who has never seen a town, a church, a clergyman, the sea!...[28]

SACRM Sunday School work continued in a variety of guises throughout the whole of the Mission's history. One innovation was 'Sunday School by Post', started in the late 1940s in the Orange Free State and Transvaal by Monica James, a Woman Worker. The scheme was for isolated Anglican children and was 'a great labour'. Each child had an exercise book and Miss James wrote in it, in the form of a personal letter, a 'Sunday School' lesson and stuck in pictures to illustrate. Work was set and then the book went backwards and forwards. The whole scheme was very personal, with enquiries about the family and pets. An examination was held at the end of each year, with a prize given by the relevant bishop. Until her recent death, letters were still exchanged, some fifty years on.

Guilds

A hangover of the Victorian Church was the suspicion, by some Anglican clergy, of the Sunday School Movement. Although the Church of England Sunday School Institute had been founded in 1841, resulting in Sunday Schools being founded in most English parishes, some Tractarian clergy felt that Sunday Schools were often a separate, almost rival, institution from Church. This was, of course, often the case in the larger nonconformist Sunday Schools. The Anglo-Catholic clergy were often happier with a Guild where instruction would be given on the Prayer Book Catechism. It was 'more Anglican' and more a preparation for Confirmation. 'For the Church of England [there was]...a growing concern for secure effective agencies for channelling members of an internal constituency into full Anglican membership.' [29]

In England many Guilds and Fellowships were set up which served as a bridge for the newly confirmed as they entered the full communicant life of the Church. In South Africa, where very many Anglican clergy were products of the Oxford Movement, it was entirely Anglican and 'normal' to found Guilds both for children to prepare for Confirmation and, to a lesser extent, for older post-Confirmation young people. As in England, it was seen as a priority that the Church 'devoted its energies more and more to activities which promised the most predictable and regular flow of confirmees and communicants.'

The Guild of the Good Shepherd was started by the Grahamstown Diocesan Railway Mission and continued into SACRM days. In the 1897 Annual Report, Douglas Ellison wrote: 'I am framing the rules of a Guild for Railway Children, which will, I trust, be the means of helping many of our boys and girls onward and upward.' Ellison was clearly expressing the Victorian self-confident view on the progress of the civilising value of Christianity (particularly Anglican!), as well as showing genuine concern for the young 'parishioners'.

The following year 'over 50 children enrolled themselves as members of the Guild of the Good Shepherd.' Subsequent issues of the GDRM 'Quarterly' wrote of the steady life and expansion of the Guild. By 1903 the Guild, 'because of its size .. [was] forced to assemble in the open air' and a missioner could report: 'The attendance continues to be excellent, and the interest of the children remains unflagging. When we see such enthusiasm among church-people it only makes us more eager to provide them with permanent Church accommodation.'[30]

Although it was always hoped that members would proceed to Confirmation, this was by no means certain, particularly when the children were not living in a railway centre or small town. Mr Herbert Wright, a lay-worker 'On the Grahamstown Coach', wrote about one trip:

> On the main line, from Bethulie to East London, and on the branches to Aliwal [North], Tarkastad and Middle drift, more than a hundred gangers' cottages were visited. The names of fifty children were added to the Guild [of the Good Shepherd], and of these ten or twelve came forward as candidates for Confirmation. [31]

As with all organisations and Societies, local - even idiosyncratic - variations developed in the Branches of the Guild. At least one imitated a Masonic Lodge, certainly reflecting the affiliation of its leader:

> At Volksrust I found myself present at a wonderful meeting of the Guild of the Good Shepherd, and if anyone wants hints as to how to work a branch in any of the bigger Camps, I can safely refer him to Mr. Urquhart. The branch is worked on the lines of a Lodge, with its own secret signs and full ritual, and it did one good to see a leading doctor among the children and taking one of the principal parts in the Guild Lodge. If ever there was work for <u>men</u> to take up in the Camps it is this ...[32]

Ritual appealed to the heirs of the Oxford Movement, although it does seem that this Guild was neither one thing nor the other. As to the exact role of the local doctor in what was supposed to be a children's Guild, one can only wonder.

Local Branches of the Guild, also known as 'The Children of the Good Shepherd', continued into the 1920s and 1930s, though not in great numbers. The pages of the *Quarterly* and of *Light for the Line* gave greater prominence to Sunday Schools, Confirmations and membership of 'Children of the Veld' than they did to the activities of the diminishing numbers of the Guild of the Good Shepherd. Little evidence remains of lesser-known Guilds. A large SACRM card recently came to light outlining Sunday worship, in both English and Afrikaans, for the Companions of Christ the King (Die Kamerade van Christus die Koning). This, however, seems to be the sole extant witness to this 1920s/30s' Guild.

Children of the Veld (C.O.V)

Most of SACRM's work among children was based on similar activities in Britain, with all the adapting and flexibility noted earlier. One branch of its work was, however, completely innovative - the 'Children of the Veld'. This one movement linked children in parishes in England and those in town parishes in South Africa with the isolated 'railway children' living on the veld. The idea came to H.B. Ellison whilst he was visiting England in 1908 for the Pan-Anglican Congress, during which he was appointed the new Head of SACRM. A small girl gave him half-a-crown (12p) for 'the black babies' in South Africa. He felt that he could not do much about 'the thousands along the line' but it did make him think about 'those dear little white cousins of ours along the Line in South Africa.' In the children's leaflet, *Letters from the Line*, he wrote: 'It made me wonder whether we might not have a Children's League for the Railway Mission.'[33] He envisaged children collecting for SACRM and praying for the (white) isolated children. Ellison took the idea back with him to South Africa, though his first few months as Head were taken up with the expansion of the Mission northwards, across the Zambezi.

The July 1909 *Letters from the Line,* addressed for the first time to children in both England and South Africa, announced the formation of 'Children of the Veld'. To become a member the children had to contact the Local Representative in their parish, or write to the Children's Secretary in England (Barnet, Herts) or in South Africa (Grahamstown). The red and black Membership Card had a picture of a ganger giving a lift, on his trolley, to a missioner. The missioner's dog scampered along, just to give added appeal. Two Africans stood behind, working the trolley. At the side of the track were the children with whom the Members were encouraged to identify - a small girl in a pretty dress and bonnet, holding the hand of her smart Scout brother, who was raising his hat as the trolley passed. Both of them were very white and English:

> Their home, miles from anywhere, on the great lonely "Veld", is in the background. ... You will see how pleased they are to see their friend on the trolley; and then you will look at the top of the Card and you will read the beautiful words from Isaiah: *"The Wilderness and the solitary place shall be glad for them."* Those Children are living in the "Wilderness" and in "a solitary place", and you are going to help, by your prayers and by your money, to make them "glad"...

No 'black babies' were in evidence. The Members were urged to become friends of the veld children and to write to them and to pray for them daily, using the C.O.V. prayer.

Within three months, eight Branches had been started in England and two in South Africa. Thirty-one children 'along the line' had asked for letters from English C.O.Vs. When H.B. Ellison invited the children of the first Branch in South Africa (Orchards, in Johannesburg) to the Mission coach for tea, his expected 'dozen or so' turned out to be thirty-six. It was a good start. By the time the 1909 Annual Report of SACRM was produced, early in 1910, eleven Branches were reported in England and six in South Africa, with an ever growing number of children wanting to become Members but not having a Branch where they lived.

One very practical help that was soon established was that of C.O.V. members sending toys and books to the Railway Mission at Christmas time for distributing to the 'railway children', mainly at the gangers' cottages. The custom grew up of the missioners travelling the lines each December and often into January or later, giving out (or even having to throw out of a moving train) parcels at each siding and cottage. 'Father Christmas' came to the children in the form of the chaplains, men and women, without whom most of them would have had few, if any, presents. This practice continued for the rest of SACRM's time in South Africa, long after C.O.V. had petered out. Children were asked to write individually to those who lived along the railway lines and to send them specific presents. Friendships sprang up, some of which continued over the years. Most of the Branches, whether in England or in South Africa, held Sales of Work and organised other activities, such as Fetes, to raise money 'for the care of the children living on the railways which [ran] .. through the "limitless veld".' The 'care of the children' did not just mean letters, toys and books; but also the support of a SACRM 'Children's Missioner', to have specific responsibility for work among railway children and groups who supported them. Other children, such as those at Sunday Schools, who were not in C.O.V Branches, also raised money and were encouraged to pray for 'their own Missioner.'

In the early years, particularly before 1916, various (Anglican) Schools in England formed their own C.O.V. Branches. The First World War had the effect of limiting the numbers of new Branches being formed, though matters improved a little after 1918. As time went on there was less support for C.O.V in South Africa itself, other than among the railway children recipients, and by the time of the Second World War the Organisation was almost entirely centrered in England. The work and support continued in ever smaller amounts until 1948, when 'C.O.V Branches' disappeared from the cover of the *Quarterly* and may therefore be taken as the official end of 'Children of the Veld'.

The South African Church Railway Mission had proved that it was not only willing to change and adapt its English Church practices, but to introduce and develop new ideas. The limits, as always, were those of lack of money and lack of workers, coupled with the constraints of the class, background and education of the workers.

Clubs and uniformed Organisations

Most of SACRM's work among children and young people was, as we have seen, with organisations or movements which catered for mixed (boys and girls) groups. However, just as there were separate, mainly uniformed, organisations in England for the two sexes, similar patterns emerged in southern Africa.

As early as 1908 Missioners were recruiting girls for the Girls' Friendly Society. The G.F.S., an Anglican Society, was founded by Mary Townsend in 1875, for young girls who had left their homes in rural areas for domestic service in towns and cities. She aimed to 'rescue the vulnerable from the social evils of the time.' It pre-dated the Guide movement by over thirty years and was more Church based and less 'outdoor'. Some of the Railway Mission women workers were themselves members of the G.F.S.

Miss Nott-Bower, one of the first women workers (and a former matron at Guy's Hospital), wrote about her visits in 1905 to the Railway Camps, work which included having meetings of the G.F.S, 'helped ... by an old G.F.S friend ... in every way she could ...'. Miss Nott-Bower's work, like so much of SACRM's activity, was multi-faceted and she had to be involved in various organisations. The Mothers' Union was one such. She wrote, 'I do all I can to promote these two excellent Societies [M.U. and G.F.S] of which, on the Line, I am the representative; but I believe that direct Mission work is really what is most needed ...'[34]

Some of the Railway Missioners would have maintained that promoting the activities and membership of Societies such as the G.F.S was 'direct mission work.' They certainly felt that about the Scout and Guide Movement, which we shall note below.

The Head of SACRM, writing in 1911 of prospective members of the staff, stated:

> We already have had a very welcome accession in the person of Mr. A.C. Bickerdike, so well known to many of the Railway lads in Johannesburg. He is now giving up his Bank work entirely and, as a member of the Mission, will give the whole of his time to the Railway Lads' Club, and to starting alongside of it the Young Men's Club [similar to YMCA] which is urgently needed to supplement the work among the boys. It is good to find Mr. Hoy [later, Sir William - General Manager of South African Railways] and the Railway authorities very genuinely keen on this scheme ... making over for the use of the two clubs the excellent premises of the old '[Railway] Staff Club' in the Railway Avenue ...[35]

In time the Railway authorities themselves, as well as established parishes and city and town groups, undertook the welfare of young people in centres such as Johannesburg. After its pioneering efforts, SACRM was then able to concentrate on the more isolated line and veld work.

Between 1907 and 1909 the (Boy) Scout Movement was launched by Baden-Powell, along with the (Girl) Guides, started by Baden-Powell's sister, Agnes, and then taken over by his wife, Olave. The Movement was quickly adopted in South Africa, although it took over twenty years of disputes before young people of the different races were allowed to be part of one organisation and wear the same uniform.

A Railway Missioner wrote from Waterval Boven in 1916,

> I have finally decided to take the plunge and start with the Boy Scouts. Very little is done for Boven boys, and I think all are agreed today about the value of Baden Powell's movement. Recently I was appointed chaplain to a Scout troop ...[36]

SACRM workers, however, became much more involved with 'Lone Scouts' and 'Lone Guides' than with Scout or Guide troops. The 'Lones', as such, were not an adaptation by the Railway Mission itself, but rather a natural development within Scouting to take account of vast distances and isolation. New Zealand and Australia had similar methods. Describing a weekend visit to railway workers, Miss Porter, a SACRM woman-worker, wrote:

> On Saturday morning ... I spend the time with Girl Guides and Brownies, Scouts and Cubs. They are 'Lone', not attached to any Company, but we are able to do all the work of the Guides and Scouts, and it is a very valuable movement and these lonely boys and girls are very enthusiastic. They take up my whole morning - teaching them to play, teaching them to work, ... to give way to others, which is a very real thing in our work out there as well as elsewhere. [37]

Miss Norah Short, a colleague of Miss Porter's, spoke at the Annual Meeting of SACRM the following year:

> The Guide Movement ... means much to our lone children to feel that they belong to a world-wide body of young people ... So we have our 'Lone Guides'. We cannot run flourishing Companies, or do great things, but we just work quietly on our own. In two [Railway] Camps, Lone Companies have been started. They are lone because the members are always changing, the fathers being frequently shifted from place to place. A Lone Company may have 18 Guides one month and 8 the next, and so on. ... Then there are a number of quite isolated Lones. They cannot do all the Guide work, but they do as much as they can ... [38]

So here was an innovation by SACRM. The available 'Lone Scout' literature, such as 'The South African Lone Scout', assumes a membership of isolated Scouts, with some very small family patrols of three or four. Scouts in larger settlements or Railway Camps were expected to be in normal (static) Scout Troops. The Railway Mission realised that, when children were frequently moving - because of their fathers' railway work, it made sense for such children to become 'Lone' scouts or guides.

Lone Scout and Lone Guide Camps were held, as well as expeditions, in order that the isolated members could occasionally meet with their fellow 'Lones'. SACRM missioners were frequently involved in running these camps and in encouraging the young people, scattered along the railway lines, to attend. Archive films, taken as late as the end of the 1950s, show Railway missioners organising camps for Lone Scouts.

There does not seem to be any record of SACRM supporting Scouting for non-white young people, either before they were allowed to be an official part of the Scout movement, or subsequently. As the Archbishop of Cape Town was the man to whom SACRM clergy swore canonical obedience, and he had openly stated that 'the Boy Scouts would be destroyed in South Africa if [Baden-Powell] allowed blacks to join'[39], it was perhaps not surprising that they did not support black or coloured

Scout work. There was also a fear that the Afrikaners would opt out of the Scouts and form their own movement (which they did, in any case, in 1931 with the 'Voortrekkers'). The unified, non-racial, South African Scout Movement, which came into being in 1935, did not noticeably alter SACRM's position.

Although the Railway Mission supported these uniformed organisations, particularly when they were Church-centred/sponsored, it is clear from all the literature and letters that the missioners who became most involved and did most to promote groups were those who enjoyed Scouting and Guiding, as in Britain. Staff who did not care for outdoor pursuits with young people were not short of other work which they could promote, including the various Church organisations and Movements, as noted earlier.

Catechism and Confirmation

All the priests in the early years of the Railway Mission, and most of those who followed later, had been made Deacon and ordained Priest in the Church of England according to the Form and Manner as laid down in the Book of Common Prayer. At the Ordination Service when admitted Deacon, aged twenty-three or older, the man would have heard his bishop exhort him to 'instruct the youth in the Catechism.' After serving one year (exceptionally longer) as deacon, the clergyman, usually a curate assisting a vicar in a large parish, would have then been admitted Priest in another Ordination Service. The bishop would have given him another exhortation, this time to '... teach and to premonish, to feed and provide for the Lord's family; to seek for Christ's sheep that are dispersed abroad [= 'at large'], and for his children who are in the midst of this naughty world ...'[40]

In particular, the would-be priest, standing facing his diocesan bishop (sitting in his 'cathedra' [chair]), was told,

> ... never cease your labour ... until you have done all that lieth in you ... to bring all such as are or shall be committed to your charge, unto that agreement in the faith and knowledge of God, and to that ripeness and perfectness of age in Christ ...

After the long exhortation came the Declarations, when answers had to be given to the bishop's eight questions. After 'thinking' that he was truly called to the 'Order and Ministry of Priesthood', to the question '..are you determined out of the said Scriptures to instruct the people committed to your charge..', the man would have replied, 'I am so persuaded, and have so determined by God's grace.' There would have been no doubt in the minds of the priests who sailed for South Africa to join the Railway Mission, that one of their main duties would be that of giving instruction in the Church Catechism and then presenting candidates for Confirmation. Whatever came their way in the form of 'Occasional Offices' (Baptisms, Weddings, Funerals), or of pastoral or social activities, the task of 'seeking out' those to be confirmed remained a constant. The High Church background of most of the missioners gave this task an extra urgency and delight.

The Catechism was the 'Instruction to be learned of every person before he be brought to be confirmed by the bishop.' It was basically a series of questions and answers, to be learned, on promises made at Baptism; plus the Creed, the ten Commandments, duties towards God and Neighbour, the Lord's Prayer, and the Sacraments of the Church - all as laid down in the *Book of Common Prayer*. When a person came to a 'competent age' and could recite The Creed, the Lord's Prayer and the Ten Commandments, and could answer various questions in the 'Shorter Catechism', he or she could then be presented to the bishop. It was not unknown, even at the turn of the century, for clergy and Churches to adapt the Catechism or to have their own version of it, although the basic 'recitations' would remain.

Alfred Long, Railway Missioner at Jansenville from 1897, wrote, 'In visiting the schools or the cottages I have enrolled children as members [of the Guild of the Good Shepherd] and many have undertaken to learn the Church [=BCP] Catechism.'[41] References to Catechism classes are frequently made in the SACRM *Quarterly,* but are often very brief. Catechism 'happened' before Confirmation - all the readers knew that - and there was not normally much difference in what took place in southern Africa from what was happening in every parish up and down England. It rarely needed comment, unlike Confirmation which involved a bishop, a gathering together (usually) of a whole group of people from across a region, coupled with all the transport and logistical difficulties. Catechism, involving only the priest-missioner, did not encounter all the problems raised by having to have a bishop present.

However, on one occasion, the readers of the *Quarterly* were informed of the 'Method' used for Catechism, as devised by the Rev. H.B. Ellison and the Rev. Lionel Sparks in about 1907. The account makes clear that the catechists (white teachers, not African 'Catechists' - who had a far greater responsibility and role) had a considerable amount of preparation to do in the week before the Sunday Class, including visiting those who were 'absentee scholars'. Scholars were encouraged to decorate the Church on special occasions and even to 'cultivate the borders in the Churchyard.'[42] The writer, Miss Attlee, a SACRM Woman Worker whom we shall meet later, noted the constant difficulty in South Africa of keeping helpers.

Some of the missioners wrote of the difficulties encountered in attempting to hold Confirmation Classes, and how they had to adapt methods and change plans almost constantly. A not untypical Class was that held by the Rev. Percy Barnes, in 1912. He took seven Services one Sunday and then travelled all night to be at a Station on the Monday, for 'there was never a school train that day' and he would be able to see the Confirmation group. On arrival he found that the train had, in fact, come and so 'Tom ... and the other children ... had gone to school.' The boy's father then decided that Tom and his sister would not be confirmed, despite their long preparation. The chaplain went on to the next station, where he discovered that the Station Master and his wife had gone on leave (with the children) 'taking with them ... chance of a meal and a bed.' The ganger's wife, a candidate for confirmation, was ill with neuralgia. Percy Barnes then walked overnight to a farm, where he was expected to take a Communion at seven p.m. The two African 'kitchen girls' at the farm had already had some Confirmation lessons on previous occasions, and so an hour was spent in further instruction, though 'Rachel had not got far with the ordinary Catechism as she had had to leave her book at home [twelve miles away].' Barnes commented, 'Out here we try to do the [Confirmation] preparation as carefully as at home [England], but there are great difficulties and we just do what we can.'[43] During the instruction they were visited by a ganger's son, the young son of the (Jewish) storekeeper, the wife of the storekeeper (in search of her son), and then the farmer for his dinner! But at least the missioner felt that the illnesses and absences had resulted in him giving more time to the African girls, bringing forward their presentation for Confirmation.

The GDRM monthly Letter, sent to supporters in England, was replaced by a much fuller *Quarterly* in April 1902. The first issue gave details of the visit of Bishop Cornish to Cookhouse railway camp - 'always an event of supreme importance when God's chief minister comes into our midst.' Almost a whole page is given over to an account of the first of two Confirmations that the bishop held, a Confirmation that they had been 'preparing for ... for many months.' This was for Whites (only) and took place in the suitably decorated and transformed schoolroom - 'something as nearly resembling a church as is possible.' The candidates, nine boys and nine girls 'most of whom were of full age', are named and details given of their first Communion. The article ends with the information that, 'The Native Confirmation was held in the little mud Church in the Location at 9 a.m. on the 18th March [the morning after the Whites' Service], when six candidates received the Laying-on of hands [ie. were

Confirmed].'[44] These African candidates were not named, nor further details given.

The missioners, when involved with children through Sunday School work, or the Guild of the Good Shepherd, or with Children of the Veld, were constantly on the look out for suitable candidates for Confirmation - those whom they felt would be willing and able to learn the Catechism, and who expressed a desire for the sacrament. We have noted earlier how, when a missioner visited a hundred gangers' cottages from the 'Grahamstown coach' in 1904, of the fifty children who joined the Guild of the Good Shepherd 'ten or twelve came forward as candidates for Confirmation.' In the whole period of the Railway Mission, a proportion of about a quarter was typical for those who went forward to Confirmation out of the total of children and young people who attended any of the Church/Mission-run groups or organisations.

Herbert Hale wrote home to his sister about the visit of the Bishop of Chichester to Rhodesia, which included a trip to the Victoria Falls and the first Confirmation Service in 'N.W.R.' [North West Rhodesia]. Hale's letters allow us to understand something of the frustrations encountered by the railway missioners, both in organising Confirmation Services and in dealing with the visiting church hierarchy. About five weeks before the visit he writes, 'I have got a Confirmation candidate for the Bishop of Chichester when he visits the Falls next month; the first in N.W.R.' A few days later he mentions spending a morning having 'a long "indaba" with a candidate for Confirmation, one of the nurses at [Hartley] ... Hospital.' The luxury, in England, of having many months to prepare candidates was not something available for an itinerant missioner:

> She seems a good girl, but I feel the responsibility of presenting a candidate to whom I can give but little preparation. I have written her a paper, consisting of three .. sheets, full of facts about Confirmation, and pointing out in the strongest language the solemnity and responsibility of coming forward. She certainly will not be in the dark as to the importance of the step she is taking. For the rest, I must leave it to her conscience to decide. ... I have another candidate at Livingstone for [the bishop], of whom I have seen more.[45]

Two days after his "indaba", Hale 'spent the morning ... in looking up another candidate for Confirmation ... [but] as she seemed inclined to draw back, [he] decided not to attempt to present her.' He points out that by the time he had done with 'His Lordship', he (Herbert Hale) would have travelled, in six weeks or so, '2,300 miles, held about 20 services at 15 different places, ranging from 4 to 500 miles apart, and [would] then probably take a run down to Headquarters at Grahamstown to talk matters over.'

After an eight and a half hour slow journey by train over the ninety miles from the mines at Gwanda to Bulawayo, Hale had little time to change, collect mail and eat before he joined the northward train, which had on board the Bishop of Chichester and the Archdeacon of Mashonaland. His letter home takes on a Trollopian air:

> My first impressions of the Bishop were not too favourable. The Archdeacon said, "He is very tired. Leave him alone, and only go and see whether he has everything." So when I had settled my baggage, I knocked at his compartment. The door opened, "This compartment is reserved. I am just going to bed. Can't see anyone tonight." Bang goes the door. When I find that, owing to the Bishop having a compartment reserved, I and two other first class passengers have to occupy a very miserable 2nd class compartment, where there was no table to eat meals at, I felt a little disgusted. But the Bishop improves on acquaintance, and is charming socially; but singularly uninterested ... in Church work out here. He never once talked about it.[46]

Later, at the Falls, Fox, the Bishop's host, 'took the Bishop and Archdeacon to his Camp', leaving Hale as a 'mere "trek" parson' to fend for himself. The two final straws came with the Sunday Communion Service at the D.C's [Mr. Sykes'] Camp:

> The Archdeacon took [the Service], having borrowed my robes. To my surprise, he announced that the collection would be for a nucleus of a Church Building Fund. Excellent, but where does the Railway Mission and I, as priest in charge, come in? He had never spoken to me about the matter, nor considered that the Railway Mission is footing the bill of the man who is taking the Services up here.

The archdeacon and bishop then went off to the other side of the river Zambezi [Livingstone Drift] with Hale's confirmation candidate, and proceeded to confirm the man without his sponsoring priest being present. This was unnecessary and also irregular. As Hale noted, 'it show[ed] some want of consideration on the part of both the Bishop and Archdeacon.' It is worth observing that, in the published account in the *Quarterly,* Hale states: 'The Bishop of Chichester ... helped us greatly at Hartley and Victoria Falls. At each place he held a Confirmation and gave a stirring address. The candidates were adults...' [47] The readers were given no hint of the difficulties or differences of opinion. No doubt

Douglas Ellison (the Head) was suitably informed the following week when Hale travelled down the 1200 miles to Grahamstown. Hale's last comment on 'My Lord of Chichester's visit', was to his sister:

> I left Bulawayo as arranged ... and had as far as Kimberley the Bishop of Chichester for a fellow passenger. He was very agreeable, but I cannot say I was very sorry to see the last of him. He was too patchy in his moods to be pleasant for the under dog.[48]

The questions raised nowadays about Confirmations in Boarding Schools, where pupils are inevitably divorced from their home parishes and where the risk of 'rubber-stamping' is ever prevalent, were not an issue in an earlier period. It was rather the reverse, for it was seen as advantageous to have a number of candidates already together. In the vastness of southern Africa it was a positive bonus to be able to hold Confirmation preparation in one place for many candidates, and for the confirmands not to have to travel to the Confirmation Service. Hale, writing 'On board train to Gwanda', in May 1905, states that he was 'to start a Confirmation class down at Plumtree [School] as soon as possible and [was] trying to fix the bishop to a date for it.' He noted that this would involve him having to 'put in a solid week' at Plumtree, in order to concentrate the Confirmation preparation.

As with the Bishop of Chichester's visit the previous year, Bishop Gaul of Mashonaland's stay was not straightforward. En route to Plumtree, from Francistown, Hale heard that the bishop was only arriving at Plumtree on the Sunday (later than expected). When Hale's train reached Plumtree 'a further telegram awaited [him] saying that [the bishop] was ill and could not come for the Confirmation on Sunday.' He wrote:

> Great consternation, great disappointment and I fear some resentment. People had come in for miles to meet him and could not stay. Personally, I was not sorry to have some extra time with my candidates. Still, it landed me with the Sunday Services and two addresses at short notice.[49]

People were quite used to lengthy train delays and other problems with transport, and were well acquainted with sickness and illness. Bishops, then as now, were somehow expected to rise above these difficulties. Bishop Gaul arrived on the Monday and the Confirmation Service was held, though not before the only boy in the school who was already confirmed used some extremely bad language, in the bishop's hearing. Hale put it down to the 'evil spirit' or the Devil in the boy, fighting against the Holy Spirit which the other boys were about to receive! The following day the missioner drove the bishop out to a farm ten miles from Plumtree, where there was a 'woman wishing to be confirmed but who [had] a baby and was afraid to venture in on account of the scarlet fever [at Plumtree].' The journey entailed driving 'a pair of frolicsome horses.' Hale continued, 'The Confirmation was quite an impressive service, though it took place in a rough mud hut. They were Dutch people and afterwards regaled us on roast sucking pig ...' [50]

SACRM chaplains were later discouraged from preparing members of the Dutch Reformed Church for Confirmation. The Mission's 'Vade Mecum' stated:

> Confirmations in the D.R. denominations are prolonged, exacting, and expensive: so ... their people apply to us for that, and then cheerfully go back to their old church. So all such applications from them should be refused, unless you first have from them their letter of resignation from their church, and you have sent it to their predikant.[51]

It is more than likely that the Mission's 'rules' were only formulated out of experience long after the time of Hale. A bishop, in any case, was free to decide for himself whom he confirmed. It would have been most unlikely that a DRC predikant was at all available, and it made pastoral sense for the Anglican Church to give the 'Dutch woman' the sacrament. It was possible, though unlikely, that these farmers were Anglicans.

The following week Herbert Hale and the bishop were on the north side of the Zambezi, across from the newly opened Victoria Falls Hotel [52], where they had each paid six shillings for 'soup made from Bovril, a little cold goat mutton or beef', and were at the D.C's Camp. Hale wrote:

> I called on the people, who were living in a tent, and found there a girl who was very anxious to be confirmed. So I said I would see the Bishop, and if he was willing to confirm, I would try my best to prepare her. It is a great problem, this preparation, and one has to take the candidates "on spec", or leave them unconfirmed. One asks oneself, "Are they in earnest", and if so present them. This girl was going with her father into the Hook of the Kafue [river], 2 or 300 miles N[orth] away back from the railway, even when it is made, in an unholy climate. Surely what gift we can give her, she needs.[53]

A few days later the bishop did confirm the girl, though not before giving Hale and the parents quite a scare by turning up three hours late and 'minus coat and waistcoat.' But this was surely a case of Anglicanism at its best. Despite its rules and regulations and the strictures of its Prayer

Book, both bishop and railway missioner were caring and flexible enough to 'bend the rules' when common sense and compassion prevailed.

Confirmations were not only held in Churches, school chapels, or even a schoolroom transformed to 'resemble a church.' Huts, houses and the *stoeps* of houses were used on occasions, particularly in the days before many parishes were formed, or churches built. In 1908 the readers of the SACRM *Quarterly* were given a vivid description of 'A Confirmation on the Veldt.' Visions of the Ceremony taking place open-air, in the middle of a 'tree-less burning veldt', were soon dispelled as the Missioner went on to mention a farm house 'standing in isolation away from anything resembling a town or village.' The farm house was by the banks of the Klip River (a dried-up track at the time), with a single railway line, running from the Cape to the Transvaal, some half a mile away. A small station, with 'three houses, an S.A.C. "Camp", a Store (of sorts) and two or three tin shanties' formed the nearest habitation. The *stoep* of the farm house was chosen for the Confirmation Service when the special visit of the bishop had been arranged:

> ... many of the railway gangers would have found it extremely difficult, if not impossible, to leave their work for the time required to travel [to some bigger centre] some 20 miles by train and back, and when once the Class was started and it was known that the bishop was coming, a regular "boom" resulted, and out of at the most some 20 houses within a radius of 10 miles, no fewer than 17 candidates came forward for presentation. The classes were held at the ganger's house at the station, where we generally had to adjourn outside owing to lack of accommodation inside ... [They were] such a mixture of ages and nationalities. The limits of age were 47 and 13, and the nationalities included English, Dutch, Scotch and Welsh. To help in the preparation of the Dutch, some of whom could speak but little English, I had to get hold of Catechisms, Prayers, etc., in Dutch, and to procure the help of the ganger's wife as interpreter and instructor in the Catechism. [54]

Here again, therefore, the Railway Mission (and the bishop) were not too worried about 'Dutch' people being Confirmed by the Anglican Church. The morning of the special day was spent in decorating the *stoep*, which ran the whole length of the house, and the piano was brought out, along with a small table suitably covered with a white cloth. A basket chair became the bishop's 'throne', with an assortment of chairs, planks, boxes and tins for the sixty strong congregation. 'The hymns went with a real swing, and the whole service was impressive, the Bishop's strong, practical addresses being followed intently by all ...'

The Railway Mission existed as the 'Church between the Churches' and as the 'Travelling Church'. In its unconventional way it fulfilled both roles very well on this occasion. In many ways all the Confirmation classes and Services that continued to be taken and arranged by the SACRM Missioners were variations on a theme - that we saw expressed by Percy Barnes in 1912 - of surmounting great difficulties and 'doing what we can.' The problems that were encountered usually involved bishops! Although the mission did try to move in the direction of its constituents, and be flexible and accommodating, this often created a tension between it and the hierarchy. For Confirmation Services, tension was virtually built into the structure. Generally speaking, in southern Africa during the time of the Railway Mission, the bishops who 'dropped in' from time to time were the least adaptable of Church servants - they did not live as the missioners did. There were, also, occasional personality clashes, and yet there were a few individual bishops who were extremely flexible in their approach, as we shall later observe. Yet basically, especially with Confirmation, there was a clash between the formal structures of prelatic Anglicanism (dealing with static groups) and the unconventional methods of the South African Church Railway Mission (dealing with people on the move).

---

1 Simeon, 1925, 7
2 Lewis & Edwards, 10
3 Hinchliff, 1963, 20
4 *Mother Cecile,* 1930, chronology
5 *Mother Cecile*, 1930, 51
6 White, 1987, 41
7 *Mother Cecile*, 53/4
8 *Mother Cecile*, 71
9 GDRM, 1894, 3/4
10 Maclaren, 1981, 212
11 Clarke, 1983, 96
12 Plumtree School Archives
13 Grain, 1985, 40
14 Vickery, 31
15 Hale, Letters, 18.12.1903
16 Maclaren, 214
17 Clarke, 83
18 Hale, Letters, 11.5.1905
19 Plumtree School Archives
20 Clarke, 83
21 Hale, Letters, 27.10.1906
22 QP 22, 1909, 2
23 QP 26, 1910, 14
24 QP 44, 1914, 9
25 *Letters from the Line* (LL) no.32, 1911, 3

[26] QP 57, 1917, 9
[27] QP 25, 1909, 11/12
[28] QP 52, 1916, 8-10
[29] Gilbert, 1976, 20
[30] GDRM/SACRM No. XIX, Apr. 1903, 2
[31] QP 3, 1904, 12
[32] QP 30, 1911, 13
[33] LL no. 21, 1909, 3
[34] QP 8, 1905, 7
[35] QP 30, 1911, 13
[36] QP 50, 1916, 9
[37] QP 76, 1923, 20
[38] QP 79, 1924, 16
[39] Jeal, *Baden-Powell*, 1989, 492/3
[40] BCP, 'The ordering of Priests'
[41] GDRM, 1998/9, 17
[42] QP 42, 1914, 16
[43] QP 37, 1912, 12
[44] GDRM no.XV, 5
[45] Hale, 'Letters', 22.6.1904
[46] Hale, 'Letters', 2.7.1904
[47] QP 5, 1904, 9
[48] Hale, 'Letters', 1.8.1904
[49] Hale, 'Letters', 15.6.1905
[50] Hale, 'Letters', 15.6.1905
[51] SACRM, 'Vade Mecum', 1949, 17
[52] The Victoria Falls Hotel opened in June 1904. It was a simple building of corrugated iron and wood - a long structure raised up from ground level. At first there were 12 single rooms, 4 doubles, a dining room, a bar and offices. Two engine sheds from Mandegos (Beira line) were then dismantled, one becoming the new dining room, and the other an additional bedroom. The railway line passed between the hotel and the Zambezi gorge until a torrential storm in 1908 washed the line away, after which time it was relaid to pass behind the hotel (as today).
[53] Hale, 'Letters', 24.6.1905
[54] QP 19, 1908, 8

5. Welfare and pastoral work

- 'a tremendous difference in their lives'

The parishioners of Chattenden and Upner, at the end of 1930, were given the following insight into 'women's work':

"Along the Line": Episode 1. A Ganger's Cottage.

RUTH. O mum, there's a private coach at the station. I thought it was the District Commissioner or Railway Plumber or Inspector of Weights and Scales, but Joyce and I went and peeped inside, and we saw a lady.

MRS. CAMPBELL. A lady?

ALL CHILDREN. It was a lady! ...

DANNY. And I asked the Stationmaster who it was, and he said it was the Lady Missioner.

RUTH. And he said she was going to have a lantern service at the School tomorrow night. Do you think we can go, Mum?

MRS. CAMPBELL. I'm afraid that is out of the question, it's much too far.

(A knock is heard)

DANNY It's the lady ...

MISS DIXON. How do you do, Mrs. Campbell? I'm glad to have found your cottage at last. I thought I was never going to come to it. I saw your children at the station, and I thought they must live here, and well, here I am.

Episode 2. A Railway Waiting Room at Sandfontein Station

(After the entry of the Railway Mission chaplain, Mr.Merryman, plus various local families and the Campbells)

MRS. CAMPBELL ... I used to be so lonely and miserable, and I found it such a job to manage the children. But ever since Miss Dixon came to see me about six months ago it's all been so different. She's been several times and cheered me up. She has had a Sunday School for the children, and Ruth has improved so much. We do so look forward to her coming ...[1]

One can only imagine what audiences in Church Halls in England made of this fifteen to twenty minute play which included a 'kaffir girl', Katie, and a 'Dutch' [=Afrikaner] girl, Anne, in its cast. Reading its somewhat formal and stylized dialogue is rather like watching a Ministry of Information film of the late 1930s. But the Play was designed to depict typical situations in South African isolated railway life and to show how useful was the work of the SACRM Women Workers and Chaplains. It was hoped that more support, such as money, prayer and even would-be workers would be forthcoming after a successful performance of the Play. The SACRM films of the 1950s were to have a similar, yet more realistic, role.

This Chapter will deal with three aspects of pastoral work, namely: nursing in southern Africa, the involvement of the Railway Mission with the Colonial Nursing Association, and the more general Women's Work undertaken by the South African Church Railway Mission. As with the educational work, we shall note how SACRM had to adapt existing patterns of work, challenge systems and officials, and become innovative in dealing with women and families often neglected by the Railways and by wider society. The women missioners felt compelled to do whatever they could to help and comfort those who lived extremely lonely and isolated lives.

Nursing

> I have suddenly had a move to fever-stricken, desolate Sterkstroom, deserted by all but the Depot people, and a sadly over-crowded Hospital, 140 cases in, and 100 of these fever. There is no military glory about it, and no chance now of getting to the front; but I am glad to be here, for I hope to be able to make myself of some use to the hospital and its patients; there is nobody else to visit the men in the wards at all.[2]

Thus wrote the Rev. W.A. Hewett on the 10th March, 1900, some six months or so after his arrival from England to work on the Railway Mission, the third assistant chaplain to be employed, after Douglas Ellison. He had hoped, and Ellison had wanted him, to be visiting the railway men on the lines of the Eastern Cape, but with his arrival coinciding with the start of the South African War the hospital work took precedence. ('We badly want him back on the line; but there can be no asking him to throw up work like this.') Three months later Hewett was writing from the tent which had become his temporary home in Naauwpoort,

> The fever ... has not confined itself to the Hospital, but has overflowed into many of the homes of our Railway folk, causing the

> Railway Doctor and Nurse to be much over worked. For a short time Miss Brooke Hunt kindly helped in the nursing of our sick, until the [Railway] Mission was fortunate enough to secure for the people here the services of Sister Catherine, of St. Peter's Home, Grahamstown.[3]

Young readers were reminded in August 1900 that Naaupoort was not only 'a big and growing railway centre' (hence the Mission's involvement there), but also 'the site of a great Military Hospital.' Three of the Mission's seven staff were working there, including 'good old black Josiah ... looking after the natives ...', as well as 'Sister Katharine [or Catherine], a trained nurse.' We have already noted how, by 1891, the Grahamstown Sisters were helping the Railway Mission and railway people by educating girls. The second time they came to the rescue of the Mission was with nursing. The biographer of Mother Cecile reported:

> On May 6 [1900] an urgent appeal for a nurse was received by the Mother from the Naaupoort Hospital Camp. A nurse, Sister Catherine Emily, was fortunately on the spot and was sent immediately. The following letter of thanks arrived in August:
>
> *"Hospital Camp, Naaupoort,*
> *August 17, 1900*
> *Dear Sister Cecile,*
> *It is being the greatest possible boon to have Sister here; she is looking after the sick splendidly and making friends in all the houses she goes to ... I am looking out for a chance of making her more comfortable ... The Hospital keeps very full, varying between 700 and 800 patients, nearly 300 of them with enteric.*
> *With much gratitude for sending us Sister Catherine Emily,*
>
> *Believe me,*
> *Yours sincerely, W.A. Hewitt* [Hewett] [4]

As we shall see, below, it was only in 1902 that the Railway Mission first employed its own nurse. However, here in 1900 it is clear that the care of the sick was a concern of the missioners - not unsurprising, given the history of nursing and the involvement of the Christian Church.

A comprehensive history of medicine and of nursing in South Africa is beyond the scope of this work. Suffice to mention that, beyond the 'normal' needs of a population and particularly of those living a 'frontier' and pioneering existence, there were the special health and living problems associated with diamond and gold digging, not least the poor diet and poor sanitation causing 'camp fever'. Other health problems came with the later railway construction and working.

By 1896 there were forty two hospitals in Cape Colony (2000+ beds), six in the Orange Free State (166 beds), eleven in the South African Republic (Transvaal) (431+ beds) and sixteen in Natal (390+ beds), along with hospitals at Leribe, Mohale's Hoek, Mafeteng and Maseru in Basutoland, and at Bulawayo, Gwelo, Salisbury, Umtali and Victoria in Rhodesia.[5]

The Railway Mission felt it important that they had their 'own' nurses, rather than relying on occasional ministrations by clergy or on the (welcome) help of the Grahamstown Sisters:

> Trained nurses were the primary and imperative need, not only for ... wives and mothers ... stranded [in isolated gangers' cottages] in their hour of need, but also for their sick children and the never-ending accidents to their men-folk.[6]

Careful readers of the GDRM 'Monthly Letter' of February 1902 would have noticed that Douglas Ellison mentioned 'a trained Nurse' in his list of thirteen staff. They might well have assumed that this refered to Sister Catherine and we cannot be sure that it did not. However, the first *Quarterly* Magazine of the Grahamstown Diocesan Railway Mission (April 1st, 1902), in its cover Headings of staff ('Chaplain', 'Assistant Chaplain', etc), gave as *Nurse:* Nurse Joyce Eardley. By April 1903 the post was marked as 'Vacant'. Ellison's sister noted that the conditions which then prevailed were daunting for most nurses:

> ... but to Nurse Eardley, who joined the Mission in 1902, belongs the honour of making the venture; and thereafter, till hospitals and other nursing schemes came along, she and her successors, several of them voluntary workers, continued their labours of love.[7]

The change and expansion of the Grahamstown mission work into the South African Church Railway Mission, in 1902, coincided with the ending of the South African War and the amalgamation and return to civil use of the railways in the Transvaal and the Orange Free State. Sir Percy Girouard remained as the Commissioner of Railways, which had now become the 'Central South African Railways' (CSAR). Ellison was delighted to report in the first SACRM *Quarterly*:

> The authorities of our South African Central Railways [sic] have already sanctioned the appointment of three trained Nurses, for the

service of our isolated people along the line. They will have no direct connection with the Mission; but we shall be at work over the same ground, and ought to see a good deal of them. The experiment will be no easy one ... but if crowned with success, it should soon spread far beyond its present restricted area: indeed I already have more than one promise to that effect.[8]

It seems clear that Ellison wanted nurses to be supplied, at no cost to the Railway Mission, basically to be working in the same areas as the missioners and among the railway men and families that the Mission considered 'theirs'. It was not a carefully worked out scheme. Six months later Ellison had to report, 'the railway authorities are apparently in rather a tight corner ... They are obliged just now to cut down expenses all round (I am afraid the Nursing Scheme is hung up, amongst others) ...'

The CSAR's 'tight corner' was almost entirley due to their 'white labour' policies. Not only had the government and the mining industry called on the CSAR to hire more white (and Indian) labour, so releasing Africans for mine work and for the vast reconstruction work in the aftermath of the War, but also the 'Railways were obliged by government to absorb some 3000 whites impoverished by war ... even though white labour cost between two and three times as much as black labour, that is, between £1500 and £2000 extra per mile of railway constructed ...'[9]

However, in the same issue as the announcement that the Nursing Scheme was 'hung up', a small paragraph at the back gave details of a 'Home Meeting' in Old Headington, Oxford:

An announcement of much more than local interest was made during the lecture, and that was that Miss Fuller was going out to South Africa, and had offered her services to the Mission as a qualified Nurse.[10]

Meetings of the SACRM London Committee confirmed that Miss Fuller would have her Second Class passage paid and would go out under the 'usual conditions' of service (ie, staying for two years [later, three]), and that her request for £5 'to lay in a store of medical appliances'[11] was granted. She had sailed by October, knowing that her work would be 'watched with the keenest interest by all .. who realise[d] ... the isolation of railway women.'

Nurse Fuller's arrival in South Africa gave new impetus to the nascent 'Nursing Scheme', although her first task was to work at the Cookhouse Railway Camp, dealing with injuries after a train crash almost as soon as she arrived.[12]

Nurse Fuller gave an account of her work, in August 1905 and, incidentally, left her readers in no doubt as to her views about (black) Africans:

> I am at present making Cookhouse my headquarters, as it is important to be at a place where one can make use of what trains there are to be had ... I came with an introduction to the railway doctors stationed there ... As in England with district nursing in a new district, it takes some time to get the confidence of the people, and for them to realize that even an English woman fresh out from home can fall into their ways, and have patience with stupid Kafir servants.[13]

Nurse Fuller explained that most of her work was maternity nursing, having to travel 'by any means available when called out in a hurry' and often by goods train, in the guard's van, if no passenger train was available. She continued:

> I have been pretty constantly occupied in nursing since the middle of March; and as I get better known I feel sure I shall have my time taken up nearly exclusively in nursing railway folk. At present I also nurse storekeepers' wives and farmers' wives, under the railway doctor, and truly their need for good nursing is quite as great, if not greater. ... Some of the women [on the line to Rosemead] were much interested in the nursing scheme, and I hope ... it may become a real help and comfort ...

The Railway Mission was attempting to respond to obvious medical need both by co-operating with the Railway authorities, supplementing their work where possible, and by initiating its own methods and schemes, with obvious limits of money and man/woman-power. No nursing scheme as such was going to be at all effective, given the mileage of the railway network, while the Railway Mission could only afford one nurse and while the Railways themselves were not willing or able to provide itinerant nurses to work with the Mission. Nurse Fuller continued with SACRM until 1912, leaving 'after seven years of devoted work among the railway people in the Grahamstown Diocese.'[14] However, although in 1905 the London Committee felt it 'not adviseable to send another nurse [to South Africa] for the present', both they and the Head, Douglas Ellison, had accepted that a new approach was vital and turned to the Colonial Nursing Association, with whom Ellison had been corresponding since 1903.

Douglas Ellison was in England from June 1902 until May 1903, mainly for the purpose of 'recouping his health', but also to appeal for 'clergymen, laymen and laywomen'[15] and for funds, all especially needed as the Mission was poised for the move northwards. It was only at the very end of his stay that he started his approach to the Colonial Nursing Association (CNA).

On April 14th 1903, Ellison had a talk with Miss Rosalind Paget, a member both of the Executive and the Nursing Committees of the CNA, 'with regard to providing Nurses for [the] S. African Railways.'[16] The following day he wrote to Miss Dalrymple Hay, the Secretary, requesting a meeting with either Mrs Piggott (the founder) or Mrs Antrobus (member of the Executive, Nursing and Finance Committees). Miss Paget wrote a hasty letter to the Secretary to appraise her of the situation. It warrants an extensive quotation:

> I have suggested that the Rev. W [sic] Ellison who has charge of a railway mission in the Transvaal [strictly this Transvaal sphere of work was only from mid-1902. He was, of course, the Head of all the work done by the Mission] and who came to see me on the subject of nurses and midwives should interview you and, if possible, Mrs Piggott & Mrs Antrobus. He has two schemes in his head. One is to induce the Colonial Office to supply nurses, as well as doctors to the railways; the other is to begin in a small way himself with one or two midwives. Either scheme could I think be far the best dealt with by the C.N.A than any other organisation, and so I told him ... I do not think he has at all matured his ideas but if he is going out there ... it is very important that we should feel we understand each other's ways of looking at things. One thing was satisfactory. He is fully aware of the way in which women exposed to those undesirable [word illegible, but altered to 'influences'] that we know of go to pieces.[17]

The maturing of ideas was rather dependent on what was practical and possible in southern Africa, which was why Ellison was turning to the Association. The 'undesirable influences' were not specified. However, in an 'Open Letter to Nurses and their friends' in 1909, the Association did mention 'personal points connected with life outside England, when home ties and influences [were] often for the first time completely severed.'[18] The nurses were reminded to bear in mind their 'religious duties and responsibilities' (though the Association was not a Church-based one); to have 'moderation' in the matter of 'amusement and recreation'; and to be careful in the choice of friends. Then came the 'difficult point':

> ... at home nurses are warned and know well how necessary it is to avoid indulgence in stimulants or drugs. If this warning is necessary in England, it is .. trebly so in a tropical climate, where circumstances tend to increase the desire for anything that will give temporary strength or relief, and from desire to craving is sometimes a short distance ...

Miss Dalrymple Hay received a letter, dated 8 May 1903, from an Oliver Williams, asking for information about Ellison, on behalf of Lord Grey (under-Secetary of State for Foreign Affairs [Foreign Secretary in 1905]). Lord Grey wished to know how far Ellison was 'a practical man, etc.,etc.'[19] If the answers were satisfactory, Lord Grey would be pleased to receive any communications that were sent by the Secretary of the CNA to Williams and to forward them 'to the Rhodesia Railways, Limited':

> As you are aware, in Rhodesia the Railways are built with black labour, and the Railway Contractors, I think, make adequate arrangements for looking after the Hospital requirements of their sick, both black and white.

The CNA Secretary informed Ellison of Oliver Williams' letter, and its contents, and received a reply dated 12th May. Ellison told Miss Dalrymple Hay that he was going to send some Mission papers and leaflets to Lord Grey, and that he hoped that two missioners would be starting work in Rhodesia by October. For the nursing, he felt that 'Mr Williams' was correct [a misunderstanding - the comments were those of Lord Grey]:

> I expect one will find that Rhodesia has less need of such a scheme than other parts of the country [ie. South Africa] - if only because of the greater sparesness of its population, & because / I would like to think / the Chartered Co have had an eye to such matters throughout ... I have drafted a short statement about the Nurses for the Colonial office, & shall hope to send it in tomorrow.[20]

The BSA Company were, of course, responsible for any 'adequate arrangements' in Rhodesia (as the Company's territories were known from 1895). The European advance into the country was not something that the British Government would deal with, though the High Commissioner at the Cape would have preferred more direct control from the Colonial Office.

Ellison's faith in the British South Africa Company was to be short-lived. The Company, which had invested heavily in railway expansion, hoped to see a return for this in its gold mining in Mashonaland. Hopes of a second Rand were not realised. It also became deeply embroiled in the whole question of land ownership. The settler population was never happy with the BSA Company's spending on social services, such as schools, hospitals and nursing - services which, by their very nature, did not show profit but were necessary for civilised living.

The letter to the Colonial Office, referred to by Douglas Ellison, although dated May 9th 1903, was sent a day or so after his l0th/l2th May letter to the CNA. It is a crucial document in this area of SACRM's history, in that it shows the Head's views on nursing development; the existing arrangements with the railway authorities; and the social and work conditions of railway workers in southern Africa. As with Miss Paget's letter (above), it must be quoted virtually *in extenso*:

> To the Under Secretary of State For the Colonies.
> Sir,
> I desire to bring to your notice the need and the opportunity which I believe to exist for some well-considered Nursing Scheme along the Railways of South Africa ... as one who has spent .... eleven years in close and constant touch with the life of the Railway-side population.
>
> The dominant note of that life is its utter loneliness: and it would be hard to exaggerate the isolation of our [sic] scattered cottages, stations, and even camps. At the same time it is true that, relatively to the rest of the country, there is a fairly thick fringe of people along the entire Railway system, consisting not merely of Railway employees, but of farms, stores, hotels, police-camps, and the like.
>
> In the Cape Colony, and I believe further North, the medical needs of all Railway servants are ministered to by a succession of Medical officers - roughly one to each 100 miles or so of the Line - who travel through their section in a private coach once a week, and are further available, so far as distance and circumstances permit, in any case of special urgency. Of trained nurses, except possibly in the immediate neighbourhood of the larger towns, there are none. The women, in their confinements, are usually dependent upon the kindly but unskilled offices of a neighbour, or even of a native woman; accidents and other acute cases often involve a cruel journey to some distant hospital; and the medical men on the spot would bear me out in saying that valuable lives are lost and much suffering entailed for the want of a few such Nurses as I am venturing to plead for now.
>
> Some few years since, I was allowed by the then General Manager of C.G. Railways to draw up a scheme, which aimed at placing one

> Nurse under each Railway Medical Officer. It was submitted to the Medical Board ... but was shelved ... on the score of expense. Three nurses were, however, appointed - 2 at De Aar, and 1 at Naaupoort ; but they were Nurses of the old order, without proper qualifications; and the venture therefore never had a chance. A little later, in despair of adequate action on the part of the authorities, I myself brought out a fully trained and certificated monthly Nurse; and though her work was a good deal hampered by the [South African] War, the experiment was of a kind that one would like to see widely extended.
>
> A special reason why this Nursing problem may well receive careful attention ... is .. the fact that the new Railway construction works in S. Africa ... will presumably extend over a thousand miles or so; and the crop of accidents is bound to be a heavy one. Is it .. asking the impossible that, in the Transvaal and Orange River Colonies, there shall be established at some early date groups of trained Nurses - let us say a minimum of six for each Colony - under a duly qualified and responsible head; whose ministry shall be confined to the Lines of Railway, and perhaps to certain small temporary Hospitals for Construction workers.
>
> Such a scheme ... guaranteed at the outset by the Railway authorities, might, I believe, soon prove to be very largely self-supporting. The men would themselves make regular payments, and would give generously on the special occasions when a Nurse's services are required. If the scheme were also extended to include the new Construction works, my own experience goes to prove how open-handed a Railway contractor usually is in his giving.
>
> But ... I do feel strongly that ... the men have some claim upon the Department for help and sympathy. Where it becomes necessary, as in S. Africa, to pitch-fork a large class of Government servants, both white and coloured, away into the Veldt, with the smallest possible chance of organising themselves for purposes of this kind, it is surely not unreasonable that they should receive assistance in so fundamental a need as that of proper Nursing?
>
> May I ... add my deep conviction of the importance of making and keeping the Railway-side community thoroughly well-affected at the present time? In a true sense the Railways are the very arteries of the life of that new Country... I would respectfully submit that the carrying out of some such Nursing scheme as I have here advocated might perform its own special part in promoting the well-being and contentment of S. Africa ....[21]

Ellison certainly left the Colonial Office in no doubt as to his feelings about the nursing situation in South Africa. It is clear that his concern was not only for the ('white and coloured') railway workers themselves, but also for their families, particularly their wives. Much of this concern would have been expressed to him by the SACRM women workers. The black African staff obviously were not on Ellison's agenda ; the phrase 'even ... a native woman' betraying a racial attitude not very compatible with the Railway Mission's declared ministry to all races. The Mission Head's frustration at the lack of medical action taken by the Railway authorities is apparent. Apart from the obligatory, occasional and fleeting visit of the Railway Doctor travelling along a line, the authorities were more than happy to leave other medical care to groups such as the Railway Mission. Many gangers and other railwaymen had started to contribute to the Railway Mission's 'Sustentation Fund', giving small amounts of money to help pay for the work of the Mission. In 1909, for example, £336 was given by the men in nine centres or areas (separate from the £211 donations and £311 collections in South Africa). It was not unreasonable of Ellison to assume that many would contribute something towards nursing, although he was somewhat optimistic regarding railway contractors, who were not in fact generous with their money. The contractors did, of necessity, have to have doctors available.[22]

Exactly one year before this letter was written, the South African War had come to an end and Britain, at a cost of 22,000 lives, had taken the two Boer republics. It was little wonder that Ellison saw the need to keep railway workers 'well-affected'. Even as he wrote, the South African Chamber of Mines had just resolved to recruit Chinese labour, in an attempt to keep low labour costs and maintain a high ratio of unskilled to skilled labour. White workers, Afrikaner and English, were extremely angry and disatisfied with the post-War policies, the Afrikaners particularly so with the 'Anglicisation' policy of Milner, the British High Commissioner in South Africa. Railwaymen were caught up in the whole turmoil of the period. Any scheme that could help to keep them better disposed towards the authorities, railway or political, was likely to be viewed favourably.

Three weeks after Ellison sent his letter to the Colonial Office, he was able to report to Miss Dalrymple Hay at the CNA that he had received a reply from 'Mr. Secretary Chamberlain', and that his letters had been forwarded to the High Commissioner for South Africa, Alfred Milner, 'for his consideration and report.' Other correspondence indicates that Mrs Chamberlain also wrote to South Africa supporting the CNA's link with the Railway Mission. On returning to South Africa, Ellison was obliged to report, eventually, that 'the nursing scheme... [was] hung up... on account of the general depression and retrenchment.'[23] By June 1905 Miss Astley, SACRM's (hon) secretary, was writing to the CNA regarding the possibility of a grant for a (Railway Mission) nurse. She was informed that the Association did not give grants to nurses other than those selected by the CNA, but that their Committee would be happy to 'make a substantial contribution towards ... [the] passage money out & home and .. salary for two years' of a nurse so selected. A subsequent letter quoted the passage cost as £23. 12/6d [£23.62], with a salary of about £50 a year, minimum.[24] Although negotiations with the Colonial Nursing Association had been proceeding since April 1903, it was only at the Quarterly Meeting of the SACRM London Committee in July 1905 that the CNA was formally minuted, although it may have been unofficially discussed prior to that meeting. The Committee was delighted with CNA's offfer, which included a list of suitable nurses. Nurse Pearn was accepted to work for SACRM in April 1906, being funded for three years by the Colonial Nursing Association.

This first CNA nurse working with the Railway Mission sailed for South Africa in May 1906. Douglas Ellison's letter from Grahamstown to Miss Dalrymple Hay, dated August 20, 1906, brings to an end his 'wooing' of the Association and is, incidentally, the final extant letter in the CNA-SACRM correspondence file. He reports the safe arrival of Nurse Pearn and states, 'It is a real encouragement to know that you are working with us in this matter.'[25] Her base is given as Cradock, and Ellison was intending to visit 'this little nurse' on his way from the Transvaal, three weeks later.

Nurse Pearn's appointment came just in time for Sarah Tooley, in her *The History of Nursing in the British Empire* (London, 1906) to write, 'Recently a nurse has been selected for work with the South African Church Railway Mission, which is doing such useful work in ministering to the large British and Dutch population scattered along the South African railways.' Ten years invaluable cooperation between the two organisations had begun.

We have observed earlier how the heading 'Nurse' first appeared on the GDRM magazine cover in April, 1902. Issue No.18 of the SACRM *Quarterly* (Jan. 1908) was the first to distinguish between 'Lady Workers' (five were listed) and 'Nurses' [Nurse Fuller (Cookhouse); Pearn (Cradock); Ross (Rosmead)]. Twelve clergy, one (European) Evangelist and three ('Native') Evangelists were also listed.

In 1908 H.B. Ellison took over as Head of SACRM from his brother, Douglas. In that year Douglas Ellison read his Paper at the Pan-Anglican Congress, entitled 'The Pioneer Work of the Church: A Plea for the gripping of the railways.' In the Paper he commented:

> Several experienced lady workers are caring for the interests of the women and girls; while three fully trained nurses, soon, I hope, to be

> augmented, are busily bringing their own peculiar blessing, more especially to the womenkind, in many of our lonelier railway homes.

The 'Blue Quarterlies' of 1909 made several references to the Colonial Nursing Association - 'the perfect fairy god-mother' in that sphere of the Mission's work. SACRM's Annual Report of 1909, a very full account of all the Mission's activities and hopes for further expansion, gave a paragraph to nursing in the general section of the Report:

> The Nursing Work ... has extended, and we now have a second nurse in the Transvaal. As every one knows, this has been made possible almost entirely by the generosity of the Colonial Nursing Association, a generosity made all the more helpful by the quietness and business-like method of its working. One seems only to need to press the button by a letter to their Committee ... and another new nurse appears like clockwork! It seems likely that another gentle pressure of the button may soon be necessary, as I have had lately a request for a nurse from Crocodile Pools ...- the name suggesting a possibly busy time for a nurse.[26]

A more detailed comment on 'The Nursing Work' appeared later in the Report. After noting the 'comings and goings' of the nursing staff, it stated, 'the services of the Nurses are getting appreciated the more they become known.' The Reports were always careful to include appreciation of the Railway authorities (usually deserved, with any criticism rarely aired publicly). This Report added: 'The action of the C.S.A.R. authorities in extending the passes of the two Transvaal Nurses so as to cover the whole of the Transvaal and Orange River Colony was much appreciated, and needs special mention.'[27]

It was well understood that SACRM staff were given free passes by the Railway authorities to travel up and down the lines. This Report makes clear that the new-style (CNA-sponsored) Nurses were naturally afforded the same privileges.

The following List, appended to the comments on 'The Nursing Work' speaks for itself. Suffice to comment that the difference that the CNA Nurses made, with their arrival in 1906/7, is clearly tabulated, and that the nurses had between a quarter and a half of their work taken up with 'private', ie. non-railway, cases. A similar situation always obtained with the rest of SACRM staff, ministering to the store-keepers, police, officials and farmers who lived by or near the railway lines:

Cases Nursed by the Mission Nurses.[28]

1905.	Railway,	3	Private,	11	Total	14
1906.	„	16	„	7	„	23
1907.	„	23	„	10	„	33
1908.	„	13	„	11	„	24
1909.	„	32	„	12	„	44

[1910 was to list Railway 53 Private 10 Total 63]

The pages of the SACRM magazines are filled with stories from the clergy and lay missioners, as well as from the Lady Workers. Although the Nurses are frequently mentioned, and occasionally have the odd paragraph of their own, they rarely gave, or perhaps were rarely granted, full accounts of their work. The almost sole exception is the three and a half page account, 'A Nurse in Cape Colony', written by Nurse Marlande (Rosmead Junction) in July 1910. Although much of the account is similar to the picture of railway and veldt life painted by her non-nursing colleagues, Nurse Marlande does see the work and the life with different eyes and emphases. She also makes observations about railway-life that other SACRM workers took for granted and her account is therefore an invaluable document for researchers and social historians today:

> To begin at the beginning, I have been sent for to go and nurse at a certain station-master's house on a certain day. So after some study of the railway time table "subject to alteration without notice" ... I find out the train I must go by. I may have to travel all night, or my journey may be quite a short one. The 1st class carriages are however very comfortable ... From Port Elizabeth to Rosmead is under 250 miles, and it takes fifteen hours ... Well, in course of time I reach my destination, and am greeted by the station-master: "Well, here you are Nurse, we are expecting you. You go over to the house and I will bring your things over when I have sent off the train." So I walk over to be welcomed by the station-master's wife and perhaps some children, who gaze shyly at "Nurse", and I am offered some refreshment ...
>
> There may be only the station-master's cottage near the station, or there may be a second in which his foreman lives, and who does all the night work, ...And perhaps when the train that brought me has gone, there will be no other train till the next day. At one place where I stayed several weeks there were six trains in the week, three up and three down on alternate days. At each station there is a post office, the station-master performing post-master's duties. Even at the smaller stations there is a good deal of traffic. Away from the

line, behind the kopjes, are many farms, and the farmers bring their stock and produce to the station

Now let me tell you how our days were passed. At 6 a.m. a native girl brought coffee, then I looked after my patient if I had one or else took a walk on the veldt, and I might have to see after the children, and get and cook the breakfast at 8 a.m. After breakfast I finished any work I had to do [and] perhaps washed the baby ... Then perhaps cooked the dinner for 1 p.m., then rest for self and patient till 3.30 afternoon tea ...

It is a very lonely life out there on the lonely stations, but once a year husband, wife and children can get free first-class passes on the railway, so they generally go away every year. Sometimes the station-master possesses a gramaphone [sic]. It is curious to be listening to a solo from Clara Butt, or marches ... far away on the veldt. The station-masters and their families have but few opportunities of attending any religious services ...The members of the Railway Mission Staff are warmly welcomed, and their visits much appreciated by those living at lonely stations ... The question of food may be interesting. Milk, butter, eggs, and perhaps fruit are procured locally. Sometimes a farmer will send in an ostrich egg, when there is a grand making of cakes and omelets; bread is always home-made; meat (generally mutton) sent from the nearest town twice a week: grocery, &c., is obtained once a month from the pay train. If the nurse acts as housekeeper, towards the end of the month she must take care not to be extravagant, or she may find herself left without tea, sugar, matches, &c.

The houses are far away from medical aid, except iust when the trains run. The Railway Medical Officer (R.M.O) comes up the line in his coach at stated times; in cases of life and death, the railway management provide a "special" for the doctor's use. The telephone is a boon, and the doctor thereby keeps in touch with his patients .. [29]

Nurse Marlande concluded her article with a page or so describing 'the natives' who worked at the houses she visited, and wondered what the future held for them.

We may observe from this account, and other evidence, that the Nurses did not normally have the use of a Railway Mission caboose, but travelled, usually 1st class, by passenger or goods train. The time spent at a station, coupled with the taking over of the cooking and housework by the nurse, suggests her presence during 'confinement' (as Ellison suggested, above), or during a time of lengthy and severe illness. The length of her stay - and this was not untypical - is one of the main differences between her work and that of other SACRM staff. Clergy,

Women Workers and lay workers certainly ministered to a far greater number of people than did the nurses, but their visits were often only for a few hours, or even minutes if on the Pay Train, though these visits might well be frequent. The nurses visited less often, saw fewer people, but stayed longer.

Nurse Marlande's reference to the 'Pay train' is a helpful reminder that the one guaranteed visit (of only a few minutes) that the gangers and their families had, was the monthly arrival of the Pay Train on its long journey up the Line with the wages for the railway staff. She mentions 'groceries', but other items such as newspapers, magazines and clothing would often be delivered by the same train. An unatributed article, possibly by the SACRM Head, Maurice Lancaster, appeared in the *Quarterly* in 1949, giving a brief account of the Pay Train:

> The principal means of communication with the outside world for these people [lonely railwaymen and families] is the monthly Pay Train, on which travels the Paymaster, a Medical Officer, a Storekeeper, and frequently the Railway Missioner, all of whom are accommodated in travelling coaches ... The Paymaster pays the European Gangers and Pumpers and their African labourers, the Storekeeper issues the rations for the Africans and the materials required by gangers, pumpers and station masters, the Medical Officer attends to minor ailments and issues medical supplies, while the Railway Missioner does what he can in the time at his or her disposal to minister to the spiritual needs of the Railway staff living along the line, their wives and children, during the short time the train is at the siding, or wayside station.[30]

The SACRM nurses, like the railway doctors, had to deal with emergencies and accidents on the railways. A major accident, known as the 'Gaika Loop Railway Disaster', took place on the Eastern Line in the Cape shortly after Christmas, 1910. Nurse Roberts happened to be on a train that was prevented, by detonators on the line, from running into a wrecked train. She was able to assist the injured and comfort the dying, all in difficult circumstances in early morning darkness. Fifty or so were injured and twenty two were killed. The nurse reported that she was 'very pleased to have been able to render the little help that [she] did.'[31]

The provision of staff, especially of women workers and (particularly) of nurses, was a taxing problem from 1911/12 until the end of the First World War.[32] The first hint that all might not be well regarding nursing, came in September 1912. Fred Rogers, the Head, in his quarterly letter, after mentioning that three members of staff were leaving, went on to warn of other departures:

> Mr. Thurlow and Nurse Marlande finish their three years with the Mission at the end of September, and ... Nurse Borradaile has left us quite suddenly. ... Now this is a very serious list of losses and I quite realise that some of our home supporters may feel that if workers are going to leave us at this rate it argues something very rotten in the state of the Mission. But I would point out ... that it was quite impossible for us to go on as we have been, incurring fresh debts every year, and that a reduction of the staff was essential ... [33]

In order to keep nurses on SACRM staff it was vital that the CNA continued its financial support. The first blow came in 1913. The Head reported:

> Miss Brownlow has been kept busy and there is no doubt that a fairly large number of people would very much miss our nurses if we had to give them up. The Colonial Nursing Association has, however, withdrawn its grant, and I am very doubtful whether we shall be justified in keeping up this part of the work much longer.[34]

Ellison does not indicate why the CNA began to withdraw its support from SACRM (it continued for a short while, until its last nurse had finished her contract). Two of the Association's publications give a clear hint regarding inadequacy of funds. The first comes in *The Story of the Colonial Nursing Association,* written in 1909/10:

> ... [an] interesting and rather out-of-the-way extension has been in connection with the supply of nurses for work among the employees on the Cape to Cairo Railway [sic] under the local management of the South African [Church] Railway Mission. Those already sent out have won their way and done excellently well, and the Association has already expended on this branch of its work £231 14s .6d. [£231.72] The question ... now arises how large a sum it would be justifiable for our Executive Committee to grant to any one place without a special appeal for funds ... These nurses ... are partly self-supporting but not entirely so, and the passages are a great expense ...[35]

Mrs. Robinson, the author of the article, seems to have been giving a warning shot across the bows. In a short history of the Association, written in 1917 by the Founder, Mabel Piggott, there is stated:

> the CNA undertakes to select and forward nurses to any place requiring them, on the understanding that a representative local

committee does its utmost to raise sufficient funds for the maintenance (ie. board and lodging and salary) of the nurses so sent out. The Association ... guarantees any yearly deficit which the locality may be unable at first to meet.

I would suggest that one reason that the CNA withdrew from supporting the Railway Mission was due to the 'at first' condition being well and truly passed, after a number of years. SACRM, at that time, was in a permanent 'yearly deficit'. Also, the Association was having an increasing number of calls made upon it and perhaps the Committee did not feel that it was any longer justifiable to grant funds to one particular place/ organisation, as stated in the earlier of the two articles just quoted. It may be that there were tensions between the two organisations that were not stated, such as that the Railway Mission were normally dealing with the 'type' of people that the very upper/middle-class CNA Committee members might not want to deal with. There were differences in the sense of isolation; for the CNA this was, to a certain extent, isolation from England, whereas for Ellison and the Railway Mission the spheres of work meant isolation from Grahamstown and Cape Town.

However, the chief reason for the 'parting of the ways' was, I believe, the 1910 Act of Union. On 31 May, 1910, eight years to the day after the Peace of Vereeniging, when the Boer generals had signed the surrender of their republics to the British Empire, the four colonies (Cape, Natal, Orange River, and Transvaal) became the constituent provinces of the Union of South Africa. Louis Botha formed a government and became the first Prime Minister of a united South Africa. The 1910 Act meant that South Africa was no longer a mere Colony, but rather a self-governing British Dominion. It was generally assumed, certainly by white South African and British politicians, that eventually other southern and even central African territories would be absorbed into the Union. 1910 was the first step on the road both to the 1948 elections and the advent of the first exclusively Afrikaner Government, and to the 1961 break with the British Commonwealth.

The CNA, after 1910, would no longer have seen nursing in South Africa as their responsibility. This, of course, left the Railway Mission with a huge bill if they were to keep nursing staff. The start of the First World War changed the whole situation in any case. Nurses were needed for more immediately important work than ministering to ill or pregnant railway folk. At the beginning of 1915 the Mission Head reported:

The Railway-side people of the Grahamstown Diocese have shewn their appreciation of the work of the Mission Nurses - Miss Fuller, Miss Marlande, and Miss Brownlow (now Mrs Griggs) - by their

> generous support of a Sale of Work which was got up practically as the last Nurse was withdrawn and took place after the outbreak of the War.'[36]

Later that year the people of Grahamstown Diocese were, apparently, still clamouring for a Nurse, preferably the one they had lost! Eventually a new nurse, Nurse Deeks, was secured for work in Grahamstown and George, although there is no indication whether or not this Nurse came via the CNA. The 1918 SACRM Annual Report continued to show income and expenditure for Nursing. By 1919 this ceased to be mentioned.

Although there is occasional mention of nursing, mainly by women workers, in the years between the First and Second World Wars, the days of the official Railway Mission Nurses, funded by the Colonial Nursing Association, were clearly over. There had been a successful 'wooing' of the Association in the early days; the 'marriage' had been an important and useful one, certainly appreciated by those who were helped by this unique co-operative venture; the 'divorce' came after ten or so years and the two organisations went their separate ways.

SACRM 'Native Hospital', Naauwpoort

The Railway Mission nurses, both before and during the involvement of the Colonial Nursing Association, dealt primarily with white and coloured railway workers and their families. In the same way that most missioners 'passed by' the great numbers of black Africans, the SACRM nursing staff did likewise. Given the terms of their employment, as well as their scarcity, this is not surprising. With one exception, noted shortly, the Railway Mission did not involve itself in running hospitals and the like for Africans; a 'medical mission' was never its remit.

The exception was the Railway Mission Native Hospital, at Naauwpoort. However, even here, there was a difference from the 'normal' mission hospital.

> The opening of a mission hospital or dispensary was an occasion for elaborate ritual, expressing many fundamentals of the medical missionary endeavour in colonial Africa.[37]

So writes Vaughan, in her book on Colonial power and African illness. She is right to state that mission medicine could not simply be subsumed under the 'western-medicine' heading (itself a catch-all term), and also right to warn that the 'division between "missionary" and "secular" medicine in colonial Africa was never clear-cut.' However, the thrust of her chapter on 'The Great Dispensary in the Sky' is the role of mission hospitals having long-term care for patients, and thus 'opening up greater possibilities for evangelization.'[38] She quotes the triumph of mission medicine in East and Central Africa with its treatment for ulcers - a lengthy hospitalization, allowing an intensive period of Christian instruction. ('Ulcers have one great recommendation from the Mission point of view - they take a long time to cure.'!)

It is surely debateable whether for medical missionaries, as Vaughan states, 'the healing of the body had always to take second place to the winning of the soul and the fight against the "evils" of African society.'[39] I do not believe that all mission doctors and nurses prioritised their beliefs and practices in this way. Most of the time they simply got on with the (healing) job in hand. In South Africa also, there was less difference between the ideas and practices of medical missionaries and the state medical practices which followed them, than there was in East Africa.

It is, I believe, important therefore that SACRM's one venture into African medical missionary work should not be viewed as an evangelical venture to convert 'the African', but rather as a genuine response in active pioneering welfare work, done in the name of the Church. This, of course, was not dissimilar to all the other areas of Railway Missionary activities.

Before De Aar became the 'Clapham Junction of South Africa', Naauwpoort was the principal railway junction, the point where the Port Elizabeth - Bloemfontein line met the line going west to De Aar to join the Cape Town - Kimberley and the North trunk line. As well as a railway junction, Naauwpoort had grown from a 'mere handful of cottages' in 1892 to a very large railway camp and, eventually, railway town. It was one place where the Railway Mission was, from the beginning, involved with ministering to the many African workers and their families, and the first SACRM African evangelist, Josiah Ngcambu, was employed there.

At the end of 1937 the Head of SACRM, Father Eustace Hill, C.R., reported that the South African Railways had offered the Mission a great opportunity:

> An outbreak of enteric, resulting in the death of three Europeans, led the authorities to open a hospital for the natives employed there by the S.A.R., and the hospital was handed over to the Mission to run, with the result that the epidemic was quickly dealt with and stopped. The S.A.R. have offered to leave this splendid bit of work in the hands of the Mission and are paying the native nurses at present in charge ...[40]

The writer urged his readers to 'find a European nurse with real missionary-hearted zeal' for the work. It is unclear whether it was the fact that Europeans died in the epidemic that made the authorities open a hospital, or whether this was the writer's way of expressing the seriousness of the situation. He obviously could not envisage an African nurse / Sister being in charge.

The 'Blue Quarterly' of Spring 1938 reported that 'A hospital ... opened in Naauwpoort last December for natives and coloured.' (A September opening was more likely, given that the previous Magazine had been written in September and published in October.) The SACRM missioner at Naauwpoort, Rev. Harold Insley, stated that the Mission had persuaded the Railway Administration 'to build a small hospital in the native location ... for the use of natives and coloureds.' This explanation for the building of the hospital, with the initiative apparently coming from the Railway Mission, is slightly at odds with details given earlier. Insley, after describing the hospital, with its two small wards plus various rooms and disinfecting station, continued:

> The hospital is a railway institution; that is, it is primarily for railway employees, though natives or coloured people who are not employed on the railway may also be admitted provided there is room. The Mission has undertaken to help with the hospital for the first twelve months, at the end of which period the whole situation will be reviewed ...
>
> In the past no accomodation existed in Naauwpoort for natives or coloured, and if one of these people was hurt or was sick they had to be sent to Middleburg, which required a train journey and where the accomodation was very limited and often meant sending cases to Port Elizabeth, a distance of 270 miles ...
>
> [It] also means that a qualified nurse is always present in the location ... Another offspring ... is the Children's Clinic, which has also been opened in connection with the hospital ...[41]

A qualified African nurse, Mrs. Violet Mama, was put in charge of the hospital and no more was heard about a 'missionary-hearted' European nurse. The hospital became officially known, in correspondence if not in speech, as 'The South African Church Railway Mission Hospital, Naauwpoort'. Nurse Mama gave a full report on the hospital in April 1939. She wrote of how ignorance and fear of hospitals had vanished among many of the 'non-European population' [she was the only SACRM correspondent at the time not to use the term 'native'], and that they had come to accept the hospital as a place where they could go for advice and services. She was pleased to announce that the death rate among babies had been greatly reduced. Her report and the commendation given to the hospital and Nurse Mama by Naauwpoort's (European) Doctor [42], show

how the small hospital had succeeded in preventing the spread of infectious diseases, had treated many patients and undertaken minor surgical work - all this alongside the running of the non-European Child Welfare Clinic. No mention was made in these or subsequent reports of any evangelising work taking place within the hospital. The 'winning of the African soul' was not mentioned; Nurse Mama's pleasure in the banishment of superstition being the nearest this 'medical-mission' came to any ideas about 'salvation'.

Theodore Franklin, the missioner in Nauwpoort in 1941, wrote that, although the 'Native Hospital' was still doing valuable work, SACRM felt that they had done their work of establishing and getting the hospital going, and should let others carry on:

> This Mission is essentially one which does pioneering work: ... we must step aside ... as our job is done. ... I hope when I next write to you I shall be able to give you some definite news as to what has finally been decided as to who will take charge of the hospital.[43]

The hospital had been under the Railway Mission's care for four years. However, it was over two years later (February, 1944) before a Meeting of the Home Committee, in London, minuted:

> Naauwpoort Hospital: The Head reported that the Municipality [of Naauwpoort] was taking over the Hospital and that our responsibility would then cease. [44]

The Railway Mission had been responsible for the 'Native Hospital' for just over six years. By the Summer of 1944 readers of the SACRM magazine were informed, 'Our work at Naauwpoort we have passed over to the Diocese because it has grown too big and responsible for the Mission to oversee properly: the [Railway] Mission cannot undertake the oversight of large Missions [to Africans], we have to be away travelling too much.' And so the Railway Mission ceased to be responsible at Naauwpoort not only for the 'Native Hospital' but for all its work - over forty years - among Africans who lived in that Railway camp/town.

We shall note shortly how SACRM's women workers, who were not usually trained in medicine, frequently had to deal with sickness or injury. In this account of 'Nursing' ('a specific and separate sphere of work') it seems appropriate to conclude with a note about the two Railway Mission's workers, briefly mentioned in Chapter 3, who died nursing Africans during the Spanish influenza pandemic of 1918.

Agnes Burt had been Principal of the Diocesan School for Girls at Grahamstown and was very involved with other educational work in the

Diocese. When she retired she became the SACRM Children's Secretary in South Africa and edited the Mission's 'Light for the Line' for many years. The First World War brought a reduction of staff to the Railway Mission, and Miss Burt offered her services as a travelling missioner, a work she did for two years. During the flu epidemic she cared for African patients in one of the temporary hospitals used in Grahamstown. This work resulted in her contracting the disease, from which she died. The Head of the Mission buried her on October 30th. Two days later, far to the north in Bulawayo, Ralphe Seacombe also died from the same disease.

The Rev. Ralphe Seacombe had arrived at Cape Town on February 15th 1916. He immediately entrained for Bulawayo. As a SACRM missioner he was first responsible for the portion of the line from Francistown to Victoria Falls, including Plumtree School. He would also visit the Fred Mine and Filabusi and the West Nicholson line. Later arrangements gave him the line from Bulawayo to Victoria Falls, the West Nicholson line and Raylton railway township. During the epidemic he did everything he could to help 'his' African and white railway workers. Mr. Bain, organist of St. John's Church, Bulawayo, gave a detailed account of Seacombe's death:

> The last I saw of Ralph, before he went into hospital, was on Monday, 21st. of October, and I noticed then how tired and worn he looked. It appears he had been down to the Railway Natives' location on the Sunday, taken Services there, attended to them, and generally acted as head of the relieving force who were there endeavouring to improve the terribly sad conditions. Incidentally ... he had only got to bed after midnight for several days.
>
> During that week Ralph volunteered to go out along one of the local branch lines with medicines to do what he could for the poor white ['poor-white'?] people outside, also for the large number of natives who were in an indescribable state. He was the first man to undertake this work of mercy, but I fear that his strength - already overtaxed by travelling in the frightful heat - was not equal to this further arduous call. He had to go into hospital at ... Gwanda, but insisted upon getting up after being only two days abed, and managed to get as far as Balla Balla on his way home when he collapsed ... He gave his life for others just as though he had died on the battlefields of Flanders ...[45]

The Railway Administration, in appreciation of Seacombe's life and work, paid all the funeral expenses.

Women's Work

The first official mention of Women Workers was on the cover of the SACRM *Quarterly* for October 1904, when Miss Nott-Bower and Miss Fuller were designated as 'Lady Workers'. Rather confusingly, Miss Fuller had not, at that time, set sail for Africa, but was to work as a Nurse. However, Miss Nott-Bower, although formerly a Matron of Guy's Hospital (and an experienced Parish worker), was not engaged in nursing work for the Railway Mission, but was 'measuring up the problem of supplying the spiritual and moral need of [the] women and girls.'[46]

Douglas Ellison wrote to the Bishop of Grahamstown in 1904/05 to report on the work of the Railway Mission in that particular diocese. There was some concern about the effect on the diocese of the mission's expansion towards the North. Ellison noted:

> An important feature of the last three years has been the development of work among women. We now have two lady workers ... [one] is directly concerned with the spiritual interests of women and girls, and is laying the foundations of a work full of promise, on the lines of the Mother's Union and Girls' Friendly Society.[47]

Miss Nott-Bower was instrumental in forming the first Branch of the Mothers' Union on the Railways in southern Africa, on September 17th 1904, in Naauwpoort, shortly after her arrival. In *Light for the Line,* circulated on the Railways in South Africa, she wrote:

> I am inclined to think that on the Railway, with its peculiar difficulties of isolation and uncertainty, the thing that will help us most is a strengthening of the bonds of Christian fellowship, of love, sympathy, and prayer, and this is just what the Mothers' Union seeks to foster. It seems to me that in many ways the Society meets our needs out here even better than in England.[48]

The same issue contained a letter from Mary Sumner, founder of the Mothers' Union, to 'All Wives and Mothers connected with the Railway Mission' - a standard letter, however, that made no reference whatsoever to the particular circumstances of her readers.

Miss Nott-Bower, in an article headed 'Work among Women', wrote of her visits along 250 miles of line from Alicedale to Naauwpoort. Like her male colleagues she had occasionally to travel by engineer's trolley (a fairly rare occurence for most women workers) in order to visit some of the gangers' cottages. After describing having meetings of the Guild of the Good Shepherd, Mothers' Union, G.F.S, and Sunday Schools (mentioned in the previous Chapter) in the various Railway Camps, she went on:

> One day we [herself plus a G.F.S. friend] arrived at a lonely siding where the nearest house was a Boer farm half-a-mile across the veldt, and the nearest cottage nearly two miles up the line. At this cottage we received a particularly warm welcome, and I asked the mother of the family - English - how long she had been there; she said, 'For two years, and the *only* visitors I have had have been from the S.A.C.R.M' ...[49]

The next issue of the *Quarterly,* emphasizing Miss Nott-Bower's description of her work, made a strong appeal for 'another lady' to go out and share the work among the women and girls.

During the latter part of 1904 and the early months of 1905, the London Committee of SACRM was negotiating an agreement with SPG for closer co-operation. At first the term 'affiliation' was used, but then the Committee had second thoughts. John Ellison, the Chairman (and brother of Douglas and 'HB') had had discussions with Miss Mackenzie of the SPG and they had agreed that Women's Work was not developed sufficiently for SPG to take any responsibility.[50] The SPG had previously, in 1902, given a grant of £1000 for three years, and SACRM was also attempting to have this renewed. The Scheme for closer co-operation between the Mission and the Society was adopted by the SPG Standing Committee on March 2nd 1905, and was then published. The small-print at the bottom of the printed Scheme stated:

> Note.- *It is understood that at the present time the Women's Work of the Mission has not sufficiently developed to make it necessary for the Society to undertake any responsibility with regard to it. In the event of any considerable extension of the work, the Mission will approach the Society on the subject.* [51]

Although the October 1905 Quarterly Meeting of SACRM's London Committee reported that both SPG and 'the Chartered Company' had withdrawn their grants, SPG soon reinstated their grants, and continued to support the Railway Mission financially and in other ways throughout its history. The relationship was, at times, troublesome, as we shall observe. There is no extant record that the Society was approached 'on the subject' of Women's Work. However, SACRM's accounting methods ensured that grants received could be used for any of its work. A sub-committee, meeting on December 11th 1906, decided that 'a special fund for Women's Work ... be started', and subsequent Annual Reports showed

'Women's Work' in Income and Expenditure, as they did with 'Nursing Work'.

Miss Nott-Bower returned to England for a short break during 1907. She was exhausted, not least because of the unavailablity of a permanent base to where she - and any other women workers - could retreat, relax and recuperate after a period of weeks 'up the line'. She attended a Meeting of the London Committee in the April, during which she

> ... explained her scheme for starting a cottage as a centre for the lady workers, explaining how it arose through the D[octo]rs having forbidden her to go back, unless she had some place where she could have a thorough rest at intervals ... Letters from Mr Douglas Ellison were read, showing his strong approval of the scheme, the only obstacle being the financial part. ... The Committee decided that they could not promise any actual grant of money towards the scheme - but they advocated that it should be "pushed" as much as possible.[52]

To jump ahead briefly, the 'pushing' proved to be rather slow, almost twenty years in fact. Miss Elise Astley, the Secretary of the London Committee for twenty years, died in 1919, and a Fund was set up in her memory. By 1923 it was 'decided that the Memorial to Elise Astley [would] take the form of a Mission House at Naauwpoort - to be the residence for the Chaplain and to contain rest rooms for other workers.'[53]

The women workers, clearly, were not deemed as important as their male colleagues. By the time the house was basically completed (1924), and opened (1925), Naauwpoort was already a dwindling community as far as the Anglican Church was concerned. The financing of the house, as well as of the Church buildings, in Naauwpoort, was a continual problem for the local supporters of the Railway Mission. By 1930 'the one central home [had] become impossible owing to the dispersion of the workers.' Although many of the women workers had longed for the 'home base' that Miss Nott-Bower had proposed in 1907, the reality was far from ideal. In 1927, two years after the opening of 'Astley Memorial House', the then Head wrote:

> Our women workers all live in "rooms", and very small ones they are in some cases. How they stick it I do not know, but I have never heard one of them grumble over the matter ... It is not thrilling .., after a tiring trip up and down the line, to come back to a small room hidden behind a house and to have to go out for your meals, or else rejoice in a cup of tea made on a "Beatrice" stove ... There is usually a pile of letters waiting to be answered, and the idea of a rest at headquarters is a bit of a snare and a delusion.[54]

We have noted above how, at the Pan-Anglican Congress in 1908, Douglas Ellison promoted the efforts of women workers and of nurses. Ellison's ill health had forced him to resign from the Headship of SACRM and to return to Britain. In his final letter (as Head) to the *Quarterly,* he stated:

> In two directions ... they [SACRM workers] have a right to expect strong and vigorous leadership at the present time:
> (a) *Women's* work requires careful thought and close supervision if it is ever to be established on a firm and lasting basis, and (b) our *finances* ...[55]

The financial difficulties were not spelled out at that time, but, when Douglas Ellison's brother ('HB') took over as Head, it was made clear that lack of funds prevented appointments of staff. It was also apparent that clergy were more 'useful' to the Mission than were the women!

> It is good to get so many offers from lady workers that we cannot on financial grounds accept them all, but it would be better still to be embarassed with offers from Priests. Will that time ever come, I wonder? ... There would not be many refusals at this end ... There are developments ahead of us in the ladies' work ... Going on the principle that old friends are the best ... it seems a sound policy to try and develope our work in the Grahamstown Diocese ...and then to extend that development, as workers and means come in, to the newer work north of the Orange River ... Not the least important part of this plan is an arrangement made with the Mother Superior of the Community of the Resurrection at Grahamstown by which two of the Sisters will in October, start work on the Eastern System ...[56]

And so, for the third time in the Railway Mission's life, the Grahamstown Community came to its rescue. The Annual Report, at the end of 1909, noted that Sister Emily and Sister Muriel would look after the Midland and Graaf Reinet lines south of Rosmead, but that 'owing to the refusal of the authorities to grant two free passes for lady workers over the same section, a season ticket [had] been purchased for Sister Muriel. The writer hoped that the railway authorities would 'at a future time' see the 'reasonableness of the request' and so save the Mission heavy expense. A different writer, in the Report, looked forward to the arrival of a Miss Watson, a lady worker from England, to 'work in the eastern half of the Orange River Colony.'[57]

Within three months of her arrival, Miss Watson wrote a two-page 'Letter from the Line', describing her 'first impressions' of railway work.

This included a rare glimpse of 'women's work' on a construction line, somewhat reminiscent of the accounts by the Navvy Mission during the 1870s' and 1880s' railway-construction time in England:

> My first trip was to Bethlehem, and there a very novel experience awaited me, as a new line is being made from there to Reitz [52 km, on the Bethlehem-Balfour line, linking with the line from Durban and Ladysmith to Johannesburg] and in the Archdeacon's absence I was allowed to use his cart and horses to visit the tents of people working on the new construction. I spent four days in this work ... making acquaintance with the gangers and labourers and their wives and children - most of them living in tiny tents, many of them with a bedstead as their *only* bit of furniture, doing their cooking over a fire made of "mist" (in other words dried cow-dung) and baking their bread in ovens made by hollowing out ant heaps.
>
> I had a nice lot of English books and papers to distribute and these were eagerly welcomed, but I wished I had some Dutch ones besides. I found nearly everyone pleased to see a visitor ... In this way I visited between forty and fifty tents, revisiting some on the third and fourth days to improve my acquaintance and deliver commissions of mending wool, lozenges, tobacco, etc, which were not brought out to them by the weekly provision waggon.
>
> Since then I have been doing more ordinary visiting ...[58]

Miss Watson stayed with the Mission for a number of years and was a popular member of staff among the railway families. Uniquely, in July 1912, a letter from a ganger's child appeared in the *Quarterly.* Headed 'G.C. [Ganger's Cottage] 477 Transvaal', the letter was sent shortly after the family had moved from the Orange Free State:

> *To Miss Watson.*
>
> *My Dearling Friend,*
>
> *I was truly glad to get your dear welcome letter ... Dear Miss Watson, can you not come to see us here, we are far from our friends, and no one comes to see us, not even a Minister. There is no school to go to, and if we get on the train, Miss Watson is not on it, to talk and show us pictures.*
>
> *My mother is always sick, and my father say if Miss Watson comes to see her it is better than the doctor and much medicine. If you do not come please send another lady as kind as your dearling self, and tell her that we have no friends here. Maggie and I shall pray to God to send one ...*[59]

A letter such as this surely sums up the isolation of the gangers' families, and the worthwhile work and friendship of the Women Workers, far more than a magazine-full of letters written by the SACRM staff.

Before leaving Miss Watson, it is worth noting the fact that, like many of her women colleagues, she was called upon to undertake minor nursing duties on occasions. The fact of happening to be where the need arose, and of being a woman ('better than the doctor'), invariably persuaded railway workers and others to ask for nursing help. A particular opportunity presented itself to Miss Watson in December 1914. This was the period during the final stage of the rebellion by over 11,000 Afrikaners, successors to the 'Bitter-Enders' of the Boer War, against the pro-British stance of the government of Generals Botha and Smuts, whom they regarded as traitors. Miss Watson wrote on December 14th, 1914:

> I got to Lindley Road [Bloemfontein Diocese] (in the coach) on Friday for my regular visit every two months, for Sunday School, &c., to find 3,000 troops assembled in various camps, and the whole place occupied, the object being the capture of the last two rebel commandoes of any Size.
>
> On Saturday morning about 7.30, as I was finishing jobs and washing up breakfast things, &c., an officer came up and asked if I was a nurse and if mine was a Hospital Coach. I explained; and he said, 'I wish you'd come and look at some of my men.' So of course I said I would, and from 8 a.m. till 7 p.m. (about) I was popping in and out of the tents, dressing wounds and sores, washing, cooking, bossing ambulance orderlies, and making myself generally useful. I think it was the hardest day's work I have ever done ...There were six or seven camps, but I could only tackle two of them; and I persuaded a Miss Holmes from the Station to go and see what she could do for another lot. ...Then yesterday they were entraining all day, and I had my Sunday School as usual ...
>
> By this morning [Monday Dec.l4th] there were barely 1,000 left, and the good news came in that Steai, one of the rebel leaders, had been captured ...[60]

Miss Watson was thanked by the officer for her help, and the troops contributed six tins of jam, six tins of milk, two packets of tea and 'half a pocket [packet?] of sugar' for the families she normally ministered to. When she left Lindley Road Station, in the Mission coach / caboose, many of the men cheered her off with 'For she's a jolly good fellow'!

The same issue of the *Quarterly* contained a similar account of nursing undertaken by Miss Watson's colleague, Miss Heddy. The rebellion had resulted in a greatly reduced train service in the Orange Free State, with the consequent halting of 'normal' Women's Work. The Head commented that the women were 'being of more use in nursing the wounded than in waiting for trains that never came.' Miss Heddy gives a vivid description of the rebellion and how it affected railway work, as well as her own. She notes that 'most of the wives and children of ...railwaymen had been sent into either Bloemfontein or Kimberley' and that she visited (in Bloemfontein) 'the wives of the many railway men in the camp who had been recalled to the colours ...' She eventually moved out to a farm, near a dorp which was then surrounded by the rebels for eleven days. Summoned back to Bloemfontein, she found that 'a large number of wounded, both loyalists and rebel prisoners, had arrived unexpectedly at the National Hospital, and help was required with the nursing.'[61]

Miss Heddy eventually left, once it was possible again to use the Mission coach on the Bloemfontein - Kimberley line. At the first station, de Brug, the coach was shunted off, so that the missioner could visit people. In torrential rain the officer in charge of the loyalist commando stationed there asked what Miss Heddy and her coach were doing, and pointed out that 'the coach was the only warm and dry place in de Burg [de Brug].'[62] The missioner took the hint and spent the afternoon supplying relays of men with tea, bread and butter, cakes, jam and biscuits - at one stage with thirteen squashed into the small living area. She was pleased to report, 'They departed warmed and fed and very grateful, and enough bully beef was sent in from their mess to last generations of railway missioners.' As she pointed out, at the end of her letter (and after mentioning a wash-away on the line, with water coming into the coach) 'life on the Railway Mission may be hard and rather rough, but no one can say it is dreary or monotonous.'

Miss Heddy became the first 'lady speaker' at a SACRM Annual Conference - in 1915. It had taken eleven years for the Women Workers to achieve that standing. The chairman did note that it was the first time they had listened to stories of babies' feeding-bottles.

We shall note, at the end of this Chapter, how one woman missioner felt that she and her colleagues 'made a tremendous difference' in the lives of the lonely families of railway men. There are quite a few lengthy and interesting accounts of 'Women's Work' in various SACRM publications.[63] Many of these accounts are, inevitably, similar in their descriptions of the work among the gangers' families and others, the isolation, and the friendship that developed between the women workers and the women and children they visited. Two of the longest serving workers and best-remembered are Miss Agg-Large and Miss James. It was generally agreed that:

> the most outstanding of all the Mission's noble army of Women Workers [was] Miss Maud Agg-Large. "Aggie", as she was always .. known, trained in early life as a school-teacher ... She threw herself into the [Mission] work with boundless energy, determination and love of evangelism. Her proven ability and success resulted in her original three year contract being extended again and again ...[64]

Miss Agg-Large served sixteen years as a Woman Worker and then eight years in London as Organising Secretary. In a private letter she described her work:

> I was accepted [by SACRM] and went out in October [1929] ... to what was then Southern Rhodesia. My Section also included Bechuanaland and, for many of my sixteen years, as far as Beira. How lucky I was to be able to include the folk at Victoria Falls as part of my "Parish".
>
> I soon realised that for both Chaplain and worker, the job was a full time one, returning to one's base perhaps every 4-6 weeks for a few days. I think that the following anecdotes may help to give a picture of the varied sides of what the work entailed for me -
>
> 1) I was once sent for late at night to go to a cottage where a child was very ill with malaria. On arrival at about 2 a.m. I found the whole family round the bed side and the girl in great distress. On my request the family left me with her, and she said that she was going to hell when she died. I was able to comfort her, and we thought together of the love of God and of our Saviour. She died peacefully a few days later. After her death, her mother wrote and said that she didn't realise the love of God before.
>
> 2) The friendship of many of these people in many instances was shown in lovely little homely ways. I was spending the day at a small Cottage when the little boy came and said, "Do you know what? We are going to have pudding for lunch, because you've come."! (Probably the pudding meant more to him than I did!).
>
> 3) Lone Guides ... Once, when we allowed the boys to join in the Tracking games, a youngster went excitedly to the Head master and asked, "Isn't there a Mister Agg-Large who could take us for Scouts?
>
> 4) Christmas was spread over two months - the Christmas story with the Crib, the party following, with presents given by the town children at their Toy Services ...[65]

Maude Agg-Large died in 1985, aged ninety-one. As noted earlier, she had been awarded the M.B.E for her work in Africa with the South African Church Railway Mission.

Almost hidden among the Minutes of a London Committee Meeting of April 1940 is the sentence: 'The Secretary reported various movements of the Staff, especially with regard to Miss Agg Large and her accident caused by too vigorous shunting; and the treatment which Miss Monica James had received at the hands of the Dutch in the Orange Free State.'[66] What, I wondered, was this 'treatment' that Monica James had received? 'Oh', she told me, 'Many of the Boers there had become pro-German and anti-British in the War, and some of them had been verbally attacking me.'[67] Monica James' account of her work (a letter dated 13.4.1985, and my interview in 1992) throws an interesting light on the relationship between the (English) SACRM workers and the Afrikaner railway folk to whom they frequently ministered (until the late 1950s):

> I joined the SACRM in 1935 to work in the Orange Free State. In those days it was still the British Empire with a Governor-General & two flags flying side by side ... My HQ was Bloemfontein where the shops bore English names and Afrikaans was hardly spoken in the cities. I lived there for 9 years and saw the Afrikaners emerge into urban life. Their first department store was called "Sonop" - sunrise.
>
> When the War came things changed. My life in the O.F.S., as a "Rooinek", was not easy ... Afrikaans was largely spoken, & it was imperative to learn it. Some of our chaplains went off to the South African forces & there was no question, for any of us, of overseas leave ... I left the O.F.S. in 1944 & returned again in 1948 to work, this time, in the O.F.S. & Transvaal. The backveld once more &, by this time, Afrikaans had become a very pronounced language & the people a formidable nation ...I should like to pay my tribute to the Afrikaner South Africans. They form one of the happiest memories of my life in their unfailing kindness [this was written before Miss James was reminded of the incident mentioned earlier].
>
> Work at a Station: - Coach 8044 would be "put off" at a small station with a bump and a crash & put into a side line. The first job of the day would be to visit every house. The station master, day & night foremen, the ganger & six labourers. In my early days these were "poor-whites", they were very poor and almost illiterate. In later days they were Africans. These poor-Whites - it was after the Depression. There were thousands of children, mostly illiterate. The 'Blacks' looked at them with contempt. But they [the Whites] had the vote, and so that was a cause of dissension. I used to get clothes for them.

There might be near-by farmers who would welcome a visit, a store-keeper, very often Jewish. I was there, for a day in the coach, & at their service & under orders from the station-master. The white children came to the coach in the afternoon for "Spiel uur" - roughly a Play hour with a religious swing to it. I carried toys on the coach, Scripture painting books & jig saw puzzles. Little texts in Afrikaans, cool drinks & biscuits. The children called me the "snarks Tannie" - funny aunty, & the afternoon ended with singing "Hy is welcom" & the "onse vader" ['Our father']. Those children had been taught in school of the atrocities of the Boer War & the hated British, & I like to think that, even today, they sometimes remember the English woman, in the coach, at that remote railway station, who played with them, long, long ago.

The "Spiel uur" was held in the "living room" of the coach. First of all there would be the white kids - their parents were Dutch Reformed Church. Then would come the coloured ones - they were the children of the gangers. After that, there would be the black children. They wouldn't come together. The kids would rush all over the railway lines.

In the evening there was a Service arranged by the station master - in his house, [or] in a goods shed, [or] in the coach. We had a Service Book compiled by us all [the 'Line Book'] ... The great difficulty was that, with a mixed congregation, each would sing in their own language at their own time & they did not fit!

In an article written for children in England (undated, but most likely the 1940s, while still in the Orange Free State), Monica James gave colour to the account of the typical Service mentioned above:

We must tidy up the coach before the evening service to which everyone has been invited, Afrikaans [sic], English and Coloured, and the African rail-worker families will stand round the coach outside ...The Service is in both languages ... and the singing is led by the Africans outside who harmonise as easily and lightly as our English birds.

The children are all on the floor, some in pyjamas and nighties ready for bed. It's all very simple but have you ever felt God nearer even in our most beautiful cathedrals?

It's bed-time and we must make a cup of tea for them before they go home. We watch them go, the farm family get into their car and their lights die away in the distance, the lamps of the ganger and rail-workers bob away up the line; torches lead the station families home and Potfontein sleeps. The only sound is the bark of a jackal.

> We, too, must go to bed because at 3 a.m. another Goods train will pick us up to take us to the next lonely place. We shall be woken and shaken and knocked about ...[68]

A different kind of 'knocking about' was frequently suffered by railway women - that of battering by their husbands. As Pirie noted, 'The men on the line suffered solitude and drank; their wives suffered solitude and drink.'[69] Given the loneliness of their lives, coupled with the heat and work, it is little wonder that many gangers and labourers took to drink for some relief and entertainment, as well as to ease pain when they were injured. The Rev. E.G. Holden, on his 'Rhodesia and Congo patch', wrote in 1914 that on one section there were 'no less than five gangers who never [saw] a white man to speak to except the Permanent Way Inspector, who passe[d] through once a week, and the Pay Train ... monthly.'[70] He went on to note that it was not hard to understand the temptations that such men had to face: 'A case of whisky, they feel, makes all the difference to the loneliness of their evenings ...' Alcohol abuse 'struck a powerful chord among religious missioners'[71] and SACRM did what it could to help the men and to help their wives and families - frequently the victims of abuse.

On occasions this help was somewhat extreme and unusual. One missioner told me of Mary Attlee, who went to be a Woman Worker with SACRM in 1911, when she was thirty-two. Mary, four years older than her more famous brother - Clement, the future Prime Minister - was the fourth child (of eight), in a typical family of the professional class brought up in the atmosphere of Victorian England. Both parents were Anglican - a 'deeply religious home' stated Mary - and philanthropic. Mary, along with her sisters and Clement (until nine) had been taught at home by the same governness as had taught the young Winston Churchill. She later stated that they all knew the Gospels and Acts of the Apostles by heart. Mary Attlee was with the Railway Mission for almost ten years. On one occasion, when she called to stay the night at a ganger's cottage, the ganger was worse the wear for drink and was being physically abusive to his wife. In order to protect the wife, Miss Attlee offered to sleep with the ganger, believing that he would not harm her, as a Church missioner, or take advantage in any way! Her offer was taken up and her faith was justified. The ganger's wife was given a peaceful night's sleep and the husband went off to work on his section at 6 a.m., no doubt with muddled views about the previous night's events. The story became well known among other women workers, who were full of admiration for Mary Attlee, though they felt that this was devotion to duty considerably over and above what was expected. Unsurprisingly, it never appeared in any SACRM Reports or Letters.[72]

Monica James, in an unatributed article (Appendix A) in the *Quarterly* in 1950, gave a very full account of four 'typical days on the line.'[73] She had 'no time to pray, let alone think, not much time to eat and no water to wash! No services taken.' Yet the number of people, mainly wives and children, visited, helped, comforted and listened to was phenomenal.

In his account of 'Gang Society', Pirie, drawing on the SACRM Quarterly magazines, details the kind of lives that most of the gangers' wives led. They 'busied themselves with domestic chores ... [and] some cooked, sewed and cleaned for the unmarried railwaymen.'[74] He is right in observing that 'the absence of husbands for large portions of each working day [often a ten-hour working day, excluding travelling] was made worse by the lack of other adult company.' Childbirth and bereavement, along with all the other trials of everyday life, had to be endured with very little support of any kind. One missioner could 'instance a case of a ganger's wife who had not spoken to a white woman for three years.'[75] Lady missioners, as Pirie has noted, 'argued that this double isolation - place and gender - gave special meaning to their visits.' However, he goes on to comment: 'The contact was no doubt stirring, but it may have been unsettling rather than rousing if it reminded women of what they had lost.'[76] Admittedly, almost all the accounts of visits made by SACRM women missioners to gangers families were written by those women themselves. Sadly there are no known extant letters written by gangers' wives. There is, however, one letter written by a Transvaal farmer's wife, in August 1928, that exemplifies the feelings of all the isolated women to whom SACRM ministered. She wrote about the loneliness, of the visits of the chaplain and of his teaching the catechism and taking Communion, and then wrote about 'our lady worker, Miss Short':

> Besides the actual Christian teaching which she brings so wonderfully to the children ... she has taken trouble to set up her lantern to show five very small people the meaning of Christmas in pictures ... And she knows the need of us lonely souls ...
>
> The blank our precious visitor leaves would be overwhelming if it were not that one knows thousands of others are also alone, far from all spiritual comforts and all the loving help, and perhaps they are needing her just a wee bit more than [we] who love her and bid her God-speed ...[77]

Other evidence does strongly suggest that gangers' wives were extremely grateful and delighted that the SACRM women workers visited and cared in the way that they did. Nobody else showed any interest in them, and although they may have been 'reminded ... of what they had lost', with the visits of the missioners, that was surely preferable to being completely forgotten.

Some comments from Miss Porter's address, made at the Annual Meeting of the South African Church Railway Mission in 1923, give a helpful summary for this section:

> In the afternoon I visit one of the ganger's cottages ... there are two families there, one is a ganger and one is a white labourer. There are many children in the families. They all belong to the English Church, and I have been able to prepare and present both the Father and the Mother for confirmation during the time that I have been working on the line, and that has made a tremendous difference in their lives and in that particular cottage; but I must go and visit them because ... they never see anyone. The woman has many children, and she can't go out because there's nowhere to go ...
>
> In the evening, when I have got back to the station ... perhaps once in three months I give a lantern evening. Everybody comes. They walk for miles. They would not miss it for worlds. It is only an old-fashioned magic lantern.
>
> ... these people are very, very lonely, and they need visits. They have many difficulties in their lonely lives, and the women need the friendship and the bond of friendship that we are out to hold to all. ...you must be able to enter into their lives. 'You know', [said the wife of a ganger (reformed from constant swearing)] 'you do so much for our home.'[78]

The ability to 'enter into their lives' was an attribute that the women missioners possessed in a way that few (male) chaplains did. There was this 'bond of friendship' and real empathy between the Women Workers and the Railway wives and mothers. It was, I believe, largely a question of gender and of position and role in society. SACRM clergy, both as men and as ordained (and therefore 'set aside', 'different') people, could rarely empathise with the railway men, 'enter into their lives', in the way that their female lay colleagues could when they visited wives and families. The ministry of the Women Workers of the Railway Mission was remarkable, as was that of the chaplains, but its uniqueness lay in the involvement and close friendship offered to the Railway wives and families.

---

1 SACRM Play, Rev. Beer, 1930, (QP 106, 1931, 39,49; QP 129, 1937, 28/9)
2 GDRM, Apr. 1900, 2
3 GDRM, Jul. 1900, 2
4 *Mother Cecile*, 74

[5] Statistics based on Table 6.3, Searle, 1965, 90/91
[6] Ellison, 1930, 118
[7] Ellison, 1930, 118
[8] QP 1, 1903, 7
[9] Pirie, 1992, 104/5
[10] QP 3, 1904, 19
[11] SACRM, Lon.Com. 20.5.04, 5.7.04, X582, RHL
[12] It was thought at that time that Cookhouse would become a great railway junction, where the South-North Alicedale to Naaupoort line crossed the East-West line being built from Cape Town to East London. The 80 mile gap between Klipplaat and Somerset East was never to be linked.
[13] QP 9, 1905, 7
[14] QP 34, 1912, 7
[15] GDRM, XVI, 1902, 2
[16] ONA Box 126 (MSS. Brit.Emp. s400, RHL)
[17] ONA Box 126, 16.4.1903
[18] ONA Box 120/1, f70
[19] ONA Box126.
[20] ONA Box 126, 10/12 .5.1903
[21] ONA Box 126
[22] In his (unpublished) 'The Story of Livingstone Anglican Parish', Canon Whitehead notes: " Dr. Sweetlove became District Health Officer [of Livingstone] in 1904, succeeding Dr. Clayton. But the railway had arrived at the Falls and there was a large party building the bridge and many more railwaymen extending the line to Kalomo and beyond, so Dr. Sweetlove was invited to work for Paulings, the railway contractors ... In 1905 Dr. Thorton Combes was the doctor [in Livingstone] while the railway doctor was Dr. E.A.Parsons. Dr. Combes later took over from Dr. Parsons at the railway depot ..'
[23] ONA Box 126, 2.1.1905
[24] ONA Box 127, 29.6.1905
[25] ONA Box 127, 20.8.1906
[26] SACRM Ann.Rep. 1909, 28
[27] SACRM Ann.Rep. 1909, 52
[28] SACRM Ann.Rep. 1909, 52
[29] QP 28, 1910, 10-14
[30] QP 164, 1949, 9
[31] QP 31, 1911, 19
[32] Sadly, the SACRM Committee Minutes between 1908 and 1938 have still not been located, and may have been lost or destroyed at the start of the Second World War. The period 1912-1917 is also a fallow period for letters, diaries and Annual Reports. Fortunately the SACRM Quarterly magazines are extant (except between 1919 and 1922) and therefore are almost the sole source of information for that period.
[33] QP 37, 1912, 7
[34] QP 41, 1913, 6
[35] ONA 120/1, Item 4, .5/6
[36] QP 46, 1915,.7
[37] Vaughan, 1991, 55
[38] Vaughan, 1991, 61
[39] Vaughan, 1991, 65
[40] QP 132, 1937, 9

[41] QP 134, 1938, 16/17
[42] QP 139, 1939, .9-11
[43] QP 147, 1941, 17
[44] X583, RHL, 2.2.1944
[45] Appendix to 'Seacombe Letters', X1441/1, f10, RHL
[46] QP 5, 1904, 4
[47] Cory MS 16811-12
[48] LL Oct. 1904
[49] QP 8, 1905, 7
[50] X582, RHL, 3.2.1905, Spec. sub-Com.
[51] X582, RHL, 2.3.1905
[52] X582, RHL, 23.4.1907
[53] QP 75, 1923, 6
[54] Ellison, 1925, 121
[55] QP 20, 1908, 1
[56] QP 25, 1909, 3
[57] SACRM An.Rep. 1909, 51
[58] QP 29, 1910, 13
[59] QP 36, 1912, 16 [orig. spelling]
[60] QP 46, 1915, 10/11
[61] QP 46, 1915, 6-12
[62] QP 46, 1915, 12
[63] These accounts are notably the reports of Miss Porter and Miss Short at the Annual Conferences in 1923 and 1924, respectively; letters reproduced in 'In Journeyings Often' (1925); one chapter in *God's Highwaymen* [sic] (1930); the leaflet No.5, 'A Woman Worker's Job', in the 1941/2 series of leaflets about SACRM work; one section in 'The Happy Travellers' (1954); and one chapter in the (post-Railway Mission) *Mission Unaccomplished* (1985).
[64] Grain, 1985, 89
[65] Agg-Large, priv.letter, ?1980
[66] X583, RHL, 19.4.1940
[67] oral interview, 1992
[68] James, M, spec.article, 5/6
[69] Pirie, 1993, 70
[70] QP 43, 1914, p.13
[71] Pirie, 1993, 70
[72] Interview with Monica James, 1992.
[73] QP 171, 1950, 10
[74] Pirie, 1993, 71
[75] QP 87, 1926, 23
[76] Pirie, 1993, 71
[77] QP 96, 1928, 21/2
[78] QP 76, 1923, 19-21

6: Far flung places

- 'a little touch of God now and then.'

UP WITH THE RAILWAY

Who goes up with the railway, northward from Capetown,
Into the golden desert, out of the veld so brown?
Into lonely country, where the white man looks in vain
For a comrade's answering laughter, or his soothing hand in pain

Trade goes up with the railway, as it's always gone before,
Where the boy with the big ambition, sets up his little store,
And the eye of the great financier sees gold and treasures rare,
Whilst the thousand hands of labour are stretched to grasp their share. ....

God's Church goes up with the railway, and her voice is ever heard,
Bringing bless'd sounds to the silence with the preaching of His Word;
And the priest stands at the Altar to give the Living Bread
To the two or three who are gathered in the presence of their Head.[1]

The original poem, with seven verses, appeared in the SACRM *Quarterly* during 1908. The work of the Railway Mission was expanding and moving northwards across diocesan boundaries; the original 'Head', Douglas Ellison, had resigned and the new Head, H.B. Ellison, was shortly to investigate the possibility of SACRM work north of Livingstone.

We have noted in Chapter 2 how, after 1904, when the 'Cape to Cairo' railway reached Victoria Falls (from Wankie), various expansions of the railway system in southern Africa took effect. For example, in the north, Stanley and others had realised the need for railways in the Congo, both to close the gaps between navigable sections of the rivers and to exploit the Katanga copper and other minerals. The furthest that ocean-going ships could proceed up the River Congo was to Matadi, on the south bank, some one hundred miles from the sea. It was therefore from Matadi, in March 1890, that the 'Congo Railway' was started towards Leopoldville. The 240-mile line took exactly eight years to build (even at a 2 ft. gauge - later, in 1932, converted to 3 ft. 6 in.), and 1800 African and Chinese labourers died in the construction, along with thirty two Europeans.

The Bas Congo-Katanga Company (BCK) was incorporated in 1902 'for the establishment of a railway extending from the Rhodesian frontier to the head of navigation on the Upper Lualaba River and branches.'[2] The line from Broken Hill, in Northern Rhodesia, had reached Bwana M'Kubwa, on the Congo border, on December 11th 1909, and construction work continued without a break until Elizabethville was reached, the first train arriving on September 27th, 1910 (though the official date is given as October 1st 1910). Kambove was reached in 1913 and Bukama in 1919. The Bukama-Port Francqui line was started simultaneously from both ends in 1923, being completed in 1928.

In South-West Africa, the originally German-built railways had to be linked to the South African system as quickly as possible after Britain had declared war against Germany in August 1914.

> The line was started from Prieska, at the end of a branch running north-west from De Aar, and was pressed on in the same direction at high speed. Upington, 146 miles away, was reached after a race in which 2 1/4 miles of railway a day were built. A ferry was started across the Orange River here while the bridge was being built, and the work went on. On one day, 5 1/5 miles were laid, and the railways of South and South West Africa were linked at Kalkfontein on June 25, 1915.[3]

The complicated history of railway-building in Mozambique and Malawi was summarised in Chapter 2 and will be examined in more detail in the Section on 'Beira and the Sena Sugar Estates'. We must note, however, that the great expansion of line mileage in 'German South West', in the Congo and in the East gave the Railway Mission whole new areas of work. As in the last third of the nineteenth century, so in the first third of the twentieth, the Mission ministered to construction workers along the lines and in the camps (with the exception of the Nyasaland and trans-Zambesia railways), as well as to the different groups under 'traffic', 'locomotive' and 'permanent way'. As we shall note later, the available evidence shows SACRM's first visit to Beira in 1925 and to other districts within Mozambique in 1930. We may assume that lack of available missioners in Rhodesia (one or two covering vast areas) accounts for the Mission's absence from line-construction, and that of the Zambesi Bridge, in 'Portuguese East'.

The major change in SACRM's operations was the broadening of its remit. Not only was it now crossing diocesan boundaries, at one time a radical move, but it was also crossing international ones. Instead of having to deal with officials who, though working in different countries or colonies, were nevertheless British and therefore shared a common culture as well as language, the missioners were increasingly having to relate to Belgian, French and Portuguese railway and colonial staff. Yet, as we shall note, important as the wider remit was, this was not just a matter of an increase in mileage covered, or of more interesting journeys undertaken, or of encountering more interesting officials. The real difference was the culture shock experienced by the Railway Mission staff, particularly in places such as Luabo where people of many different nationalities, races and classes met together for worship. Divisions in society were broken down in a way that the missioners had never experienced before or elsewhere. Once again the SACRM experience was unique and the Mission's workers were obliged to radically re-think their ecclesiology.

When 'Up with the Railway' was read by the Mission's supporters in 1925 the pioneering and relatively frequent visits to the Congo were drawing to an end, though occasional trips occurred for the next thirty years; the eleven year period of work in South-West Africa (Namibia) had come and gone; the visits to Beira and subsequently to Sena Sugar Estates in Lower Zambezia and, later, to Nyasaland were reported for the first time; and only Maun and Lake Ngami (Bechuanaland/Botswana) remained on the horizon - nine years hence - to be included in the 'far flung places'.

In one sense, of course, almost all the places visited by SACRM staff were 'far away', not only from England, but even from Cape Town. A list of the missioners in 1934 has Cape Town, Grahamstown, Johannesburg, Naauwpoort, Alicedale, Beaconsfield, Queenstown, Pretoria, Volksrust and Irene (Transvaal), Bloemfontein and Kroonstad (O.F.S), Bulawayo and Salisbury, Lusaka and Broken Hill as bases from which the twenty staff operated. Their 'patches' often stretched hundreds of miles from these bases. Yet most of these places and lines were visited frequently, often weekly, certainly monthly and were not deemed exceptional. The railwaymen and their families who lived in the Cape and in Natal, in the Orange Free State and the Transvaal, and in Bechuanaland and Southern and North-Western Rhodesia formed the bulk of the Railway Mission's 'congregation'. They were the 'normal' parishioners of this itinerant Church. Yet, as in most settled and static parishes, so in the Railway Mission there was always a concern about and, when possible, care for those who lived well outside the normal geographical limits and who were otherwise denied the ministrations of the Anglican Church.

In the history of the South African Church Railway Mission the ones who lived 'well outside', those in the 'far flung places', were the railway workers and residents, the traders, farmers, cattle-buyers, store-keepers, officials and plantation workers in the varied territories of South-West Africa, Ngamiland, the Congo and central Mozambique. The Staff 'Vade Mecum' (Handbook) stated that SACRM 'had the care of the few in many miles, while the parishes ... care[d] for the many in few miles.'[4] The

Handbook also stated that one of the ideals of the work was 'to assert the inestimable value of one single soul by [their] seeking for it.'

The searching out of the few and even of the 'one single soul' was the main *raison d'être* of this aspect of the Railway Mission's ministry. We shall look at the four areas of work 'well outside' the usual spheres of operation and end the chapter by asking whether or not the time and effort was 'worthwhile' being spent on so few people.

The Congo

> I only got two days in Elizabethville and that little stay revealed about three communicants amongst the residents, one of whom was away on holiday. Then there were a few British Tommies at the hotel where I put up, and one of these, a devout young Yorkshireman, came for his communion to a Mass I celebrated in my bedroom just before leaving. What gratitude on his part, well worth the 300-mile journey backwards and forwards from the Rhodesian border.[5]

The 'Blue Quarterly' that gave the account, in the Winter of 1940, of Hobson's visit to the Congo, also reported the death of Herbert Hale, the pioneer Railway Missioner chosen to be with the railway workers as the railhead moved northwards to Victoria Falls and beyond. Herbert Hale left Rhodesia in 1906. Three years later railhead crossed the border into the Congo.

Various copper mines, including The Star of the Congo (Etoile du Congo) mine, were started by the Union Miniere in 1907. With the arrival of the railway from the south, the Star became the headquarters of the mining company, and Elizabethville mushroomed from a shanty town to a modern European city. The rapid development of the area

> brought a flood of immigrants to Katanga. Lured by tales of a new Eldorado, they came from England, South Africa, Australia, as well as the poorer countries of Europe. Many of them brought their families. They built their own houses in rudimentary fashion, opened shops, hotels and bars. Soon their ranks were swelled by several thousand Belgians, recruited under a scheme of assisted emigration.[6]

In the years following the First World War, despite the world-wide slump, Katanga, with its increasing copper production, was transformed. New towns appeared, with their missions, schools and hospitals. Black Africans were promoted to positions that had previously been reserved for Whites, and which still were in southern Africa. Exceptionally, the civil service resisted 'Africanisation' of its higher grades until 1959. By nature of the Congo being a Belgian colony, the British community was never large. The British who were there, and who were to be the 'draw' for the Railway Mission, were initially railway construction workers, gangers and engineers; then, as the Congo was developed, mining engineers and management, Bank workers and British Consulate staff, along with one or two railway people and farmers.

The South African Church Railway Mission started its preliminary 'Congo work' in 1909. By July that year the Rev. Fred Rogers, missioner in North-West Rhodesia, was reporting on his ministry in Broken Hill, which had been the railhead for four years. He informed his readers of the decision to 'push on the railway another 150 miles to Bwana 'Mkuba [M'Kubwa] and eventually to the Star of Congo copper mine just over the Congo border.'[7] Apart from his 350 miles-long 'parish' between Livingstone and Broken Hill, with a white population of five hundred (gangers and their families, settlers and government officials), Rogers was concerned about the many construction workers employed by Pauling & Co. for the line to the north.

Rogers, along with a friend from England, Mr. Swinnerton, spent part of July and August 1909 on an exploring trip to Bwana M'Kubwa, a trip that was to be a severe test of endurance, three attacks of fever also having hindered the start. Although he was not the first SACRM pioneering missionary (Simeon, Douglas Ellison and Hale held those honours), nor was he the first to visit construction workers during the laying of a line, this initial 'trek' of Rogers to the Congo was remarkable for his determination to battle his way to find the railway workers, and for his vivid description of the visit. Few, if any, missioners would ever again need to set off on a trip equipped as a minor 'Stanley' or 'Livingstone'! (A similar trek was made that year, with an equally vivid description, by George Pauling, accompanied by Sir Charles Metcalfe, 'to go on beyond the railhead as far as the Congo border ...[the] object being to select a suitable route for the railway.'[8] Pauling's 'three hundred native carriers' contrasted with the twelve employed by Rogers). The missioner explained:

> We wanted to go along the proposed [railway] route as far as the Congo border, and as the tsetse fly kills all horses, mules and oxen, and the rails are only laid for 60 miles north of Broken Hill [ie. to Kashitu Siding], we had to depend on native carriers. We were very fortunate in being able to travel with Mr. Worthington, the Secretary for native affairs ...

... I think it is rather creditable that 12 carriers managed to convey all our belongings, including a tent, two camp beds, a canvas table, bath and washhandstand, canvas chairs, rugs, pillows, clothes, books to read, books for services, books in large quantities to give away, a bicycle, a rifle, a 12-bore and collector's shot gun, cooking pots and pans, crockery and cutlery, and provisions for three weeks!

Messrs. Pauling & Co. kindly gave us a free pass as far as the trains would carry us (no small consideration, as their ordinary fare at that time was 1/- [5p] a mile). We turned out at the Railhead at 7 a.m., on Thursday, July 22nd, had a cup of cocoa and some biscuits, and started off in a most imposing procession, Mr. Worthington and Mr. Swinnerton walking and myself cycling, followed by 60 natives, each laden with a package weighing about 50 pounds. A ten mile tramp brought us to the first Railway Camp, where we found three white men and over 100 natives building a bridge [near Katanino]. They gave us a warm welcome and an excellent breakfast of wild pig and buck ...

[Then follows the description of the daily routine of meals, ten or twelve miles trek in the morning and five or six in the afternoon, camp life, and going to get 'something for the pot'.]

Collections are difficult in a land where stores are 100 miles apart, and the currency consists of limbo (ie., calico) and salt. Few men carry any money, and a cash collection of nearly £2 came as a pleasant surprise, which was increased by further offerings the next day of the wages of my carriers for the entire trip, amounting to something like £5, two tins of cocoa, a bicycle pump (of which I was in great need), and sundry stores and provisions.

On the journey up we did not follow the construction, but took a better path which was made for the mine. It consists of a track about a foot broad ... [and] from a cycling point of view leaves something to be desired ...

Some of the rivers have rough log bridges, but most of them have to be crossed on the shoulders of carriers, one of whom gently sank with me into a pool ... At Bwana M'Kubwa my previous companions left me.

On the return journey we kept to the path made by the surveyors of the Railway. First of all, on leaving Bwana M'Kubwa, we had five miles through a wood. The only signs there of the prospective railway were a series of small pegs twenty-two yards apart. Then we reached an embankment about a mile long, which was almost ready to receive its sleepers and rails ...

> As we came south, embankments became more frequent ...[and] at last, when I was within a mile of the train at the Railhead, my bicycle gently collapsed ... it broke clean in two ... Everywhere I met with unbounded hospitality and kindness, and I hope to repeat the trip in October ...[9]

Shortly after this trip Fred Rogers was very ill with enteric fever and had to return to England for a while. In writing his report he anticipated the inevitable query over the wisdom and the cost of his Congo journey, knowing that supporters at home would ask, 'This sounds a delightful picnic, but where does the Mission work come in?' His answer was clear:

> On paper it certainly does not seem worth while to spend four weeks and about £35 in covering 250 miles merely to see 40 Railway employees, and 130 other white men, and hold three services.
>
> The work of constructing the Railway is divided up among contractors and sub-contractors, each of whom is responsible for a mile or a few miles. He may have anything from 50 to 150 natives working under him, but there are seldom more than two white men together; consequently anything in the way of a formal service is out of the question as a rule. On the other hand one gets to know the men, and there is every chance of meeting them again, and the bare fact that a clergyman has come along to look them up, goes for something and shows that they are not forgotten. At ... Bwana M'Kubwa, near the Congo border, there is a copper mine which has raised the population to 15, and the congregation on Sunday night consisted of 14, which is not a bad proportion.[10]

The Annual Reports of 1909 and 1910/11, whilst rejoicing in the 'northward extension' of the Railway Mission's work, reminded readers that, once over the Zambezi, SACRM work was no longer in an Anglican area under the jurisdiction of South Africa (CPSA), but, as noted in Chapter 3, in the missionary sphere of UMCA [Universities' Mission to Central Africa], with whom they were happy to be associated. Also, the work in the north was 'a big venture of faith financially'.[11] It was realised that a new mission house would be needed eventually, if the work was to grow. H.B. Ellison, the Head, asked that supporters be content with the advance made and be able 'to consolidate [the] existing work before thinking of further extension ...'

By the end of 1911 Fred Rogers had taken over as Head of the Railway Mission from H.B. Ellison and a new missioner, Geoffrey Douglas, appointed for North-Western Rhodesia. Douglas's first trip to Bwana M'Kubwa (November 1911) was the monthly pay train, which also took the Railway Doctor and his coach. Clergyman and Doctor shared the coach, which leaked, necessitating the missioner to spend some time sleeping under a table, though the five minute stops at gangers' cottages meant two one-hundred yard sprints each time, as the Doctor's coach was at the opposite end of the train to the pay coach. There were various breakdowns on the way, and the notice about a Sunday Service did not arrive at Bwana M'Kubwa. Douglas commented, 'it was not a very cheerful person that [returned to] Broken Hill ... in the Doctor's coach.'[12]

In Chapter 5 we noted the Rev. Holden's comments on his 'Rhodesia and Congo' patch about the especial loneliness of (single) gangers in the northern areas, of temptations and the resort to drink. He also commented that, as the line penetrated into new and sparsely-populated districts in the Congo, it carried with it 'a class of men, not necessarily vicious (although in many cases that [was] the case), but rather of the wild buccaneer type ... attracted by the romance of a new country ..'[13] SACRM pioneering work in such distant places was not something for the faint-hearted!

During 1912 the Railway Mission started its bi-monthly visits to Elizabethville. As the missioners crossed the border at Sakania they were 2150 miles from Capetown and almost a thousand miles from the northern Headquarters in Bulawayo. These distances limited more frequent visits to the Congo. As he established himself, Geoffrey Douglas commented:

> ... there are a number of British residents living either in the town [Elizabethville] itself or at the smelting works, a mile and a half away, and the copper mine, the Star of the Congo, six miles away.
>
> Of these there is quite a good sprinkling of keen Churchpeople [= Anglicans], who, if it was not for the Railway Mission, would be entirely deprived of the ministrations of the Church.[14]

Inevitably the chaplain had a busy round of Services on a Sunday. It is worth noting, in passing, that almost all the visits to 'far away places', not just Elizabethville, were timed for weekend arrivals, though this did not always work out in practice. As we have seen earlier, a visit to a lonely farm on the South African veld could and did take place on any day of the week, and a Service be held, and a 'Sunday' School be held on another day. However, the groups of men living and working together in such places as Katanga, Sena Sugar Estates and Beira not only expected Church Services to be held on a Sunday, but would have been generally unavailable to attend on any other day. They could, of course, be visited on other days. Geoffrey Douglas gave an account of a typical Sunday for him in and near Elizabethville:

> ... a Celebration [of Holy Communion] at 8 o'clock at Lubumbashi (the smelting works), with a congregation of 10 or 12; then Mattins at 11 o'clock with a congregation of about 20; and in the afternoon a native service at which about 30 boys [sic] attend, most of them from Likoma, on Lake Nyasa. In the evening there is a service in the town itself, with a congregation of about 40 or 50 ...[15]

During this visit, the missioner was able to 'pay a hurried visit to the Railhead ... 48 kilometres north of Elisabethville [ie. just south of Tumbwe].' The 'boys' from Likoma, mentioned by Douglas, were Africans from the island of Likoma, which was the central mission station of the UMCA. Approximately half of its 4000 population, in 1908, were Anglican.[16] Martelli noted that copper from Lubumbashi foundry flowed for the first time on 30th June 1911, though 'an increasing shortage of native labour [had] slowed down all work until a solution was found by importing Africans from neighbouring territories.'[17]

As the Railhead moved ever northwards from Elizabethville to Kambove and Bukama and eventually to Port Francqui, the Railway missioners, 'the only Anglican priests within 800 miles', continued visiting the construction workers. The SACRM Quarterly Magazines noted '60 miles north of Elizabethville', '100 miles north', '130 miles north' and so on, in succeeding issues. On one visit Geoffrey Douglas was joined by the Head, Frederick Rogers. As they journeyed to Railhead, the Head noted:

> ... we hardly met a man whom we had not come across somewhere before. In a visit of two or three days one can hardly hope to get hold of men who have not seen either Church or Clergyman for anything from one to ten years ... When we got to Lufira, about 11 degrees S. of the Equator, the rails stopped. But for another 50 miles the earthworks are made ... Every five miles or so we found one or two white men camping, who were contractors or engineers.
>
> ... On construction trains we do not enjoy the luxury of passenger coaches, and when we had asked the General Manager of the Chemin de fer du Katanga to run our private coach from the Belgium border to Elisabethville, he replied that he would be pleased to do it for £48, so we had to leave it behind, and travel (when on the construction) on open trucks. This has its drawbacks when the thermometer stands at something over 100 in the shade, and there is no shade ... [18]

The difficulty encountered with the CFK Manager no doubt was a result of various Belgian factors. Firstly, the colony was by then being run as a Belgian colony, under their administration. Secondly, although the line to

Elizabethville had been a British construction, when 'the contract to Elizabethville was finished, Belgian interests decided to continue the construction under the aegis of a Belgian firm, and for that purpose was formed the Societe Coloniale de Construction [though Paulings] ... were offered and accepted a material interest in the new company.'[19] Lastly - and this may have been the crucial factor - the South African Church Railway Mission, itself a strange title in Congo territory, was both English and Anglican. Its declared interest was in ministering to the needs of the British, particularly Anglicans, in Katanga. The free transport of a (Rhodesian) caboose was not likely therefore to be high on a list of priorities for a French-speaking General Manager in the Belgian Congo.[20]

The association of SACRM with UMCA has been observed above. Bishop Alston May was enthroned in Mapanza Church, then the pro-cathedral of Northern Rhodesia, on 27 September 1914. After some initial visits in his diocese 'up the line to the Congo border and beyond it' he wrote in December (1914) about Railway Mission work, the article being printed in the UMCA journal the following March. After commenting on the great opportunities that lay ahead and the influence of the white population (a recurrent theme in all mission articles), he made an urgent appeal 'for a priest ... [to] devote himself primarily and at first to work amongst white men.':

> ... the work has been undertaken hitherto by the South African Church Railway Mission (though of course we are beyond the limits of the South African Province), and I have every reason to hope that they will continue to make themselves responsible for it, thus relieving the diocese of a difficult task and a serious financial burden (We ought, I think, to bear part of the cost.) But Mr. Holden [SACRM] ... has had to return home ... and Archdeacon Rogers, the Head of the [Railway] Mission, has kindly invited my assistance in securing a good man ....
>
> It has occurred to me that, amongst the supporters of U.M.C.A., there must be some young priests who do not feel called to native work but would welcome the opportunity of serving the Mission in this necessary branch of white work ... ministering, say for two or three years, to the white men on and near the line from the Victoria Falls to the Railhead in the Congo territory, and doing, perhaps, in addition such little native work as he finds himself able to tackle.
>
> Unless some special arrangement were made, he would be a member, not of the U.M.C.A., but of the Railway Mission - appointed by them, drawing his stipend from their funds, and acting under the direction of the Head of the Mission, who would be to him *in loco Vicarii.* But, on the other hand, he would be approved by my

Commissaries and, as holding my licence, he would be on the staff of the Diocese ... in all respects as one of ourselves ... The life is a hard and trying one ... but it has many attractions for a vigorous person, who is anxious to do useful pioneer service and is not afraid of his fellow men.[21]

The First World War had already started by the time the bishop made his appeal and, inevitably, it fell on deaf ears. Would-be chaplains were joining the army, to serve as chaplains to the Forces. Railway chaplaincy lost some of its appeal and urgency. The Rev. E.F. Winnington-Ingram was already the missioner for the Bechuanaland Protectorate, with the line up to thirty miles north of Bulawayo. His colleague, the Rev. E.G. Holden, had had responsibility for Wankie, Northern Rhodesia, and the Congo. His departure, mentioned by the bishop, left Winnington-Ingram with the whole section (Southern and Northern Rhodesia and Congo), which task he continued until 1916, when Ralph Seacombe arrived to look after the Southern section of this work.

The first visit by Winnington-Ingram (June? 1915) gave the missioner a new experience in having to pay his fare, from Sakania, as well as having to practise his rusty French. He noted that the 'new experiment ... tried at night ...[that of] holding a service at the workmen's quarters at Lubumbashi'[22], produced a congregation of forty. The voluntary offerings paid for all the expenses of the journey. In August 1915, while again in the Congo, the missioner took a Service in the British Consulate in Elizabethville and 'had the unusual honour of welcoming there the officers of the British Naval Expeditionary Force to Tanganyika ...[which] was almost like a Parade Service.'[23]

The reference to the Expeditionary Force was to one of the most unusual and fascinating episodes of the East African Campaign of 1914-18. Two gunboats were sent to Lake Tanganyika from England via Cape Town and then up the railway line to the Congo and then by 'road' and river to the Lake, where they achieved two decisive victories against German ships. Despite Belgium's invasion by Germany, it had kept a neutral pose in Africa. The sinking of Belgian canoes by a German gunboat on the Belgian side of Lake Tanganyika led to a change in policy and to official cooperation with British war efforts in East Africa.[24]

Winnington-Ingram, in the course of his report (above) on his August 1915 visit, and also in a subsequent account, published in October 1916, made disparaging remarks about the railway north of the Rhodesia-Congo border. He referred to 'that terrible Belgian railway to Elizabethville' and to the 'peculiarities of the Railway', though acknowledging that the authorities could be generous with 'concessions', ie., free or reduced rail travel. Issues of *Light for the Line* at that period, and later, not infrequently criticised the customs and border officials and the running of the railway, safe in the knowledge that such comments were unlikely to be read by the people concerned. Although *Light for the Line* was published for mission supporters and railway workers in southern Africa, and therefore comments had to be more guarded than in the 'Blue Quarterly', this English and Anglican journal was unlikely to fall into the hands of French-speaking officials in the Congo. It would, however, have been read by the '40 or so Britishers employed by the C.F.K. (Chemin de fer du Katange)' whom Winnington-Ingram found 'difficult to discover, but they [were] there: some on the trains, some sleeping in cabooses, others staying at hotels, others in camps of their own ...'[25] They would have read the comments of Winnington-Ingram's predecessor, E.G. Holden, when he complained of 'difficulties ... [due to] the Belgian influence on the British in the question of Sunday observance.'[26] He found that Sunday evenings were always 'reserved for dinner parties and the cinema, [producing] a so-called gala show on that night' to which everyone went.

Canon Thornely Jones, who took over as Head of the Railway Mission at the end of 1915, made a fourteen thousand mile trip, over three months, visiting all the workers 'on the Line', the Congo being the furthest extent of this staggering 'visitation'. He was pleased with what he saw and, on returning a year later, reported that at Elizabethville the Anglicans had 'decided to have Lay Services in between the monthly visits of the [SACRM] Priests.'[27] For the earlier bi-monthly visits, themselves generous, given the distances involved, to have become monthly ones was quite remarkable. This proved to be an exceptionally generous provision on the part of the Railway Mission and was not one that could be sustained for very long. There was a greater need for the services of the missioner in the railway and mining towns of Northern Rhodesia. The fact that lay people (most likely civil servants in Elizabethville, rather than railway workers) were willing to take Services in between the missioners' visits, is itself an unusual occurrence in the Anglican Church of that period. They were, however, geographically outside the normal constraints of diocese and hierarchy, and made best use of their 'freedom'.

Even by the following year (1918) Winnington-Ingram, although feeling that the monthly visits had justified themselves, was expressing some reservations. Part of his report is worth quoting in full:

> The Congo is full of money and wickedness, as usual; the population continues to increase, but it seems likely that the English element will not increase very largely. The tendency to replace English by Belgian labour is always very strong, and whatever increase of British population there may be, it will be of a floating nature, artizans coming and going, and the position of the Church will not be altered

very much. That does not alter the fact that the next thing to work for is a resident Chaplain in the Congo mainly supported by the local residents, and responsible to the S.P.G., or the Railway Mission, as circumstances may decide. Besides Elizabethville and Kambove, there will shortly be large mining centres at Likasi and Fungarume, and possible elsewhere, with a total British population of, perhaps, 500. Enough to give a man plenty of work ...

> ... the trouble [with the monthly visit] is that the number of supporters has proved so small that the Church Council [in Elizabethville] has been somewhat discouraged. What the outcome will be this year must decide. It is the same old difficulty - that of trying to teach English Church people the principal of regular support to their Church, apart from collections.[28]

The writer seems oblivious of the fact that his 'floating' English population, coupled with their lack of support and unwillingness to contribute much financially, were hardly likely to help the viability of having a resident chaplain. The 1918 Annual Report, published in 1919, notes that Anglicans north of Rhodesia were entirely without the ministrations of the Church. One year later, visits were no longer regular. The 'wickedness' referred to by the missioner no doubt related to the heavy drinking and gambling, and to crossracial sex which was commented on by some observers.

Over the next fifteen or so years the various publications of the Railway Mission give occasional glimpses of chaplains, or the Head, or lay workers making the journey to Elizabethville and beyond. Long trips for few people continue to be the order of the day, though always justified, and the railway in Katanga continued to have its dubious reputation. By 1934 the Northern Rhodesia chaplain, Norman Faull, was reporting,

> From Kafulafuta, on to Sakania, the "vorder" station for the Belgian Congo. There are few English people left there now; but we found an empty house for services, and had a very jolly little Evensong, and Communion the next morning. Then ... I went up by mail train, with enough kit to last several days, to Elizabethville ... I stayed with the British Consul, and we had our services, as usual, in his house. The British community in the town is decreasing very fast, and it looks as though there will soon be no "Britishers" left at all.[29]

The next six years saw Elizabethville, with the 'remotest Church people', visited annually by the Railway Mission. After 1940 no recorded visit occurs until 1945, when Arthur Hobson made his 'eight weeks trip for eight communicants.' Writing from the river steamer, S.S. "Kigoma", tied up for the night at a small station on the Kasai River (tributary of the Congo), Hobson gives a full account of what proved to be the last substantial visit to the Congo by a member of the South African Church Railway Mission. He was on the 'homeward trek ... back to [his] NR [Northern Rhodesia] Section', reflecting on the trip:

> from Ndola ... there was a stretch of about 1,000 miles, four days in the train, to the little town of Port Franqui on the Kasai. The kind Belgians gave me a free pass for that railway journey. There we boarded this two-funnelled, stern-wheeled, four-decked vessel with accommodation for over 100 passengers, without counting the native travellers on the lowest deck ... The distance from Port Franqui to 'Leo'[poldville] ... is about 550 miles, mostly on the Kasai River ... We had a Sunday on board. There were several families of American missionaries, mostly Presbyterian, making their way home to the States on long overdue leave ... I was asked to conduct a little service for them, so we had a gathering of about twenty men, women and children in the saloon ... In 'Leo' I discovered several nice Anglican families, some who had been there for years and years, but they don't ever remember having had a mass of their own. So I think we may feel that the good old S.A.C.R.M made history there, as we set up our altar in the Baptist Chapel and gave the Holy Sacrament to eight souls, amongst them the Consul-General and his wife. I was the guest of the Baptist Missionary Society, who were really quite angelic in their treatment of me ...
>
> Leopoldville is a surprisingly beautiful city on the banks of the great Congo ... I took a ferry-boat one day over to the opposite side and visited Brassaville ... and I was glad to pay a call on our British Consul there and have lunch with him ...
>
> I had a ... borrowed Baptist bike, and went out some miles to a perfectly amazing sight, the rapids of the Congo River ... The riches of this huge Belgian territory are quite untold .. [and] it's grand to hear on so many sides the good things that are said about the Belgian Administration. The missionaries, for instance, are loud in their praises. The Africans do everything up here; no such thing as a colour bar ...[30]

Leopoldville and Brazzaville were the furthest places ever visited by the Railway Mission. There is no record of any missioner travelling there again. Four more years were to elapse before Elizabethville witnessed the ministrations of a SACRM chaplain, followed by a visit in 1953 and one in 1954. This latter visit merited half a sentence in the report of the Head, Ray White, - 'a delightful week in the Belgian Congo, at Elizabethville'[31], and appears to have been the last time that the Mission made the journey. Sakania, on the border, was visited once or twice over the next few years, but the Congo was no longer to see the Anglican Railway chaplains, nor were the Belgian officials to be pressed or pestered for free Passes.

By 1955, the rise of nationalism in the Congo and the demand for independence, which gathered force after a new government was elected in Belgium in 1958, inevitably resulted in the Railway Mission being an anachronism in that area. There were increasingly fewer Europeans living there and virtually no British. The secession of Katanga in July 1960 and the disorder and chaos which resulted in the Belgian Congo, ensured that that 'far flung place' would no longer have the ministrations of the Rhodesia and Nyasaland Railway Mission (as SACRM had become in 1957, after the withdrawal from South Africa).

South-West Africa (Namibia)

> In 1860 Bishop Gray, preaching in Holy Trinity Church, Cape Town, spoke ... of his hopes for the future: "There is a great field beyond this diocese on the west coast among the Ovambos untouched. I have long been anxious to found a mission there." ... He hoped, he said, to see a Church Mission, "if my life is spared", beyond British territory on the west. "I should rejoice to see the C.M.S. undertaking it." [32]

After early CMS failure in Natal, noted in Chapter 1, that Society withdrew from South Africa; the other main Anglican missionary Society, the SPG, had no spare money for west coast missions; and no would-be missioner stepped forward to offer himself for work in the arid and semi-arid south-western portion of Africa. Bishop Gray's words (and, although Metropolitan, he was never Archbishop - that title only came to his successors) had fallen on deaf ears.

The Rev. A.R. Hoare was the first priest appointed by the Diocese of Cape Town to go to visit 'Great Namaqualand and Damaraland' . In 1898 he went on the steamer "Taal" to Walfisch (Walvis) Bay, the English enclave some eight hundred miles north of Cape Town. The ship called at Angra Pequena (Luderitz), where the priest found a German settlement of 'a few soldiers [and] one or two traders living in small wooden houses at the head of the bay ..' He noted that, at Walfisch Bay, 'besides the magistrate [Mr. Cleverly] and his family there [was] a police sergeant and constables, two trading stores, Mr. Boehm, a German missionary, and a number of Hottentots [Khoi].' [33]

Three miles inland at Landfontein, a Khoi settlement, he found the only vegetation on his visit. At the time, a light railway was being built from the port to the oasis of Rooibank on the River Kuiseb:

> This short 2-ft. 6-in. gauge line, with its single British-built 2-4-2 tank locomotive 'Hope', shortened the wagon haul by a few miles when it was put into service in 1899, but was quickly put out of business by an all-German line further north.[34]

In the account of his visit, Mr. Hoare wrote:

> We set about looking for a church in which to hold a service on Good Friday, and chose the drawing-room in Mr. Cleverly's house. We arranged a temporary Altar and had Matins, Litany, and Evensong for congregations of about 20. On Easter Eve we had preparation for Holy Communion, and the "Church" looked lovely on Easter Day at the early Celebration, and the singing was hearty.[35]

This was the beginning of Church work among the English Anglicans of Damaraland. Mr. Hoare next went the hundred or so miles to the north, to Cape Cross, where he found a Mr. Elers managing a guano works, with its camp of '60 whites and 150 blacks':

> We had service in the men's dining room, and 9 were present at the Holy Communion service, 70 came to Matins, and a good many to Baptisms, the dedication of the cemetery, and evensong. The singing was splendid, and the number at Matins swelled by the crews of sailing ships anchored outside.

After this, Mr. Hoare returned to Cape Town, leaving the magistrate to continue the Confirmation classes that the priest had started.

Bishop Gibson, the coadjutor (assistant) bishop of Cape Town, was the next Anglican cleric to venture north-west from the Cape. In 1901, three years after the Rev. Hoares's visit, the bishop went to Windhoek and Swakopmund, finding plenty of work that could be done by an itinerant priest among the three to four hundred English folk in the areas in and around those centres. He did not think then that there was an opening for Anglican 'native work', as other missions were clearly present; he changed his mind after subsequent journeys. Then came the First World War and the German South-West campaign.

The First World War came nearer to the Diocese of Kimberley and Kuruman than to any other part of the Church of the Province of South

Africa. 'German South-West' was technically part of its mission work. The diocese had been created in 1912 from part of the huge Diocese of Bloemfontein, the awkward northern part of that of Cape Town, the distant north-western part of Grahamstown Diocese, plus a slice of Southern Rhodesia. The Dean of Pretoria, Wilfrid Gore-Browne, was elected as the first Bishop of the new See. He had originally gone from Darlington to South Africa in 1902, having been recruited as a member of the Railway Mission. Within a few weeks of his arrival he was persuaded by the Church authorities to be Rector of Pretoria, subsequently Dean.

After a visit to England, Bishop Gore-Browne returned to his diocese in December 1914, and wrote: 'I saw Prieska under a very new light. Sleepy, sunburned Prieska resounding with the hurrying hoofs of horses, the streets full of mounted men.'[36] The parish of Prieska took in 40,000 square miles and included the Prieska-Upington line of rail. During the first twelve months or so of the 1914-18 War there could be as many as 10,000 troops at any time in Upington, with others continually passing through. It is therefore little wonder that Frederick Rogers, Head of SACRM, wrote in the January 1915 'Blue Quarterly':

> I have ... been asked by the Bishop of Kimberley to send a man to the Prieska-Upington line, a most important bit of work at the moment, as it is being pushed forward rapidly and used for the conveyance of troops to German S.W. Africa.
>
> I could only reply that if the Bishop would find the man, I would do the rest.[37]

We have noted the details regarding the building of this line and the linking of the two railway systems. Rogers' remarks about the bishop's request are the first mention in SACRM history of South West Africa, though the line in question was not, of course, in the colony. Three months later, the Head was able to report to his readers that he was sending a Mr. George Houghton Thorne to represent the Railway Mission on the line 'which has come into special prominence as it is our only entrance by land into German S.W. Africa.'[38] It is not clear whether the 'our .. entrance' referred to that of the Railway Mission or that of the Union Defence Forces (ie., with the transport of troops).

Details of the work of Mr. Thorne only appeared the following year, January 1916, in an edited letter written by Thorne himself. He points out that, although he did not join the staff of the Railway Mission until February 1915, he had in fact begun his work in the previous November. He had received his licence from the Bishop of Kimberley, with the instructions to work among the railwaymen and troops along the line [Prieska - Kalkfontein (Karasburg)] 'but not to leave the line to go after the troops.' At first he talked with the troopers he met on the train going on the line north west from Prieska, towards railhead, including some German prisoners. He held well-attended Services at Putzonderwater, his congregations including the station foreman and details of Parkinson's Horse and of the Veterinary Corps, then, he wrote:

> I went on the railhead, at that time about 120 miles out from Prieska. The first night I held a service for a gang of about 120 boys, most of whom attended. The next day I walked along from the construction camp to actual railhead. On the way I chatted with some of the men.
>
> At Christmas [1914] I held services at Upington for the 8th Midland Rifles, Cape Field Artillery, S.A.M. Corps, Scott's Horse, Hanover and Coleberg and Philipstown Commandoes; also a service in hospital for the convalescents. Directly after, I worked along the line to Prieska, holding services at several camps, mostly amongst contractors' boys ...[39]

George Houghton Thorne had been on the staff of SACRM for only six months or so when he had to leave the work because of heart trouble and related illnesses. Unlike most workers on the Railway Mission he had not been recruited in England, but was, unusually, a bishop's appointment in South Africa. The Church structure and SACRM itself were both able to be flexible when the urgent need arose. The bishop had 'found the man' and Rogers had 'done the rest'. Rogers' next letter, written within a day or two of the German surrender in S.W. Africa (9 July, 1915), hoped that he was not premature with his title of "British S.W. Africa":

> I do not know what steps the Church of the province will take to minister to the English people who are now occupying what was "German S.W." We have already, I believe, taken over something like a thousand miles of line, and I quite expect it will be an opportunity for us to show what we are worth ...[40]

It seems that with the use again of 'we' and 'us', the SACRM Head was identifying the Railway Mission with the British/Union forces, or at least not distinguishing between them. Similar, somewhat loose, thinking often identified 'the Church' with the Anglican Church, and by extension with 'white', 'Britain' and 'civilisation'.

Two Reuters reports in the *Morning Post* of 27 June 1915, are of note:

> Pretoria, June 25th: The extension of the Upington railway line to Kalkfontein [=Karasburg], north of Warmbad, has been completed, thus linking up the German lines with the Union system.

1. An old-time ganger, the Cape, 1890s

2. A Coloured platelayer and his 'gang', Rhodesia, 1955

3. World record-breaking track laying, Broken Hill (Kabwe), January 11, 1906

4. First wedding in N-W Rhodesia, Livingstone, August 25, 1906
Dr Thomas Donaldson and Sister Elizabeth Fry, with Herbert Hale and witnesses, Court House. (Reception at Victoria Falls Hotel)

5. A ganger and his family, 1904/5

6. "Ganger's wife - a communicant", 1904/5

7. Philip Barrington Simeon, 1885-1892, originator of the Railway Mission

8. The Staff, plus 'pill-box' coach, 1899
Leonard Moxon, Ambrose Leefe, W A Hewett;
Henry Forshaw, Josiah Ngcambu, Douglas Ellison, Fred Rogers

9. Staff on Retreat, Irene, 1940
Theodore Franklin, Harold Insley, Arthur Hobson, Stephen Skemp;
Gwen Bliss, Hilda Venables, Maude Agg-Large, Monica James,
Helen Paterson, Arthur Lee

10. Staff on Retreat, Irene, 1954
Lavinia Roberts [Fidgin], Lilah White, Connie Saunders [Piers];
Arthur Hobson, Richard Hughes, Ray White, J L Durant (Secr.),
Stephen Easter; Michael Fidgin, Charles Sutton

11. Herbert Hale and railway folk on pump trolley
on the "72 mile straight" near Wankie, Rhodesia, 1904

12. Pay Train, near Gwelo, Rhodesia, 1906

13. Herbert Hale, with bike, bags, books and camera, Gwanda, Rhodesia, 1905

14. Transport to Maun, Ngamiland, 1954

15. Station Master and children, Dullstroom, 1952

16. Mission coach in its siding, Dullstroom, 1952

17. "Mission coach on the back of 1504 Up", Santa, 1952

18. Inside a Mission coach (Bulawayo Railway Museum), showing portable organ, with the altar next to the fridge!

19. The Victoria Falls Bridge nears completion, April 8/10, 1905
"Loose planks laid down on the open girders" (Hale)

20. Opening ceremony, Victoria Falls Bridge, September 12, 1905
Sir George Darwin, son of Charles Darwin, performed the opening ceremony as President of the visiting British Association. Herbert Hale preached at the Association's Church Service in Bulawayo

21. A Rhodesia Railways' train crosses the Victoria Falls Bridge

22. Missioners and African carriers at Livingstone station, 1905

23. Lone Afrikaner Sunday School boy, Rayton, 1935
(Pretoria - Lourenco Marques line)

24. 'Lone Scouts' at camp, Transvaal, 1953

25. Sunday School party at Mission coach, Rhodesia, 1970s

26. Family gathering after a baptism at a Mission coach, Rhodesia, 1970s

27. Serowe ("Khama's Town"), August 23, 1905

28. "The parish for the day", the Karroo, 1952

29. Paddle steamer for Sena Sugar Estates, 1942

30. Sena Sugar Estate's "Whizz-bang" to Marromeu, 1953/4

31. The Mission coach, with Norman Faull, visits Lusaka, 1930
Lusaka's only place of worship until 1932

32. Laying the foundation-stone of St. Mark's, Lobatsi, July 29, 1934
The stone was laid by Sir Herbert Stanley, High Commissioner for South Africa. The Service was conducted by the Bishop of Kimberley, with the Mission Head, Lawrence Hands (on bishop's left), and missioner Allen Rusbridger (by the stone).
The Head died suddenly just three weeks later.

33. The Railway Mission's first African priests, 1960
Noel Borerwe and Willie Sigeca

34. 'Altar of railway sleeper' - one of SACRM's postcards, 1904 & 1940s

S.A.C.R.M.—Altar of railway sleeper, the ganger the one communicant in the "bush" alongside Line, Rhodesia.

35. Railway worker and observer at Beira, 1968

36. "Lady Missioner (Rachel Davies) meets Railway Staff"
Michael Fidgin filming at Palapye, 1960

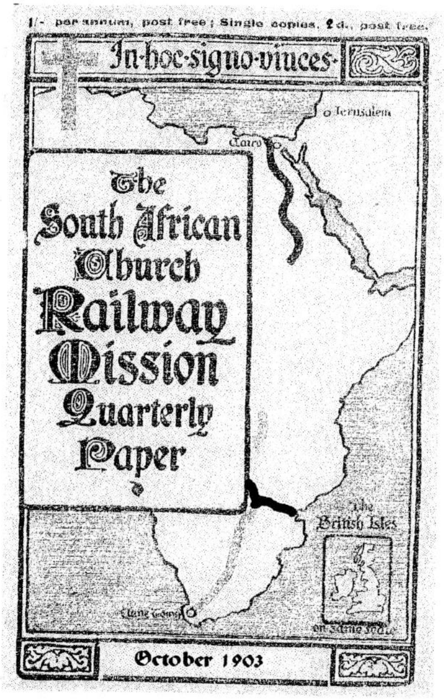

37. First issue of the 'Blue Quarterly', October 1903

38. Final issue of the 'Blue Quarterly', December 1964

39. THE SPIRITUAL RAILWAY

(By a Ganger on the C.S.A.R.)

The Line to Heaven by Christ was made,
With Heavenly Truths the Rails were laid:
From earth to Heaven the Line extends
To Life Eternal where it ends.
The Station is Repentance true,
Where passengers can all book through;
No fee for them there is to pay,
For Jesus is Himself the Way.
The Bible is the Engineer,
It points the way to Heaven so clear;
Through tunnels dark and dreary here,
It does the way to glory steer.
God's love's the fire, the steam is Truth
Which drives the engine well, forsooth.
All you who would to glory ride,
Must come to Christ, in Him abide.
No first saloon, or third or second,
All classes one by Him are reckoned.
By penitence, faith and holy living,
To God alone the glory giving,
You must the way to Heaven gain
Or you with Christ can never reign.
Come then, poor sinners, now's the time!
At any station on the Line,
If you repent, and turn from sin,
The train will stop and take you in.

(*Quarterly* No.25, October 1909, p.1)

40. Railway Mission Christmas card

> Johannesburg, June 26th: The linking-up of the Union railways with the German South-West Africa system is a remarkable record, all material having been brought four hundred miles. It will be an enormous advantage to General Botha's advance northwards, assuring regular food supplies, and it will also mean a considerable saving, as the costly item of sea transport now disappears.

Just fourteen days later, on 9 July 1915, the Germans surrendered to the (South African) Union Defence Forces, led by General Botha, the Prime Minister of the Union, and General Smuts, his Minister of Defence. The Union government had been given the 'go-ahead' by Britain, three days after the declaration of War, to occupy and seize vital parts of 'German South-West'. Many of the Boers strongly disagreed with the actions of the Union Government, and some, with the approval of Germany, rebelled against the Union in order to rid themselves of British rule. The Boer rebellion was crushed (by February 1915), the German forces surrendered and Botha issued a Proclamation notifying the conquest of Deutsch-Sudwestafrika, and placed the country under martial law.

Almost immediately Archbishop Carter and the Anglican bishops of the Province of South Africa wrote:

> It must be a matter of deep thankfulness to us all that hostilities have ceased and the campaign in S.W. Africa has been brought to a close without serious bloodshed. We are now faced with the responsibility as churchmen of seeing that the civil and military population of the occupied territory is not left without the ministrations of the Church, and also that the opportunities of direct mission work among the natives are not neglected. [41]

It was clear that these bishops, along with the Bishop of Kimberley and Kuruman and the Head of the Railway Mission, wanted clergy to minister to troops and others along the line into the newly conquered territory. Yet, at the end of August 1915, printed in October, Frederick Rogers could only report: 'I still have hopes that we may be allowed to take our part in the spiritual work of S.W. Africa, but at present the arrangements are still under discussion.' Presumably he had been hoping that Mr. Thorne would have been able to continue his work. Rogers was, at the same time, stepping down from being the Head of the Railway Mission. He had been a missioner since 1899 and Head since 1912. He was to continue helping SACRM, and be a vice-Head, into the mid-1920s. Canon Thornely Jones took over as the new Head of the Mission.

In March 1916 Thornely Jones gave a full report on the work of the Mission at the AGM in London. His remarks about South-West Africa, particularly regarding the initial coolness from the governing authorities about mission work, and the isolation of railway people, have been detailed in Chapter 3 in its overview of the development of SACRM. However, in the same issue of the *Quarterly* that gave the AGM Reports, there appeared a full account of the start, by Everard Esdaile, of Railway Mission work in South West Africa. The Rev. E.G.K. Esdaile had joined the Mission in 1913 and had been based latterly at Waterval Boven in the Diocese of Pretoria. His letter about his first month's work is lengthy and was quoted extensively in Dorothy Ellison's *God's Highwaymen.* However, it is so full of interest that its main features need quoting here, or this account would be distorted:

> Kuibus. S.W.A. Protectorate, Feb.22nd, 1916;
>
> I ... arrived at Keetmanshoop on Thursday night, 20th, at 11 p.m., unheralded ... I spent Sunday there, and was lucky enough to get through to Windhuk in thirty hours by two specials, the second from Marienthal conveying seventy-five camels. It was my first experience of protracted travelling by box-truck, which is the normal rule in this benighted land, and I needed the wash and shave at the drinking-fountain at Windhuk Station, ... the only alternative to a German hotel ... I am quite looking forward to getting back to Windhuk to enjoy the quarters allotted to me, a notable clergy house called "Six Men House", including three military chaplains, Anglican, Presbyterian and Wesleyan, and myself .... Massive German furniture showered upon us ... As all three chaplains were either north of Windhuk or moving north, I arranged to go right away (without waiting for my camp or caboose equipment) to Ludoritzbucht [Luderitz], which I did in comfort owing to the kindness of a [Railway] boiler-inspector, in sharing his reserved coach ... A considerable proportion of the dunes is pinned down with canvas to prevent the waste of time and labour caused by sand drifts on the line. Gangs of boys and several sand-dredges are going all the time keeping it clear. In Ludoritzbucht the evening service was held in the German Lutheran Church, and the new Constabulary swelled the numbers to over a hundred ... A school has been started for English and Dutch [Boer] children on Shark Island, close to the Hospital, connected by a causeway with the mainland. About thirty children attend, and it was a pleasure to find a Sunday School already started. I stopped at two small stations, Tschaukaib and Garub [42] on the way up to Aus, and enjoyed the hospitality of the Station Masters (in each case without a staff). An early morning

Intercession Service [Prayers for those fighting in the War - in Africa and in Europe - and for civilians] and an Evening Service were held, the latter in the open-air for ten Europeans with a background of thirty Ovamba railway boys, who helped to make the service still more impressive in the moonlight by their reverent silence.

Then three days Camp at Aus, where I was made most comfortable, rather enjoying the novel experience of "visiting" in tents. I held [Holy Communion] Celebrations in the Reading tent and in Hospital, and about two hundred men were present at the evening service ... As soon as I get my caboose, and the Archbishop of Cape Town sends another man to be stationed in the South, I can begin on my proper work, which is the visiting of small stations all over the Protectorate. It is a hard country, and many Railwaymen, I am sorry to say, have been broken by it. I can see many others who are going the same way ... Quite a few I already know ...[43]

By the time that Esdaile wrote again, in July 1916, he was able to report that he had been able to welcome Archdeacon Fogarty at Windhuk, who was taking with him two or three priests, giving a 'brighter outlook to the English Church.' In the October *Light for the Line* Esdaile acknowledged that the arrival of Archdeacon Fogarty and the other clergy had 'modified considerably [his] plans as a Railway Chaplain.' This was because all the large centres were therefore 'properly provided for' and he was free to 'devote [himself] exclusively to reaching the small stations and sidings, of which there [were] some 67 still untouched by [his] brother clergy.'[44]

The missioner had met many railway people at the stations along the line, some of whom had been ministered to by SACRM in the Union of South Africa. He also reported: 'I am now the proud possessor of a German [railway] truck, 1017, converted, with kitchen, pantry, and bed-sitting room ... The P.W.D. have supplied me with stove, bed, mattress and chair, and the Railway Truckfitters put in a bookcase ...[45]

Nelson Fogarty had been among the first ten Railway Missioners, joining the Grahamstown Diocesan Railway Mission in 1896 and mainly working with the men building the line to Bulawayo. During the Anglo-Boer War he had been a military chaplain and then in 1901 became the Principal of St. Mary's Training College at Thlotse in Basutoland (Lesotho), going on to be the Director of the Government Industrial School in Maseru. Archbishop Carter, in 1916, asked Nelson Fogarty to undertake new work in Damaraland (he was currently a chaplain to the Union Defence Forces in South-West Africa) and he became Archdeacon, and subsequently vicar-general and finally Bishop.

Archdeacon Fogarty gave an account of his work in October 1916, mentioning that he had travelled 3,275 miles by train and 142 by mule-cart, and that at every place he had been 'most kindly received by the people and [had] had Celebrations of the Holy Communion and other services. [He found] people thankful for the ministrations of the Church and glad they [were] not forgotten.'[46]

In the second half of 1916 Canon Thornley Jones, SACRM Head, travelled 14,000 miles visiting most of the Railway Mission work and staff. At Karabib, in South West Africa, he found 'Mr. Esdaile "gone in", and no wonder when one thinks of what his eight months in the Captured Territory involved.' He was obliged to send the missioner to the south coast (Grahamstown Diocese?) to recuperate, noting that the authorities had appreciated Esdaile's work and had withdrawn the converted truck, 'fitting up for future use a German saloon ...'[47]

The same issue of the *Quarterly* (January 1917) contained a letter from the Rev. Martyn Harries, temporarily moved one thousand miles from his SACRM work centred on Cradock, to relieve the sick Esdaile. He points out that, 'for the time being, [he was] acting as a Military Chaplain, as well as a Railway Chaplain.' This is a helpful reminder of the fact that the crucial part of the Railway Mission work in South West Africa was linked with military chaplaincy. Once the First World War had ended, SACRM work, as we shall see, was to be more limited and occasional.

Bishop Chandler of Bloemfontein made an extensive tour of South West Africa, after Easter 1917, at Archbishop Carter's request. After commenting about the continuing 'Germanness' of the country, he wrote:

> The work of the Church is carried on under great difficulties. Perhaps the greatest is that we have not a single building of our own in the whole country, and cannot begin to put up any till the destiny of the country is determined. [It was still in doubt at that time whether the country would return to Germany or become part of the Union of South Africa. The 1919 Treaty of Versailles established the Mandate.] The result is that the clergy as they travel round have to take with them all the necessary plant .. it is genuine pioneer work.[48]

Railway Missioners were, of course, quite used to having no permanent church building and to taking with them 'all the necessary plant'. South West Africa gave some parochial clergy and their hierarchy a useful insight into the 'normal' working conditions of their Railway Mission brethren. After his six months' enforced rest, Everard Esdaile returned to his work in 'SW.' He was helped by a 'Cape boy', to whom the Administration had granted a free Pass. With the arrival and work of Archdeacon Fogarty and his assistant priests, Esdaile could report:

All the big centres have Services monthly, Keetmanshoop two Sundays a month, and Windhuk every Sunday, and it becomes possible for a Railway Chaplain to devote himself to his real work amongst the people living at the small stations and sidings. I have just spent a month between Keetmanshoop and Windhuk, and I would have liked to have spent longer. Six out of fourteen children baptised [by him] were of an age to receive instruction ... There were Confirmation candidates ... and isolated Communicants who needed more encouragement than one could give in a day or so.

I have had the pleasure of completing the work of distributing Christmas toys to some 80 children between Seeheim and Nakop [in June!] ... In one way I think in S.W. we are ahead of the Union, and that is in the employment of female labour. Most of the small stations are shut up, and the ganger's [gangers'] wives answer the telephone. In some cases they supervise coal stages and water stations, and have a certain amount of bookwork involving the handling of cash ...[49]

The employment of women during both that War and the Second World War was also a very noticeable change in Britain itself. Shortage of men was not confined to South West Africa.

The editors of *Light for the Line* came to realise that there was a great deal of interest in the 'South-West' among their readers in southern Africa. In the July 1918 and the following two issues they reprinted, from the George *Diocesan Magazine),* the account by the Bishop of George of his visit to the Protectorate in the early part of 1918. He went at the request of the Archbishop of Cape Town, and his report ran to twenty four pages, almost 15,000 words. The bishop's account is a fascinating and detailed journal. As most of his travelling was done by train, the railways and the stations and their personnel, including gangers, are all especially singled out. The work of the Anglican Church, namely that of Archdeacon Fogarty and his clergy, is commended. Yet, nowhere is there a single mention of the South African Church Railway Mission. The writer cannot have been ignorant of Esdaile's work, particularly as he spent part of his time visiting the Protectorate in the company of Archdeacon Fogarty, the former SACRM missioner. Perhaps this member of the Anglican hierarchy, the first South African-born Anglican bishop, was one of those who were suspicious of the itinerant 'trek parsons'. In stark contrast to the extremely lengthy account in *Light for the Line,* the visit went unreported in the 'Blue Quarterly'.

Other than one or two very brief mentions in 1918 and 1919 *Light for the Line* magazines, the final (extant) account of Railway Mission work in South West Africa during the 1914-18 conflict appeared in the July 1918 *Quarterly.* Esdaile had been continuing his itinerant ministry, taking

Services in many different centres, as well as in scattered, lonely communities. Confirmation instruction had taken place, particularly at farms, though this had proved difficult because of various interruptions. He pointed out, after a ganger had been seriously injured, the difficulty of getting medical attention in emergencies. This was due to 'the distances between stations in S.W. [combined] with scarcity of doctors corresponding to the very thin population.'[50] There was no weekly trip of a Railway Medical Officer, as in the Union. The missioner was attempting to start 'two Circulating Libraries in the South' for the use of gangers and their families. There were, in fact, two schemes already in operation, that of 'Comforts Committees' and that of the 'Institute Library'. These schemes, however, seemed to by-pass the railway workers in the southern part of the country. It is unclear whether or not Esdaile's library scheme worked out, for the lack of Minutes for the period and a gap of five years in the known copies of the *Quarterly* currently prevent the question being resolved.

Thornley-Jones resigned as Head of SACRM in April 1923 and was replaced by the Rev. Harold Rolfe. Shortly after the obligatory visit to Britain, on taking up his responsibilities, and the visiting of his staff, he reported:

> Mr. Rogers [former Head] is up in South West Africa at the moment helping Bishop Fogarty. The railway work formerly done by the Mission in this part is now being done by the Bishop and his staff. This is most advantageous, as it relieves an already overworked Mission Staff from one of the Sections [railway areas]. Mr. Rogers writes that his admiration for the Bishop and his staff increases in inverse ratio to his admiration for the country ...[51]

Two years later, in his 'Letter from the Head', Rolfe reported that 'Mr. Robinson, now at Naauwpoort, [will be enabled] to do some work in the Free State and part of South-West Africa that has been waiting for some time to be done.'[52] Reginald Robinson's own report, in the next issue of the *Quarterly* (May 1927), was destined to be the very last account of any work in the territory undertaken by the Railway Mission. Even the words 'South-West Africa' are only mentioned subsequently in a work such as *God's Highwaymen.* Writing from Naauwpoort, Robinson reported:

> Since writing my last letter I have had a trip up into South-West Africa and shall be going again next week. I formerly thought that around Naauwpoort was one of the most desolate spots in Africa, but I have now changed my mind ...

> The country [after De Aar] seemed to get drier and more desolate every mile (except at Upington where we crossed the Orange River), and one scarcely saw a human being except at sidings and stations. Even there one found only half-a-dozen or so white people and about a dozen natives. This isolation is fearfully trying and especially for the women folk. There is nothing to do except work.
>
> On arrival at Keetmanshoop, my destination, I went to my room at the hotel and after some breakfast started to visit the English Church people. ... I was surprised at the number of Churches in Keetmanshoop. In addition to our Church there was a Wesleyan, Dutch Reformed (the largest congregation), German, Seventh Day Adventists, Roman Catholic, Jewish Synagogue, and one other ... Considering the population is about 1,000, some of the congregations cannot be very big. Another port of call in S.W.A. is Kalkfontein [= Karasburg] ... even worse than Keetmanshoop ... The English people in Keetmanshoop are hoping shortly to have a priest stationed amongst them ...[53]

We may assume that Mr. Robinson did go the 'next week' to re-visit places along the first two hundred miles of the railway as it entered the 'South-West' from Upington. It is clear that his heart was not in that particular work. He was used to far busier and less lonely railway centres, such as Naauwpoort and De Aar. The diocesan and parochial structures had taken over the bulk of such Anglican work as was then possible in the Mandated territory. The South African Church Railway Mission had completed its task there and it needed to use its slender resources of staff and of money where they could be of more use. The Rev. Reginald Robinson's closing words in his report (with reference to Keetmanshoop, or possibly to Kalkfontein/Karasburg) are a suitable and pleasant finale to SACRM work in South-West Africa:

> The Church is a lovely building and they all seem to love it.

Maun, centre of Ngamiland (Bechuanaland/Botswana)

> It was sad to have to leave Maun today on our return journey - this country is so fascinating and the idea of returning to that hole Mafeking is most unwelcome.[54]

> ... at 12.45 we arrived at the dreadful village of Maun, chief village of Ngamiland, and the most desolate and forbidding of villages in the country.[55]

The contrasting views of Colonel Charles Rey, Resident Commissioner of Bechuanaland Protectorate from 1929 to 1937, regarding Maun are not too surprising - given his strong, contradictory and blunt nature. To go on a month's 'great trek' to the north-west of his 'domain', away from the administrative headquarters of Mafeking, which were not even in the Protectorate, was a refreshing change. Heat, drought and sand, coupled with endless 'troubles' (political and 'tribal') resulted in Maun loosing its attraction for Rey.

However, for thirty years - 1934 to 64 - Maun was to be a magnet for the Railway Missioners whose Section was on the line between Mafeking and Bulawayo. Although, as we have seen, SACRM had always brought the Church's ministrations to non-railway people who lived within a reasonable, cycling distance of the railway, Maun was the great exception, for it was over four hundred miles by road, west of the line.

Khama's appeal to the British Government for 'protection' against the land-hungry Boers and the South-West African Germans, resulted in his country becoming the Protectorate of Bechuanaland in 1895. Through a large part of 1895 Rhodes and the British South Africa Company 'negotiated with the imperial government for the transfer to the Company of territory in the Protectorate. Ostensibly this territory was required for colonization and the further extension of the railway.'[56] It soon became clear that the BSA Co. wanted possession of the narrow 'railway corridor' on Bechuanaland's eastern border in order to launch the invasion into the Transvaal (the Jameson Raid). Despite the political disaster of the ill-advised and bungled Raid, railway development continued, even with a new sense of urgency. As we noted in Chapter 2, the line north from Mafeking was started in late 1895, and reached Bulawayo in November 1897.

> Maun is the administrative centre and principal village in the Ngamiland district ... There are four European stores, representing wealthy trading interests as this is a great cattle buying centre. But the Europeans mostly a bit mixed in blood, are a ghastly crew ... hardly anybody from the outside ever comes here ...
> ... after lunching at the Residency I went back to Camp and met all the European men - traders, cattle-buyers, and storekeepers, mixed blood mostly, some Greeks and a couple of Jews - no self-respecting person could live here through the rains ...[57]

Rey's somewhat extreme views of Maun's European population were fortunately not shared by the Railway missioners. They were quite used to ministering to all kinds of people in whatever circumstances they found them. The 'challenge' of Maun and district was the journey entailed in reaching the people, not the inhabitants themselves.

In April 1934 subscribers to the SACRM *Quarterly* may have been surprised to read the letter from the Rev. Allen Rusbridger. Towards the end of his account he put:

> In the Bechuanaland Protectorate the railway only traverses a narrow strip of it near its Eastern border. To the West of the railway is the Kalahari Desert, uninhabited save for bushmen and white settlers at the few-and-far-between water holes. One of the places where there is quite a number of white people is at Lake Ngami, five hundred miles west of the railway - a spot mentioned by Livingstone on his journey to Central Africa. A lorry goes there once every two or three months from Palapye Road, and through the kindness of the owners, I hope to be able to make a trip there in April or May. It will be an opportunity of ministering to very isolated people ...[58]

It is not clear when Rusbridger first had the idea of going to Lake Ngami. His Diaries show that he had met the SACRM Head twice in early 1934, and it may be that this was discussed then. His very detailed Diary for 1932 (one page to a day) and the, smaller, Diary for 1933 make no mention of discussions regarding trips away from the line of rail, other than Serowe. In a private letter (Nov. 9, 1980) Allen Rusbridger stated:

> ... a few notes about the time, 1932-1938, I was a chaplain on the S.A.C.R.M.
>
> I had what was known as the Kimberley section since I was based at Beaconsfield - a suburb of Kimberley. My section went from just above De Aar to just below Francistown ... 800 miles.
>
> I had no coach as there was sufficient hospitality to make sure that I was adequately fed & housed ... it meant that I had to trundle suit-cases, portable altar & bicycle during my six-weekly trips up the section.
>
> I visited 36 places with congregations varied from one to forty. The one was a coloured ganger whose family were in Capetown for schooling, to the Sunday services which were attended by railway staff, colonial service personnel, farmers & traders. We built two churches ...
>
> My schedule revolved round 5 Sunday places, Modder Rivier, Warrenton, Lobatsi, Mahalapye & Palapye, with the isolated farms & cottages having services during week days ...[59]

The planned trip to Lake Ngami in April/May 1934 did not take place, possibly due to the fact that the missioner had his suitcase, which contained most of his clothes, stolen from a train. From the start of his SACRM work he had made short trips, by car, away from the railway line. These were to the 'native stadt' at Mochudi, just east of the line above Gaberones, and to Serowe, the Tswana capital in the Bamangwato Reserve, some sixty miles north of Mahalapye, or thirty north-west of Palapye Road. On his first trip to Serowe, Rusbridger recorded:

> Track road very jolty, one slight breakdown ... Serowe - very large native camp about 20,000 strong, second largest in Africa ... Service in European Church at 8 ... H[oly] C[ommunion] at 7.30 [a.m., next day]. 2 others present ...[60]

The first visit to Maun and Lake Ngami did not take place until January 1935. Rusbridger's Diary for that year has not been preserved, but fortunately the 1934 diary included the first two weeks of January 1935 - the only extant account of this visit:

> January 1935: Serowe, MONDAY 7th - Waiting for lorry, but no word yet. Chance tomorrow...
>
> Serowe, TUESDAY 8th, The Road:
> Left at 7.30 for Lake in Gov.nt [vehicle]. 3 of us.. heavy going about 7 mile an hour. Slept at Co[?] Camp.
>
> The Road, WEDNESDAY 9th:
> Travelling all day. Through salt pans Mopipi, Rakops & slept about 30 miles out. Plenty of eland ...
>
> Maun, THURSDAY 10th:
> Arrived 10.30. Stayed at Capt. & Mrs. [?] ... Met several people ...
>
> Maun, FRIDAY 11th:
> H.C. 7.30. 9 cc [communicants]. 1st time in history E.C [English Church, ie. Anglican] service here. Left at 3pm ... stop at 11.
>
> Road, SATURDAY 12th:
> Breakfast Rakops. Drove all day until about 8.30 when slept 10 [?] miles out of Serowe. Fast travelling not much game ...[61]

This pioneering visit by the Railway missioner went unreported in the 1935 *Quarterly* magazines, although at the SACRM Annual Meeting, on May 14th 1936, supporters were told:

> In the south the chaplain had occasion last year to go up to Lake Ngami where there was a temporary Government Camp, amongst whom were camp inspectors, border police etc. The chaplain was asked to go up, and it involved for him a journey of three days by lorry, and there was no one but he who could have gone up, because there were no other priests for four hundred miles.[62]

There was almost a two-year gap between the first and second visits by SACRM to Maun. In November 1936 Allen Rusbridger went on his next trip across the Kalahari, a trip that was fully reported in both the Spring and Summer 1937 issues of the *Quarterly.* Along with a travelling dentist, a young Afrikaner ('Dutch') cattle driver and two Africans, the missioner travelled in a 3 1/2-ton Dodge post-lorry across the deep sand track, and slithered along the sticky 'black turf', following torrential rain.

> We had taken a day to do about forty miles, and as the post lorry was under contract to get to Maun by Saturday, 1 p.m., or else be subject to a fine of l0s [50p] for every hour late, we had to get a move on. Next morning we left about 6 a.m., ... we drove all that day and most of the night, reaching our destination between 3 a.m., and 4 a.m., on the Saturday morning .
> ... We had the service of Holy Communion on the Sunday morning, and nine came to make what will have to be their annual Communion. There is a London Missionary Society worker stationed here, so the free church people are able to have services occasionally ["when his native work allows it". [63]] Motor transport has enabled us to come now and do in three days what formerly took over five weeks by ox-waggon ... [64]

We may assume that the reason for the trip being only an annual one was the fact that there were no railway workers at the receiving end. The difficulties of the journey were not a limiting factor. Rusbridger told his readers, in the first account of that trip, that 'the railway do not mind us going off at a tangent occasionally when there is no one else to go.' The issue of free Passes by the Railways to SACRM staff did limit their non-railway work. There is no known account of any Anglican work at Maun before this period, so the comments about 'five weeks by ox-waggon' seem rather superfluous in the context. By contrast, in more recent times priests would go by plane from Mahalapye, leaving after breakfast, taking a Service at Maun, and then return by lunch! Transport development has reduced a journey from five weeks to five days, and then to five hours. However, anyone who travels by car or lorry is still likely to have problems, despite the tarmacing of some sections.

The Rev. Arthur Lee took over Rusbridger's section when he left at the end of 1938. Lee made the annual trip to Maun in August 1939. He noted that there were about 'twenty-four white people (civil servants, traders, police)'[65] in the area. He stayed with the LMS missionary, Mr. Anderson, and his wife, who were 'very kind' to him. Lee was replaced the following year by the Rev. John Alliston, who was able to make three annual visits to Maun.

Alliston remarked how the various Europeans appreciated the visit of a priest. On his second visit, in August 1941, he was asked to go beyond Maun 'to a place called Nokannen ... for a baptism.' This entailed crossing a dried-up Lake Ngami. His third and final trip (September 1943) coincided with a Day of National Prayer, on the anniversary of the start of the Second World War, and he joined in a large open-air service at Maun, attended by hundreds of local 'Batawana' as well as most of the Whites in the area. On his return he travelled in a convoy of seven lorries 'full of natives from Ngamiland, Ovamboland and Angola'[66] who had been recruited by W.N.L.A for work in the South African mines. After taking his leave of them in Francistown, Alliston was moved to question whether or not the system was right - 'plenty of black labour, plenty of organisation so that the dividends can be paid.' This is a relatively rare example of a missioner raising such a moral / ethical question in the pages of SACRM's official journal. He did not, of course, go on to question the role of the Railway authorities in African labour recruitment.

The Rev. Fred Naylor joined the Railway Mission at the end of 1940. His chief work was on the Bulawayo to Salisbury (Harare) to Beira sections, with periodic visits to Sena Sugar Estates, as we shall observe later. However, added to his normal work was the annual trip to Maun and Ngamiland and he gave readers of the 'Blue Quarterly' vivid accounts of his journeys.

His first account was in 1948, a five year gap following Alliston's last report, though it is clear from his opening remarks - 'The Maun trip, as I always call it..' - that this was not his first journey to Maun. Thirteen years had passed since Rusbridger's pioneering trip and the visit now took in far more than just a short stay in Maun itself. Naylor, travelling 'in a convoy of nine lorries which were returning "Boys" who had finished a period on the gold mines', carefully names all the villages and rest camps they passed through - Moseke, Nata, Odiakoe, Kanyu ('Where [he] met the only white person on that route between Francistown and Maun'), then Maun, Tsau and Norkanen. At Maun, a scattered 'town', with 'the recruiting depot at one end, and the hospital, five miles away, at the other end [with] ... the Hotel approximately half way', Naylor did what visiting he could, as well as arrange Services for the following Sunday.

A good one hundred and fifty miles north of Tsau was Shakawe, on the extreme northern border of the Protectorate:

> Wednesday afternoon saw us at Shakawe - often called Mohembo, though Mohembo is really the police camp a few miles farther on [by the crossing into the Caprivi Strip]. Shakawe is another recruiting depot with a couple of trading stores and a large African population.[67]

Fred Naylor had a day and a half at Shakawe, talking, visiting, showing that 'the Church' cared for people. What is not immediately obvious from the account, and we may surmise that few readers were aware of, is that this had been a journey over six hundred miles, from Francistown to Shakawe, travelling in a bumpy lorry 'through the dust and heat of the day and the piercing cold of the late evening and early morning ... denied proper facilities for washing and shaving ...' Readers were aware that 'the Congo' was a far off place, yet even the single trip to Leopoldville entailed a shorter and more comfortable (boat) non-railway section of the journey than this road trip to Shakawe. This, most certainly, was the furthest that the Railway Mission ever went away from the line of rail.

I asked Fred Naylor what he thought were the strong points of the Mission, what was its real work and purpose:

> It was keeping people in touch with religion, because they didn't see a parson ... They'd say, " Good Lord, a parson! I haven't seen one for years!" And I remember when I went off across the desert, the Kalahari, to Ghanzi ... to Maun. I remember there was another outpost further up [Shakawe] and they used to have a telephone ... The woman in Maun would ring up this chap at the other end, higher up, and I remember the conversation, "Oh, is it all right if the padre comes?" "The what?" "The padre." "Oh, send him up if he's got a tennis racket!" On those trips I started from Francistown - staying at Riley's Hotel - went in a convoy with the WNLA people repatriating African workers. They would come back with new recruits. I sometimes went with the Education man in his Bedford, or with the doctor.[68]

Naylor's next trip to Maun (June 1949) broke new ground in that a woman missioner, his wife Gwen, also went along. At Sehitwa, seventy miles south-west of Maun, they spent a short time with 'a lonely trader and his wife'[69], most likely the first time that another European woman had visited the store. Constance Saunders was the next SACRM 'woman worker' to visit Maun and district, in the early 1950s. By then WNLA were augmenting their system of recruiting 'by flying [the Africans] from the various centres instead of doing the long journeys by lorry' and so the Railway Mission staff were usually spared at least one 300 mile leg of the return trip.

The visit of the SACRM Head, Ray White, and Constance Saunders in January 1954 is the final one recorded by Railway missioners. It is quite possible, however, that the Railway Mission did make further trips to Maun and Ngamiland. By 1957, when SACRM became the Rhodesia & Nyasaland Railway Mission, the work in Botswana was curtailed for a while. From then, through the period of 'The Railway Mission of the Church of the Province of Central Africa' (1964-1970) and that of 'The Railway Mission of Rhodesia & Botswana' (1970-1980), a single missioner would normally make a monthly visit to places on the line, such as Lobatsi, Gaberone, Mahalapye, Palapye and Francistown. Anywhere more than a very short distance from the line was out of the question.

The last issue of the 'Blue Quarterly' was in December 1964 (No. 215). After a short gap, Railway Mission news continued to appear in *Partners,* the journal of the Transvaal & Southern Rhodesia Missions (T & S.R.M.). Not every issue contained something about the Railway Mission, and when it did it had to be contained within a page or so. The days of the twenty-two page *Quarterly* were truly over. Maun made its final appearance in *Partners* in May 1964. On this occasion, instead of the Railway Mission coming, as it so often did, to the aid of a parish or diocese, we read of the Rector of Francistown, with his wife, responding to a request from the Mission. The Rev. Peter Bloomfield had already been taking Communion, on the Railway Mission's behalf, to a few stations on the line south of Francistown. He was allowed the use of the Mission coach for this. The trip to Maun was different:

> Every week Wenela [WNLA] run a Dakota to Maun, returning the same day, and it was through this service that I was able to visit Maun just after Christmas.
>
> I get to the airport at 5.30 a.m., and all is ready for the take-off ... for the first 100 miles or so, we fly at a fair height ... for the rest of the 300-mile trip, we are flying at 150 feet, first over a vast salt pan ... Just before Maun, we ascend again for the landing, and at 7.45 we touch down on the grassy air-strip ...
>
> The "terminal buildings" at Maun consist of a pole carrying a wind-sock. [A photograph of the airstrip taken by a missioner shows a pole with the notice attached: "If you require a motor car or other

assistance please wave your handkerchief in direction of town." Landing at a much-enlarged Maun airport today, a visitor will find up to twenty or more light aircraft parked by 'real' terminal buildings.]

Here the District Commissioner, Ian Gass, is waiting to take me to the Court Room where we are to hold the service. Our congregation is again very small as it is a working day, and many of the men-folk are out on duty in the bush ...

During the morning, I go to the local hotel where I baptize the child of the hotel proprietor and his wife. A salad bowl serves as the font ... Then back to Ian and Ruth Gass for an early lunch ... As soon as the plane is heard approaching, we hurry off to the air-strip as they don't wait for any length of time... At 3.30 p.m. we begin a slow descent to Francistown ... [70]

Almost thirty years had passed since Allen Rusbridger had first taken the ministrations of the 'English Church' to Maun. The South African Church Railway Mission had started its limited response to the perceived needs of the white population of Ngamiland in the years just prior to the Second World War; it bowed out of the work just before the first general elections were held in Bechuanaland, and Seretse Khama became the first President of the Republic of Botswana.

Beira and the Sena Sugar Estates

In the interest of both Powers, Portugal agrees to grant absolute freedom of passage between the British sphere of influence and Pungwe Bay [Beira] for all merchandise of every description, and to give the necessary facilities for the improvement of the means of communication.

The Portuguese Government agrees to construct a railway between Pungwe and the British sphere ... [alternatively] will give the construction of the railway to a Company ... The said Company shall have all requisite facilities for the acquisition of land, cutting timber, and free importation and supply of materials and labour. [71]

Visits by Railway Missioners to the port of Beira and to officials and families working for the Sena Sugar Estates owe their origin to the 1891 Anglo-Portuguese treaty and the concessions which followed in its wake.

The Beira Railway Company started its construction of the line from Fontesville, on the Pungwe River, towards the Rhodesian border in 1892. In April 1895 the Beira Railway Company transferred its rights to construct the line east of Fontesville to the Paris Exploitation Company

Ltd, which then formed the Beira Junction Railway (Port Beira to Fontesville) Limited. It was this Company which constructed the 35 1/2 mile section from Beira to Fontesville, with the Beira Railway Company building the remaining 168 1/2 miles to Umtali, six miles across the Rhodesian border. In 1930 the Beira Junction Railway was absorbed by the Beira Railway Company, with the whole 204 miles being owned by that Company, controlled by the British South Africa Company, and being worked as part of the Mashonaland and Rhodesian Railways. The Mashonaland Railway Company was absorbed by the Rhodesia Railways Ltd in 1937.

The sovereign powers of the Companhia de Mocambique were due to expire in July 1942, and the British and Southern Rhodesian Governments were concerned that Portuguese changes might prejudice Rhodesian interests. Rhodesian Railways were asked to formulate a statement of the general position. In their memorandum, dated 23.9.1941, the Rhodesian Railways stated, of the line:

> It is the railway directly connecting with the Port of Beira, the eastern terminus and sea outlet for over 2,500 miles of railways operated in the territories of Northern and Southern Rhodesia, Nyasaland and Mocambique.
>
> Beira is the chief port for the Rhodesias, and some 90 per cent. of their imports and practically the whole of their exports go by this route ... It may ... be taken for granted that the Portuguese Government will, after it has taken into its own hands the administration now being carried on by the Companhia de Mocambique, continue to respect the various agreements with the British Companies affected which handle the traffic ...[72]

The line from Beira - Machipanda/S. Rhodesia border was eventually purchased by the State (P.E.A) on 7th April 1949, and was administered by the State from October of that year (C.F.M - the Caminhos de Ferro Mocambique). The construction of the Central Africa Railway lines and of those of the Trans-Zambesia Railway, making the link between Beira and Nyasaland, has been detailed in Chapter 2.

There were two other routes of relevance to this study: firstly, the purely Portuguese 175 miles-long Tete Railway, which ran from Dona Ana, on the north bank of the Zambezi, via Entroncamento to the coalfields at Moatize, just across the water from Tete on the south bank. This line was started in 1939 and, after various delays, due to Pauling and Co. defaulting and to the problems associated with virtual slave labour that the contractors used, was completed in 1949. ('The last of Oury's indelible-pencil doodles had been written across central Africa.')[73]

The other relevant route was the 56 miles-long narrow-gauge private line which connected Caia, on the Trans-Zambesia line, with Marromeu, running along the south bank of the Zambezi. This line, always mentioned, as we shall note, by the Railway Missioners, was built mainly for the sugar traffic from the Sena Sugar Estates.

Anglican Diocesan boundaries in most of Africa have rarely corresponded with national boundaries, dependent as they were on the growth and history of missionary societies. Where a state was under British influence or control there was some resemblance of correlation between the 'secular and the sacred', but where, as in Mozambique's case, the country was not British colonial territory, then Anglican work was piecemeal and tidy diocesan structures and boundaries were not possible.

When Bishop Smyth, first Bishop of Lebombo, visited his new diocese in 1893 he found in this southern part of Mozambique only two communicants of the Anglican church in the whole diocese; 'there were no clergy, no churches, no schools, no organisation, and no property whatever belonging to the Church.'[74] The northern part of his diocese was at Machanga Point, at the River Save. Across the river, Anglican work was under the Diocese of Mashonaland and Bishop Knight-Bruce, shortly, in 1895, to be replaced by Bishop Gaul. In this central area of Mozambique the Diocese of Mashonaland extended to the Indian Ocean, between the rivers Save and Zambezi; the area to the north of Chinde and the Zambezi being part of the Diocese of Likoma, then recently (1892) separated from Zanzibar Diocese. The final four hundred miles of Portuguese East Africa coastal area remained as part of the Zanzibar Diocese. There were, in other words, four Anglican dioceses and bishops in Mocambique (until 1959) and these basically corresponded to the Portuguese administrative boundaries.

> By the Treaty of Berlin of 1885 and the Anglo-Portuguese Convention of 1891, the southern part of the eastern lakeshore [Nyasa], where UMCA was most active, was allotted to Portugal. So, almost by accident and a quirk of history, Anglican missionaries found themselves working in an area that was included within the Portuguese Eastern African colony of Mozambique.[75]

The UMCA missions kept a low profile in this part of northern Mozambique, and relations between the Anglicans and the few Portuguese administrators remained fairly cordial, with occasional suspicion of each others' activities. The lakeshore area was allowed to remain exclusively UMCA/Anglican until the 1940s. By then, Salazar's "Estado Novo" had made the Portuguese presence felt much more.

The Witwatersrand mines have attracted the labour of Africans in the Sul do Save (southern Mozambique) for over one hundred years. From the earliest days, many of these workers came in contact with the Anglican Church while they were in South Africa and became Christians. This was partly the reason why the Diocese of Lebombo was created, so that the new converts could continue to have the ministrations of the Church on their return home. Swiss Presbyterians and American Methodists started work in the Sul do Save at the same time as the Anglicans. All were very conscious that they were working in Portuguese territory 'and were careful not to proselytise outside the families of their converts.'[76] Salazar's Colonial Act gave to Roman Catholic missions in Mozambique a privileged position from the 1930s onwards. To some extent the Anglican Church in much of Mozambique officially was one 'Protestant sect' among others, though all their workers would have been horrified at the term 'sect'. Having said that, it did have advantages over most of the other Protestant missions: the churchmanship of the Anglicans was 'high' and therefore understood by the Portuguese; it had the British monarch as its 'Head'; and often enjoyed a greater prestige than non-Portuguese Roman Catholic missions. Lebombo, as a diocese entirely dependent upon 'missionary giving', inevitably remained extremely poor.

The central section of 'Portuguese East', as far as the Anglican Church was concerned, was that covered by the Diocese of Mashonaland, as seen earlier. More so than for the rest of Mozambique, this was a Church for the diaspora. The concern of the bishops was for those Anglicans, mainly expatriate English, who visited or lived in the Port of Beira (seamen and the diplomatic corp), those who worked along the lines of rail, and workers on the Sena Sugar Estates. Most of the Anglican ministry was undertaken by the Railway Mission or by the Missions to Seamen. In 1959 this area ceased to be part of the Diocese of Mashonaland, being incorporated into the enlarged Lebombo Diocese. In stating that Mashonaland 'lost' the port of Beira, the Sena Sugar Estates and the line of rail, 'all of which were served by the (Rhodesia) Railway Mission', J.Paul, in the 1978 Edinburgh Seminar on Mozambique (p.34), seems to infer that the work itself ceased. As we shall note below, this was not so. The diocese changed, but the work remained, at least until Independence.

The SACRM Leaflet No. 2, of 1939/40, stated:

> The Headquarters of this Section of the [Railway] Mission are at Beira, quite a large and important sea-port now ... The population is about 18,000, including European, Asiatic and Native peoples, of whom about 350 are British. To these we minister, in Beira, where

> we have the care of the little War Memorial Church built in 1924, holding services there twice monthly in normal times.
>
> From Beira the Chaplain goes out along his Section, and once a quarter he takes a trip to one of the remoter parts of the territory, to the Sena Sugar Estates on the Zambezi River, near its mouth ...[77]

The 'normal times', mentioned in this leaflet (one of four or five produced to show the different aspects and spheres of work by the South African Church Railway Mission), were presumably a reference to pre-War conditions. The leaflet gives a full description of the missioner's travels in lower Zambesia, ending at Chinde, to stay with 'some Swiss people and visit the only four British people there; celebrate Communion and conduct Evensong for ... [arguably] the smallest and remotest congregation in the Anglican Church.' The 'travel-stained, sometimes weary, but always happy' Chaplain then retraced his steps, finishing with a few days in Beira, before setting out to visit gangers, farmers and miners in his Section.

Almost certainly the Railway Missioners visited Beira in the first quarter of this century, although current research of the available evidence prevents a date earlier than 1925 being posited. The first reference in the 'Blue Quarterly' appears to be that of April 1926, when the Rev. Reginald Robinson, chaplain of the Southern Rhodesia Section, wrote (in March): 'For about two months it has been impossible to get to Beira on account of the abnormal rains.'[78] It is clear that this was not the first occasion that readers were informed about visits to Beira.

No further mentions of SACRM work at the port are evidenced until the issue of *Light for the Line,* in April 1930, with reference to a visit in December 1929. The missioner, H.S. Ram, visited 'the Portuguese East section of the line' as part of his final trip after three year's work on the Mission, and noted that the services he took at Villa Pery and Villa Machado were the first services ever to be held there 'as far as the British population [was] concerned.'[79] He borrowed the engineer's coach and visited Beira, 'which [was] regularly served from Umtali ...' In those early days the missioners usually travelled in the guard's van on scheduled mixed-goods trains. A mission coach, "pill-box" No.89599, first made a trip to Beira in April/June 1930. This was the Rev. Francis Synge's first visit to the eastern part of his Section, 'having been in Rhodesia ... for just seven weeks.'[80] Synge's next few reports suggest a pattern of quarterly or four-monthly visits east of Umtali. By 1934 the British population of Beira had grown to about five hundred. A small amount of work was undertaken among some of the Africans in Beira. The Rev. J.H. Henwood, missioner in Southern Rhodesia in 1935, wrote: 'Also, I take Native Services in

Beira as well as European, for some Nyasa boys who are working down there and were brought up by the U.M.C.A.'[81]

The indefatigable Maude Agg-Large visited many railway families along the line from Victoria Falls to Bulawayo and on to Salisbury and Beira, in an extended 'tour' in a mission coach during July and August 1931. In Beira she had 'a busy six days, seeing many fresh people.'[82] A Mr. Crowther placed his car at her disposal, enabling "Aggie" to get around the town and visit the British community in their homes. Her male colleague, Francis Synge, on his return from Beira within a week or two of her visit, officiated 'at the first wedding in the chapel of the Victoria Falls Hotel [83] [17 August, 1931].'[84]

At this period Beira was officially part of the parish of Umtali, some 203 railway-miles distant. The priest in Umtali was the Rev. A.C. Kibble and 'monthly visits [to Beira] were arranged between Mr. Kibble and the railway padre alternatively.'[85] By the end of 1934 the Railway Mission had sole charge, due to the arrival of an additional chaplain, and this 'part-time resident priest' spent half of each month in or near the port. By 1936, with the arrival of the SACRM missioner, Donald Leavey, the port had its 'only resident [full-time] English padre and the first to make [his] headquarters there.'[86]

Two attempts were made by SACRM to make some linkage with the (Anglican) Missions to Seamen. Evidence suggests that these attempts failed, although individual chaplains of the two Societies respected each others' work. The first attempt was in 1936, with the Archbishop of Capetown, as SACRM President, writing to the General Superintendent of the Missions to Seamen, in London:

> Dear Mr Trench ... I am writing to enquire whether it is possible for the Mission[s to Seamen] to give a grant to Reverend Donald Leavey who is on the South African Church Railway Mission and is also working at the port in Beira. The Railway Institute there is open to seamen and a steam launch helps Leavey to visit the ships. But he finds the expenses there more than can be met by the Diocese of Southern Rhodesia and the Railway Mission, and if he does not get rather more ... he might have to be withdrawn.
>
> ... he cannot be the whole time at Beira as he has to do the Railway work as well; but if a subsidy could be granted him it would be a great help in keeping the Seamen's work going. The Head of the Railway Mission thinks that some of Beira's Steamer Companies Officials would subscribe if the Seamen's work were made more of, and it might be on a £1 for £1 basis. But this I leave to you ...[87]

Nothing came of this. Leavey appears to have been the only Railway Missioner to have paid ship-visits. The situation changed, as we shall note, when the Missions to Seamen started to have their own chaplains in Beira.

The first Anglican ministry to the Sena Sugar Estates (SSE) was not undertaken by the Railway Mission but by Bishop Paget. It is unlikely that most readers of SACRM's *Quarterly* had ever heard of the Estates until Francis Synge wrote in February 1932:

> Another line has been added to my length [ie. not a newly-built line, but an addition to his 'Section']. When I was in Beira early in December [1931] the Bishop came down on his way to some sugar estates on the Zambesi. There are a number of keen Church people working on the estates who receive no attention from the Church owing to the difficulty of reaching them. The Bishop was doing pioneering work in ministering to them. From Beira he went up the Trans-Zambesi line and, by a variety of conveyances, reached them on the Saturday night. He had time to give them Evensong then and Communion next morning, and then returned. He has asked me to pay them a visit when I can, and I have promised to go in May and October, when there happen to be five Sundays ...[88]

The Bishop made clear, in a letter written in November 1947 from SSE at Luabo, that his first visit was in response to a telegram from 'the Secretary of [the] estates, himself the son of a Bishop.'[89] This was Mr. John Eden (strictly, the Assistant Manager) who became responsible for arranging the visits of Railway Missioners, until his promotion to the London Office in mid-1934. As we have noted in previous chapters, the South African Church Railway Mission frequently initiated new work when it saw the need. Equally, it tried to respond to requests from others for its help. In the case of the Sena Sugar Estates, the initiative was clearly made by the bishop responding to a request, who then realised how SACRM, already visiting Beira, could take over this ministry. From time to time in the next twenty years, when Railway Missioners were on leave or busier than usual, Bishop Paget returned to Sena Sugar on their behalf - a reversal of roles.

John Eden later related that they (SSE) had initially asked 'if it would be possible to send the Blessed Sacrament carefully down the river for those who wanted it.'[90] He had received a reply from Bishop Paget stating that such a request could only be granted by the Archbishop of Capetown, but that 'he himself would come on the 19th December.' These two sentences, tucked away in the extra small print of a lengthy Annual Report, are remarkable for what they imply. Firstly, the devotion and

Churchmanship of the Anglicans at SSE was clearly of a high order, with their need and respect for the Holy Communion, even when it had previously been consecrated and then given without the physical presence of a priest. Secondly, despite the fact that Paget was bishop of his own diocese, he felt that such an unusual request, involving - as it did - the most sacred elements of the (Anglican) Catholic tradition, could only be granted by his Metropolitan in Cape Town. The practicalities of sending the consecrated wafers 'carefully down the river' must have been mind-boggling. Any irreverent picture of the scene, that now comes to mind, must be tempered by the knowledge of the seriousness and sincerity of that request.

Synge apparently gave an account of his visit to the Sugar Estates when he next wrote for the 'Blue Quarterly', though sadly the relevant issue and the following two issues have not been preserved in known archives. The Annual Report for 1932 surprisingly makes no mention of SACRM's first venture to the Estates. *Light for the Line,* in December 1932, reproduced Francis Synge's colourful account of his second (or third?) visit:

> I found the Sugar Estates hard at work and hot and somewhat handicapped at sunset by the Portuguese ban on the import of whisky. It is surprising what hardships and deprivations the human frame can survive.
>
> Beira was considerably perplexed by the decree ordering every firm to employ 70 per cent Portuguese. The Shell Oil Company, at whose bachelor mess I stayed, had done nothing to comply with the law. If the decree can be enforced the British population of Beira will be greatly diminished.[91]

The Portuguese ban on spirits was due to Salazaar's new colonial policy (Colonial Act, 1930). The same Colonial Act limited the role of non-Portuguese personnel, referred to by the Rev. Synge, and prescribed the use of Portuguese as the language of instruction.

The first reasonably detailed account of a railway missioner's trip to Sena Sugar was that given by the Rev. Hugh Wilson [92] , Francis Synge's successor, in August 1934. Many such visits over the next twenty five years echoed Hugh Wilson's account and experience, though many were detailed at far greater length. His (edited) letter can stand as an exemplar for the rest:

> [The visit] ... to the Sena Sugar Estates ... proved to be one of my most enjoyable experiences up here. At Beira I had the good fortune to meet the manager of the Estates and we travelled up to Caia together, which was reached after an all-night journey at about

> 4.30 a.m. At daybreak we set off by car on a 30 mile run to the River, which we crossed while breakfasting on one of the Sugar Company's ferry boats. After the customary formalities with Immigration and Customs officials, necessitated by the fact that we were entering the Province of Quilimane [sic] from Mozambique Company's territory, we motored another 10 miles to Mopea [Mopeia]. Here I spent three days and had services on the Sunday morning. In the afternoon I was driven down to Luabo, some 60 miles distant, in time for an evening service. After two days at Luabo I boarded the ferry again, and a three hour's journey up the Zambezi brought me to Marromeu, where I had an evening service for a congregation of four. Torrential rains were responsible for the fewness in numbers. There was a rainfall of just over seven inches during the two days I was there! Despite this I got safely over the 54 miles back to Caia by motor rail trolley. Climatic conditions make life "on the River" particularly unbearable during the hot season, so I was unable to meet most of the womenfolk as they were enjoying more congenial conditions elsewhere ...[93]

Hugh Wilson made it clear to readers, in a later report (November 1934), that the reason for visits to Sena Sugar being infrequent was 'the expense of the journey', for the Estates were reached by the Trans-Zambezi Railway. 'This', he said, 'is the only line on which our free passes will not carry us.'[94] This comment may be queried, as he went on to state that 'the expenses [of the journey had] always been amply covered by the collections.'

John Eden, mentioned above, when he addressed the one hundred-strong SACRM supporters having their Annual Festival at South Africa House in Spring 1935, gave a 'thank you' for the work of the Railway Mission. He said, 'You cannot imagine what it means to us, when we have no chance of a service from year's beginning to year's end, to get four services a year - a little touch of God now and then.'[95] He went on to state that he had great hopes that the British employees would start a fund and build their own church, which would be a 'fitting house for the Railway Mission padres to ... carry on the work they helped to start.' It would appear, from later accounts, that this particular project was still-born.

Over the next twenty five years - 1935 to 1960 - the pages of SACRM's magazines contain detailed and fascinating accounts of visits to Sena Sugar Estates paid by a succession of missioners - Donald Leavey, Dennis Charlton, Maurice Lancaster, Fred Naylor, John Oldham, Stephen Easter, Richard Hughes and Hugh Palmer. Supporters of the Railway Mission learned that, 'no electric massage could equal the jolting of the sugar train', that most missioners called at Chupanga (Lacerdonia) to visit Mary Livingstone's grave 'in silent salutation to the memory of a very noble lady', that the padre might be met at Caia 'by a tall West African native interested in politics [and who] had lived in London', and that frequently 'coloured boys [sic] were under instruction for Baptism.'[96]

On the 5th November 1938 'at Luabo, Zambesi River, the little child of Mr. and Mrs. Coton of the Sena Sugar Estate Co., was baptised by the Rev. J.D.B. Charlton.'[97] This notice was given some prominence in the *Quarterly* as it was 'thought to be the first Christening of a European child on the Sugar Estates.' Molly Ada's baptism at the home of the General Manager, Mr. Thurnheer, was attended by twenty five guests. The first annual donation - of £25 - from Sena Sugar was noted in 1939. This gift continued for many years. The Tete railway, mentioned earlier, was not ignored by SACRM. Dennis Charlton informed his readers in May 1941 of the construction of this Portuguese line by Messrs. Pauling and Co. and stated, 'There are a certain number of British people connected with Pauling's firm there [Dona Ana], and I have consequently added Dona Ana to my Section ... the people are very appreciative of the services, and do all that they can to help...'[98]

Although the missioners sometimes gave the impression that they were mainly visiting 'the British' when they were on the Sugar Estates - and in one sense this was true, in that house-visiting was usually, though not always, confined to that community ('sick-visiting' could include anybody) - this was not the case regarding worship. Bishop Paget's account, referred to earlier, written from a different viewpoint from that of the missioners, was a carefully constructed article giving as much information about his trip (November 1947) as possible. En route to Chinde in the Company's paddle steamer, he stopped for one night at Luabo:

> In the evening we had a service to which about twenty people came. At the services during this visit there have been English, Scottish, Irish, Portuguese, a Czecho-Slovakian, an Hungarian, a Swiss, a Hollander, a Cape Coloured, Mauritians, people from St. Helena, Demararians, Africans, Chinese, Greeks, and so on.
>
> There is no colour discrimination in the worship here, and no difficulties arise from this indiscriminate mixture of races in the worship of the Church. The services are held in private houses, as we have .. yet no churches on the Estates. There is no allotting of special places for peoples of different colours - and I am assured that no one takes advantage of this practice and no embarrassments arise. [99]

In many ways this paragraph is one of the most remarkable accounts in the whole history of SACRM's work, albeit by a bishop! Perhaps it needed a man of Paget's vision and episcopal experience to comment as he did. The list he gives includes 'English' - managerial staff; 'Scottish' - engineers, who worked and maintained the sugar mills; 'Irish' - possibly working on the railways; 'Portuguese' - a mixture of groups, some of whom worked in the Offices (and some Portuguese ladies were married to English managers); 'Swiss' - the Manager, or the General Manager (Max Thurnheer); 'Demararians' - field work overseers from British Guiana; 'Mauritians' - fitters and pan-boilers in the sugar factories; 'Chinese' - often from Hong Kong, many of whom were Anglican, and mostly carpenters and brick-layers; 'Africans' - "Niassa boys" referred to earlier, and general labourers, among whom were the Ngoni (the 'aristocracy' of the labour force), the Sena, Doto and Podzo, and the various Anguru migrants; along with individual members of other nationalities.

The SACRM staff frequently encountered a mix of races, but Bishop Paget's tally was one that witnessed to the catholicity of the Anglican Church and is the largest such list ever given in SACRM's pages. What is even more remarkable about an act of worship conducted with such a group present, is how dramatic an occasion this must have been. The fundamental divisions of society there were broken down, as people, from the perceived highest (the Manager) to the lowest (African labourer), came together in one room for a common purpose. This was unique in Sena Sugar's history.

The bishop's final sentence, referring to 'no ... special places', and 'no one [taking] advantage', is (in 1947) virtually a plunge into the future of a race and class-tolerant Africa. Yet, he is ambiguous. We cannot be certain whether Paget meant that people 'knew their places' and no humble African cane-cutter was going to sit in the best arm chair; or whether he was suggesting that, although the Services welcomed all, there was a danger in mixing in such a unique way, lest people imagine it was possible outside the house - once worship had ended.

The SACRM chaplains also encountered similar mixing of workers and nationalities. John Oldham, for example, writing in 1949, two years after the Bishop, stated: 'There is a very cosmopolitan congregation at these services. British, Dutch, Swiss, Swedes, Portuguese, Danes, Mauritians, Demeraras, Chinese, and Africans. It is certainly a witness to the catholicity of the Church'. [100]

One may add that the order in which the groups were listed by Oldham and the bishop was a witness also to imperial attitudes. 'Special places' may not have been 'allotted' when the heterogeneous groups came together, yet they were still clearly (unthinkingly?) placed in 'order' by the British clergy.

In theory, such a hierarchical group could have worshipped together in Southern Rhodesia, from where Paget had travelled, though in practice it would not have. Worship at the Sena Sugar Estates was a very novel experience for the visiting Anglican priests, as clearly shown in Oldham's 1951 letter, noted below. It was utterly new for them and must have had a tremendous impact on their thinking and their work. The visits to 'far flung places', especially Sena Sugar Estates, although basically straightforward (travel problems apart), broadened the ministering experience of the missioners in a way that nothing else could have. Sadly, glimpses during worship at SSE into a brighter future were inevitably clouded over as the west-bound train, back to the Railway Mission base, arrived at Umtali.

In their travels down the Zambezi the missioners usually travelled in the paddle-steamers, as noted above. These were flat-bottomed boats with two decks and a large paddle at the back, and on each side a barge was tied. The barges contained the cargo of sugar and were usually loaded up on the top with wood. This was for the fire for the boat's boiler. The rest of the space on the barges and on the steamer's lower deck was taken up by African passengers with luggage that often included goats and hens. 'At the front of each barge [was] an African with a measuring stick; ... to measure the depth of water, and see that if possible the barges [did] not run into sandbanks.'[101] They frequently did!

The longest and best-written description of the work undertaken by the South African Church Railway Mission in the Sena Sugar Estates is that by the Rev. John Oldham, in July 1950 (see Appendix B). It would be incomplete and unfair for any account of SACRM's ministry to omit Oldham's article, for to do so would lose the detail and colour, even romance, of the trips undertaken by the missioners. More than any other writer, he also answers the would-be questioners regarding the validity of that work:

> It is thus that we of the Railway Mission are trying to minister to the isolated communities of Christians in this part of the world. Without the Railway Mission those people would probably not receive any ministrations. It is not an easy task for these people to lead the Christian life in their isolation, and with many real temptations which that isolation causes.[102]

Most visits to the Sugar Estates took in a few days of visits and Services in Beira. Missioners noted how it changed from the 'poor decrepit place with its few buildings planked down on the thickly sand-strewn streets, and the only means of locomotion little two-seater trolleys [featured in post-cards of the time] pushed up and down on miniature tram lines by

[Africans]..'[103], to a port having the fine docks on reclaimed land, with modern roads and 'picturesque bungalows'.

In 1950 Beira became the jumping off point for SACRM's new venture into Nyasaland, to visit the African and British employees of the Nyasaland Railways. Writers marvelled at the great railway bridge which bridged the Zambezi from Sena to Dona Ana, opened some fifteen years earlier, and how the journey from Beira to Limbe had been reduced to a twenty-four hour one. John Strouts informed me how his father (General Manager and, later, Manager of the Nyasaland Railways from 1953-1963) and mother would have the visiting Railway Mission padre stay quite often. They lived in their smallholding ten miles south of Limbe, the Headquarters of the Railway.[104] Occasional visits of the missioners continued into Nyasaland until 1961. In his lengthy report on the whole work of the Railway Mission, following an extensive tour, in which he shot the very last SACRM film, 'The Church in a Changing World', the Rev. Michael Fidgin (former missioner, and subsequently Chairman of the London Committee) commented on the work in Beira, Sena Sugar Estates and Nyasaland. Towards the end of his Report he stated:

> We still go to the Sena Sugar estates, and up to Salimia [Salima], Chipoka and Monkey Bay in Nyasaland, although I doubt if we shall continue doing the Nyasaland work much longer ... It does seem to be a most wateful [sic] and un-economical use of time and manpower to send a Missioner right round from Salisbury via Beira and up from Portuguese East into Nyasaland, and then right up the whole Nyasaland railway system, just to reach two small communities at the very far end, who are within 25 miles of large U.M.C.A. Mission stations ..[105]

As we have seen, in much of the Mission's work in the 'far flung places' there was nothing unusual in the vast distances travelled to see but a few communicants. However, this was a case of work gradually extending from one centre (Beira) without thought given to the possibility of others working from the 'other end'.

Richard Hughes, as the only inter-diocesan priest in the area, was the first bearer of the 'new Primatial Cross of Central Africa at the service at which the Bishop of Mashonaland [Paget] was proclaimed Archbishop of Central Africa [June ? 1955].'[106] The inauguration of the new Province meant that Matabeleland and Mashonaland Dioceses left the Church of the Province of South Africa (CPSA), and the Dioceses of Nyasaland and Northern Rhodesia (UMCA missionary dioceses) ceased to be under the jurisdiction of Canterbury. Bishop, now Archbishop, Paget could thenceforth take his own decisions regarding the transport of the 'Blessed

Sacrament carefully down the river' if such a request were to be made again! In the same letter as he outlined the part he played in the inauguration of the Province of Central Africa, Richard Hughes broke the news that 'another milestone in Mission history [had] passed.' He reported (July 1955):

> Beira, which has been in our care ever since there was a British population there, was handed over to a Missions to Seamen chaplain who is stationed at that large seaport permanently. Mr. Roberts, the new chaplain, arrived in November [1954] ... We have lost some staunch supporters and I have lost my monthly visit to the sea and the round of golf with my Churchwarden [Clarence Izard, the British Consul].
>
> The [Railway] Mission is still responsible for the Sena Sugar Estates so I still pass through Beira every four months.[107]

It is rather surprising that the change in Beira was not reported earlier. A lengthy letter from Bishop Paget to the Missions to Seamen (the Chaplain General?), in December 1953, gives a very clear picture of the new proposals:

> You may have been wondering why I have not been writing to you before this, in reference to the appointment of the Rev. R.S.J. Roberts as Missions to Seamen Chaplain at Beira.
>
> ... As you will know, our work at Beira in the past has been carried on by Chaplains of the South African Church Railway Mission; and when I was down in Natal recently, I had an opportunity of a talk with Canon White, Head of the South African Church Railway Mission, and I asked him if he would write to you to open up negotiations to see how far the Railway Mission could work with the Missions to Seamen.
>
> Canon White felt that it would be to the advantage of your Chaplain in Beira if he had a link with the Railway Mission, as it would enable him to get a free pass on the railways, both in Nyasaland and the Rhodesian railways, and the South African railways - which would enable him to attend any Retreat or gathering of clergy in Salisbury or Johannesburg, and visit people in Portuguese East Africa without any travelling expenditure ...
>
> We hope very much that you may now decide to send the Rev. R.S.J. Roberts out to us as Missions to Seamen Chaplain at Beira, to be also Rector of the Parish of Beira, and - we hope - Manager of the Seamen's Club.

As I think I have already told you, the Parish of Beira undertakes to put up £150 a year, the Sena Sugar Estates would put up another £150, and the Seamen's Club would put up £500, making a total of £800 a year, towards the cost of this venture. ... We estimate that the total cost of salary and rent would be in the neighbourhood of £1,200. Rents are very high in Beira, and the cost of living is very high too .

It has recently been brought to my notice that your Chaplain in Lourenco Marques was expected by the State authorities there to be able to talk Portuguese, and that the same thing might apply at Beira. Nobody in Beira has brought this question to me; we have had Railway Mission Chaplains resident in Beira in the past, and the question of the Portuguese language has never arisen. ...The Chaplain's work there would be entirely amongst Europeans, though there are a few Africans converted here in Southern Rhodesia who now live in Beira and have a service occasionally in St. George's Church.

St. George's Memorial Church, Beira, is in a sense an inter-denominational church, though the Anglican Church holds the title deeds and the church was consecrated by my predecessor! The Presbyterian Minister at Umtali goes down occasionally for a service there; but arrangements can easily be made for that visit to fit in with your Chaplain's plans - perhaps for the week-end when your Chaplain is visiting the Sena Sugar Estates, for instance.

I look upon this scheme as a sort of pilot scheme. A licensed Lay Reader ... could hold services when your Chaplain was away up the line at the Sena Sugar Estates ...

Edward Mashonaland [Paget]. [108]

It is apparent that the bishop hoped for a chaplain who could undertake more than the traditional port work associated with the Missions to Seamen. This was a forlone hope, as was the wish that such a chaplain would receive free Passes from the Railways. The Railway authorities did not lightly allocate the Passes, and they certainly would not grant one to a chaplain whose main remit was with sailors and non-railway workers. (As far back as 1949 SACRM had reported, 'The Portuguese have taken over the railway from Umtali to Beira, so that in a few months' time there will be no more English-speaking railwaymen left outside Beira, and only a very few in Beira.')[109] The Missions to Seamen could hardly appoint one of their chaplains to spent time visiting workers on a sugar plantation, especially as Beira was becoming an increasingly busy port. The £150 promised from SSE is a surprising figure, given their normal annual donation of £25 to the Railway Mission.

The letter from Richard Hughes, above, makes it clear that the Missions to Seamen chaplain (Rev. Roberts) was 'confined' to port work, and the Railway Mission continued with visiting the Sugar Estates - via Beira. The bishop's plan certainly did make sense from a diocesan / parochial point of view, but he had not contended with the narrower viewpoint of the Missions to Seamen, who were far less flexible, by Constitution, than the Railway Mission.

As if in compensation for losing his monthly brine and golf at Beira, Richard Hughes was given money from the bishop's Discretionary Fund to buy a B.S.A. Bantam motor cycle for use in the Salisbury area! In his recent 'Reminiscences' of his time with the Railway Mission (June 1953-July 1956), Canon Hughes mentions the uniqueness of the trip to Sena Sugar, complicated by having to travel on three different Railway systems (four, if the Company's own 'rickety line' is included). At Marromeu he was housed in the Company's guest house, as at Sena:

> ... a double storied mansion with very high ceilings, ceiling fans in every room to help alleviate the very hot and humid conditions, and a team of servants to wait on one's every need. I was given a list of people to visit, informed who my hosts would be for dinner and given the venue for the service on the following evening, usually the manager's house.
>
> When the visit was concluded, the next stop was the Luabo Mill, the larger of the two, some miles further down the Zambezi ... On arrival I would be met and escorted to the home of the Company's Field Manager, Neville Usher and his wife. This was for me the most enjoyable part of my visit ...[110]

His main complaint, shared by other missioners, was the 'notorious ... bureaucratic regulations [of the Portuguese] concerning visas and ... their brutal application of rules, regardless of circumstances.' On one occasion he was ordered off a train as he returned from Blantyre to Sena - 'bundled off ... around 10:00 pm in the pitch black starry night', as his visa apparently did not allow re-entry into Mozambique. He spent the night under a ganger's trolley in a very remote siding, until a goods train arrived at 6 a.m. bound for Blantyre, where he was 'met by a very sympathetic and angry General Manager [Mr.Strouts], furious that such a thing could happen to the Railway Padre.' Richard Hughes had then to fly back to Salisbury, obtain another visa, travel back by rail via Umtali and Beira to Sena, 'just about ten miles from where [he] was ordered off the train' in order to fulfil his commitment to conduct the Christmas Services at

Sena![111] It is doubtful whether, on this occasion, the collections covered the expenses of the journey, as they had done with Hugh Wilson twenty years earlier. Although the Portuguese authorities were frequently criticised, it must said that most missioners commented on the friendship and help they received from other Portuguese expatriates.

Over thirty years have now passed since the Railway Mission paid its last visit to the Estates whose sugar was first milled just a century ago. After 1961 SSE had some seventeen troublesome years of life left; the Mission, which had begun in 1885 - eight years before Pitt Hornung's first sugar crushing - outlived it by two years, similarly troublesome. Four of the missioners who made those occasional trips to Sena were able, through interview and/or letter, to give their reflections on their work. Fred Naylor, Hugh Palmer, Stephen Easter and Richard Hughes all agreed that this part of their work was the most enjoyable, something which they always looked forward to, even with Portuguese officialdom, although the 'loss' of Beira took the edge off the trip.

Just as John Oldham's written contemporaneous (1950) account (Appendix B) must stand for all those written over the thirty years, Fred Naylor's 'conversation' can represent the four SACRM-Sena witnesses. In the course of a two and a half hour interview he referred to what happened once he arrived at Caia, at 4 am. on a Friday:

> I'd be given a cup of tea by somebody sent to meet me, and then put into a tiny coach - the "whizz-bang" - attached to a railway engine which ran on a very narrow gauge railway track. After much "tooting" to warn people and animals to get off the track - they would walk between the rails - we came to Marromeu. Mind you, there were delays occasionally due to the engine-coach connection breaking. The African driver and his mate seemed to fasten everything together with pieces of wire or rope!
>
> I was in a little coach - it would only hold about four people - like a little cab. If the "string" broke - I was left stranded until they came back and picked me up again ... The only time I got through without any effort was when the General Manager was going by the same coach, and so they had to make sure that it was tied up properly. ... At Chinde my host and hostess were a [German-speaking] Swiss couple. He managed that end of the Sugar Estate business and lived "over the shop". They had one invalid son. Each morning [that I was there] father took his wife, son and me to spend the day about a mile away at a cottage with a lovely garden and tennis court - near enough the sea for me and the boy to go for a paddle. Father came out for lunch and supper and took us home at night ....

.... [We] got plenty of baptisms to do, not many weddings. The banns had to be published in the nearest parish, like Umtali . Now and then ... I would drop off at Inhaminga [about forty-five miles south of Caia] on my way back from the Sena Sugar Estates. The train only ran twice a week from Blantyre to Beira and back, and arrived at Inhaminga at two o'clock in the morning; but there was always someone to meet me and help me with my luggage - Service books, portable organ and so on. Sometimes I stayed with the Station Master and his wife, [who were] British, or more often with Johnny Creef and his wife. He was a Dutch timber man, she a former American nurse ... Inhaminga was usually Portuguese. But I gave the Station Master and his wife Holy Communion and usually held an evening Service to which most English-speaking would come, regardless of nationality. Many Portuguese could speak English ...
.... [Bishop] Paget was a six-foot something chap ... grand really, though a trifle boisterous now and then. I remember being at Umtali station in the Mission coach when Bishop Paget came along the platform with a cooked chicken which he thrust through the open window of the coach. 'Hang on to that,' he said, 'I'll be with you in a minute.' He was coming to Beira with me for a Confirmation. There was only one knife and fork, so we tossed a coin. The winner - the bishop - got the body of the bird and I got the legs and wings. I lost my fear of bishops, being abroad! ...

Amando, my 'boy', travelled with me in the [Mission] coach. At the back end of the coach was the "Boy's" room, then there was the sitting room, then there was my bedroom and the loo ... Amando would smuggle anything. The Customs men at Beira, when they saw me, they would waft me through, but I often dreaded that they'd take one of my cases - opened it - what they'd have found in it, because Amando packed them the night before. The next day I'd think, 'By jove, there's more in than [I thought].' And there'd be shoes, there'd be bicycle covers, there'd be all sorts of things packed in my case. And I'd say to Amando, 'Amando, don't you do that again. They'll have you - smuggling you know...' And he'd say, 'No, Customs are my brothers.' They let him through all right.. Mind you, he was probably smuggling for them! [112]

We have noted that, in 1961, Michael Fidgin reported that the Railway Mission (the 'Rhodesia and Nyasaland Railway Mission', since 1957) still visited the Sena Sugar Estates, although Nyasaland trips were likely to cease. In November 1961, Kenneth Sims, the new Head of the Mission, wrote: 'Father [Dennis] Charlton, a former Railway Missioner who is now Chaplain at S. Stephen's College, Bala Bala, has kindly offered to help us out with the Christmas Communions. He will visit the line down to Beira and go on to the Sena Sugar Estates.'[113]

The evidence presently available indicates that this is the last reference to the Sugar Estates, either in the 'Blue Quarterly', which ceased in 1964, or in *Partners* into which it was incorporated, or in the Minutes of the London Committee. Anglican ministry on the Estates had started in December 1931 with a visit of the bishop who handed over the work to the Railway Mission and frequently himself gave assistance; it ended just thirty years later with an ex-Railway Padre helping out his former Mission.

Some 20,000 Renamo troops invaded the area, from Malawi, in late 1986, resulting in the towns of Sena, Mopeia, Marromeu and Luabo being 'systematically levelled.' A visitor today to Luabo sees a mostly ruined town, with the Sugar factory a wrecked and rusted monument to European enterprise and greed.

'A waste of time?'

It is clear from the many accounts given by the Railway Missioners that "God's Church" did 'go up with the railway'. The question needs to be asked whether or not this was a waste of time, whether the effort was worth while.

From time to time, as we have seen, the clergy themselves questioned the amount of time, effort and expense involved in taking the ministrations of the Church to but a few, if for no other reason than to forestall the inevitable question marks likely to be raised in England. It was not always easy persuading supporters 'back home' to visualize the difficulties involved in 'normal', more localised SACRM work, or to understand the needs of railway workers and families. The task was so much harder with respect to the mission's work in 'far flung places'. It is significant that the Railway Mission staff found far less need, when writing in the *Light for the Line,* to justify their work in these distant areas, than they did when writing for home consumption in the 'Blue Quarterly'. In the areas in southern Africa where they worked, their ministry was generally appreciated and understood. The geography and topography of South West Africa, of Ngamiland, of the Congo and of the lower Zambezi, coupled with the sparseness of parochial / diocesan clergy, did not need lengthy explanations to railway people and Anglican supporters in the regions where SACRM ministered.

We have noted how the Railway Mission usually responded to a request or to a perceived need. They were willing to be the 'church between the churches', the 'travelling church', until such time as a diocese could take over. At times, however, the dioceses were too willing to let SACRM continue for too long, and SACRM itself did not question enough.

In the Congo, the South African Church Railway Mission, already moving northwards with railway construction, had a justifiable care and concern for the construction workers who would otherwise have been denied the ministrations of the Anglican Church. Fred Rogers, in his pioneering trek to 'find' the workers in the Congo, did not want them to feel forgotten. This was, surely, laudable? Exceptional trips to Leopoldville and Brazzaville made for fascinating reading, yet, after the initial work among the railway construction workers and gangers, SACRM was ministering to British expatriates, Consular and banking staff, for example. SACRM was a Railway mission, that was its *raison d'être,* and it seems that at times it allowed itself to expend manpower, time and money on doing work - good and noble in itself - which others (such as UMCA, for example) should have undertaken.

The ministry in South-West Africa, the shortest period of work undertaken in one area, evolved from special circumstances. Without the First World War and the campaign in 'German South-West' it is highly unlikely that SACRM would have ventured into that territory. Its ministry to the troops and railway staff was at others' request. Once it became clear that the bishop and his staff, ie. diocesan and parochial ministry, were available and beginning to duplicate the work of the Railway Mission, SACRM withdrew, its task completed.

Ngamiland, because of its remoteness and sparseness, was always going to be a difficult 'parish' for whatever system the Anglican church devised. The fact that other missions, particularly the LMS, were already working in the area did not deter the Railway Mission. As Fred Naylor observed, they felt the need to keep people 'in touch with religion'. It seems that they took the LMS more to be concerned with the African population, and this was its priority, and themselves more concerned with Europeans. Perhaps the need of the few British residents in Maun and Ngamiland was more one perceived by SACRM than by the people themselves? Yet, it is clear that, apparently, the missioners' visits were appreciated. Certainly, as in other areas, British Anglicans felt spiritually enriched when they received Holy Communion from their 'own' denominational minister. The sacrament was very important to many of them. For SACRM, to travel six hundred miles away from a railway line was not an easy option, reliant, as it was, on its Railway Passes and goodwill of Railway management, hence the limits of an annual visit. Of all the Railway Mission's work throughout its history, its excursions into Ngamiland are the most difficult to justify. This is not to say that it was wrong or that its ministry there was not worthwhile. I do, however, believe that it was distracted from its real mission, its purpose. When, in earlier days SACRM had been tempted, indeed asked, to become a 'veld mission', it firmly rejected the notion. That work was for others, not for a Church Railway Mission. In Ngamiland, it yielded to the temptation, and only escaped censure because of the relative scarcity of visits.

On the surface, SACRM's involvement in Beira and the Sena Sugar Estates was a logical extension of its work on or near the railways in Rhodesia. Instead of turning round at Umtali, the missioners had to keep going until they met the sea. While Beira could be serviced from Umtali by parish clergy there was no need for Railway missioners at the port; and once the Missions to Seamen had made a base in Beira it was clear, even to the missioners whose trip to the port was the highlight of the quarter, that SACRM was not needed there.

The evidence has clearly shown that the Mission responded well to the initial request from the local bishop to visit the Sugar Estates, the bishop himself having acted on the initial plea for a sacramental ministry. SACRM were better placed than anyone else to undertake the work involved. The ministry of the chaplains was appreciated and it almost seems churlish to query the efforts of those dedicated missioners. They did not confine themselves to the British employees of the Estates, even when giving Communion, for there were Anglicans of other nationalities. Other Services and visiting, particularly where there was illness, included non-Anglicans of many nations and races. However, nowhere in all the great number of letters and accounts which were written, in Annual Reports or official literature or even in the current oral testimonies, is there one single query about the system employed by the Sugar Estates. Housing, diet, labour policy, racial discrimination - all these were ignored or overlooked by the visiting missioners. Head's study of the 'Sena sugar Estates and migrant labour' is required reading for any realistic assessment of the situation that obtained in the Estates. [114]

In SACRM's work in South Africa and in Rhodesia the question of racial intolerance, of a colour bar in worship, of wage differentials and working practices did surface from time to time in the ministry and letters of the SACRM staff. Often they had to be pragmatic. If they 'rocked the boat' too much they were likely to lose their free Passes and their Railway privileges. But they did question 'the system' and some got into trouble. A weekend at Marromeu, Caia or Sena, spent in querying the Hornung working policies, was not, of course, going to change the whole of SSE's system of sugar production. Yet, there is no evidence that the SACRM workers were even aware that things were not as they ought to have been, and that, in some ways, they themselves were helping to perpetuate inhumane working conditions. Evidence suggests that few chaplains ever saw the cane being cut or the sugar being milled. That they were given lavish hospitality is more evident.

The missioners could answer that they were not there to change the system. Their role was to take the ministrations of the (Anglican) Church to those who needed it. This they did in a marvellous way and often after almost horrendous journeys. Swimming in the Indian Ocean at Beira was, certainly, a welcome break and mini-holiday for very many hard-worked SACRM staff, but the trip to Sena Sugar was anything but a sinecure. Yet we may wish that they had shown some awareness of what life was like for the majority of SSE's workers, as opposed to the cushioned life of 'the bosses' with their ceiling fans. There was concern and care for those outside the normal boundaries of the Church, but this concern was focussed too narrowly on a minority, with little (apparent) concern for the wider community. Perhaps, if Hugh Wilson's many letters home had been preserved, we would be able to paint a more positive picture. As it is, the record must stand - heroic, inspiring, worthy - but with a question mark hanging over it.

Of their ministry generally in the 'far flung places' the Railway Missioners would have had no problems with the sentiments expressed in the poem 'Up with the Railway', quoted earlier:

> God's Church goes up with the railway ...
> ... And the priest stands at the Altar to give the Living Bread
> To the two or three who are gathered in the presence of their Head.

---

1 'In Journeyings Often', SACRM, 1925, 28
2 Railway Gazette, 5.12.1927, 107
3 Day, 1963, 49/50
4 SACRM 'Vade mecum', Sectn. 28
5 QP 145, 1940, 6
6 Martelli, 1962, 191
7 QP 24, 1909, 7
8 Pauling, 1926, 1969, 206
9 QP 25, 1909, 5-8
10 QP 25, 1909, 6/7
11 SACRM An.Rep. 1910/11, 19
12 QP 34, 1912, 16
13 QP 43, 1914, 13
14 QP 36, 1912, 17
15 QP 36, 1912, 18
16 The Diocese of Likoma was originally a part of the field of UMCA and was separated from Zanzibar diocese in 1892. The diocese included territories under three

governments - the British (British Central Africa/Nyasaland), German (part of German East Africa) and Portuguese (part of Portuguese East Africa).
[17] Martelli, 1962, 191
[18] QP 40, 1913, 16
[19] Pauling, 1926, 1969, 213
[20] It was not until 1954 that the province of Katanga was added to the Diocese of Northern Rhodesia. 'This was done,' wrote the bishop, Oliver Green-Wilkinson, 'at my request, and is the formal recognition of a situation which had already developed through our call to minister to Anglican Christians in Elizabethville and in the villages along the left bank of the River Luapula ...' (Blood, 1962, Vol.III, 307)
[21] UMCA, *Central Africa*, March 1915
[22] QP 49, 1915, 14
[23] QP 50, 1916, 12
[24] A full account of the two gun boats and their extraordinary journey - and eventual success - is given in Sibley's book on the East African Campaign (Sibley, 1971,36-83).
[25] QP 53, 1916, 12
[26] *Light for the Line*, LXVI, Jan. 1915, .5
[27] QP 57, 1917, 7
[28] QP 59, 1918, 5/6
[29] QP 117, 1934, 4
[30] QP 155, 1945, 10-12
[31] QP 189, 1955, 2
[32] Lewis & Edwards, 1934, 785
[33] Lewis & Edwards, 1934, 785
[34] Day, 1963, 52
[35] Lewis & Edwards, 786
[36] Lewis & Edwards, 523
[37] QP 46, 1915, .7
[38] QP 47, 1915, .7
[39] QP 50, 1916, 13/14
[40] QP 48, 1915, 6
[41] Lewis & Edwards, p.788
[42] Garub station was built by the Germans who dug a well there in 1908 to water the steam locomotives of their newly-built railway. It was patrolled by cavalry, whose horses were supplied by Baron Hans Heinrich von Wolf - a wealthy horse-loving officer. When the German colonial era in Namibia came to an end in 1915, their horses stayed - left to their own devices. Garub's new station master and his family became the only people allowed into that diamantiferous area, leading solitary lives (as did all such families) and keeping a trough supplied with water for their goats, and maintaining the water supply for the locomotives. More recently, diesel engines replaced steam engines, and Garub became a wholly forgotten place, its station a crumbling ruin. But 'the descendants of the German cavalry horses never strayed far from the old trough, as they roamed for grazing among the sparsely scattered tufts of grass. That is where they are today.' (*Independent on Sunday*, 'Review', 13.8.95, 13)
[43] QP 51, 1916, .9-11
[44] *Light for the Line*, LXXIII, Oct.1916, 10
[45] QP 53, 1916, 1
[46] 'Bloemfontein Quarterly', 1917, in Lewis & Edwards, 1934, 788
[47] QP 54, 1917, 7
[48] 'Bloemfontein Quarterly', 1917, in Lewis & Edwards, .789

[49] QP 57, 1917, 12-14
[50] QP 59, 1918, 10
[51] QP 81, 1925, 4,(wr. Nov.1924)
[52] QP 89, 1927, 2
[53] QP 90, 1927, 9/10
[54] Rey, 28.6.1930, in Parsons & Crowder, 1988, 35
[55] Rey, 16.6.1933, in Parsons & Crowder, 133
[56] Maylam, 1977, 30
[57] Rey, 26.6.1930, in Parsons & Crowder, 35
[58] QP 118, 1934, 9/10
[59] Rusbridger, priv. let. /JMR
[60] Rusbridger, Diary, Jan. 26/27, 1932, RHL
[61] Rusbridger, 1934 Diary, Jan. 1935, RHL
[62] QP 127, 1936, 8
[63] QP 129, 1937, 4
[64] QP 130, 1937, 7/8
[65] QP 141, 1939, 18
[66] QP 152, 1944, 9
[67] QP 163, 1948, 6
[68] Naylor, oral. int. 23.1.1992
[69] QP 168, 1950, 3
[70] Partners, IX, No.2, 12/13
[71] pt. of Article XIV, Anglo-Portuguese Treaty, 11.6.1891, OURY Box 1, York
[72] OURY Box 2, 3,1
[73] White, 1993, 201
[74] SPG Atlas, 1908, 46
[75] Paul, 1978, 32
[76] Paul, 1978, 33
[77] SACRM Leaflet No.2, 1939/40, 1/2
[78] QP 86, 1926, 9
[79] *Light for the Line*, CXXVII, Apr 1930, 18/19
[80] QP 103, 1930, 8
[81] QP 122, 1935, 4
[82] *LL*, CXXXIII, Sep. 1931, 18
[83] This was in the newly-built extension to the Hotel. The chapel was not, in fact, officially consecrated until 28 February 1932, when Bishop Paget of Mashonaland performed the ceremony.
[84] QP 108, 1931, 11
[85] QP 121, 1935, 4
[86] QP 126, 1936, 20
[87] AB940, WITS/CPSA, 7.8.1936
[88] QP 110, 1932, 6
[89] QP 160, 1947, 8
[90] QP 122, 1935, 15
[91] *LL*, LXXXVIII, Dec. 1932, 12
[92] Wilson wrote home frequently during his many trips to Sena Sugar Estates and sent back a considerable number of photographs. His widow threw these away, because of a house move, a few weeks before being first contacted by the writer!
[93] QP 120, 1934, 15
[94] QP 121, 1935, 4

[95] QP 122, 1935, 15
[96] QP 128, 1936, 20; QP 134, 1938, 13; SACRM leaflet 2, 2; QP 136, 1938, 6
[97] QP 137, 1938, 10
[98] QP 147, 1941, 8/9
[99] QP 160, 1947/8, 9
[100] QP 168, 1950, 8
[101] QP 168, 1950, 8
[102] QP 172, 1951, 7 (See App. B)
[103] QP 149, 1942, 5
[104] JMR corresp. 8.1994; 9.1994
[105] QP 206, 1961, 20
[106] QP 190, 1955, 2
[107] QP 190, 1955, 3
[108] SACRM Papers/JMR
[109] QP 166, 1949, 1
[110] Hughes/JMR corresp. 1993
[111] Hughes/JMR corresp. 1993
[112] Naylor/JMR interv. 23.1.1992
[113] QP 207, 1961, 2
[114] Head's study of the files in the SSE archives has made clear the reluctance, on the part of the management, to provide decent housing or diet for their workers. Many aspects of the various laws governing labour were ignored, even deliberately flouted. A Colonial Health Inspector, Manuel Saraiva Junqueiro, visited the Estates at Luabo in September 1956. In his report he stated, 'We are left with only one conclusion, that the worker is not thought of as anything more than a simple, cold and inanimate part of a huge machine. ... with only one end, that he produces the income which is expected of him, and who is substituted mercilessly once he is worn-out or useless.' (Head, 1978, f.n.39, 73, her translation)

Although the Sena Sugar Estates are now confined to history, an almost parallel operation still exists in Usina Serra Grande, north-east Brazil. Like Sena had, it has its own private rail track, with the sugar cane being transported by steam train. The 100 square mile plantation contains within its borders the vast majority of workers, who live like serfs and cut the cane by hand. The manager is quoted as saying, 'We keep things like they were at the turn of the century. It will be like this for another 500 years.' (Full report in the *Guardian*, 6.3.1999, p.18)

7: African work

- SACRM is 'a ministry for all races.'
- 'The Mission was just one-sided - for Europeans.'

> There have always been a small number of African Catechists, working among their own people, under the kindly wing of the [Railway] Mission. Experience has taught that Evangelistic work among the African people is better done by their own people, or by Europeans who are specially trained and fitted for that sphere of work, so the primary duty of the Mission has always been to keep the things of God before the white people employed upon and living near the Railways ...
>
> Experience, also, has taught that where the Christian Faith of the white people is defective, and the witness of their life is unworthy of their privilege, the impact of "Western Civilisation" upon the African is a disaster rather than a benefit. (*The Happy Travellers*)[1]

Apart from a folded leaflet ('Your Travelling Church'), published in 1959, the twenty-two page booklet, *The Happy Travellers,* which appeared in 1954 (revised 1955), was the last official publicity material put out by the Railway Mission for the general public. (The *Quarterly* Magazine was for subscribers). So, seventy years after its inception and two years after its withdrawal from South Africa the Mission was clearly stating that its priority was work with Whites. The emphasis was to change in the final two decades, as we shall note, and is, indeed, reflected in the 1959 leaflet referred to above.

However, from the very beginning, the stated aim of the Railway Mission was to bring the ministrations of the Church to people of all races. Yet, throughout its whole history there was a constant awareness that 'the natives' were being neglected, and that when the Mission did try to improve matters it came up against white resistance or hostility. The bulk of SACRM's work was, in practice, with white and coloured railway employees and families. The reasons for this emphasis were many and various, and will be outlined during this examination of 'African work'. One constant factor, however, during SACRM's history, was the so-called 'language problem'. It is useful therefore to reflect on this at the outset.

The South African Church Railway Mission and each of its successors was fundamentally different from other Missions in southern or central Africa in its operation. Whereas other Missions normally had their staff based in one area at any one period in order to evangelise (on a narrow or broad basis, depending on the particular Society) the local African community, the Railway Mission was - by its very nature - an itinerant mission. The missioners travelled, as we have seen, hundreds of miles per month. The majority of them went out from England for a 'tour' of three years, though this was extended for some. Wherever they were based, the missioners would see, meet or 'pass by' Africans who spoke a variety of languages. There was no way in which any Railway chaplain could learn even two or three languages before or during the relatively short time he or she was employed by SACRM. All of those based in South Africa learned a little Afrikaans, even if that was only the basic greetings and the ability to speak parts of the Services in the language. A few of the staff, such as Monica James, progressed further with Afrikaans, where much of their work involved ministering to the Afrikaner railway people.

For other Missions, the learning of a local language was a *sine qua non,* and lack of linguistic ability caused problems, as noted below. Knowledge of one language could often lead to evangelising a people whose language was similar or related. Livingstone and Coillard are two such examples:

> When Livingstone came to the Makololo (1850), he knew Sechwana, and had no need to study another language in order to understand and make himself understood. So it was also for Coillard with the Sesuto. When in 1878-79 he first came to Sesheke [Barotseland / Western Zambia], he could perfectly understand the people and be understood by them.[2]

This initial evangelizing via a related language is not without its critics. Isichei, in her broad sweep of Christianity in Africa, is critical of the Paris Missionary Society using seSotho in Bulozi, though, ten pages further on, comments, 'They [the PMS missionaries] came with Sotho co-workers, with the precious advantage that they knew a closely related language.'[3]

The Railway Mission was almost entirely dependent on interpreters for any work it did among the many different African groups, although considerable numbers could speak English as a second language. Fred Naylor had the lovely story of how he was using his catechist, a miner, as interpreter during an extremely lengthy Baptism Service in a Church near Umtali. The catechist, Paul Tembo, wanted to retire, and asked Fred Naylor to choose one of the two candidates he had put forward:

> I'd been in that corrugated-iron Church nearly two hours in a temperature of more than one hundred degrees. I was wearing a pair of new shoes and my feet were killing me! So I said, 'Choose which you like - they're both rogues anyway!' This was followed by roars of laughter; I'm sure they all - the whole congregation - spoke English as well as I did ...

The question of lack of interpreters and of not knowing African languages was one that SACRM clergy frequently returned to. It could be, at times, a convenient excuse for lack of ministry towards African workers, though there were these genuine problems.

Perhaps the most helpful comment on the SACRM staff's need for interpreters is that given by the Rev. E.D. Smith, writing from Naauwpoort in 1926:

> The Head has asked me to say a word or two about our Native work, and I am glad to do so because I think I am the only Missioner on the Staff who has any Native work at all. [He was one of ten clergy, six women workers, one nurse and two native catechists then employed by SACRM] ... I am quite sure that the S.A.C.R.M. would do more if it were possible, but the rush of a short three years spent chiefly among isolated Europeans makes it practically impossible for our Missioners to acquire a working knowledge of the Native language or to gain that experience which is necessary for the simplest work among them. Native thought, customs, manner of life bristle with difficulties, so that the missionary should be an expert. In the towns - where we do not work - the language difficulty can be overcome by means of an interpreter, but along the line if a Native boy [sic] understands any language but his own it is Cape Dutch, or as we call it now, "Afrikaans." And this is the medium I use chiefly at Rosmead, Naauwpoort, and Norvals Port [Pont].[4]

During the period that the Railway Mission was in South Africa, particularly once the emphasis changed from English to Afrikaans-speaking railway workers, many SACRM staff learned to 'get along', as they put it, in Afrikaans, as noted above. A similar effort was not made with any of the African languages.

The African priests, who were employed in Rhodesia by the Railway Mission during its last twenty years, used either Shona or Ndebele as their main medium for ministering to Africans. They also used English. Most priests and railway workers would have been conversant with Chilapalapa, the pidgin form of Shona/Ndebele/English/Afrikaans, although this would not have been used in worship, and was used mainly by white employers.

In looking at what may be termed 'African work', it is possible to distinguish between the question of the Railway Mission's ministry to the African railway workers, and that of the ministry itself of African workers employed by the South African Church Railway Mission and its successors.

A new constituency

Ray White, Head of the Railway Mission when it transferred to Rhodesia in 1957, accurately identified the changes facing the Mission: the different (increasingly African and Coloured) constituency of the missioners; the influence of the independent Churches; and the politicisation and increasing radicalism of the African railway workers. It is needful, therefore, to examine this 'new constituency'.

We noted, at the end of Chapter 2, how in Rhodesia the Railways had first recruited from Britain and then taken in the 'regular stream' of white manual workers from South Africa. The major part of skilled and semi-skilled railway work remained in white hands for many years. In 1920 the 'European workers' went on strike and won an award of '25 per cent. on substantive pay, increased overtime pay, a shorter working day, a cost-of-living allowance, better leave, and other concessions.'[5] This was more successful than the strike nine years later. On that occasion the white population in Rhodesia were warned about their duties, living, as they did, '.."among thousands of natives," implying that the door had been opened for an African rising.'[6] Volunteers manned a paramilitary force to protect the railway, although 'no evidence arose that Africans had contemplated rebellion during the railway strike.' The strike collapsed under the weight of hostile public opinion.

In August 1934 the Rhodesia Railways Conference was held in Cape Town. A complicated scheme worked out at the Conference ensured that, with the birth of a unified 'Rhodesia Railways Ltd.' in 1937, the railway revenue increased considerably. This was mainly at the expense of Northern Rhodesia, which took strong exception to the 'maintenance of a rating policy and system which discriminated against [it].' Success 'depended upon Northern Rhodesia's continued use of the southern route [rather than using the Mozambiquan ports].'[7]

The 1939 Bledisloe Commission Report on Rhodesia and Nyasaland noted Prime Minister Huggins' speech outlining his protectionist policy for white workers:

> While there is yet time and space, the country should be divided into separate areas for black and white. In the native areas the black man must be allowed to rise to any position to which he is capable of climbing. Every step of the industrial and social pyramid must be open to him, excepting only - and always - the very top ... In the European areas the black man will be welcomed, when, tempted by wages, he offers his services as a labourer; but it will be on the understanding that he shall merely assist, and not compete with, the

> white man. The two races will develop side by side under white supervision ...[8]

The largely African audience listening to Huggins' speech in March 1938 would not have returned to their homes or 'kias' particularly encouraged about their future prospects.

The Bledisloe Commission restricted their comments of 'The Asiatic and Coloured Communities' in the three Territories to one paragraph. They pointed out that the Coloured communities were 'under some disability' in that they were often 'regarded as forming part of the native, rather than the non-native, population.' These circumstances were seen to 'bear especially hardly upon the more enterprising amongst the Coloured peoples ...'[9]

As we shall note below, the creation of the Federation of Rhodesia and Nyasaland opened up new opportunities for Africans working on the railways. However, ever since the first railways were built in Rhodesia, thousands of Africans had been employed in a variety of jobs. They have been largely ignored in all historical accounts, other than, as Lunn noted, being 'subsumed in more general analyses of industrial labour.'[10] Lunn is one of the very few commentators who has sought to rectify the historiographical gap. As he notes, 'Throughout the period 1892 to 1939, the railways were the largest single private employer of black labour in the Rhodesias.' At their peak, in 1930, the figures for African railway labour reached just under eighteen thousand.[11] Many of these were indirect labour, ie. Africans employed by the railway contractors, such as Pauling and Company, and sub-contractors. Even when the initial construction work had been completed, 'there still remained large-scale tasks of repair, maintenance and improvement which periodically necessitated the temporary mobilisation of great numbers of black workers.'[12] As the railways, during the 1900s, started to take over the management and working of the network, more direct labour recruitment became necessary. In moving up into Northern Rhodesia the railways made sure that 'the privileged access to North Western Rhodesia given for the purposes of indirect labour on construction, was extended to recruiting for direct labour.' Every year thousands of men from Barotseland made their way to Livingstone and the Victoria Falls, in order to be recruited, mostly for railway work. For many of them this was preferable to the virtual 'slave labour' of Lewanika, the Lozi Paramount, in his canal and dam-making projects. Increasing numbers of workers in the 1930s were Angolan migrants, who also entered Southern Rhodesia by the Falls route. In the eastern part of Southern Rhodesia (Umtali[Mutare] area) the majority of workers came from Nyasaland, from the districts of Mzimba and Kotakota.

Most of the African workers were employed in unskilled manual labour, such as the maintenance and repair work along the line of rail. A few did find semi-skilled Railway employment, but this was 'hidden and unacknowledged, in order to protect the sanctity of the informal colour bar on the railways.'[13] The 1945 Railway Strike was the first such strike to be organised by Africans. However, in 1919, at the end of the strike by white railway workers, their African assistants and subordinates came out in what was dubbed an 'imitative strike'. The settlement benefited the permanent and long-service workers. The majority of unskilled African employees, working on line-maintenance and repair, received no benefits from the settlement. During the period 1920-1939 the average European earnings on the Rhodesian Railway System varied between £33 and £39 per month, with an African average wage of between £1. 1s [£1.05] and £1. 5s. 11d [£1.29].

In 1926 Brigadier-General Hammond, an experienced railway administrator, submitted to the Legislative Assembly a report on the Railway System of Southern Rhodesia. He had been asked to see whether a reduction in overall railway working expenses could be made without loss of efficiency. He reported that an increase in African employment could be one answer. He wrote:

> There is a very large class of so-called skilled work, which ... can be performed by natives under periodical supervision after a short period of instruction ... the work of firing a locomotive is easily within the scope of the native, and he is probably better suited physically for this work than the men of English descent.[14]

This 'threat' to White employment on the railways, followed as it was by the slump of 1930-31, received short shrift from the settler community.

The strong position of Rhodesia Railways at the outbreak of the Second World War changed dramatically with the escalating mineral demands of the Allied war effort. There was a fifty per cent increase in total tonnage carried between 1939 and 1944, at a price of engines, coaching and goods stock 'being flogged to the uttermost.' Phimister notes that 'white labour became increasingly difficult to recruit and retain.'[15] One result was the steady increase in semi-skilled and skilled work being allocated to African and, more especially, to Coloured workers.

On Rhodesia Railways there had been, as we have seen, considerable prejudice against employing Africans or Coloureds in any work that was normally done by the Whites. However, with the creation of the Federation of Rhodesia and Nyasaland in 1953, developments took place on the railways, in management, rail communications and opportunities for the advancement of non-white workers. A major policy change was the decision to 'open to Coloureds, Asians and Africans recruiting for grades such as firemen, shunters, lorry drivers and dining-car waiters; progression to the grade of driver and guard was also provided for.' [16]

These changes naturally affected the work and attitudes of white railwaymen. The writer interviewed two who had worked in both Northern and Southern Rhodesia in the 1950s and 60s; Dick Nyenhuis (DN), former Driver, First Class, and Murray Thompson (MT), former Chief Clerk and Station Master:

> DN: In the main the platelayers were Coloured - not Black. So that was already a community of itself, and I can give you names - there was the Orange family, ... the Bismark family - they were all platelayers. It was not only that one person in a family was a platelayer - the father was a platelayer, and if he had four sons - in most cases - like the Oranges and Bismarks - they were all platelayers.
> MT: Same as miners in this country.
> DN: So, these people were all Coloured. We greeted them. The Whites used to greet the Coloureds and the Coloureds [would greet] us - on Section. And if there was trouble they would help each other.
> JMR [JM Roden]: What was their language?
> DN: English, mostly English. they were fluent in the native languages, and I think a lot of them could speak Afrikaans ... If there was trouble we would help them and they would help us. We used to supply them with water. We used to bring them a lot of things. Let us presume that if the coloured platelayer would come to a place like Kafue or Mazabuka, he could not come into the Bar where the Whites were. He was not allowed. But things changed all the time.
>
> Now again, looking at the platelayers - the Coloured community - in the 50s there was not that amount of transport, the amount of motor cars as nowadays, so that the only way that these men could come into one of the bigger places was to travel in the van of a goods train .. or, on a passenger train. You stopped the passenger train for [them] ...You blokes [to Mr. Thompson] used to give an instruction to such and such to pick them up at .. a cottage.
> MT: Slow down ... stop .. have a one minute stop. They might want to go to Hospital or anything ...
> DN: But, of course, you've got to understand - if there was trouble - they would help each other [ie Coloured platelayer & White driver]. And they would greet each other - have a big laugh - but they would not socialise. These things came in ... from the middle 60s, then they started more or less .. socialising came in. These men - they knew the job, no two ways about it, and if, for instance, you could get a

situation that there was a derailment on a Section - locomotives derailed ... trucks derailed ... these men, they were so experienced at re-railing it.

MT: Plus the fact that they would get more work out of the nat.. [sic] the Africans .. than what the white man could.

DN: They were living in the gangers' cottages. And very close to the ganger's cottage you had the labourers' compound - the labourers' Location. And usually, at 6 o'clock in a morning, one of them would hit that big bit of rail - and that's when everybody would come to work ... Let us presume there would be a derailment at a place called Nega Nega [Siding, between Kafue and Mazabuka] you would get the platelayers from Kafue, Nega Nega, Lubombo and Mazabuka, - they would all come. They used to work the little pump-trolley - now it's all motorised, and even the platelayers will say it's not the same as what it used to be. But, what has also happened ... the condition of the track has deteriorated. These men only had about ten miles to look after and they were proud of it - that was their own ten miles. You could look along the footpath along the railway line and all the gravel and stones was one direct line.

MT: You wouldn't see one out of place.

DN: Absolutely straight. There [were] no weeds - there was nothing there. The footpath was there, and that ballast was one straight line ... You would never have to tell these men, 'Listen, we think you've got a bad neck in the track somewhere.' Because they examined that track - they were proud of their own bit of Section.

MT: There was competition between them.

DN: Prizes were given out for the best Length.

The discussion then centred on the Railway Missioners and the use of the coach. The driver of a train was (normally !) told by the guard that he had a Mission Coach on his train:

> DN: ... sometimes he would overcarry it [ie forget to drop off Mission coach] ... he would get there eventually ... and then .. as far as food was concerned ... although the missionary had all the food with him, I don't think he had ever to worry about fresh meat, because the platelayers - they were living where there was a lot of game ...and a lot of the Stations Foremens [sic] - they knew how to get their meat - so he [the missioner] would get his meat alright, and also the platelayers and the station foremens - they had their own gardens with vegetables - so he got his meat and his eggs and so on. Yes ... 'scoff'.

MT: We always used to get a box ... the eggs were packed from the farms ... sending them away to the towns ... they were all 45 dozen boxes - we used to always get one given.

DN: Even the box you carried .. was known as the Scoff Box ... and, again, you had African labourers who would carry all those boxes onto the locomotives and to the Guard's Van ... they were the box carriers.. all they did - that was their job. Then you had the 'tea boys', in Section, all over ... all they did was to keep the fire going and over that fire was a big tea pot with water. Then you had the 'fire boys' - they were cleaning the fires out ... During that time, the 50s and 60s, they were all still known as 'boys'...

MT: We used to go on about them being badly treated .. when we were at Bwana M'kubwa ... we had a coal fire - we'd no lights - we had paraffin lamps - across the road in the Compound ..[by?] the copper refinery - electric lights .. the lot! ...

JMR: Their wages wouldn't be what yours were though.

DN: When I joined as a fireman in 1953, my monthly wages [were] £38-l0s [£38.50] - I'll never forget it (MT: Mine was £24) ... and I'm almost certain the 'Garratt boys', which we had - the Garratt boy - the coal trimmer - he travelled with us on that locomotive all the way to the destination and back again - all he did was trim the coal and then break the coal up. I think they got about two pound, two pound-ten [£2.50] a month - so, already - look at the difference ... But then, of course, from that £38-l0s, we had insurance. I think we had to pay something like eleven shillings [55p] for accommodation, and then tax, which they ['Garratt boys'] didn't pay, but then, still - two pounds ten! There was an enormous gap in that ...[17]

A Railway Training Centre was opened in Bulawayo in 1953 'to give intensive theoretical and practical courses of instruction for the grades of guard, shunter, fireman, station foreman, clerk, checker and platelayer.'[18] The men were then sent out to depots and stations to complete their training. English language classes were held in the Bulawayo Training Centre and these were not just for the benefit of non-white Rhodesians, but also for the Dutch, Italian and Greek staff who joined the British and South African railwaymen being recruited in the 1950s.

We shall note later, when looking at the Railway Mission work of African priests, the involvement of the Rev. Willie Sigeca in the 1945 strike by Africans working on the railways. This was not the first strike that Africans had initiated in Rhodesia. Shona workers in 1895 had refused night-shift work at a small mine; African workers downed tools at the Camperdown Mine in December 1910, following a wage reduction; a walk-out was staged at Wankie colliery in 1912 in protest at the brutality of the acting compound manager; and, in September 1927, 3,500 African mine-workers at the Shamva Mine (which had an unsettled white labour history) went on strike for higher wages. The 1927 strike was

> a bold declaration that a comparatively sophisticated African labour force, with many of the characteristics of a fully-fledged proletariat, had emerged on the Shamva Mine. Because of the nature of Southern Rhodesia's political economy the strike carried vital political and social implications for the territory's European population ... From the Government's point of view it was essential that the Shamva strike be broken, and with it the pretensions of the African workers to an articulate voice in industry. [19]

Various social/welfare, religious and recreational groups existed at Shamva, as in all mines. The role that (imported) independent Churches have played in African industrial unrest has never been explored fully. There were many members of the Watch Tower Church, for example, at Shamva, although Phimister has concurred with the findings of others, that the movement did not seem to have been involved in any 'agitation' there. The territorial governments, as well as the Anglican Church (linked as they were) were suspicious of independent Churches.

However, the 1945 strike was the first railway strike organised by Africans. It started on 20 October and involved over 2000 black railwaymen. A unilateral and unexpected introduction of a new system of overtime pay was the immediate cause. The strike started in Bulawayo, quickly spreading to the Copper belt in Northern Rhodesia. Eight thousand men were eventually involved and the management had to negotiate

> by the promise of a commission of enquiry into workers' grievances ... 'The Railway Strike', exulted Jasper Savanhu, 'has proved that Africans have been born ... Africans realize as never before that united they stand and divided they fall ...We have found ourselves faced a ruthless foe - exploitation and legalized oppression the white man for his and his children's luxury ... The days when a white man could exploit us at will are gone and gone for ever.' [20]

Although the strike was successful, Rhodesia Railways, 'backed by the Southern Rhodesian Government, was able to maintain strict control over African labour organisation and prevented the foundation of an African railway union in Southern Rhodesia.'[21] The Government in Southern Rhodesia wanted African labour to be represented by Europeans. By 1952 the labour laws in Southern Rhodesia had been amended to recognise two

African railway unions, the African Railway Workers' Trade Union (ARWTU) and the Rhodesia Railways African Workers' Union (RRAWU). These amalgamated in July 1955, to become the Railway African Workers' Union, with its headquarters in Bulawayo. The formation of this Union

> represented the end of an era of Rhodesian history when African workers were men without power. They had had virtually no hope of promotion, their colour had barred all occupational, economic and social advance. They had been a working caste. After the strike of 1945 the workers became conscious of themselves as a pressure group. The struggle to develop an effective union created a craft consciousness among the [African] railway workers of the two territories. [22]

Two aspects of African railway trade-unionism history, which at first seem contradictory, are worth noting. Firstly, as Turner has demonstrated:

> Rhodesian railway workers did not interact closely with other urban Africans even during strikes. When Rhodesian railway workers went on strike they continued to live in their isolated railways compound housing and to receive railway rations ... Along the railway line, workers stationed at small depots could not have contact with other industrial workers. [23]

This may give the impression that any action taken by railway workers would be slow, fragmented and lacking in unified effort. The reverse was true. All accounts of the 1945 strike emphasise the speed of the strike's spreading. Phimister stated, 'Starting from Bulawayo, the strike quickly spread along the railway system and across the Zambezi to include Broken Hill (Kabwe) and the Copperbelt, as well as other towns in Southern Rhodesia itself.'[24] Turner acknowledged that, on 25th October, as the last trains made their runs, 'word of the strike passed up the line from Bulawayo. Because African crews changed trains at mid-points between major depots [not always the case], they returned home each day and it was easy for them to spread the word in their compound.' It was, in fact, this mobility, rather than isolation, that was the crucial factor in railway trade unionism as well as in strike action.

In Botswana, the railway - as we noted in Chapter 2 - runs from south to north through the eastern side of the country. Since it was first constructed, the running of the railway has been variably linked with that of Rhodesia Railways. In 1959 operational responsibility was divided at

Mahalapye, the northern section coming under Rhodesian control. In 1966 the entire line became operated by Rhodesia Railways. However, in spite of the railway's importance to the economy and transport of Botswana, 'there has been virtually no railway expertise within the country. Most of the eight hundred Batswana workers employed on the railway [1980] are unskilled, and are engaged on track maintenance.'[25] After 1974 Rhodesia Railways began to train Batswana for skilled and supervisory positions.

Although the Railway Mission had been active in Bechuanaland and the Rhodesias since the lines were laid, work among African railwaymen had not been a priority, notwithstanding Seacombe's death in ministering to them in 1918. It was only with the Mission's withdrawal from South Africa and the employment of African priests that a 'new constituency' was recognised.

Mission to Africans?

We have noted, in Chapter 3, how Douglas Ellison stated in 1896 that one 'Object of the Mission' was what 'with more men and money, should ... be a great work among the thousands of natives ... along the Line.' In December of that year the first 'Native Catechist', Josiah Ngcambu, was appointed - 'an earnest ... of what is yet to be among the thousands of natives up and down the Line.'[26] Josiah Ngcambu's work was frequently mentioned, and will be detailed below. A (white) Lay Evangelist pointed out in 1902:

> The success of our native work depends very largely on the help that we get from friends at home, for it is hard work to keep our other Churches out of debt, and our White Congregations are not perhaps quite as much enamoured with mission work as they ought to be.[27]

Clearly, work among Africans was to depend on availability of money and man-power once the needs of the 'White Congregations' had been met. Such ministry as was undertaken among Africans in the Grahamstown Diocesan Railway Mission days was often that of attempts to fund the building of 'Native Churches', always after the 'Parish Churches' (ie. for White use) had been erected. A typical note in the GDRM 'Quarterly' was:

> So far we have been unable even to touch work among natives along the line, the numbers of whom are now increasing considerably; but the completion of the Church of St. Margaret for Natives at

Jansenville [Graaf-Reinet line], is meant soon to operate in that direction.[28]

Letters and other correspondence of the period indicate that Railway Mission supporters in England, as well as white congregations in South Africa (mentioned above), needed persuasion to help support the building of African churches. The Rev. Eustace St.C. Hill, in an unusually openly frank letter, spelled out the situation. In reference to the building of St. Agnes' Church, which the Railway Mission had started building near the 'Native Location' at Naaupoort, he wrote:

> The Natives out here seem to have an unqualified claim on our help, and that for many reasons. We have taken their country; we have practically destroyed their old religion, such as it was, and their moral code; we need them as servants and employees, and so let them congregate in Locations by our towns where they live in rag huts, compared to which the huts they lived in when in their heathen state are perfect. In such Locations they learn European vices ...[The] one hope of raising the Natives to be a sober, moral race, is to bring them under the godly discipline of the ... Church.
>
> ... I feel that by helping forward this Church we are in a small way trying to give to the South African Natives what those who are absorbed only in the pursuit of wealth have not given to them, namely, Christianity rendered practical by the Church. They are like children [sic], and need the strong, loving discipline of the Church; but if the Church is slow to do her duty they will chose fancy religions of their own, and thus add to the sadness of our unhappy divisions.
>
> I do then ask most earnestly for help in building this Church, which will cost £700 ... [29]

Some of the sentiments expressed by the missioner are certainly 'politically incorrect' for a reader today, yet were radical and caring by the standards obtaining in South Africa in 1904. The Church was completed and dedicated at the end of the year, funds having been forthcoming. The 'unhappy divisions' referred to were a cause for concern over another denomination. As noted in Chapter 3, at the end of the Boer War the Railway Mission bought various huts from the authorities. One was bought for 'a Native Church and School at Cookhouse.' However, Douglas Ellison had to report in January, 1905:

> I have recently received a refusal from the Railway Department to my request for a small plot on which to place this urgently needed building. It is intended almost entirely for the service of their own

> Native people, who would probably be hundreds of miles away had not the requirements of the railway drawn them there; but the application is courteously refused, on the express ground that other religious bodies may come asking for a similar concession .. We have indeed come to a pretty pass when "the illimitable emptiness" of Africa cannot hold us all![30]

Six months later Ellison was able to report that the Railway authorities had had a change of heart and had given them a prime site on railway land. Perhaps not unconnected with this 'change of heart' was the fact that Ellison was on good terms with Mr. Price, the (Baptist) General Manager of the Central South African Railways, and had received a cheque for Mission funds from him in April 1905.

Mission work among the African employees of the Railways does not seem to have been of immediate concern to the London Committee of SACRM. Although the Committee was formed in 1899 (GDRM days) and they may have discussed 'Native work' in some of their quarterly Meetings, the first minute to note this was in June 1907, when a sub-Committee suggested that an appeal be inserted in the July *Quarterly* for a memorial grave-stone for the Evangelist, Josiah Ngcambu, who had recently died.

The question has to be asked why most importance was given by the Railway Mission to bringing the Christian Church (first) to Europeans who were normally deemed to be Christian already. Speaker after speaker at the SACRM Annual Meetings in London left the hearers and, subsequently, readers in no doubt at all. The pattern at all the AGMs, certainly up to 1939, was to have various current or former missioners and the Head, when possible, talk about their work and experiences; to have a returned or visiting bishop lend some colour and episcopal blessing; but to have the main speech - the 'keynote address' as we would term it now - given by a most prominent 'Africanist'. These speakers, usually titled, and most of whom were vice-Presidents of the Railway Mission, were eminent in finance, or railway management, or railway surveying, Colonial Governing, politics, or the army. Much of the thinking of the Railway Mission, especially the policy towards work with Africans, was determined by these annual Addresses. Excerpts from four such speeches illustrate their theme.

On March 20th 1908, Lord St. Aldwyn presided at the AGM and gave the main Address. After outlining how the railways were pushing further and further 'into the wilds' of Africa, dependent on the 'essential pioneers of everything that we mean by civilisation', he went on to state:

> If you want to push the Gospel among the heathen; if you really believe it is your duty as members of the Christian Church to do the work and to spend money on that object, depend upon it you will never succeed unless you do your best to keep in connection with the Church the white men to whom the heathen look for an example. (Hear, hear) ... I should say, so far from thinking that the first work of the Missionary is among heathen and barbarous natives, I should think his work is to keep up the spirit of religion among those who have begun as Christians at home. Those are the objects of the South African Church Railway Mission ...[31]

Bishop Gaul, who had just retired from Mashonaland after thirty three years in southern Africa, followed Viscount Aldwyn. He gave a fascinating account of pioneering work and particularly the contribution of the Railway Mission, but avoided any reference to the previous speaker or his comments.

Sir Walter Hely Hutchinson, a 'great Colonial administrator', addressed a 'large gathering of friends and supporters' at the AGM in March 1910. His was a short speech, as he said that he had only one particular point to make, regarding missionary work:

> One of the strongest reasons why I am glad to support the Railway Mission is that it is particularly addressed to white people. You must not be shocked at hearing this. I yield to no one in desiring the improvement and evangelization of the black races; but it is our duty to attend to our own people first, if only in the interests of the blacks ...[My] experience as an administrator in South Africa leads me to think that the white man's interests are often neglected in favour of the black man, to the ultimate detriment of both ... It is a fact that if a white man falls in South Africa, he falls to the bottom. He goes underneath the black man, and there seems to be no means of getting him up again. [32]

The following year, 1911, Lord Selbourne told those at the AGM, 'These railwaymen [in South Africa] are living to a very great extent among the heathen, and every white man is a missionary for good or for bad, and, therefore, although this is not a Mission to the heathen, it is a Mission to the white men who will have a permanent influence on the heathen.'[33]

Various problems had been considered at the Pan-Anglican Congress in South Africa in 1908, one of which was 'The Church's Missions amongst white settlers in South Africa'. E.C. Baxter, in a Paper under that title, wrote:

> Whilst the Anglican Church raises certain sums and obtains volunteers for Missions to coloured [=African/ 'Coloured'] people, should not an effort also be made to provide for shepherding the British colonists and to give them all the assistance possible in their religious life? The temptations to commit certain sins when so far removed from Christian influences are strong, and many a man who possesses sundry good qualities sets a bad example to the natives around him ... it is an admitted fact that the natives imitate the vices of their superiors [sic] much more readily than their virtues ... What a help it would be to the advancement of Christ's kingdom on earth if the Englishmen who rule, employ or trade with the natives were to influence them by leading consistent Christian lives ...[34]

This 'setting a good example' was a constant theme of European Churches in Southern Africa. Archbishop Davidson referred to 'Civilisation, as represented by the railways, pushing itself into the heart of the mysterious continent.' Therefore they (the Church) had to see to it that 'the Christian faith ... is preserved among the white people who are going out as colonists, as well as that the Word of Life is taken to the dark races.'[35] At the Annual Meeting of SACRM, in London in 1920, Sir George Parkin, Secretary of the Rhodes Trustees, was in the Chair. He spoke of the rapid advance of the railways into Africa and of 'the absolute necessity of the whiteman being kept in touch with religion if he was to stand against the terrible temptations of a life lived in close contact with weaker [sic] races.'[36] It was obviously unclear whether 'the natives' were likely to 'imitate the vices' of the whites, or 'the whiteman' be tempted by his contact with 'weaker' races. Whichever view was held still led the European Churchmen to emphasise the necessity for the Whites in Africa to be 'kept close' to their religion, to 'save them from falling right back', as we noted earlier in the days of the Grahamstown Diocesan Railway Mission.

To most Europeans, 'Christianity' and 'Western civilisation' were synonymous. Evangelicals were not alone in believing that 'all people shared equally in the depravity of original sin, [and] .. found hard to resist the conclusion that centuries of Christian influence within a society had held in check the human sinfulness that was given a free rein in "heathen" countries'.[37]

Some of the SACRM reports indicated just what the 'vices' and 'sinfulness were, namely 'drunkenness and immorality.... (because of the presence of natives with their low moral code)..'[38], though most reports left it to the readers' imaginations. One missioner, Gray Hopkyns, visiting workers near the railhead of Newington, on the construction of the Selati line (North West from Komatipoort, eventually through Acorn Hoek and Tzaneen), clearly believed in spelling matters out:

> [There] is also the darker side of the picture; drunkenness is fearfully common, and many so-called white men are living with native wives. Think what this latter thing means: the presence of half-caste children, who are shunned alike by natives and whites, the dragging down of the white man to the native level, and the almost certain desertion of the native wife if the white man leaves the district. Religion means "holding back" from falling into these abominable sins. In the district of which I write the Railway Mission has been the only religious agent at work ...[39]

We may assume that Mr. Hopkyns' use of the term 'wives' was not suggesting that the people he had in mind had been formally married. This was not, of course, unknown at that time, and some of the Railway Chaplains officiated at such 'mixed' marriage Services. It seems unlikely that this missioner would have approved of anyone following the example of Johannes Van der Kemp, a century earlier!

The Railway Missioners, most of whom, in the early days at least, shared the prevailing views as outlined above, were therefore left in no doubt about their responsibilities to their fellow Whites. The differences and the conflicts came in their attitude to the Africans.

Douglas Ellison had felt regret at 'passing by the native huts.' Herbert Hale wondered whether the Bulawayo Christians' devotion to 'the Gospel' was limited to white people. He noted 'the bestial lives lived by so many white people' there, and felt that the 'black man ... does more credit to his savagery [sic] than the white man to his Christianity and civilisation.'[40]

At the 1908 Pan-Anglican Congress, Ellison, in his Paper 'The Pioneer Work of the Church: A Plea for the Gripping of the Railways', stated: 'Finally, it is only the serious dearth of competent European priests for Native Mission Work throughout South Africa which has prevented us hitherto from evangelising the great mass of railway-side natives on some really comprehensive scale.'[41] Work with Africans was not ruled out, given the man-power. Percy Barnes, missioner for the Alexandria Line in the Diocese of Grahamstown, reported that 'a lot of natives [went] into Zuney for service, but as there was no interpreter [they all] had to be content with hymn-singing and a prayer or two.'[42]

Geoffrey Douglas, on a trip to Elizabethville and the Congo (examined in Chapter 6), observed:

> It is not possible for the Railway Mission to do any regular native work in the Congo, but perhaps some day a regular priest may be placed here, to look after the spiritual welfare of the British people and of the native christians of the Anglican Communion.[43]

Again, the impression is given that 'native work' is an admirable hope, but that it had to take second place to the more urgent needs of 'the British'. However, Geoffrey Douglas was succeeded by the Rev. E.G. Holden in his 1,650-mile Section from Mafeking to the Congo Railhead, 250 miles within the Congo. Holden spoke at the Annual Meeting in 1915 and effectively turned the received SACRM wisdom on its head. He spoke at length about the difficulties of the work and the many problems faced by gangers and their families. At the end of his speech he addressed the question of the Railway Mission and 'native work':

> ... the ultimate aim of all our work must be native ... [and] really the Mission is helping as much in the native problem as the people of the Universities Mission [UMCA] which you come across in Northern Rhodesia. Yet compared with what there is to be done our help is comparatively small. We pass through so many countries, so many different tribes, having so many different languages, that we are confronted all the time by the language difficulty ..sometimes we try .. through interpreters. I would ask you to do your best to [help us] arouse the interest of people who so far have not been interested, so that this great black Central Africa and South Africa may be won for Christ.[44]

This evangelical call for the conversion of Africans and for 'native work' to be the 'ultimate aim' of the Railway Mission was certainly rather different from the usual calls to save the white people from 'falling right back'. Little wonder that the Chairman, at the end of the AGM, was moved to observe, 'I think most of you will agree with me that we have never had such speeches at any Meeting before as we have had this afternoon.' UMCA supporters were unlikely to be thrilled with Holden's implied suggestion that their missionaries, specifically employed for work among the Africans, were no more effective in Northern Rhodesia than the Railway missioners.

However, there is little evidence to indicate that Holden's words were heeded. He was no longer 'in the field' and, for those who did continue to serve the Railway Mission, the perennial problems of shortage of workers and money and the honouring of their commitment to railway workers and families prevented any major attempts at converting great numbers of Africans. Their efforts regarding 'native work' were more concentrated in providing worship and in conducting the 'Occasional Offices' of Baptism, Marriage and Burial, with or without the assistance of a 'native catechist'.

At isolated gangers' cottages Herbert Hale, for example, had few problems in holding Services for folk of different races and colour, particularly as all were of the same 'class'. At the larger centres and in churches he was obliged to hold separate celebrations of Holy Communion; an early one for 'natives', followed by a later one for 'whites'. Although he did champion the cause of education for Africans, in the face of much settler opposition in Rhodesia, he was not averse to giving his African servant a sjamboking for allowing another 'boy' to share his 'kia' [hut]. He records that the 'boy ... quite recognised the justice of his punishment' and that 'it would have been a very much more painful experience under another white "boss" ...[45]

Many of the missioners made attempts to bring together the different communities in worship. Sometimes this worked as a 'one off', and then they would be told by some of the Europeans that it ought not to happen again. In order to continue their work, and not 'rock the boat' too much, they acquiesced. It is difficult to know what else they could have done, given the overall prevailing views of the time. The Church of England's first 'Missionary Bishop', Charles Frederick Mackenzie, when he called in Natal en route to the Shire, 'spoke most openly on the treatment of the natives ... as a shame to the white people ...'[46] He believed in evangelising 'native heathens' and that there should be equality between the races. He advocated 'mixed Churches'. His friend and biographer, Dean Goodwin, felt him to be in error over this, yet 'the error was a noble one. It was the love of the weaker race.'![47] In some ways little progress was to be made in the next one hundred years, although we have noted the exceptional circumstances obtaining at the Sena Sugar Estates.

Protests were, of course, made. One missioner wrote of taking Communion Services at private houses and finding 'some devout old Native, baptised and confirmed, kneeling outside in the passage, not allowed to come in. Clean enough to .. handle and cook the food, .. but not clean enough to receive the Bread of Life with fellow Christians of another race and colour!'[48] Presumably the missioner did not feel incensed enough to refuse to give communion to the Whites unless they allowed their African worker to join them. Or, more likely, he knew that if he made such a stand, then he would lose his ministry to the white railway people. This would inevitably threaten the whole stated policy of SACRM. Compromise was inevitable. Ellison notes, after the above printed outburst, 'Thank God the South African Bishops have made and are making themselves felt on the side of the Native, and a Church conscience is being aroused.'[49]

Ralph Seacombe, in one of his early letters home, wrote on March 13th 1916:

> On train near Figtree:
> ... I had my first experience of native work yesterday -
> - The native catechist at Francistown came up on Saturday to ask whether I would celebrate for them in the native Church on Sunday: they wanted it fairly late, but I compromised on 10.30 a.m. as I had to be up for the White Celebration soon after 7 ... After the Creed I preached to them and Peter interpreted sentence by sentence: I found it rather easier than usual as the break gives one time to collect scattered thoughts! ...[50]

Here was one missioner at least who was happy with having to have an interpreter. Sixteen months later and Seacombe had still to rely on the language skills of others:

> On Monday I went to Ramaquabane and had a nice little Service under the Church tree ... The following morning I was away at 7 for the Native Stadt, the two mile bike ride being intensely cold: Celebration there, and back at 8.30 for one on the farm. Then over to the Stadt for eight Baptisms (5 adults) and a Native wedding, which kept me an hour and a half in Church with all the interpreting ...[51]

The great reduction in English-speaking railwaymen did mean that some of the SACRM staff had to re-examine their work, at least until the time came when the Mission withdrew completely from South Africa. It meant, for some, that they could spend more time ministering to Africans, as Eustace Hill, C.R., (Head) seems to be saying in his Letter in September 1935:

> I realize that the Railway Mission must keep to the rail, and where the railway natives are not ministered to by missionaries [ie. other Societies] and where the services of the S.A.C.R.M. are welcomed by the Bishop, these make up for the loss of British railway men by serving the Bantu far better. [52]

It was still, clearly, a matter of 'native work' being undertaken as a kind of second best. Hill's somewhat pointed remark about bishops is indicative of his troubled relationship with hierarchy and his idiosyncratic views of the Railway Mission, both of which led him to being 'persuaded' to resign from the Headship, as will be detailed in Chapter 8. He finally 'went over' to the Roman Catholic Church, to the surprise of no-one.

The same issue of the *Quarterly* which published Hill's letter contained an account by the Rev. Roy Sinker of the actual work among Africans that was being undertaken in the Alicedale Section:

> More and more on this Section the Mission is taking up work amongst the natives; their spiritual needs are tended from three centres where there are native churches, and we are trying not to neglect their bodily needs. Soup kitchens for the native and coloured school children have been started in Alicedale and Sandflats, and we hope start one at Addo in the near future. Both the local doctor and the schoolmasters felt that there was a tremendous need for some such scheme, as it is almost impossible to teach children who are hungry, and hungry children are easy targets for any germs .. about.[53]

The Minutes of a Meeting of the London Committee, held in July 1938, include the cryptic sentence: 'Letter from Rev. H. Insley concerning Native work was not dealt with.' Six years were to pass before the Committee discussed Insley's concerns, as we shall note shortly.

In the meantime, Harold Insley gave a colourful account of another aspect of SACRM's ministry to Africans:

> The most interesting event of the last few months [written in February, 1940] has been my camp for Naauwpoort and Rosmead native children at Port Elizabeth. ..Thirty-three children - boys and girls - attended camp and had a right royal time and lots of fun. ... ten whole days by the sea - - I might even say in the sea.
> ... For some it was the first long train journey; for all, except three, it was the first time that they had ever seen the sea ... A concert given by the children in camp ... was witnessed and enjoyed by over eighty people from Port Elizabeth. On Wednesday, January 10th, we all went ... and sang Evensong in St. Mary's Church (the Port Elizabeth - European - Parish Church). It was the first occasion that a native choir had sat in the choir stalls of St. Mary's ... I hope [the camp] will be the first of many more in the future. We have the distinction of being the first Mission to have organised a native camp in the Eastern Province of South Africa ..[54]

Edward Winckley, who arrived in South Africa at the beginning of 1942 to work on the Railway Mission, was very soon aware of the 'colour problem'. He admitted in his first letter that he had been advised (not by SACRM) not to say publicly what he found to be 'horrible':

> The things I refer to have to do with irrational colour prejudice and misguided ideas of racial prestige ... In the matters of housing and education of natives at Naauwpoort, for example, much is left to be desired. Yet the Europeans' houses and schools are up to date. There are houses on the native locations literally tumbling to pieces ... Why should not a black man be allowed to drive an engine (if he is competent to do so) if a black woman is good enough to nurse a white baby? Yet all the higher paid jobs on the railway are reserved for Europeans ...
> ... At a Capetown Church I attended, the natives went up for their Communion when all the Europeans had been communicated. I believe this is quite usual out here, but what a shame! [55]

Winckley's criticisms were those made by many who had recently arrived from England, though it was not very often that such comments appeared in SACRM literature. He was careful not to write in this way in *Light for the Line,* particularly with his comments on railway-worker policy. At the Annual Festival in July, 1943, Francis Synge, a former missioner, told his audience that it was felt that the Mission should 'confine its activities either to white or to black people.'[56] He believed that the prevailing view in South Africa, that there could be no mixing, was wrong, but that the Mission could not ignore the situation. He went on to say that 'the Railway Missioner had not the time to minister to both. He had had about 1200 miles to cover, and his time had been fully occupied with white folk.' His final point concerned the Passes issued to Missioners. He felt that, 'if the Railway Mission ministered regularly to the natives' the Railway authorities could withdraw the Passes. There is no evidence to suggest that this would be so, unless, of course, the Mission entirely abandoned its ministry to Whites.

Harold Insley's concerns about SACRM's work with Africans returned to the Agenda of the London Committee in 1944. The Minutes of the Meeting in June that year record: 'Cable from Head - reference "to an erroneous statement made by Mr. Insley to the effect that the SACRM was no longer ministering to the Railway Natives".' The cable, and Mr. Insley's comments, had to wait another two months before they were discussed. The Minute, in full, reads:

> At this point [in the Meeting] the letter from the Head re the Rev. H.M Insley's statement that the Mission was not going to do any Native work in future was read. This letter was a follow up of cables between the Head and the Secretary and explained the situation, which showed that Mr. Insley was entirely wrong in his statement that the Railway Natives were to be left out of the Mission's care in

> future, and the Head [by cable had] asked that a statement to this effect might be inserted in the next Quarterly Paper. [57]

Monica James, whose future with the Mission happened to be discussed at that Meeting in August 1944, informed me that 'Insley's comments were true - up to a point.' It happened to be the time when SACRM was withdrawing from the 'Native Hospital' at Naauwpoort and Insley's views were coloured by that. Also, as this was during the Second World War, it was not possible to recruit and send out extra workers from England. Nevertheless, as noted above, Insley had been concerned for a number of years about the paucity of the Mission's ministry to African railway workers. Available evidence suggests that his pleas were ignored. No statement was inserted in any of the Quarterly Magazines following the London Committee Meeting. Few of SACRM's supporters would have been aware that the issue of ministry to Africans had even been discussed.

Each year the Railway Missioners held a Staff Conference, usually, until the withdrawal from South Africa, at the Convent of the Holy Cross, Irene. That held during February 1950 was notable in that the Head, Maurice Lancaster, gave a Statement of Policy, particularly regarding work with Africans, and in that the nine staff were addressed by the Rev. Trevor Huddleston, C.R. Speaking generally, the Head stated:

> I believe it to be the right policy of the Mission to regard all the people along the Line, within our care, as our responsibility. They have been baptized, even where they are not Anglicans, and are undoubtedly members of the Church ... Charity binds us to do all in our power for everyone, particularly for the less attractive people, or for those who are in great need.[58]

These comments were chiefly aimed at those who felt that Afrikaners, the majority of whom were members of the Dutch Reformed Church, should not receive the ministrations of the Railway Mission. The Head then turned his attention to 'The Africans', and gave an uncompromising statement, which needs quoting in full (as reported; the exact words used do not exist):

> The Head remarked that the time had come to pay less attention to the too tender susceptibilities of the weaker brethren; circumstances were now very different, and there was need for Gospel teaching to be more plainly stated. A most important point in all this was to make very sure that people were disabused of the idea that the Gospel taught that any social equality was necessarily implied. Social equality and social intercourse were based on common habits,

common interests, and a common cultural background. And the Fatherhood of God and the brotherhood of man did not necessarily imply the necessity for social intercourse with any European or African. [59]

These remarks by SACRM's Head have to be viewed in the context of that period in South Africa's history. It was less than two years since the Reunited National Party (HNP) of Malan formed the country's first exclusively Afrikaner Government, replacing segregation policies by apartheid. The Prohibition of Mixed Marriages Act was already being enforced, and the Population Registration Bill (with its definitions of 'race' and the provision for the carrying of identity cards), and the Immorality and Group Area Bills were going through Parliament, prior to becoming Acts during the year (1950). During 1948, Churches, other than the Dutch Reformed, had formerly criticised proposed apartheid legislation. The Anglican bishops, at Synod in November 1948, had stated, 'if ... Europeans seek to preserve to themselves the exclusive benefits of Western Civilisation, and to allow the non-Europeans merely its burdens, South Africans will inexorably draw apart into mutually antagonistic groups.'[60] The Rosettenville Conference in 1949, which was the first ecumenical Church Conference after the 1948 elections, was important in setting the anti-apartheid positions of the English-speaking churches for the next forty years.

In 1949 Trevor Huddleston had been appointed Provincial, for South Africa, of the Community of the Resurrection, and Superintendent of St. Peter's School (now St Martin's), Rosettenville. Although his *Naught for your comfort* was still seven years away, his crusade for African rights had resulted both in praise and opprobrium. He spoke at the SACRM Conference on 'The African Outlook'. It is probable that he outlined the points which he was making public at that time, namely that the racial divisions within churches were not a result of geographical or linguistic difficulties, but rather of fear and prejudice and outright racism. He believed that the churches had failed on the colour issue and that increasing numbers of Africans were condemning the religion which allowed discrimination to happen.

Monica James, one of the 'Women Workers' at the Conference, remembers that, at that time, there was a feeling that the Railway Mission 'ought to have been more heavily involved with the African situation.' She said that many Missions were very pro-African, but that SACRM was not, though the Mission was aware of 'the increasing vocal demands' of many Africans and of Whites such as Huddleston. That, it appears, was the reason that he had been invited to speak at the Staff Conference. His views must have contrasted sharply with those expressed by SACRM's

Head, Maurice Lancaster. Yet, Lancaster himself was to change. Monica James notes that he altered his views considerably, once the Mission transferred to Rhodesia, becoming more pro-African, with the Mission itself then admitting African priests to its staff.

Peter Garnett, who was a SACRM chaplain from 1955, recalls that when he was at Bronkhorstspruit he used his 'coloured servant as a server [ie.in the Communion Service] in the church room.'[61] The farmer who was attending the service refused to go again. On another occasion, at Komatipoort, he was asked to put on an 'early Mass', so that a Mrs. Gilmour could go and play her tennis! He suggested that she went to the 'earlier Mass laid on for the Africans'. This she did, but when he returned to base three weeks later he found a letter from the Komatipoort [SACRM] Committee stating, '.. they did not think that the time was right, nor were the Africans ready to have services for them in the same building as that used by whites, even at different times.' The SACRM Head advised him to 'give in', which he did. It was, of course, a case of the Whites not being ready, rather than the reverse. It is unlikely that African views were asked for.

Not all the discrimination was of Africans by Europeans. Ray White, when Head of SACRM, wrote of a Railway Township which had a large church consisting of 'native Africans and Coloured families'. He was approached by one of the Coloured men and told that they were collecting money to build their own church. On asking the reason, White was told ' ... Father, how can you expect us to associate with the Kaffirs? We have our own school and .. we shall have our own church.'[62]

Clearly, the Railway Missioners were frequently faced with a dilemma. On the one hand they did not condone a colour bar which resulted in separate worship Services for Africans, Coloureds and Whites, but, on the other hand, they were extremely unhappy with mixed marriages, particularly where these seemed to be short-term relationships. We noted, in the previous chapter, how exhilarating the missioners found multi-racial / multi-national worship on the Sena Sugar Estates. They were, however, never in a strong enough position to insist on such mixing. The Mission was a small society within the Anglican Church of the Province of South Africa. The missioners themselves were mostly 'imported' from Britain, whereas the majority of their 'congregations' along the line or in railway centres had settled in the country before they, the missioners, had arrived. Much of the local support for the Mission came from Anglicans in well-established parishes. Courageous and outspoken priests, such as Trevor Huddleston, did not find universal approval among fellow Anglicans, particularly among Whites native to the country. It was little wonder, therefore, that itinerant clergy, who had a somewhat lower profile, were able to make little headway with racial tolerance and acceptance.

The last account of SACRM's 'native work', prior to the first African priest joining in December 1959, was at the Annual Meeting in June of that year. During the Meeting, Peter Garnett stated:

> African work, although in many ways some of the most interesting and rewarding is, however only a small part of our work. It is a pity that it cannot be larger ... African work is very much a specialised thing, which is probably better not done at all if it cannot be done properly. ... [We] only help to keep things going where there is already a congregation, and do not attempt any evangelistic work. That is in any case better left to the Africans themselves to do.[63]

Work had been 'left to the Africans' from the earliest Grahamstown days of the Railway Mission, usually in the hands of evangelists. It is to this ministry that we now turn.

Ministry by Africans

> Catholic missionaries and Protestants alike looked forward to the time when their pupils, fully instructed in the Word of God, would spread out into the villages and preach it with the full wealth of African metaphor and simile, to the millions whom they themselves could never hope to reach.[64]

The 'missionary factor in East Africa', as outlined by Oliver in his seminal work, had many unique features, not least Livingstone's individual influence, coupled with that of the powerful Church Missionary Society. However, all missions had one common factor with those of East Africa, the reliance on indigenous Christian leaders. Ranger pointed out that 'from the very beginning, African catechists and teachers bore the main burden of conversion.'[65] Van Velsen, in his introduction to *The Life of a Zambian Evangelist,* states, of Paul Mashindo's life:

> It gives an insight into the role, the difficulties and ambivalences of the local Christian evangelists in relation to the foreign missionaries. The latter were the advance guard of the expansion of Christianity; they tended to want to retain the initiative in their own hands ... [The] local allies of the missionaries would appear to have been a crucial element in whatever successes the foreign evangelising agents have been able to register. But merely being the soldiers and the N.C.O.s,

so to say, to the missionary / officers, the role of these local allies has on the whole received less attention ...[66]

When we examine the photographic evidence of mission endeavours we notice the (white) missionary dominating the scene. 'He stands forth at the centre of ... the pictures of missionary parties and church councils ... The faces of the African co-workers to his right and to his left, standing behind him or sitting before him on the ground, are not very clear.'[67] The dust has to be removed from these 'African co-workers', who spread the Christian Gospel in their own environment.

Increasingly, the witness of these 'soldiers and N.C.O.s' is being treated seriously. It is acknowledged that the expansion and development of much of Christianity in Africa depended on African initiatives. South of the equator, 'although most of the pioneer mission stations were founded by Whites, it was African catechists, teachers traders and migrant labourers who assimilated the faith and initiated villagers, kinsfolk, workmates and strangers into [the] new identity.'[68]

A careful reading of Robert Moffat's ministry in Kuruman, of Coillard's establishing of the Paris Mission among the Lozi of Western Zambia, of Bishop Knight-Bruce's journey to Mashonaland, to pick but three different denominational and pioneering accounts, shows the indispensable role played by African evangelists and interpreters. Bible translation and the writing down, and therefore standardising, of African languages is usually credited to the great pioneering missionaries. They were, nevertheless, entirely dependent on their African 'guides'. This situation obtained until modern times, when the Europeans could become the co-workers and 'soldiers'. The Rev. Etienne Berger, for example, in his 1970 'Revision' (though basically a completely new and enlarged version) of Jalla's *Silozi-English Dictionary,* wrote, 'Our sincere thanks are ... due to Mr. Alex Silumesii Mubita who, from the very beginning, has been our much appreciated Silozi guide.'[69]

Some ordained evangelists, such as Leonard Kamungu of Malawi and Zambia, the 'priest from the lakeside', and Paul Mushindo, were ordained priests and have become famed in their own right - for who and what they were - rather than 'N.C.O.s' to European 'officers'. In many areas the evangelists were denied 'promotion' to full priestly ordination, or were made to wait an inordinate length of time.

Unlike many of the Protestant Missions, the Anglican Church in southern Africa had two separate arms to its work, the white parishes, mainly ministering to the settler community, and the missions, serving the African and Coloured communities. Most of the 'missionary ministries' became, from the time of the Provincial Missionary Conference in 1892, independent of the parochial system. The work of Anglican catechists and evangelists reflected the distinctive C.P.S.A. ethos. It is worth noting that, at the first Provincial Synod in 1870, when the title 'Church of the Province of South Africa' was adopted,

> it was ... a great deficiency that no African clergyman was at that ... Synod. There was not, indeed, *any* clergyman who had been born in [the] country with a seat in synod. [The] English Church in [South Africa], after nearly three-quarters of a century's existence, was still unable to find any priest born and bred in South Africa, of any race or colour, who could represent it at what was probably the most important synod in its history.[70]

This situation changed but slowly. Shortage of priests of any nationality meant that large numbers of men (rarely women), both black and white, were licensed as lay readers or catechists. In rural areas in particular, and to some extent in the towns, these licensed lay people preached and instructed baptism and confirmation candidates. Their job was to 'provide services in between the visits of a priest and to help the priest when he ... [came].' Many an African (ordained) evangelist started his ministry in the Anglican Church, as did others in different Churches, by being a lay reader or catechist.

Illustrative of this is the work of the African staff of the South African Church Railway Mission.

African catechists and evangelists

> In December [1896] Jonas Mcangangwa became the first Native Catechist of the Mission ... There we are then, six full workers - two clergymen, three Lay Evangelists, and a Native Catechist ...[71]

From the beginning, the seniority order was established, only to expand as the Railway Mission expanded: 'Head of Mission, Assistant Missioners, Laymen, Lady Workers, Nurses, Native Catechists and Preachers.' In the same paragraph that readers learned of Jonas Mcangangwa's appointment, they read, 'and, best of all, we now have a second clergyman in the person of Mr. Forshaw ...' Perhaps it was not too surprising that Mr. Mcangangwa immediately disappeared without trace, at least from the Railway Mission's pages! Within a few months Josiah Ngcambu was to take the place of the first 'Native Catechist' and was to feature frequently in the Mission's letters and reports. For example:

He is well, happy and doing famous work, as ever. His great ambition at the moment is to build a small Native Church in his old camp at Norval's Pont ...[72]

I have heard nothing but good news of Josiah's work amongst the natives on [the Midland] line ... and it is much to be desired that ... a second Native Catechist, like-minded, may be doing similar work upon the Eastern.[73]

The young readers of SACRM's 'Children's Quarterly Leaflet' in January 1904 were given details, by Douglas Ellison, about Josiah Ngcambu and his son, Shadrach:

Shadrach ... is the son of Josiah Ngcambu, a Zulu, and the oldest of our Native Catechists in the Railway Mission. Some years ago, when I first knew him, Josiah was the head coal-porter in one of our Railway Camps; but even in those days he used to gather his own people together, and teach them about the Lord Jesus Christ. Well! I wanted a good native to come and work amongst our black Railway folk, I thought first of all of Josiah; and he at once gave up an excellent post, and became our Catechist at Naauwpoort, for something like half the salary he was earning as a Railway man; and there he has been doing a fine work for God and His Church ever since.

Well! Shadrach is his son ... his years, I think, 13 ... His father and mother quite rightly want him to be well educated. Who knows but that, some day, he may minister as a priest among his own people? Anyway, they sent him down to our Kaffir Institute [Grahamstown] ... and I want some of you to lend me a helping hand in keeping him. Josiah is too poor to manage it ... [and] the boy clearly mustn't suffer through his father joining the Mission.[74]

The same issue of the 'Children's Leaflet' included a letter from Shadrach, written from Grahamstown. The 'Shadrach Ngcambu Fund' continued for many years, to give support for his education. His father usually had at least four Services a Sunday, with an average attendance of between sixty and seventy, and took 'regular classes for Catechumers [sic] and Confirmation candidates during the week.'

By August 1900 the Mission Head was pleased to report:

An event of exceptional interest at Naauwpoort has been the recent visit of Canon Woodrooffe, a member of our [Grahamstown] Cathedral Chapter, and one of the first Kaffir scholars in the country. I have long been anxious to see our Native work extended on wise

> and durable lines, and this visit was ... undertaken ... for the purpose of forming a reliable opinion, both as to the value of Josiah's ministrations, and as to the possibility of further developments. Canon Woodrooffe['s] .. advice is that we should aim at extending our native work, on similar lines, to other larger Railway Camps ...[75]

By July 1902 Benjamin Raba had joined the Mission as Native Catechist at Sterkstroom; replaced the following year by James Kutshwayo, with Walter Collis Belu at Cookhouse; and joined, by October 1903, by William Xesi at Grahamstown, giving a total of four Catechists (Josiah Ngcambu remaining at Naauwpoort).

The SACRM 'Children's Quarterly' (No.16) of July 1907 reported that Josiah Ngcambu had been ' "called up higher" after many years of devoted service for God and His Church ...' It told that:

> he was brought up as a heathen but that as soon as ever he heard about the true God he gave his heart to Him and began at once to teach his heathen neighbours what he had himself learnt and had so changed his life. And so God used that heart and that life to win many to Him, and he and his wife, who shared his faith and his labours, have been such a blessing to the natives at Naauwpoort that many a time those natives have shamed us white people by their love and devotion to God. I wonder how many English parishes there are, where all through Lent - at 4.30 in the morning and at 7.30 in the evening, the Church is full of working men and women on their way to and from their work. And yet this is what you would see at St. Agnes', Naaupoort, the men filling one side and the women the other, and all showing such a simple but deep reverence as one seldom sees in Christian England! And all of it under the inspiring leadership, not of a white Missionary, but of a Zulu Catechist!

Dorothy Ellison recounted how Josiah Ngcambu, as all the catechists, was 'schoolmaster as well as catechist' and of how, typically, a priest wrote 'of having to baptize at one time no less than fifty adults prepared by Josiah, all of whom had passed ... [the] examination.'[76] The Baptism Registers show the SACRM (white) clergy as the Officiating Ministers, and the Confirmation Registers give the bishops' names, yet, where those baptised or confirmed were African, it had been the 'Native Catechists' who had done all the preparation.

In discussing 'Railway Mission work with Africans' we noted Edmund Smith's letter from Naauwpoort, in which he wrote that he was the 'only Missioner on the Staff who has any Native work at all.' His letter concluded with a description of the work done by the Catechists. It is one of the very few detailed accounts written in all SACRM literature of this ministry by Africans, and merits quoting in full:

> The Catechist is a busy man. His duties are many and various. In the absence of the priest he conducts morning and evening services, and preaches, takes the Sunday School, gives the preliminary preparation to candidates for confirmation, visits the sick, in cases of emergency baptizes the sick, instructs the hearers and catechumens, collects diocesan dues and etc. Where he is trained - that is has spent a year at St. Matthew's, Keiskama Hoek, or Zonnebloem College, Cape Town - he is a whole-time catechist.
>
> Unfortunately both our men at Naauwpoort and Rosmead are untrained and through lack of means are compelled to engage in secular occupations. David Mjezu at Naauwpoort is a painter and David Lolwana at Rosmead is a labourer in the Station Gang. David Lolwana is an old man and has spent his best years in railway service and now has a fairly light job - no longer wielding a pick and shovel. The Rosmead Mission owes a great deal to him. He is typical of many acting-catechists who work for love and without any monetary remuneration. The small congregation has been gathered together and tended and cared for by him for many years. The tiny church, a low-roofed, rough-built shanty, some 25 feet by 12 feet, composed of old railway sleepers, old corrugated iron and old flooring boards and paraffin tins is his work. ... Perhaps when we have built the Church for the Europeans at Rosmead we may be able to build a permanent church for the Natives.[77]

The Railway Mission was never secure enough financially to afford the training costs and then salaries of full-time African catechists, especially as the first call on money was always for the work done by European missioners.

Peter Garnett, who was with the Railway Mission in its final two years in South Africa (1955-7) and then moved to Northern Rhodesia as the Mission became the 'Rhodesia and Nyasaland Railway Mission', has spoken and written, as observed earlier, about work with Africans. Of the work done by them, he noted:

> In my time the Waterval Boven African congregation had a regular Mass once a month, and when I arrived there was an African catechist ... Stanley Lakaje, who did his best, but he was not very good at accounts ... From time to time I visited in the WTB [Waterval Boven] location with him, trying to communicate in a mixture of English and minimal Afrikaans ... While I was there

> Bishop Robert Selby Taylor wanted a retirement post for an elderly African priest, Fr. Evelyn D'lepu, so he joined us and ministered ...
> .... At Monze [N.Rhodesia] an enterprising African had built a church in his own backyard and used the church for a dormitory for his older boys. It was remarkable how much more initiative Africans have for collecting up other Anglicans and having services. Whites would sit around and wait for a priest to do that work for them ... The African church leaders were all in quite humble positions, I forget what the Monze man did, perhaps he worked in the mealie silos. The leader at Kafue worked in the post office behind the counter. The Mazabuka leader was, as often a teacher, and at Kalomo .... he worked in a store .[78]

The work of the evangelist, Stanley Lakaje, and of the priest, the Rev. E. D'lepu, was summarised in the SACRM Annual Reports in 1955 and 1956. Of Lakaje's ministry the 1954/5 Report stated:

> This Catechist's main work is in the Railway Camp at Waterval Boven and at Machadodorp. During the year he has concentrated on strengthening the work in these centres; the other visits have been largely concerned with breaking fresh ground in Evangelisation. He has some 70 children who are regular Sunday School attendants, and he prepared 27 adults for Confirmation, and 18 adult converts have been prepared for Baptism. [79]

The Report noted that the Evangelist had paid 176 visits during the year to seven places. The following year, some seventy years since the Mission had started, the Annual Report announced: 'One further development of the Mission work has been on the African side. For the first time in the Mission's history we have an African priest on the Staff, stationed at Waterval Boven.'[80] Readers were not informed that this was a 'retirement post for an elderly African priest.' They were told that the Mission hoped soon to station another African priest at the Railway centre of Lochinvar, near Salisbury. As we shall note below, supporters had heard this before, and nothing had happened.

By the time that SACRM withdrew from South Africa there were no longer any 'African Catechists' on its staff. Missioners were still to rely, from time to time, on parochial / diocesan catechists to help them in interpreting during Services. The official Railway Mission work done by Africans during the Mission's final years was that by its priests.

African priests

> As soon as possible the Mission hopes to take on its Staff its first African priest, to work a part of the Line in Southern Rhodesia.

> An African priest was shortly to be appointed for the Railway Natives.

These two notices, the first one appearing in the 'Blue Quarterly' in August/September 1949, and the second being a Minute of the London Committee in July of the same year, would have brought some cheer to the Mission's supporters and Committee members. Perhaps, at last, those who had criticised the Railway Mission for its apparent lack of enthusiasm regarding 'Native work' would be silenced.

However, matters were not straightforward. The wish for African priests, and even increasing willingness that they be employed, came up against practical difficulties. SACRM clergy and women-workers, with only one or two exceptions, throughout its whole history had been recruited in England and sent out from there. This was not ideal and has been criticised, as we shall note in Chapter 8. Clearly this was not an option for the recruitment of African priests. If they were to be employed it would necessitate them being seconded from parochial duties, ie. given permission by the bishop. The work of the Railway Mission was not a priority for most bishops, given their perpetual shortage of parochial staff. The Mission was also entirely dependent upon the goodwill of the Railway authorities, especially regarding free Passes and other privileges. They could not assume that African priests on the staff would be afforded the same concessions, particularly in the period when the Afrikaners had taken governmental control in South Africa, racial riots were on the increase, and a Federation of the Rhodesias and Nyasaland was being actively proposed.

Three more years were to pass before the matter of African priests was again raised at a Meeting of the London Committee. The Bishop of Southern Rhodesia addressed the Meeting, thanking the Committee for its considerable help to him over the years, though complaining vigorously regarding overwork by SACRM staff, due to the lack of personnel. He stated that 'the old pioneering days would return with the construction of the new line from Bannockburn to Lourenco Marques, and he outlined a scheme for the use of African priests to work with the Chaplains along the line .., the Mission being needed in S.Rhodesia for many years to come.'[81]

We may note the suggestion that the proposed priests were to work with (European) Chaplains, he was not suggesting the independence that the white missioners had. The bishop's 'scheme' was, apparently, not marked 'urgent', for over seven years were to go by before secondment took place in Southern Rhodesia, though, as we have seen, an elderly African priest was stationed at Waterval Boven, in South Africa, during 1956.

The SACRM Head, Ray White, on a visit to England, attended the Meeting of the London Committee in April 1959. The Minutes reported:

> Head informed Committee that the Bishop had seconded an African priest, Fr. Noel Borerwe, for work with our Mission. He would be joining in January [1960] for a trial period of 1 year. Bishop prepared to lend him for 3 years. Head spoke of tremendous opportunities awaiting Fr. Borerwe, should he prove himself to be an Evangelist.[82]

It was clear that there was still some hesitancy over the new step to be taken, yet Fr. Borerwe was to 'prove himself' a far greater evangelist, in its widest sense, than anyone had anticipated or imagined. Back in Bulawayo, on the day that he gave in his resignation to the Archbishop of Central Africa, the Head was pleased to write to the supporters of the Railway Mission:

> I can ... give you a certain amount of good news, the most important being that we are to have two African Priests as Mission Chaplains, quite soon.
>
> Father Willie Sigeca is joining us on December 1st and will be stationed at the Railway Township of Mpopoma, near Bulawayo and Father Noel Borerwe will come on to the staff as soon as we can get a house built for him in the Township of Lochinvar, near Salisbury. So we shall have one each in the two Dioceses of Matabeleland and Mashonaland. ... Their work will not be at all easy, but it is a great help that they are both ex-Rhodesia Railway employees who realised their vocations to the Ministry while they were working on the Railways ...[83]

Ray White went on to give reasons why the priests' work was likely to be exacting; - the separate communities of Platelayers' gangs, few of whom had been in touch with Missions before; the influence of Jehovah's Witnesses; the frustrations felt by many African railway workers over the obduracy of white Trade Unionists; and the special problems facing the African workers who had recently moved from rural communities to industrialised city life in the large Railway Townships. White had, in fact, accurately identified the main areas of change confronting the Railway Mission in its work north of the Limpopo, changes that were examined above.

Six African priests were to serve the Railway Mission in its last twenty years. The printed letters, private correspondence and interviews with the three best known of the six can tell the story for them all. It is indeed fortunate that, not only did Africans become 'full' Chaplains of the Railway Mission, albeit rather late in the day, but that their story can be told in their own (second-language) words, rather than, as so often, being transmitted through the European screen.

The Rev. William (Willie) Sigeca

William Sigeca, whilst being interviewed in Bulawayo, in the Cathedral in which he had been ordained, outlined the period leading up to his time with the Rhodesia and Nyasaland Railway Mission:

> I was a clerk on the Railways and was a Lay Reader [in the Anglican Church] for many years - from my youth upwards. I was [later] chosen by my people for ordination. In 1945 the railway people went on strike [as noted earlier]. I was the leader - I was responsible for everything.[84] The Government intervened - they thought they could divide us - so we got a lady barrister from South Africa, for six months. During the Strike we tried to approach the D.C. for money [to pay the barrister]. Then we had to collect money - one thousand pounds - all paid by the Africans themselves, nobody else helped us.
>
> My friend, Rev. Percy Ibbotson, a Methodist, - he was one of the Strike Commission and also on the National Labour Board.[85] He told me, that when I went for ordination, if I passed my examinations, he would buy my ordination gown ... He got the cassock and surplice for me, from overseas, in 1954 ... [After the strike] the Railways were forced to build better houses for their employees...[86]

Railway authorities world-wide are not noted for being accommodating to staff involved with organising strikes. When I asked whether the Rhodesia Railways had responded in any negative way to Willie Sigeca, following the strike, he replied that they had not held that against him at all. Even when he transferred to the Railway Mission, they had issued him with a free Pass, as noted below, and were happy for him to minister to their employees. The General Managers of Rhodesia Railways were all at least nominally Anglican, and Trevor Wright, the 'G.M.' at that time, was a very devout Anglican, the Honorary Treasurer of the Railway Mission and extremely supportive of all the work undertaken by it. There is no doubt at all that, given those facts and Rhodesia's general ethos, Anglican priests, even former strike leaders, would have been deemed more preferable for ministering to railwaymen than ministers of independent Churches / sects, which were often unfairly deemed to be subversive.

The Railway Mission *Quarterly* of December 1960 included letters from both of the newly-appointed African priests, accompanied by a photograph of the two. Readers were informed: 'Fr. Sigeca, one of the two African Priests on our Staff, is doing a wonderful work in the African township of Mpopoma. Both he and Fr. Borerwe have been tremendously encouraged by the response and welcome they have received from the African Railway workers.' William Sigeca's letter was a very detailed three-page account of his appointment and his work. A flavour, at least, may be captured with an edited version of his letter:

> In July 1959 .. the Archbishop of the Province of Central Africa came to St. Michael's Mission in the Gwaai Reserve, to take Confirmation there ... Discussing with him some of the things concerning the development of the Mission, he said to me, 'I do not know yet [when] you might be removed from this place to somewhere else, but you will be told in three weeks time.'... Towards the end of October [sic] I received a letter saying ["You] have now been transferred from St. Michael's to the Rhodesia and Nyasaland Railway Mission. You have been chosen because of your previous experience with the Railways." I was then referred to the Director [Head] of the Railway Mission to consult him so as to get all the necessary information from him as I was to start work on the 1st December, 1959.
>
> On the 1st of December I left St. Michael's for Bulawayo. I found my house still incomplete, but the Builder was working on it.
>
> ... In January I started to think about going out on the Lines. On the 10th January I left Bulawayo for Dett which is one of the big stations [Railway centre / township, etc] on the North line. I stayed there for three days trying to find out what the place was like. I found only one Communicant with [a] few other lapsed Christians. I had Services in the Welfare Hall for all those days I was there. During my stay in Dett I visited Malindi which is the first place where there are some Platelayers [Rhodesian term for 'gangers'] on line from Dett to Bulawayo. I conducted the Service there for them.
>
> On my way back I visited Ngamo, Gwaai Sawmills and then back to Bulawayo. I started again during that same month ... to go out on the East Line. I went straight to Gwelo and started working backwards from Gwelo. I visited Somabula, Daisyfield, Shangani, Insiza, Kambo Lochard and Bembesi.
>
> When I arrive at these places for the first time I start by going to introduce myself to the Station Master ... or to a Ganger [in charge of

platelayers] where there is no Station Master. That I am a Railway Missioner I have come here on Railway Mission business. May I see your people, he says yes. You can see them at the Compound, or if he'[s] good enough, he calls his Headman (or Boss Boy) and says to him, here is a Priest - he wants to see you all at the Compound, tell the people to get ready.

When the people are ready the Boss Boy and I look round for a suitable place where people can sit just in the open air. I often start by introducing myself to them, telling them about my work, what it is about and so on. After that the Service begins. When I have [Service] books I distribute them amongst them, but I hardly get responses.

After the Service I ask them to sit down to find out to what Denominations do they belong. Everywhere I find [a] few people who belong to these peculiar Sects such as Zimutu (Zion) Jehovaha's [sic] Witnesses, etc., in some places I do find members of the Roman Catholic and [a] few others who belong to different denominations working in this country. But the rest belong to no denominations at all. It is obvious that the most important part of my work on these [railway] lines is to evangelise these people which some of them have been influenced by these Sects. However, it is hope that after a year or two something good will come out of it ...

[When] I am on the line where there are [a] few communicants I always arrange to have the Holy Communion administered to them (next morning) ...

Bulawayo has two Townships. Matshobana and No. 5 Township ... there are so many Religious bodies working in these townships, mostly Sects. However, that is not the thing I am afraid of. I myself have two congregations here in Bulawayo, one at Matshobana another one at No.5 Township. I hold Services (H.C.) in both of these places every Sunday, and the number of Christians is increasing every month due to the fact that those who had ceased to practise their Christianity now wish to come back. ... On weekdays when I am at home I hold Services in my office (H.C. and E[vening] P[rayer). It is not surprising because I have no Church yet, but it is hoped that I shall soon be alright .. (Signed) W.Sigeca. [87]

During interview, in August 1993, William Sigeca agreed that he had enjoyed his time with the Railway Mission, though the work had been exacting and tiring. He had always felt on equal terms with the white missioners or, rather, never noticed that he was not being treated as an equal. However, when asked whether or not he ever travelled in the Mission caboose, he replied, 'No, no, no ... what they did - they were clever people - they gave me a Second class ticket, a free Pass, so that I could go up and down the line.' The 'they' refers to the Rhodesian Railways, rather than to the Railway Mission. Although the other missioners would have a First class Pass for the times they needed to travel without the caboose, this was a period when there were four classes of carriages on the Rhodesian Railways. Even to travel by Second Class was comparatively rare for any African.

As well as the question of the 'Colour bar', that of whether or not the African railwaymen appreciated having their 'own' missioner, inevitably came into the conversation. When asked about this, the Rev. Sigeca responded:

> Yes, very much .. very, very much. You see, in my time most of the platelayers were .. Coloured people.
> JMR: And before you, they'd not been looked after?
> Sigeca: No - not at all, not at all. As I said, the Mission had started from South Africa ... it was just one-sided, and when I say 'one-sided' [I mean] for Europeans ...
> JMR: The literature said that it was 'a ministry for all races ...'
> Sigeca: It wasn't that way .. not here, but it depended on the type of missioner ... it changed ...[88]

The major factor in the change was the advent of the African priests in the Mission. At the Annual Festival of the Railway Mission, in September 1966, Harold Crane, the Missioner/Secretary, reported:

> The two Railway Missioners who have the longest service with the mission are ... the Rev. Noel Borerwe and the Rev. William Sigeca, our African Chaplains in Mashonaland and Matabeleland respectively. These two priests are veritable dynamos. They are as active and enthusiastic, zealous and diligent as they were when they joined the mission some six years ago. They are truly a blessing to the people and a wonderful example to all of us on the staff.[89]

After serving for eight years with the Railway Mission William Sigeca was, in 1967, asked by Bishop Kenneth Skelton to go to the St. Athanasius's Mission at Ngamba, Ngai. His work was taken over by two priests, the Rev. John Mhlabi as Railway Missioner for Matabeleland, and the Rev. Matthias Damasane as priest-in-charge of the church of Christ the King, Sizinda. Sizinda church had been built by the Railway Mission, under William Sigeca, and served 1,600 railway families.

The Rev. Noel Borerwe

Noel Borerwe, like Willie Sigeca, had worked on the Railways prior to ordination. He had been a 'station-guide' for five years before he received his calling / vocation to the ordained ministry. He studied in Johannesburg for the priesthood and, after completing his training, was appointed to Highfield Anglican Church. Although, as noted earlier, his appointment was announced before that of Fr. Sigeca, he actually joined the Railway Mission staff just over a month later, in January 1960.

His letter in the December 1960 *Quarterly,* although not as detailed as his colleague's, gives a colourful account of his inauguration to the work, as well as being an unintentional (?) indictment of previous Railway Mission efforts at 'African work':

> The occasion of the Blessing of the Church House for the African Priest at Rugare Township, Lochinvar, marks the real beginning of the Railway Mission service to the Africans employed on the railway line in the Diocese of Mashonaland, who have not been in touch with the Gospel Message for well over 60 years since the advent of the white people.
>
> The programme for the day began by a large crowd waiting for the arrival of the head of the Mission and his wife ..This was followed by a Sung Mass conducted by the writer ...The Mass was conducted in Shona. Father Sims, the Head of the Mission, gave a lively sermon..
>
> After the Mass we proceeded to the Blessing of the House. Father Sims was ... vested for the purpose of the Blessing and was led by two Servers while he was followed by the Priest, Catechists and the rest of the congregation to each room of the house ... After the Blessing Ceremony, the Priest and the Congregation provided breakfast to 100 guests and over. The excitement of the morning only disappeared when the chief guests were driven to the Lochinvar European township for a rest, while they wait[ed] for their next train back to Bulawayo...[90]

After he had been on the Mission staff for six months, Noel Borerwe wrote an account of his work in the Diocesan Magazine, *The Link,* although it was a year later (August 1961) before readers in England were able to read his article in *Partners.* The letter forms a helpful adjunct to that of Willie Sigeca:

> The normal living house or cottage of a Railway Mission Priest is on the train. It gives extreme joy when travelling First or Second Class on a passenger train. But it is a very different picture when you travel

in the Guard's Van on a goods train. Mission priests do not choose the trains on which they travel to please themselves: the deciding factor is the time one has to be at a certain place.

The Railway African labour is composed of various grades. Sometimes one finds it very hard to know where to begin. Some have said I was a Bishop, or an Inspector of Schools, or a Railway Official. What I usually do is to ask them to settle down so that I may ask them a few elementary questions in the Catechism. As soon as I do I find they begin to realize that I have come for a special purpose. ... Whenever I come across a couple already in the Faith the real work begins ... I am now advancing some ... catechumens to Baptism.

I am very happy because the Bishop has allowed me to administer the Holy Sacrament beyond church buildings because of the circumstances confronting us. The response is remarkable all over the line, for the Gospel has been conveyed to some for the first time in their lives on a theological level. Sect religions and other denominational teaching has touched some areas but among the greater number of the railway labourers and on nearby farms anglicanism was completely unknown. They have heard about the Bishop but never about a priest.

I appreciate the sympathy which has always been expressed by the parish priests who allow us to use their parish churches. I find European Christian brethren very friendly ...

It is happy news, which has just been disclosed, that the Head of the Mission is appealing for a Railway Coach for the use of African Clergy on the Railway Mission. This for certain will be a relief from bugs, etc., I have often brought back from the Trek. However, this does not discourage me, because St. Paul had real stripes.[91]

There was obviously no doubt in the Rev. Borerwe's mind regarding the alleged 'theological superiority' of Anglicanism! It is clear that both he and Willie Sigeca were quite scathing about Sects, such as the Jehovah's Witnesses. In many cases, of course, these independent Churches had been working with railwaymen, miners and others before the Anglican Church appeared in the shape of the (African) Railway Missioners, as was seen in the Shamva Mine strike. The Railway Mission was coming late into a ministry by African priests. While the Mission had ignored its black constituency, Christianity had been spreading nevertheless, even if its theological content was deemed to be questionable. Anglicanism, as such, had been present in Southern Rhodesia since Bishop Knight-Bruce's journeying in 1888, and his transfer as bishop from Bloemfontein to Mashonaland in January 1891.

The Rev. Borerwe's hopes for a Mission coach were to be dashed. As with the Rev. Sigeca, he had to be content with a Second Class Pass provided by Rhodesia Railways, or 'travel in the Guard's Van.'

Noel Borerwe became best known for the various churches which he constructed. He was called 'The Church builder' and eleven were erected during the eleven years he worked with the Railway Mission. During interview in 1985, Canon Borerwe spoke (and wrote) of his experiences on the Mission:

> The ground I covered was between Salisbury and Gwelo, including Branch lines, and not a single railway family was left untouched. In addition to that we also made remarkable [religious] conversions of the farm labour within three miles of the railway line. Where the conversion was in big numbers we were forced to erect some reasonable buildings for worship. And I must say, it was manageable to construct these owing to the generous farmers ... And indeed I was delighted as the late Bishop Cecil William Alderson agreed to dedicate some of them and, except one, Fr. Kenneth Sims [Head of the Railway Mission] blessed.
>
> The Churches Bishop Cecil dedicated were as follows: St. Philip's, Odzi; St. Mark's, Pounseley; St. Elizabeth's, Baddeley (Umtali line); St. Christopher's, Rugare (Salisbury); St. Catherine's, Mount Hampden (Sinoia line); St. Cecilia's, Mazoe Mine (Bindura branch); and St. Luke's, Maryland (Sinoia branch). We built eleven churches altogether within a period of eleven years I was on the staff of the Railway Mission. And I still hope that one suitable Church will be dedicated and that is St. Cyprian's, Darwendale (Sinoia branch).
>
> And one is very happy to hear that the parish Priests continue to use these buildings and above all our friends who contributed the materials will be encouraged to do more when other programmes warrant. Another distinctive factor which encouraged us was Bishop Paul Burrough who consented to travel along the line to administer Confirmations to the railway families, including farm labour.
>
> During the War of Independence I went trekking [ie. visiting for the Railway Mission] on a donkey or on foot [as well as by train].[92]

Rhodesia Railways each month published a newspaper, *Sitima* (= 'steamer', ie. steam locomotive) for their African staff. News about the Railway Mission, such as Noel Borerwe's church building, not infrequently featured in its pages. The issue for March 1967 included a photograph of Fr. Borerwe standing outside the newly-built Anglican Church at Rugare, a fine brick, 400-seater, church with an imposing bell tower. Under the title 'They built their own church: Fine example', the story accompanying the photograph stated:

> The new Anglican Church in Rugare is an excellent example of what can be achieved through self-help and co-operation. The church was built under the supervision of the priest-in-charge, Father Noel Bororwe [sic]. The site of the new church was formerly occupied by a corrugated-iron building which served the need of the local Anglican community for many years. When Father Berorwe [sic] began building operations he was assisted by a voluntary band of workers drawn from his own congregation. Their immediate concern at the time was to procure the essential building materials. Offers of assistance were readily forthcoming from several interested parties ... Today, Rugare has a fine new church that is a credit to the neighbourhood and to the self-help and co-operation of Father Borerwe and his parishioners ...[93]

Sadly, the work at Rugare was later to result in much acrimony, as we shall note below.

By early 1971 the bishop wanted to transfer Borerwe to other work. This was not a popular decision with the priest, the Executive Committee of the Mission (in Rhodesia), or the African railway workers. At a Meeting of the Railway Mission Executive Committee, held at the Railway Headquarters in Bulawayo in February 1971, a lengthy debate ensued on the issue. The Rev. James Isherwood, Missioner / Secretary, informed the Committee that Noel Borerwe had written three letters asking to be allowed to remain with the Mission. The Minutes then noted the remarks of Mrs. M. Wright, the President of the Local Associations of the Railway Mission and wife of the General Manager of Rhodesia Railways):

> Mrs. Wright, who has been familiar with the extent of Fr. Borerwe's work and the growth of his beneficial influence on his flock over a number of years, stated that Fr. Borerwe's departure would be a sad loss to the Mission. Mrs. Wright expressed the fear that failing the appointment of a replacement of equal calibre, which seemed unlikely in view of Fr. Borerwe's experience, the Mission's work would be in danger of falling away. Fr. Borerwe's position is unique in that he is the only Railway Missioner resident in the Salisbury area, consequently his particular attributes are most valuable to the Mission.
>
> The Chairman [Bishop Wood] explained the position of the African priests in the respective Diocese[s] and the control over their

> movements held by the bishops. It was appreciated that in his capacity of Bishop of Matabeleland he could not consider interfering with the decisions of his counterpart in Mashonaland.
>
> The Executive Committee decided that a letter be addressed to the Bishop of Mashonaland setting out our reluctance to lose the services of Fr. Borerwe and the reasons therefore.[94]

The letter failed to achieve its purpose, for the next Meeting of the Executive Committee minuted, 'It was advised that all arrangements had been made for the transfer of Fr. Borerwe to his new post at St. Faith's Mission.'[95] The Committee proposed a 'Resolution of Appreciation' and agreed to forwarding to Noel Borerwe a framed address and a small gift.

When Fr. Borerwe left the Railway Mission in September 1971, after eleven years, to be in charge of St. Faith's Mission at Rusape, 'one of the oldest and most successful in the country', he was again featured in *Sitima.* The article ended by noting:

> People of all denominations were very worried when Father Borerwe left because he was a father to everyone. When he was interviewed before he left Father Borerwe said that his main objective in life was to see that he brought as many people as possible under Christ's banner. He further stated that wages were meaningless when churches were empty.
>
> Everyone was welcome in Father Borerwe's house regardless of their religion. When railway folk along the line of rail heard of his departure they could not believe it and many expressed deep regret.[96]

He had certainly 'proved himself to be an evangelist'! The article was also reproduced in *Partners* in February 1972, for the benefit of supporters in England. The October 1971 issue of *Sitima* announced and welcomed the arrival of Fr. Cyprian Gwatidzo, 'a very keen and energetic person', to take over Fr. Borerwe's work.

The Rev. John Mhlabi

If Fr. Borerwe is to be known as 'The Church builder', then Fr. Mhlabi ought to be known as 'The Letter writer'. It is beyond the scope of this work to detail all the correspondence he entered into, particularly over his project of a 'railway school' at Mbizi. Few people or organisations, whether they were the Executive Committee of the Railway Mission (Bulawayo), the London Committee, the World Council of Churches, the Rhodesia Railways, the bishops, or the government, plus various individuals, were spared his constant pleas for help. Even in retirement, letters still cross the world to would-be-supporters, including the writer, soliciting help for his orphanage and other projects.

Parts of Mhlabi's letter to the USPG in London (October 1972) can well illustrate the school project and his enthusiastic pleading:

> I am an African Anglican Priest employed by the Diocese of Matabeleland along the Railway Lines in Matabeleland from Bulawayo to Victoria Falls, Bulawayo to Vila Salazar, P.E.A border to Beitbridge border and Bulawayo to Gwelo, finally Bulawayo to West Nicholson - Bulawayo into Botswana. I have done the Rhodesia Railways Mission work since 1968 up to now.
>
> Christianity is of a small beginning scale along the Rail lines everywhere in Rhodesia. My personal problem especially to the Eastern low veld areas to P.E.A. border is poverty, shortage of food and shortage of Primary Schools for our African Education in these remote places. Our Government accepts your cheques for charity.
>
> Mbizi Railway Employees African Village at the junction to P.E.A border and to Lowveld Triangle Sugar Estate - Chiredzi. Here is a Picture [photos enclosed] where the school is granted a Ground freely by the R.R. [railways] officials for African Educational Centre in a Rural Council European Area. Forms and permission have been lodged to the Government Educational Officials and I have been told to encourage the people to donate money towards the school building Projects ... Here at Mbizi, there are over 170 little children who need a school ... My bishop helped me in persuading the General Manager of the R. Railways to grant a Ground for the pupils arranging [sic] from 7 years old to even 13 to 14 without any pre-schooling knowledge at all.
>
> The R. Railways have a ground for school facilities but they have no materials and money to grant towards the building of this new Pre school classes at all ... As the school manager I appeal for money towards R.R. Mbizi African Village School which is very urgent indeed. [Details of rooms, costs, fees, facilities, etc., followed, along with details of other projects] ...[97]

The letter was passed by USPG to the London Committee of the Railway Mission. Although the Committee was sympathetic towards the appeal and felt it to be a challenge to them, they were obliged to refer it back to the Committee in Rhodesia, especially as they were unsure of the project's viability. The matter taxed the members of the Executive Committee in Bulawayo for a considerable period, the letters of Fr. Mhlabi ensuring that the project was not forgotten. The chief problem was that the Mbizi School project involved permissions and decisions from the Railway Mission, the Rhodesia Railways, the Ministry of Finance, the Rural Council and the Ministry of Education. No single authority would or could take overall responsibility. This is shown in a Minute of the Executive Committee of the Railway Mission in April 1973:

> The report submitted by the Secretary on his investigations into the feasibility of establishing an African School at Mbizi, was discussed together with the findings of Fr. R. Woods on his "on-the-spot" investigations.
>
> It was accepted that the proposed site at Mbizi was totally unsuitable and that future plans must be directed towards the site offered under certain conditions by Nuanetsi Estates. This location is situated three miles from Mbizi and had its own borehole.
>
> The Various responsibilities of the Mission and the Railway Administration in this matter were again discussed. The Chairman [bishop of Matabeleland] stated that whilst he appreciated the Mission lacked the means and the Railway Administration had no function in regard to education he did feel it was the Mission's duty to officially bring the Railway's attention to the lack of educational facilities at Mbizi for he saw it as part of their duty to their employees. The bishop added that he did not consider the provision of these facilities would be setting a precedent.
>
> In reply Mr. Wright stated that he appreciated the Chairman's point of view but was restricted both by legislation and resources as to what he could do. The Railway Administration saw quite clearly that, particularly in areas away from the main centres of population, it was their responsibility to provide housing, services and welfare facilities but schooling was never taken to be a Railway function. Under the present Railways Act he was not allowed to make any financial grant to an educational institution without the permission of the Minister of Finance. Indeed, since direct Government control of the Railway finances was instituted the Mission had become the sole recipient of annual donations.[98]

And there the matter rested, as far as the Railway Mission was concerned, for no further Minutes referred to Mbizi, nor did the proposed school gain any mention in the Mission's printed letters or information. It remains for John Mhlabi himself to give the ending of the story, a story which has some parallels with the early days of Railway Mission education, as detailed in Chapter 4, and which points forward to the final days of the Mission, which will be examined in Chapter 8. His letter of March 1995 needs quoting almost *in extenso:*

Re: Mbizi School (1971-73). -

I brought in a female teacher in 1971 and another one in 1972 and in 1973; a male teacher was in as well to teach boys carpentry and woodwork, while Lady-Teachers did cookery, basketry and washing utensils and yard-cleaning and sweeping, whilst boys did agriculture and vegetable garden[ing] and caring [for] cottage-fruit trees in the ... cottage for .. parents ..

I used to say Mass at 6pm to 7pm, then church music teaching for 45 minutes, and then give them Ndebele, Shona and Lozwi pamphlets .. [for] their own interest in the [anglo-] Catholic faith. During the morning time I used to say Mass and then group children and teach .. them stories in the Bible. Their parents used to group with their children as well.

(i) The school was just a tent of Railway sail to cover the roof of sticks and wood from wind and rain.
(ii) Music-players used to visit Mbizi to organize ... concerts ...
(iii) The money collected paid the school-teachers and paid for their food rations. The food stuff, soap, candles, utensils, exercise books, ballpoints and reading books were cheap [at] that time, and people liked the children's education, because it was free.
(iv) The huge sail classroom was along the back yard of the cottage. Some child[ren] who were in St[andard] V and VI did go to Dadaya Secondary [School], Svishavane.
(v) I was given the site of sails by the Station Master, including ... huge bundles of sails, poles which were not [being] used. The Cottage Bossboy agreed with the Station Master to choose a free site for a Primary School.

The terrorists came in and the Railway Station Master and the Bossboy were removed to Bulawayo. There was danger on their lives. In 1973 the Railway Mission was discontinued in between 1973 to 1974 because of Terrorists and all black Priests worked in Bulawayo until 1980 onwards..
(v) [vi] Railway Mbizi Station employees whose children were at school were paying Levy for the Teachers who were not trained Teachers ...[99]

This was clearly not the noblest episode in the Railway Mission's history, although it is difficult to know what more the Mission could have done, given the intransigence of the various authorities. We noted earlier how Peter Garnett had commended the initiatives invariably shown by the

African staff of the Railway Mission. John Mhlabi's tireless efforts at and for Mbizi exemplify this.

Three years after the Rev. Mhlabi's appointment in 1968 replacing, as noted earlier, Willie Sigeca, James Isherwood advised his Executive Committee that in his observation of Fr. Mhlabi, 'he had come to the conclusion that Railway Mission work was not his particular forte. He considered that Fr. John would be much more effective in a parish.'[100] He was to remain on the Mission for a further two years. No one could doubt his enthusiasm and hard work, but his energies were clearly more suited for parochial (settled) projects, such as Mbizi, and evangelising than for itinerant work. He did undertake a considerable amount of travelling, though this was a great strain.

At the priest's farewell, *Sitima* reported the remarks of the Railway General Manager, Trevor Wright, that:

> Fr. Mhlabi had [become] a worthy member of that conscientious band of Anglican clergy who have, since the early days of the Railways in Southern Africa, brought spiritual comfort to the people of all races and creeds along the line of rail. But the rigours of almost continual travelling, mainly on goods trains, with attendant trips on bicycle and on foot became a strain for him, and the executive committee decided that he had earned a respite from this arduous life. He was transferred to Luveve ... [101]

The use of a caboose would, no doubt, have made John Mhlabi's life rather less 'arduous'. It may be noted that it was unusual for the Railway Mission itself to decide that an African priest had 'earned a respite'; this was a decision normally reserved for the appropriate bishop, as observed in the case of Noel Borerwe.

Other African priests

After Noel Borerwe was transferred from Railway Mission work in 1971 his place in Mashonaland was taken, as observed, by the Rev. Cyprian Gwatidzo, 'already well-known for his energetic enthusiasm for the Gospel.' John Mhlabi was replaced by the Rev. Ernest Gwetu, based in Bulawayo. For a few months at the end of 1974 and beginning of 1975, while the European missioners were on leave, the whole of the active Railway Mission work in Rhodesia was in the hands of these two priests.

The question of a Mission coach for the African priests continued to be unresolved. Fr. Gwatidzo, in a letter to 'The Railway Ladies Association, Salisbury', in November 1974, wrote:

> There is not a caboose for an African Missioner in the Railways. We have been told many times that they will give us one, from the time of Rev. Fr. Isherwood. This needs reviewing. Many things are held up by the fact of rail, free card pass, which controls a priest. We feel the help given to a priest in this way gears him to a very slow way of moving. Also his car needs money to run it. The car does a great deal at night, like taking a woman in labour to maternity. This is one of the great difficulties in the Mission. We are grateful for those who help us, in giving whatever they have ...[102]

One unusual piece of work that the African priests did, during the War of Independence, was to visit Africans held at a Restriction Camp in the extreme south-east corner of Rhodesia. At the Annual Festival in London in September 1967, Harold Crane, the Missioner/ Secretary, reported:

> We also greatly appreciate the work that the African priests are doing, they do exactly the same work ministering to people who are out of touch with parishes. The Railway Mission is also responsible for 400 men who are in a Restriction Camp ... - Gonakudzingwa -, it was extremely difficult at first but we are now allowed to visit them once each month. These forgotten men do not know how long they are to be there .. [103]

The priest who did the visiting was the Rev. Eli Magava, who was still doing this particular work in 1971. In February that year he wrote to his bishop pointing out that his free rail Pass had been withdrawn and that some solution was needed, if the work was to continue. The bishop agreed that the work was 'terribly important indeed and must go on ...', and that, if he was unable to have a free Pass, the priest must 'pay [his] fare and re-claim it from [him (the bishop)].'[104]

The work at Rugare, so ably founded by Noel Borerwe, caused a great deal of anguish at the end of the Railway Mission's period in Rhodesia. The African priest in charge of Rugare from 1977 found 'his services ... terminated because he did not do much work, and .. did not do any travelling "along the line"...'[105] The maintenance of the work at Rugare was costing the Railway Mission 'the impossible figure of £200 per month with no contribution of any sort whatsoever from the Rugare congregation.' The Church building was, by then, 'in a most deplorable condition.' The Diocese of Mashonaland and the Railway Mission both found problems as to who owned the Rugare buildings and who was responsible ultimately for any church work there. The work was finally taken over by the Diocese.

The ending of Railway Mission work at Rugare in 1978 coincided with the ending of all such work. As far as the Mission was concerned, 1978 'was the year when it could no longer afford to pay any African priests at Rugare, Lochinvar or anywhere else; they were in fact doing the work of parochial clergy, and acting just as though that were their status; accordingly it was felt that it was only meet and right for the Diocese to pay them.'[106]

All through the Railway Mission's history, from the Grahamstown days, it had continually sowed the seeds of its own death. It was, in many ways, a "stop-gap", doing the work which the dioceses and parishes could not do. There always came a time when the dioceses had to take over. This was no different with the work undertaken by African priests. The ending was sad, yet no more so than similar 'partings' with white missioners in other places and at other times. The African priests had, as we have seen, done work which no-one had undertaken before, and their vital ministry had been appreciated. That some of them found itinerating work difficult is hardly surprising, especially as they were never afforded the privilege of their own caboose. Matters were not helped by the political and diocesan machinations during the final period of the War of Independence, as we shall observe in the final Chapter.

The work of African priests had been entirely with Africans and Coloureds. By the time that black clergy might have been accepted working among the Whites, as opposed to ministering to fellow Africans, the Railway Mission had come to an end.

---

1 *The Happy Travellers*, SACRM, 1954, 6

2 Jalla, 1914 / Berger, 1970, Pref. 1st. edn.

3 Isichei, 1995, 133, 142/3

4 QP 86, 1926, 5

5 Gray, 1960, 99

6 Kennedy, 1987, 137/8

7 Kanduza, n.d., 130

8 quoted in R-N RCR, 1939, par.392

9 quoted in R-N RCR, 1939, par.543

10 Lunn, 1986, 248

11 In 1913, 1556 European and Coloured workers were employed on the Rhodesian Railway system, with 5701 African workers. The European and Coloured figure steadily rose - usually by 100-200 per year, to 3843 by 1939. The African figure fluctuated, though climbed on average 500-1000 per year, until the peak of 17, 698 in 1930, dropping back to 8711 in 1934, and then rising again to a total of 13,762 in 1939. (Lunn, 1986, App.C, 322)

12 Lunn, 1986, 250/1

13 Lunn, 1986, 278

14 quoted in Gray, 1960,100

15 Phimister, 1981, 77

16 Croxton, 1973, 1982, 228

[17] Or. int. 13.4.1992, Dick Nyenhuis + Murray Thompson /JMR
[18] Croxton, 1973, 1982, 228
[19] Phimister, 1981, 86
[20] Phimister, 1981, p.264 (And see Vickery, K.P. in *JSAS* Vol.24, No.3 (1998) 545-560 and Vol.25, No.1 (1999) 49-71 for an excellent study of the strike and its consequences.) (And see note 84)
[21] Turner, 1975, 73
[22] Turner, 1975, 93
[23] Turner, 1975, 74
[24] Phimister, 1988, 263
[25] Colclough & McCarthy, 1980, 161
[26] GDRM, 1897, 6
[27] GDRM 'Monthly Letter', Jan. 1902, 3
[28] GDRM, XV, Apr. 1902, 3
[29] QP 2, 1904, 6
[30] QP 6, 1905, 3
[31] QP 19, 1908, 10
[32] QP 27, 1910, 15/16 (changed from reported speech)
[33] QP 31, 1911, 8
[34] Baxter, 1908, 4
[35] Ellison, 1930, 104
[36] Ellison, 1930, 140
[37] Stanley, 1990, 161
[38] QP 32, 1911, 18
[39] QP 37, 1912, 17
[40] H Hale, 7.4.1904
[41] Ellison, Douglas, 1909, 12
[42] QP 25, 1909, 13
[43] QP 36, 1912, 18
[44] QP 47, 1915, 21/2
[45] H Hale, 8.9.1906
[46] Goodwin, 1864, 286
[47] Goodwin, 1864, 182
[48] QP 79, 1924, 5/6
[49] Ellison, 1930, 143
[50] R Seacombe, 13.3.1916
[51] R Seacombe, 7.7.1917
[52] QP 124, 1935, 1
[53] QP 124, 1935, 5
[54] QP 149, 1942, 4
[55] QP 149, 1942, 14
[56] QP 151, 1943, 17
[57] X583, RHL, 9.8.1944
[58] QP 169, 1950, 6/7
[59] QP 169, 1950, 7
[60] quoted in Gruchy, 1986, 55
[61] interv. Garnett/JMR Feb .1992
[62] QP 187, 1954, 3
[63] QP 200 [1959 2nd Qu.] 14/15
[64] Oliver, 1965, 181

[65] Ranger, 1967?, 3
[66] Van Velsen ,1973, ii
[67] Verstraelen-Gilhuis, 1992, 82
[68] Gray, 1990, 81
[69] Berger, E, 1970, UCZ, ackn.
[70] Hinchliff, 1963, 116
[71] GDRM, Ann.Rep., 1897, 7
[72] GDRM, Sep. 1899, 3/4
[73] GDRM, Ann.Rep. 1898/9, 5
[74] SACRM, Children's Qu. Leaflet, Jan. 1904, 1/2
[75] GDRM, Sep. 1900, 3
[76] Ellison, 1930, 37
[77] QP 86, 1926, 5/6
[78] Garnett, P. 1985,1992, written/oral/JMR
[79] SACRM, Ann.Rep. March 1955, 8
[80] SACRM, Ann.Rep. March 1956, 4
[81] X583, RHL, 30.4.1952
[82] X759, RHL, 28.4.1959
[83] QP 201, 1959, 4
[84] 'The key figure in the RRAEA [Rhodesia Railways African Employees Association] was its General Secretary, William Sigeca, former head of the Bantu Benefit Society. An Ndebele who lived in one of the compounds but went 'home' on weekends, Sigeca had joined the Railways in 1930. He had a Standard 7 education - very high for the time - and was the senior African in the Records Office of the goods shed.' (*JSAS*, Vol.24, No.3, Sep.1998, p.550) (and see note 20)
[85] Percy Ibbotson was Organising Secretary of the Federation of Native Welfare Societies and a prominent Bulawayo 'friend of the native'. He had, nevertheless, been censured by the Salisbury Native Welfare Society for somewhat derogatory remarks about Africans.
[86] Sigeca/JMR interv. 18.8.1993
[87] QP 204, 1960, .4-6
[88] Sigeca/JMR, interv. 18.8.1993
[89] *Partners*, Vol.XI, No.5, Feb.1967, 11
[90] QP 204, 1960, 7
[91] *Partners*, Vol. VI, No.3, Aug. 1961, 6
[92] Borerwe, letter + interv./Grain, 1985
[93] *Sitima*, Vol.18, No.3, March 1967, 5
[94] Bul.Ch.Arch., R&NRM, Ex.Comm., 26.2.1971, Min.5.1
[95] Bul.Ch.Arch., R&NRM, Ex.Comm., 22.9.1971, Min.3.4
[96] *Sitima*, Oct. 1971
[97] Mhlabi corresp./JMR, letter 16.10.1972
[98] Bul.Ch.Arch., R&NRM, Ex.Comm, 6.4.1973, Min.3.1
[99] Mhlabi/JMR, corresp. 12.3.1995
[100] Bul.Ch.Arch., R&NRM, Ex.Comm., 26.2.1971, Min.6.1
[101] *Sitima*, 1973, quoted in *Partners*, Vol.XIX, No.4, 1974, 16
[102] Bul.Ch.Arch., RMR&B, 23.11.1974
[103] *Partners*, Vol.XII, No.4, Nov.1967, 24
[104] Bul.Ch.Arch., RMR&B, 8.3.1971
[105] Bul.Ch.Arch., RMR&B, 11.3.1978
[106] Grain, 1985, 105

8: Ending of the Church Railway Mission

- 'We have been privileged to play a small part in Church history, and we thank God for it.'

> In some parts of the country the new system of centralised train control (C.T.C) has done away with many of the small and lonely communities. More and more railway families are now living in railway "camps" or townships.

Thus stated the five thousand copies of the leaflet, *Your Travelling Church,* published by the Railway Mission in 1959. It was the Mission's very last publicity literature. The leaflet also noted the growth in the 'African side' of the work and acknowledged that 'in a growing and changing land [Southern Rhodesia]' they had to be 'ready to change meet new situations and new opportunities.' The leaflet ended with a 'Call to Adventure':

> *Adventure - spiced with a lot of monotony, much boredom, some frustration, but with the knowledge that you are helping to build God's Church in a growing country.*
>
> *WILL YOU HELP KEEP OUR CHURCH TRAVELLING?*

Despite the fact that the Mission was the 'Rhodesia [South and North] and Nyasaland Railway Mission', and also was working in Bechuanaland / Botswana, the various references to 'the country' throughout the leaflet referred only to Southern Rhodesia. The twenty years' life remaining for the 'travelling church' was certainly to see 'adventure', but little 'monotony' or 'boredom', given a period which saw a U.D.I, a War of Independence, and more than one country achieving independence from Colonial powers. 'Some frustration' turned out to be an understatement. Keeping the Church 'travelling' also proved more than troublesome during a time when trains and personnel were under attack.

Although, as noted previously, the Railway Mission, as with virtually every Mission, continually sowed the seeds of its own demise and had constantly to be ready to hand over its work to the settled Church, the particular changes and conflicts of the 1960s and 1970s inexorably brought about the complete ending of its activities. By 1980 it seemed that all that remained was the need for a decent and fitting funeral.

The changes, as indicated in the opening quotation, were both technological, in terms of railway maintenance and signalling, and social. Each type of change had its effect on the operation of the Railway

Mission. The increase in African and Coloured railway employment, and the changes made by the Mission to accommodate this, have been examined in the previous chapter.

To some extent there had always been conflict, certainly tension, between the Mission and the Church hierarchy and Diocesan structures from the earliest Grahamstown days and in particular from the time that the Mission moved from its confines within one Diocese. The seeds of the various frustrations and conflicts of the final years were sown in the early years of the century. It is appropriate therefore, in this final phase, to examine such conflicts in the whole sweep of the Railway Mission's history, rather than focus too narrowly or solely on terminal squabbles. The political conflicts, particularly between and within the Rhodesias, had a devastating effect on all Church work and, as we shall note, proved to be the major factor in the ending of the Church Railway Mission. The majority of missioners and commentators were in agreement that 'the Mission's days were numbered', but note will be taken of the opposing viewpoint.

In a chapter which is concerned with the ending of a unique Mission provided by the Anglican Church for almost a century, it seems right that a conclusion not only gives an overview of the work and history of this Mission, but also attempts to determine whether or not its aims and objectives were achieved. At the end of the day had it all been worthwhile?

Technological and Social change

The Principal Signal Engineer of Rhodesia Railways, Mr. D.H. Constable, read a paper to the Institution of Railway Signal Engineers in October 1969, describing the signalling and telecommunications development in Rhodesia during the previous twenty years. In this paper he gave a vivid account of the working conditions when he arrived in 1949:

> ... there were some primitive semaphore signalling installations at Salisbury (West end station only), Bulawayo (again only at the West end) and three ... installations at Sawmills, Dett and Zimba ... Bulawayo was even more frightening than Salisbury. The small standard South African Railways type frame was housed in a signalbox, if one could call it that, actually it was more like a gardener's "potting shed", situated at ground level .. [and] for 90% of the time the signal-box attendant (as they were then called) could see nothing! [At] Salisbury and Bulawayo the signalbox attendants only worked the signals under the orders of the station foremen and

> shunters; they had no control of the train working arrangements, which were made by paper order. Only in later years, when they were given control of the block instruments for train working, were they re-named "signalmen".
>
> Returning to Bulawayo I was horrified to see 1,400-ton coal trains thundering up the heavy gradient from the old North line into the station yard at 20-30 m.p.h. with the home signal off, but no detection of any facing points [for protection] and no indication of where the train was going.[1]

At the end of the Second World War a pilot Centralised Traffic Control scheme had been started on the Bulawayo-Gwelo Section, the first in the continent. The then General Manager, Sir Arthur Griffin, did not agree with the word 'traffic', and so C.T.C. in Rhodesia was named Centralised Train Control. The arguments in favour of C.T.C. were the speeding up of traffic, with the consequent lessening of hours of duty for train crews and reduction in overtime payments. (Crews had frequently to wait for hours, doing nothing, while waiting for trains coming in the opposite direction, on a single line, to pass at loops or sidings). Also, the use of foremen at intermediate stations could be avoided. 'These intermediate stations served districts that were far from settled towns, and railway housing had to be provided at each, for three station foremen - one to a shift.'[2] By installing C.T.C., at least two houses, staff and salaries would be eliminated at each station.

We noted in the previous chapter how, with the creation of the Federation of Rhodesia and Nyasaland in 1953, various developments took place on the railways, such as the advancement of non-white workers. The booming economy of the Federation (in Southern Rhodesia) strained the resources of the railways to the utmost and, late in 1957, 'it was decided to complete the installation of C.T.C. from Umtali, on the eastern border ... to Ndola, on the Northern Rhodesia Copperbelt [both Rhodesias were still under unified railway control].'[3]

> By April 1964 the astonishing situation had been attained that the *entire* main line system of the Rhodesia Railways had been converted to C.T.C. operation with 1200 route miles, with 205 [train] crossing places, controlled from ten control rooms. No more remarkable example of the complete metamorphosis of the operating strategy of a railway could be found anywhere in the world. [4]

With the Centralised Train Control and the increased line capacity came not only the reduction in personnel and buildings, but much safer train control, standardised and improved supervision by the 'central control', improvement in average train speeds, and postponement of the doubling of track, except in Stations such as Salisbury and Bulawayo. The notorious number of accidents caused by collisions on single-track lines and overturning of engines, along with irregularities in the telegraph orders issued to train crews, were considerably lessened by the safety procedures incorporated in C.T.C.

The technological changes were observed by the Railway Mission staff. The Rev. Hugh Palmer, writing from Salisbury in 1959, reported:

> After my trip to Northern Rhodesia, I moved to the line between Bulawayo and the Victoria Falls. On this section, I visited the sidings as Ngamo, Gwaai and Kennedy. At each of these places, the railway staff consists only of pumper (who looks after the water supply for the locomotives), platelayer (who looks after the permanent way) and technician (who looks after the signal and telegraph equipment) ...
>
> Until recently, guards of trains booked to cross one another at crossing loops (called "sidings") on the Dett section, had to get down from their vans, in order to turn the points by hand. When making a crossing during the hours of darkness, there was always a risk that the King of Beasts might appear at the facing points [This did happen]. Nowadays, however, the points and signals are electrically operated; they are worked by remote control, and turned by a controller sitting at a desk far away in Dett, so that it is no longer necessary for a Guard to leave the safety of his van to turn the points.[5]

The technological revolution and implementation in signalling was not the only change to affect railwaymen and their families, with the 'knock-on' effect on the Railway Mission. In all areas 'the passing years had seen steady strengthening of bridges and culverts, consolidation of ballast and sleepers and other technical improvements, doing away with the constant breakdowns and "washways" [washaways] of pioneer days ...'[6] To a certain extent the 'pioneer days' returned for the Railway Mission with the building of the 'South-East connection' to Lourenco Marques, as we shall note below.

Peter Garnett, recollecting his time on the Railway Mission, noted that, in the mid-1950s, 'Already ... there was talk of the need to reduce outlying [Railway] staff. Centralised Traffic Control was being talked of which would reduce the need for so many foremen ...'[7] In conversation, Garnett emphasised the difference that the bitumenized roads made. Both in the Rhodesias and in Botswana these roads usually followed the line of rail. Such all-weather roads had a profound impact on gangers and their families, making most of the gangers' cottages redundant. No longer did the platelayers need to live in isolated areas, ten or so miles from the next cottage, and reliant on slow goods trains to take them or their families to the nearest centre. The advent of the tarred roads meant that they could live in towns or centres and travel out in lorries or cars to work on the line.

Michael Fidgin, the last Chairman of the London Committee of the Railway Mission, in a letter written shortly before his untimely death in 1991, stated:

> At the same time as improvements were taking place in the technical ability of the railways, the same revolution was taking place along the roads. I used to see ox-carts, and carts drawn by teams of donkeys, and many of the local roads were dust roads. But tarmac replaced the dirt, and cars became more efficient and trustworthy, and whole areas that we used to visit became within commuting distance of big cities.[8]

Many people were no longer cut off from shops, schools and clinics. The railways themselves were providing more Welfare amenities as time went on, thus lessening the need for the different kinds of social service formerly given by the Railway Mission. Denis Charlton, who returned briefly to the Railway Mission in 1963 after an absence of twenty-one years, noted the differences between the 'old days' before the Second World War and those at the time of writing:

> The work has changed a little as now there are very few people living at lonely places in cottages along the line. They tend to be centred in communities, such as Dett - a large Railway Camp. Also the houses in which the people live are greatly improved. They are well constructed, concrete or brick, and many people have television, while all have wireless or radiogram. These centres are well equipped with modern facilities ...[9]

During the 1970s there was a change in the Rhodesias from all-steam traction to the partial use of diesel locomotives. As well as the obvious reduction in the need for manpower to fire, clean, and rake out the steam engines, and the lessening of the work by pumpers, other changes were caused by having fewer engines capable of easy shunting. We shall note, shortly, the effect this had on the work of Railway Missioners.

> We, of the Railway Mission, are conscious ... of the winds of change. I think we are, all of us, becoming increasingly aware of the changing pattern of Railway Mission work ... [We have] a roving

> Commission to seek out and to care for the spiritual welfare of Railway folk along the line. Nevertheless, the pattern of Railway life itself is changing, and we have to adapt ourselves to it. The introduction of the Central[ised] Train Control system has reduced the number of railway families living in remote and isolated places. All along the line one comes across empty houses once occupied by "lonely gangers" or signalmen. Moreover, the majority of those who do live at lonely sidings, now possess their own cars, and have easy access to the nearest Railway Township.[10]

Kenneth Sims, the Head of the Rhodesia and Nyasaland railway Mission, wrote the above words for the supporters 'at Home' in March 1961. It was already over a year since Harold MacMillan's 'wind of change' speech at Cape Town (3 February 1960), condemning apartheid; exactly one year since the Sharpeville massacre (21 March 1960); and but two months away from the inauguration of the Republic of South Africa (31 May 1961). Civil war had erupted in the Congo and in Angola; Tanganyika was moving rapidly towards full independence; repressive practices by the Portuguese in Mozambique were being denounced by the Church; the abortive constitutional talks on Northern Rhodesia (31 January - 17 February 1961) had just taken place in London; and in Southern Rhodesia, in mid-January, the Constitutional Conference had been held in Salisbury. Change was everywhere in the air, and the Railways and the Railway Mission were but part of a larger transformation of social, political, industrial and religious life in central and southern Africa.

In his 'winds of change' letter, Kenneth Sims went on to discuss the policy of the Mission regarding Railway Centres:

> The population of these Railway Townships is increasing rapidly, and the Railway Mission is faced with the problem of growing Communities in which everything is laid on except the Church. Take a place like Dett, for example, where you have an Institute (or Club), a swimming pool, flood-lit tennis courts, a bowling green, a Railway Clinic, a store, a hotel, a school, everything in fact needed by a civilised community except a Church.[11] I am quite sure that the policy of the Mission today must be to concentrate more on these large Railway Centres where there is no Church and no Parish Priest. Our answer ... has been to establish "bases" from which the Railway Mission Chaplain can visit the sidings and outlying places, returning regularly to his "home base" for Sunday Worship on specific Sundays in the month. This means that without neglecting the line work in the least, places like Dett, Choma, Kalomo, and Lochinvar

> have an established Church and a semi-resident “Parish Priest” living amongst the railway people in his own furnished house.

Denis Charlton, in examining the changes that had come about in railway life, observed how these affected the work of the Railway Mission:

> The Head has adopted a very realistic approach by appointing a Missioner to live in the [Railway] Centre, really identifying himself or herself with the people, and holding services where possible. In many of the Centres buildings are being converted into Churches. In other words each Centre is becoming a little railway parish on its own, which the Head visits to keep his eye on everything from time to time. ...The coach is still used to visit from the Centre any outlying people along the line, and they are linked up with people at the Centre. To my mind this is an ideal policy, making for much greater efficiency and a more corporate church life.[12]

Talk of parishes immediately raises the question of the main ethos and work of the Railway Mission. It had always been an itinerant Mission, ‘being’ the Church where there was no parish or diocesan structure or input. If changes in railway practice and life necessitated the Mission becoming parish-like, it was surely no longer the Railway Mission as traditionally understood? Here was another example of the continuing conflict, now brought into sharper focus, between the settled Church and the free-roaming Mission, a conflict which later will be examined in detail.

However, as noted above, the ‘pioneer days’ did return to the railways and the Railway Mission for one brief last fling, with the building of the ‘south-east connection’. The need for an additional rail outlet from Southern Rhodesia to the East Coast became clear soon after the 1939-1945 War. The development of both Rhodesias, coupled with rapidly rising populations, ‘was beyond the capacity of the port of Beira and its rail route to the hinterland. Discussions of the problem eventually led to the choice of the Mozambique port of Lourenco Marques as a second sea terminal ...’[13] Bannockburn, then a siding on the Somabula-Shabani branch line, was taken as the Rhodesian starting point of rail construction. The route was to be south-east to Rutenga and then to the border, where a new settlement, Malvernia (named after Lord Malvern, the Rhodesian and Federal Prime Minister), was established. The section from Rutenga to Malvernia was arid and desolate, with no roads and little water. In Mozambique the existing CFM line from Lourenco Marques to Guija was to be extended the 200 miles to Malvernia.

> The South-East Connection ... cost approximately £6 million and was opened to goods traffic on 1 August 1955. Until stone ballast had been laid both on the RR and CFM sections, it was not considered desirable, due to speed restrictions and the dust nuisance, to inaugurate a passenger service. Even when this was eventually done, on 20 July 1956, the weekly passenger train had a dusty trip, but this soon improved and the service was then increased to twice weekly.[14]

The new construction made its first appearance in the Railway Mission's journal in July/August 1953, in a letter written by the lady worker, Constance Saunders, in May. After writing about the 'at least seventy congregations ... with their own Church, who owe[d] their beginning and their growth to the work of the Railway Mission', she continued:

> But - and this is very important - as these congregations pass from our care, so the Mission is continually taking on fresh responsibilities. In Rhodesia, the new line now being built from Bannockburn through Portuguese Territory to the Coast, will add about 250 miles to that section, and the conditions for the Chaplain and woman worker will not be unlike those of the early pioneering days, for it appears that the Railwaymen stationed there will be very isolated indeed. At the moment, the Construction Camp is under the Mission's care. Then another responsibility is the large Railway Housing Estate called Lochinvar (six miles outside Salisbury) ...

One year later, August/September 1954, Richard Hughes, who had joined the Mission in mid-1953, wrote a detailed account of his visits on the new construction. At the end of his letter he states, 'I have told this visit in detail because it is a piece of work now unique on the Mission. It is the kind of work done in the early days of Mission history when the Railways were being built.'

This came to be the final such work undertaken by the Railway Mission. Although there were other constructions, such as the eighty-three mile section from Rutenga to Beit Bridge, opened in October 1974 and giving a new route to the south, none were of the length and complexity, coupled with isolation, of the Bannockburn - Lourenco Marques line, and all were built during the last gasp of Railway Mission activity. For the reasons given by Richard Hughes, therefore, it is essential that this final 'pioneering' work be quoted almost in full:

> Every two or three months I visit the siding of Bannockburn, the rail-head of the new line, under construction, between Rhodesia and Mocambique. From here, I set out, by whatever transport is

available, to visit the men and their families scattered along the 200-mile strip of country. I last visited there at the end of June.

The [Mission] coach arrives at Bannockburn in the early afternoon. It is now a large centre with railway sleepers piled high for use on the new line. The Mission is not responsible for the services [in Bannockburn] as the Vicar of a near-by parish takes monthly services, but I always visit as many families as possible before setting out for the Bundu.

The following morning I rose early, shivering because of the thick frost outside ... After a hasty breakfast, I pack some old clothes and pile them and a crate full of magazines and books, into the truck parked beside the coach. Actually it is a Land Rover I have been lent which has lost its silencer, so for the next eight hours I am almost deafened as I head for the Portuguese border through some of the wildest, unpopulated country of Rhodesia.

The road, built specially for the construction of the new line, is only a track running through the bush. After a day's travelling I shall be a brown dust-covered blob with two gleaming white eyes. My food for the journey consists of biltong (dried meat) and Coca Cola!

After about fifty miles the first camp is reached, where the men are blasting to cut through a granite koppie. There are a dozen families for me to visit here. The houses are primitive, they consist of several corrugated-iron huts. The bush grows up to the front doors and where the grass is worn by passing feet a layer of thick powdery dust remains. The children love it, but it is hard on their mothers, but despite these hardships, the houses are beautifully clean and tidy. All the people are pleased to see a fresh face. They are delighted to receive the books and magazines I have brought.

So the journey proceeds till halfway-house is reached, just 100 miles from base. Here I have made efforts to arrange an evening service but, always, the results have been disappointing. A family has always put their home at my disposal but few turn up. The difficulties are real. A number of the men work at the border only getting home for week-ends and their wives cannot come and leave children alone in the house. Then few have transport, and it is pitch dark with wild game everywhere.

That night I spent at the rest-hut with some of the engineers. Next morning, I rose, before day-break, shaved by candle-light in very cold water, then set out for the home of one of our Communicants. The service must start by 6 a.m. as he must be on his machine by 7 o'clock. After breakfast I leave again and motor into even denser bush. There are one or two small camps on the way; but for the great part there is no sign of human life at all. By early afternoon I am some fifteen miles inside the border. There are three babies to be baptised and it has to be done quickly as the only family has been told to pack their huts and move back eighty miles. A frantic rush follows. The babies are "thrown" into bath-tubs, older children have their faces scrubbed and the mothers attend to their own toilets. In half an hour we are transformed creatures. A white cassock covers my dust and the children, clean and happy, wait round the table, on which a glass bowl stands for a font, to see how their new baby gets its name. These baptism services are most impressive.

The following morning I again rise early to celebrate Holy Communion. After the service I pack my belongings but first go into the bush, with some of the men, hoping to see some wild game ... About 11 o'clock I say good-bye and start back on the rough, dusty drive to Bannockburn where I join the coach - my ever-welcome home on wheels.

The religious value [of the visit] may not be very apparent - not many services, not many attending. There are two confirmation candidates and two communicant families and there are generally some baptisms. But the main value of my visits is to get to know these people and to let them know that the Church has not forgotten them. There may well be other hidden fruits but one goes on visiting in faith and hope doing the little one can, under the circumstances ..[15]

Philip Barrington Simeon, Douglas Ellison, Herbert Hale and many others among the early pioneers would have recognised and applauded this type of Railway Mission work, even if the 'navvies' visited had now become 'construction workers' and the 'gangers' had metamorphosed into 'platelayers'. Given such commitment shown by the missioners, it is little wonder that, when the SACRM withdrew from South Africa and the new 'Rhodesia and Nyasaland Railway Mission' came into being on April 1st 1957, the first cheque paid into the new account was one for £1000 from the Administration of Rhodesia Railways, a promised annual grant. 'This extremely generous backing [was] not only a tribute to the work of the Mission in the past, but also a very definite challenge for the future ...' It also helped to make good the loss of some £3000 a year which had formerly come from South Africa.

The Railway Mission's work with the 'south-east connection' did not stop once construction had ceased. Visits continued to be paid to the railwaymen and their families, particularly those at Malvernia. A journey of twenty four hours, spread over three days, was involved in reaching Malvernia, 'with an occasional handshake or a wave at the stations en route.' Homes were visited and services taken.

More than one said, 'We need you to visit us here', and judging by the very warm farewells from Rhodesian and Portuguese as well as Immigration staff, we were left in no doubt that our interest in these people was appreciated, and the long journey back to Bulawayo was lightened with the assurance that it was well worthwhile.[16]

We have noted, above, the change from all-steam traction to partial 'dieselisation'. All journeys in Southern Rhodesia had to be arranged with the Trains Office in Bulawayo before departure. The missioners would go with their suggested itinerary, only to be told, 'You can't go with that one; it isn't a shunting train', and they had to re-plan. A shunting train was necessary for use of the Mission coach. The missioners found it difficult then to visit the smaller stations, sometimes necessitating spending '12 or 15 hours where 2 or 3 would be sufficient.' It became necessary to go by car down the Malvernia line as far as the road went, and 'with the help of the Coach for overnight, [visit] some of the smaller stations.'

Other changes were forced on the Railway Mission, but these were more a result of Diocesan financial and ecclesiastical constraints and of political changes, such as the Rhodesian UDI, than of specific alterations in railway operation or of general social improvements.

Conflict: Settled Church and itinerant Mission

We have noted, on various occasions, how the Railway Missioners were almost the equivalent of the medieval mendicant friars and 'hedge priests' who were exempt from the jurisdiction of a local bishop and were free to preach and hear confessions where they wished. Secular clergy and bishops in twentieth century southern Africa have equally had problems, from time to time, with accommodating the kind of 'trek parson/bush priest' ministry of Railway Missioners. That there were some bishops who were extremely enthusiastic for and supportive of the Railway Mission does not mitigate against the conflicts that occurred in the Mission's history.

Archbishops and bishops in southern Africa, apart from the initial and occasional forays into 'native'/mission work, were primarily concerned with 'normal' diocesan and parochial work among the white settler community. Even some of those who did see and understand the valuable work done by the Railway missioners were not averse to 'poaching' them to serve as parish priests. As we saw in Chapter 4, Herbert Hale, in his letters, made various remarks about the bishops with whom he had contact. We noted how, when the Bishop of Chichester visited Rhodesia and then went to Victoria Falls to take the first Confirmation service in

'N.W.R.' - North West Rhodesia - he almost ignored Hale, who was the sponsoring and organising priest. The missioner was not over enamoured with the bishop's apparent lack of interest in the Church work in that region or with episcopal blindness regarding Mission finances.

Later in 1904 Hale comments on the possibility of the Railway Mission working in Bulawayo Railway Camp: '... I sense an undercurrent of hostility on the part of the Church people at the Camp to this course ... I have all along had the opinion that the Railway Mission has never been fairly presented by the Bishop and clergy ...' It would be fair to say that most Anglican clergy, given the tradition of parochial ministry, find it difficult to welcome unreservedly 'itinerant missioners' into what they see as their 'patch'. Harold Crane, SACRM chaplain, was passing through Lusaka in 1965 and during a brief stop was asked to see a railwayman:

> Ecclesiastical courtesy has to be considered here since Parish priests and other ministers are readily available in a city like Lusaka ... still, the railwayman comes to feel that the Missioner is one of us, and therefore also feels more easily able to talk to him ... the next step is a discussion with the Parish Priest.[17]

What irked many of the missioners was that, so often, they would be asked to help the parochial system, but help was not always forthcoming their way. Hale, again, received a letter from Archdeacon Upcher of Mashonaland, who was acting as Vicar General in the bishop's absence, in which he wanted Hale to take charge of Francistown for six months or so, plus his railway work. Hale had to write to the Head for guidance, but he was not at all pleased.

Conflicts broke out again in 1914 when Douglas Ellison, founder and the then current Head, wrote to the Chairman of the London Committee regarding the letter from the Metropolitan in Capetown and the Bishop of Pretoria, who were advocating the closure of the Mission. Ellison's extremely strong and angry, even bitter, rejoinder was seen only by the Committee. It has never been published, other than in this writer's doctoral thesis, even in part, and it is easy to see why this was so. After regretting that he would be unable to be present at the Committee's Meeting, he continued:

> ... If either he [the Chairman] or the Archbishop had spent even a twelve month in direct touch with the problem of these isolated people of theirs, with which we have been trying to wrestle all these years, it is safe to assert that this letter or anything like it would never have seen the light of day ... I must confess .. to thankfulness that we do not stand committed, as a Communion, to any theory of the

infallibility of the Episcopate; ... thankfulness, too, that after a generation of irresponsible criticism someone in authority has at last committed himself to something definite ... This letter, stripped of its frills, involves nothing more or less than the practical extermination of the Railway Mission.

... Can you afford to dispense with the services of a strong and capable Head? I am sorry that your Heads until now have apparently failed so completely to justify their existence ...[perhaps] you need a man of blood and iron, a sort of ecclesiastical Bismarck, if you are to hold your work together in the face of lamentable indifference and powerful reactionary forces ...

... I do not think I am wrong when I say that the Bishop's [Bishops'] letter means one of two things: either (1) in their view, they are not sufficiently impressed with the essential need for our work, up to the point of being willing to pay for even a small part of it; or else (2) while fully conscious of the urgency of the need, they are at issue with our method, and believe that, on the whole, the remedy is worse than the disease ...

... It is really astonishing that men of the ability of our Bishops can travel frequently about that immense country without an almost painful consciousness of the great aggregate of professing Christian people who are falling clean through the broad meshes of their existing organisation. It is no earthly use talking about handing these same people over to the established parochial administration. The parochial clergy never have reached them, and never will; and I have no sort of doubt that the Bishop's proposal involves practically the consigning of a considerable and important section of the Community to more or less complete spiritual destitution.

I cannot pretend to any very profound sympathy with the Bishops of Grahamstown [not mentioned earlier] and Pretoria in their implied complaint that they are now left with only one [SACRM] man apiece. They have themselves to thank for it. They have not hesitated to take good men from the Mission, they would have taken many more if I had not strenuously resisted it. But they have never moved a finger, to the best of my remembrance, to find men for a work which, in any ideal order, they would have regarded as peculiarly their own.

It is better that one of two things should happen:

(A) either that the Archbishop and the Bishops of the Province should fundamentally alter their traditional attitude towards the Mission ; should frankly recognise the tremendous importance of the gap which it is trying to fill in their existing machinery; and should from this time forward make its cause their own ...; or

> (B) failing this, that with intense regret you think it best to retire quietly from the long and unequal struggle, simply because that adequate support from authority has not been forthcoming ...[18]

A 'generation of irresponsible criticism', 'indifference', 'reactionary forces', along with taking 'good men from the Mission' are not the normal polite terms used by a well-respected and honoured clergyman of his bishops, to whom he had owed Canonical obedience. There was not even a clash of churchmanship, as was so often the case in South Africa. It was, quite simply, a monumental clash between an advocate of pioneering 'mission church' work, and an imported Anglican hierarchy who were wholly wedded to the seventh century Archbishop Theodore's parochial system. The fact that Ellison was ill and 'overwhelmed by a sense of failure'[19] does not, I feel, lessen the real conflict that existed.

In the same month that Ellison wrote his letter, the then Head, Frederick Rogers, handed in his resignation to the Archbishop of Cape Town. Ellison's sister, Dorothy, in her *God's Highwaymen,* states that 'The Bishop of Pretoria had offered him [Rogers] the post of Archdeacon of Pietersburg, which he had accepted.'[20] One can imagine Douglas Ellison's reaction to that news.

The Archbishop of Cape Town and his fellow bishops must have taken 'option A', for SACRM continued, with their blessing. In 1923 they even appointed (and released) a recently-arrived parish priest, the Rev. Harold Rolfe, as Head of the Railway Mission. In that same year the two Chairmen at the Annual Conference made pertinent comments about the relationship between the bishops and the Mission. The Bishop of Pretoria stated:

> I should just like to say as a Diocesan Bishop in South Africa how unreservedly I value the Railway Mission. There have been ... in the past a certain amount of doubtful relations between the Bishops out there and the Railway Mission. I can't conceive how anyone could not rejoice in the fact of the Railway Mission, because ... we are only just touching tasks which clearly go beyond our resources. To have a little bit of something which is in addition ... oh, what a blessing![21]

Archdeacon Cameron of the Transvaal, who chaired the Evening Meeting at the Annual Conference, warmly supported the Mission, yet showed his understanding of bishops' problems:

> Bishops are a little bit of trouble because they are quite natural and human beings like everybody else, and they have their temptations, and when they have got a parish like Pietersburg ... suddenly vacant

> ... and supposing there is a very excellent chaplain working on the Railway Mission, the Bishop does not always pay the Head of the Mission the respect he ought to, and so he writes to the man and says, "I want you to accept the job at Pietersburg." Well, sometimes - even Railway Missioners are human - they succumb and off they go, and then the Head of the Railway Mission hears of it ...
>
> Now, fortunately, Mr. Rogers [previous Head] was not above making himself unpleasant to Bishops at times ... and Canon Thornely Jones is also addicted to that practice. And so Bishops have lost the habit of doing these little things. But for the fact that the Railway Mission is an extra-diocesan affair, and in charge of somebody else, you would find that one after another the men would go, and there would be hardly a man left on the Railway Mission. That is why it is important that this should be maintained as an organisation independent of the various bishops. There is no real antagonism, there is no real opposition to the diocesan scheme ...[22]

It was good, yet rare, for this problematical relationship to be so clearly stated.

Whatever the state of relationships between Church hierarchy and SACRM, the missioners were always licensed by the diocesan bishop and were under his authority. In many cases it was the Railway Mission which founded the churches subsequently 'owned' by the diocese. As Rev. Synge put it: 'It was something to be proud of when the local Church could catch up with the work of the Mission, which could then move on or close down; the SACRM was essentially a stop-gap.'[23]

Until 1957, when SACRM moved out of South Africa, the Head of the Mission was 'contracted' as laid down by the Episcopal Synod of the church of the Province of South Africa:

> His appointment, resignation, or removal shall rest with the Archbishop of Capetown.
>
> He shall hold a licence in a Diocese to be selected by the Archbishop. He shall also be granted permission to officiate in each Diocese in which the Mission works. He shall confer with each Diocesan Bishop as to the extent and nature of the assistance which the Bishop thinks desirable; and when a mutual agreement has been arrived at, the Head of the Mission shall do his utmost to secure continuity of work and workers; and the latter shall only be removed after due notice to, and with the consent of, the Bishop of the Diocese.[24]

It is clear from the above that the crucial point of contact, with its potential for conflict, between the Church hierarchy and the Railway Mission was the appointment of the Mission's Head by the Metropolitan Archbishop. Although the Archbishop would confer with the Home/London Committee of SACRM and with his fellow bishops in the Province, he was the one who 'hired and fired'. The appointment and dismissal of Fr. Eustace Hill, C.R. in the 1930s is an illustrative, if extreme, example.

Hill had been a military and Railway Mission chaplain at the end of the Anglo-Boer war and subsequently was a chaplain to the South African forces from 1914:

> His courage during the six day battle of Delville Wood, after which only 800 of the 3,000 South African troops survive, became legendary. In a later battle he asked for volunteers to follow him into no-man's land to collect the wounded, 'Do you believe in God? If you do, follow me!' He was badly wounded in foot and arm. His foot healed, but his right arm had to be amputated. He refused to wear his MC but had it set in a crucifix and placed in [St. John's College, Johannesburg] chapel. He returned to St. John's in 1919 after some tough months in a POW camp, his memory and hearing impaired, but a national hero.[25]

In March 1922 Eustace Hill became Headmaster of St. John's (The Community of the Resurrection's college for white boys), mainly as a result of his fame during the war and of the resignations of others. In 1930 he retired to the Community's home base of Mirfield, only to be asked by his Superior, with the Archbishop of Cape Town, in 1934 to return to South Africa as Head of the Church Railway Mission. Although his saintliness and courage could not have been questioned, Hill's eccentricity, age and extreme anglo-catholicism should have made the CPSA Metropolitan look elsewhere for someone to take on the difficult and tiring job of Head of SACRM.

The CPSA archives, in the University of the Witwatersrand, contain a fascinating collection of Railway Mission southern Africa correspondence for the period from 1935 to 1949. Many of these letters were not copied for sending on to the Home Committee in London, and of those that were, only the originals survive. Among the letters are those to, from and about Eustace Hill. Readers of the 'Blue Quarterly' may have been mystified, as I was initially, why the new Head (from December 1934) did not write very often in the magazine and, when he did, was frequently confined to short letters hidden within the *Quarterly,* rather than having the prime spot at the front, which was the norm. An examination of the relevant correspondence soon makes the picture clear.

Early in 1935 Eustace Hill sent his first 'Head's Letter to Quarterly', which was not published. In it, while noting the need to adapt mission work 'owing to the change from 98% British [on the railways] in 1902 to that of 10% in 1935', Hill made two radical, if not revolutionary, suggestions. He stated, ' .. just as the S.A.R is augmenting its services to the State by Road Transport so our Railway travels must be supplemented by road travel.' He mooted the idea of a motor van, though recognised the expense involved and the failure to fully use the free railway Passes. His second 'phase', as he termed it, 'looks away from the rail [to] the needs of the British farmers on the veld, who have a Church as well as national claim on us.' He believed that SACRM should no longer 'be bound exclusively to Railway folk.'[26]

In London, as the Rev. Pat Leonard, Chairman of the SACRM 'Home Association', as it was then known, digested the startling letter from the new Head, he received a letter (not preserved) from the Archbishop of Capetown. He replied by return on 17 July 1935:

> My dear Archbishop,
>
> I am most grateful to you for your letter this morning, enclosing a copy of what you wrote to Eustace Hill. It is difficult for me at this distance to have a well formed and balanced opinion about the future development of the Railway Mission. I am bound to say, however, that I have been a little disquieted by Eustace Hill's revolutionary proposals to forsake the Railway for the lonely farmer.
> .... I found that [the Executive] largely shared my misgivings that the Railway privileges, free passes, etc., might be withdrawn unless the main emphasis of the work remains on the Railway operatives .. My own feeling, even before your letter arrived, was to hold up the publication of the Head's letter until the scheme has been more adequately thought out ...[27]

The CPSA bishops were very unhappy with Eustace Hill, and Archbishop Phelps of Cape Town cabled the Superior of the House of the Resurrection, Mirfield:

> Bishops' Synod feels urgent necessity Community [of the Resurrection] should recall Father Hill from Headship Railway Mission immediately stop <Otherwise must ask for his immediate resignation stop Writing> Bishops desire avoid demanding his

> resignation stop Writing fully ARCHBISHOP [Words in parenthesis scored out in original])[28]

By asking the Community to recall Hill, the Archbishop and his fellow bishops had hoped to avoid conflict or even being seen to be involved. Phelps, as Metropolitan, spelled out, in a hand written confidential letter, the reasons for their request. It shows clearly the dilemmas posed by the conflicting authorities of bishop and Mission Head:

> The Bishops' Synod has recently been in Session in Johannesburg and had had under discussion the work of the South African Church <Institute> [scored out] Railway Mission in the various dioceses of the Province. I have the very uncongenial task of writing now to you to tell you what is in the mind of the Bishops, for the debate disclosed a very real dissatisfaction on their part with the administration of Father Eustace Hill, the present Head of the Mission.
>
> None of the Bishops doubts his great devotion to his work ... but all those in whose dioceses the Mission works are united in saying that he cannot continue as Head of the Mission.
>
> His failure to be an accepted Head seems to lie in the fact that he never allows the Clergy and Lay Workers on the Mission to continue in their work without continuous interference and the frequent interruption of their work by the introduction of new schemes and ideas which are pursued just so far as to cause unsettlement and bewilderment among congregations and then laid aside in favour of something else. Clergy who go for a holiday, leaving the Head on their section, find the section in turmoil on their return ...
>
> The Mission Chaplains find themselves continually compelled to appeal to their respective Bishops as against the Head, for they find their position so intolerable that it takes the heart out of their work ... [One Bishop] complains too that the Head, without his permission, goes to Rectors of parishes bordering upon the railway and <makes> [crossed out] consults with them as to [inserted] new arrangements for work and new redrawing of parochial boundaries, causing unsettlement not only among Railway Mission congregations but also in others which are under the parochial clergy. The Bishop hears of it when the trouble is well developed and has to try to straighten out embarrassing situations. Another Bishop says that he has never know[n] the Mission in such a state of disorder in all his - considerably long - experience.
>
> A result of this is that the Mission finds itself short of workers. Clergy will not renew their contracts to work under the present Head.

> And there seem to be some signs that the uncomfortable character of the service under Father Hill is becoming known in England and that young priests in consequence will not come out to the Mission.
>
> Bishops have repeatedly urged Father Hill to go to England to find new workers, and he declines to go... It seems clear that unless - as one Bishop puts it - the Head leaves the Mission, the Mission will leave the Head.
>
> .... It is a matter of the utmost urgency that Father Hill should be recalled from this work to which your Community has so kindly [sic] lent him. It is felt that this urgency grows daily more immediate and that is why I have cabled to you that you may feel supported by the Bishops' Synod in any action in recalling Father Hill which you may think is right to take. The Bishops ... clearly feel that Father Hill should not be the Head of the Mission for one single day longer than is necessary.[29]

The bishops must have been particularly incensed with Hill's cavalier attitude towards parochial boundaries and his 'discussions' with parish priests. This was very clearly episcopal territory. Hill, who, as a Religious, had never been a parish priest, and whose canonical obedience was first to his Community's Superior rather than to a diocesan bishop, either was ignorant of or chose to ignore parochial and diocesan courtesies.

It is unknown what response, if any, was made to the Archbishop's cable and letter. It took over a year for matters to be resolved. Bishop Edward Paget, of Southern Rhodesia, wrote to the Archbishop in February 1937 concerned that the work of the Railway Mission in his diocese might be damaged by the 'considerable discontent and unsettlement amongst the Railway Mission workers.' He had 'all along felt that [Hill] was not the right man for the post.'[30] The Archbishop replied to Bishop Paget within the week. He stated that, although SACRM was an 'imperium in imperio' [a power within a power] its strength [depended] largely upon the working of the Head with the local Bishop ..'[31] He accepted that, if the bishops were unhappy with Hill, he had the 'power of dismissing him', although he would be extremely reluctant to do that 'without a general backing on the subject throughout the Province.' Phelps assumed that Paget had put before Eustace Hill 'the way in which his action [was] clashing with the Diocesan Bishops' and suggested that the bishop write Hill a friendly letter to resolve the matter.

We may assume that further correspondence ensued between Bishopscourt (Claremont, Cape Town), London and Hill himself. It appears that the Head was summoned before the Archbishop and confronted with his 'sins'. He then wrote to the Archbishop, in his distinctive left-handed script, learned after the amputation of his right arm, on 8th October 1937:

> My dear Archbishop
>
> Distinct signs I had better let our staff know of my services being terminated 31 xii 37. I wrote to Pat Leonard [London] saying that my services were to be ended ... that the reasons given were poor, but underneath was the fact that I was not ... big enough for the job. This I am telling the staff. You didn't let me keep the paper recording my "sins" but I remember (1) Not going Home [England] to get Missioners, (2) Upsetting young Missioners work, (3) Causing unrest in Grahamstown Diocese. I must say that I should like to have faced these charges & all the rest & swept them aside & got to the unpleasant reality that I am not big enough for the job which is a true tribute to the Mission ... and not provoke controversy ...[32]

This letter was followed by one from the Dean of Salisbury, Lawrence Skey, a former Railway Missioner and one of the two vice-Heads of SACRM, expressing concern for his old friend Eustace Hill. He felt that one or two chaplains had been disloyal to Hill and wondered about his own position as vice-Head, particularly as he had not been consulted by the bishops. Hill himself then sent a highly critical and somewhat rambling letter to the Archbishop. He had come to believe, or perhaps was happier to believe, that the 'real reason for [his] unfitness for Head of SACRM', was his refusal to be licensed by any bishop not against Resolution XV of the 1930 Lambeth Conference. This resolution had given a qualified approval to contraception. Hill, and many anglo-catholics who were members of the League of National Life, which campaigned against contraception, was totally opposed to the Resolution. In his letter he admitted to feeling more and more detached from 'the English Church' and even from the C.R. Houses. He was aware of his extreme stance:

> I am very sorry that the C.R. do not endorse my extreme views & are frankly bored by them & hoped the [Railway] Mission w[oul]d modify them.

The Archbishop wrote to Pat Leonard, in London, asking for advice about a new Head. Noting that Father Hill had 'done valiant work ... with .. the Bishops of one mind in their admiration [sic] for his self-sacrificing devotion to the work of the Mission', he admitted that there had been 'certain difficulties arising through the unique character of the man himself.' The crucial sentence in his letter lies almost hidden, half-way through:

> It is necessary therefore to secure a priest [as Head] who has the faculty of enlisting the sympathy of the Missioners and also to work in co-operation with the Bishops in whose dioceses the work is going on.[33]

On the same day, Archbishop Phelps wrote to Eustace Hill a somewhat disingenuous letter which, nevertheless, brooked no argument:

> My dear Eustace,
>
> I hope I have not misinterpreted you and done you an injustice. I was quite under the impression that you wanted to retire from the headship at the end of the year and the Bishops agreed that it would be well to act on this. But your letter rather indicates that you were not ready to give in your resignation so soon; and between the two points of view I cannot decide. Certainly I thought that was interpreting the wish of the bishops when I talked with you. I am afraid therefore that the finding of a new Head must be taken in hand at once ...[34]

Suddenly, on reading through all the correspondence of the period, the reader's sympathies towards the Mission and the bishops, faced with a difficult and idiosyncratic Head, swing towards this elderly priest caught up in church politics and less-than-honest episcopal missives. That Eustace Hill had to make way for someone else was, perhaps, a forgone conclusion; but the manner of his dismissal was not entirely edifying. At the end of his time Hill had been trying to sort out difficulties in Northern Rhodesia, where one of the missioners, Charles Potts, had had a mental breakdown, resulting in an attempted suicide, partly as a result of the sexual misdemeanours of his wife, a Civil Service clerk. The Governor and the Bishop of Northern Rhodesia, as well as Hill, were involved in the various 'negotiations'. Shortly afterwards, Hill converted to Roman Catholicism.

As noted above, this episode in relationships between Church hierarchy and Railway Mission does illustrate the difficulties that arose between the two, and can stand as an example, even if extreme, of all such conflicts.

The potential for conflict was evident in the relationship between the (Anglican) Railway Missioners and members of other denominations, particularly the Dutch Reformed, encountered by and ministered to by them:

> The development of settler Christianity and churches in South Africa took place along lines which mirrored the ecclesiastical situation in Europe. The same confessional and theological differences which divided the churches there into Protestant and Catholic, Reformed and Lutheran, Anglican and Nonconformist, took root. These differences were reflected, as in Europe, in everything from church architecture and liturgy to the way in which church members related to society and politics.[35]

To read through letters, diaries and reports from SACRM chaplains is to be aware of how often they baptised, held services with, prepared confirmation for and generally ministered to members of the Dutch Reformed Church, mainly Afrikaners. Yet, the Missioners' *Vade Mecum* read:

> 1) Baptisms: Never, under any pretext, or for any reason, excepting only if the child is dying, Baptize the child of Dutch Reformed parents .. Members .. are liable to ask us .. as we don't charge for the Sacrament ...
> 2) Confirmations in the D.R. denomination are prolonged, exacting and expensive; so again their people apply to us and then cheerfully go back to their old Church. So all such applications ... should be refused ...
> 3) The [Dutch Reformed] denomination predominates in the Union [of South Africa] numerically .. [and] its officials seem to have a rooted dislike to the Anglican Church ... Avoid contact with most of their predikants; there are a few very good ones ...[36]

I have no doubt whatsoever that, although the Guidelines are suggestive of much conflict, they were actually more observed in the breech than in the keeping of them. If anything, the missioners often felt sorry for 'the Dutch'. Arthur Hobson, visiting Content, near Warrenton, in 1918, wrote:

> One cannot help feeling strongly that there is very little real love for the Dutch Reformed Church amongst their people .. Content has half a dozen families of the class known as "poor whites", Dutch people who are working as labourers on the line, the sort of work that is generally done by natives under a white ganger ...They are nice simple folk ... and I am sure can make good Christians ...

> One of them is a member of the Church [=Anglican], and came to his Communion this morning before going out to his day's toil on the line.[37]

Herbert Hale makes many references to 'the Dutch' in his letters home:-

> Yesterday I drove out 10 miles to see the wife of a farmer, who is anxious to be confirmed. She is half-Dutch, and had undergone the so-called [sic] confirmation of the Dutch Reformed Church. She is anxious for Confirmation in the English Church, especially as the door to Holy Communion ... I shall have little hesitation in presenting her ...[38]

He reports subsequently, 'the Confirmation Service went off very well .. though it took place in a rough mud hut .. they were Dutch people and afterwards regaled us on roast sucking pig ..'[39]

Baptisms get frequent mentions:

> ... after breakfast I went a short distance outside the mine to Christen a Dutch transport rider's baby ...
> ... I was faced with no less than 5 babies to christen, several of Dutch parents with scant knowledge of Church English ... I made little Christians of them all, wrote out certificates of Baptism for their parents, accepted the Thankoffering fees tendered,... then photoed the five with their proud mothers.[40]

Some tasks were sadder, such as when Hale was asked to bury the child of a 'poor Dutch woman of the "bywoner" class' whose baby had died on a train. He writes of the 'poorer Dutch people' experiencing 'terrible privations', and continues, 'Four girls from the School carried the coffin, nearly all the people at the Siding turned up, and we had a really touching reverent service.'[41]

Almost thirty years later Allen Rusbridger noted in his Diary,

> Ootsi [near Gaberones]: ... There baptised two Dutch children whose parents never saw a "predikant", man couldn't speak English & I couldn't Afrikaans. [42]

In November the same year (1932) Rusbridger was at Debeeti (on the line between Gaberones and Palapye). He wrote,

> ..arr Deb.[eeti] 4.29 [pm.]. Stayed with Vys. all Dutch here but turned up well & we had 100% of the pop. to the tune of 12: also baptised Ganger's baby. First time E[vensong] ever been held here.[43]

Most of the Railway chaplains found that, whereas at Communion Services they would have only a few, almost entirely Anglican, people present, at Morning Service (Matins) or Evensong there would be very many more, of all denominations and none, including those of other faiths. Hale frequently mentions 'all denominations' at Services; Seacombe writes of 'keen Wesleyans who want a Service', and 'the congregation was a mixture of Salvationists, Wesleyans, Presbyterians and C.of E.', or of '..a weird congregation of .. two Gentiles and two Jews! We said Compline together ..'[44]; and Rusbridger noted at one small village near Pokwani, 'E[vensong] at 7.30 & two "strolling players", one an educated Jew, came to the service & we had an interesting talk afterwards ...'[45]

When Rusbridger left the Mission in 1938 the list of 'Wellwishers' who subscribed to his 'parting gift' included: '9 Dutch Reformed, 7 Wesleyan, 2 Jewish, 1 Lutheran, 4 Presbyterian, 1 Seventh Day Adventist and 2 Roman Catholics, along with 26 Anglican families.'[46] We may safely assume that none of them had read the strictures of the 'Vade Mecum'.

A lady worker, Miss Venables, wrote from Naauwpoort in 1945, 'We had thirty; that is considered a "largish" English-speaking congregation ... But besides C.of E. we had Presbys., a Methodist, a R.C., a Jew and a few D.R's. ..[47] The presence of Jewish people, mostly storekeepers, at Christian Services is certainly an interesting and unique sidelight on Church history/Judaism. For the Jews, as for many of the fairly isolated people, the arrival of the Railway Chaplain and the coming together of a group within the community was an occasion, an 'event'. It was social as well as 'religious'. Hellig reminds us that, 'in the early years of East European Jewish settlement, Jews could be found in various parts of [southern Africa]. Many became pedlars *(smouse)* who supplied the rural Afrikaner community with commodities to which they did not have ready access.'[48] The Anglican Services of Matins, Evensong and Compline all had their roots in Judaism and were not, of course, as blatantly 'Christian' as the Service of Holy Communion.

Conflict could arise, as on one occasion when Hale was at Gwanda. He wrote,

> Sometimes the zeal of my congregation to provide me with a good congregation outran their discretion. I noticed ... that all the Jewish storekeepers were lined up in the congregation against the back wall. On enquiry I learnt that the Christian male members had roped them in much against their will, so as to give the "padre" a good show ..[49]

In the period of the Railway Mission the various Christian denominations did co-operate in Southern Africa in so far as Mission (evangelistic) work was concerned, or at least tried not to 'poach' or to enter someone else's 'patch'. The same co-operation and concern was not as marked where pastoral work with Europeans/Whites was concerned. There was often little love lost between the adherents of the different bodies. Hale, going to baptise a ganger's baby, wrote,

> The mother was a Church-woman [Anglican], the ganger a R.C. and I asked him if it was his wish that I should christen the youngster. He said, 'Yes, he was a R.C. but he was not a narrow minded man. So long as his children were baptised by a R.C. priest or a Church Clergyman, it was good enough for him. But he couldn't abide those imitation Churches, like Wesleyans, Primitives and the Salvation Army.[50]

Many would want to query the ganger's definition of 'narrow minded'.

Sister Mary Stella CSP, formerly Miss Elsie Clarke, who was a SACRM Woman Worker from 1947 to 1949, wrote of her encounters with other denominations:

> 'There was an English speaking family on the junction of a branch line [Orange Free State], but they were Methodists, and attended their own small chapel in the nearby small town. They were always most kind and welcoming, and spent a lot of time trying to persuade me to marry their youngest brother!
>
> Further trips on all the other lines proved the great dearth of English speakers, leave [let] alone Anglicans, and my Afrikaans improved rapidly ... I always had the most friendly and happy relations with everybody, but pastoral work was virtually nil. There was a Dutch Reformed Mission on the line, but I never coincided with them, though I know that they preached against me and "The High Church of England", though whether or not they would have preferred the old Colensoite church, I never discovered.
>
> There was also one other non-conformist church coach, with which I coincided from time to time, and was always most kindly welcomed to a meal and prayer session, while we exchanged news and a few goodies.
>
> The Railway also maintained a group of social workers along the line, and again we were quite friendly. So there was little for me to do, as on my 3000 miles of line there were only about 20 Anglicans, and all but one of these had access to the Anglican church in the nearest town, or was visited regularly by its Rector..' [51]

The lack of (Anglican) Railway Mission work in the region caused Elsie Clarke to terminate her contract.

It seems to me, from all the current evidence, that the Railway Missioners were far more broad minded and all-embracing than many of the people they dealt with, including the 'normal' parochial clergy. There were conflicts between Anglicans and non-Anglicans, but the Railway Mission, despite its 'Vade Mecum' and its general 'High Church' ethos, had a tolerant 'via media' concept of Anglicanism. Its relationship with non-Anglicans, though potentially (and at times) one of conflict, often was more positive than the relationship with fellow Anglicans.

Political change and conflict

> It came as no surprise ... when the Head was asked to arrange services in connection with the recent Conference on the break-up of the Federation, held at the Victoria Falls. We were able to have a Chaplain in residence at the Falls Hotel throughout the Conference, a daily Celebration of Holy Communion was possible, and on the Sunday a special Service was organized and was attended by most of the delegates. The Archbishop of Central Africa preached the sermon, and the Bishop of Matabeleland also took part in the service, which was conducted by the Head of the Mission. It was a wonderful opportunity, and I was glad that we were able to give some spiritual significance to this historic gathering.[52]

The ten year-old Central African Federation had been opposed by most Africans, fearing rightly that it would, and did, serve mainly to benefit the white rulers of Southern Rhodesia. Growth of federal government power increasingly clashed with emerging African nationalism. The 1962 elections in Northern Rhodesia, which led to a nationalist coalition government, brought the end of full federation. In January 1963 Dr. Banda returned to Nyasaland/Malawi and the following month had a 'Federation coffin' dumped before him. The Conference, for which the Rhodesia and Nyasaland Railway Mission had spiritual care, met to wind up the Federation. The 'Great Experiment' itself was not finally and legally ended until the close of 1963. It is from the break up of the Central African Federation that the major political changes took place which had direct bearings on the work of the Railway Mission and which ultimately brought about its demise.

By April 1964 the Head, Kenneth Simms, writing from Bulawayo, was able to advise supporters of how the Mission was being affected:

> I think that you all ought to know that we have been passing through a very anxious time out here. I think it is true to say that the Railway Mission has been facing the greatest crisis in its long and wonderful history.
>
> The unsettled state of affairs in this country, and the break up of the Federation has greatly affected our financial position. Our income has dropped alarmingly, and we have lost many of our best friends and supporters ... It is obvious that we shall have to reduce our staff, at any rate for the time being. We shall also have to give up some of our work in Northern Rhodesia. This work will be taken over by the Diocesan Clergy ...[53]

This was the last-but-one 'Blue Quarterly' letter, and the last one under the head 'Rhodesia and Nyasaland Railway Mission'. Later in 1964 the Mission became 'The Railway Mission of the Church of the Province of Central Africa', the Meeting of the London Committee in September that year agreeing to put the new title into force in Britain. The very last *Quarterly* (QP 215, Dec.1964) informed readers of the change.

Harold Crane, Missioner/Secretary, whose ordination-training had been sponsored and funded by the Railway Mission, wrote to the London Committee Chairman, Michael Fidgin, in November 1965, to appraise him of the situation faced by the staff in central Africa:

> That which we had fervently hoped would not happen has come to pass - a U.D.I., and at this stage we do not know just exactly what all its effects will be. One thing is certain, however, and that is that the work and the ministry of the Church, always supremely vital in any human situation, remains so in this. The Railway Mission has a big job to do, and this must go on.
>
> ... It seems quite obvious to me that our contacts with you are going to continue to be as close as ever, and that your role in London will be not only the task of raising financial assistance, but also to promote interest in the Railway Mission and co-operate with the Executive Committee in finding new workers for the Railway Mission out here. ... We are in very urgent need of a Chaplain for Zambia, and the Archbishop (who ... is also Bishop of Zambia) is most anxious to have one as soon as possible ... This really is a most desperate need. The Diocese itself is not in a position to assist with our line work because of their own heavy commitments ... Housing will be provided, and a Mission Coach awaits him in Zambia ....
>
> There are still very many little groups of people and often individual families, in out-of-the-way places in Zambia, Bechuanaland and Rhodesia ... It is true that we minister much more

> to little communities than isolated homes these days, but it must be seen that these communities are many, and vary from one Platelayer, with his compound of approximately 15 African families, to other places with a dozen European and Coloured families and a large African township. Some places, of course, have no one there but the Pumper and his family.[54]

Harold Crane was one of the very few (white) Railway chaplains who joined the Mission in Africa itself, as we noted in Chapter 1, where he gives his reasons for joining SACRM.

The course, construction and even running of railways have always been interwoven with political decisions. Government Ministers have invariably been in charge of railways, though leaving the administration and running of them to the railway professionals. Croxton, in his *Railways of Zimbabwe*, noted that 'over seventy years, the picture of the railways in Central Africa ... changed from the spreading system born from the dreams of Cecil Rhodes into more compact units organised on a national basis.'[55] The break up of the Federation meant that the ownership of and financial responsibility for Rhodesia Railways passed to the separate governments. At first the Railways continued as a unitary system, overseen by a 'Higher Authority', comprising two members from each government. With the northern partner becoming the Republic of Zambia in October 1964 and the southern one declaring U.D.I thirteen months later, it became increasingly impossible for Rhodesia Railways to function as one system. On midnight on 30th June, 1967, Rhodesia and Zambia established autonomous railways in their own countries, leaving Zambia with 669 track miles from the centre of Victoria Falls Bridge to the Zaire border, and Rhodesia with 2,040 miles, though that included the 390 miles that fell within Botswana and which were still run by Rhodesia Railways.

The Railway Mission had to move quickly if it was not to be entirely wrong-footed by the political/railway changes. Just three months after the formal split of Rhodesia Railways it was decided, at an Executive Meeting of the Mission on 20th September, 1967:

> to arrange a constitutional separation between the Mission's work in Rhodesia and Botswana and that in Zambia. The former would continue as the Railway Mission of the Province of Central Africa while the latter would become the responsibility of the Diocese of Zambia ... The London Committee would be asked to continue to assist both areas. A division of assets and liabilities would be necessitated ...The Archbishop [of Central Africa] informed the Committee that the general Manager of Zambia Railways had

expressed a sincere wish that Railway Mission work should continue in Zambia.[56]

However, sincere wishes were not enough to finance and staff mission work. Zambia Railways itself had a disastrous first year of operation. Many of its skilled railwaymen left and within twelve months there had been '369 derailments, 13 main line collisions and 53 severe siding accidents.'[57] All of which goes some way, perhaps all the way, to explain the remarks under 'Zambia' in Railway Mission News in *Partners* in November 1968:

> We have no Missioner here now... The new Railway authorities have many problems, and are unlikely to grant special travel facilities for just one church, although they might consider this if the request came from the local Council of Christian Churches. In the meantime, the old Railway Mission centres are being visited by the nearest parish priest. This involves the Diocese in extra expense to cover this travelling, and the Archbishop hopes that we could help meet this in some way, perhaps by adopting one of the churches originally founded by the Railway Mission. This plan is being examined.' [58]

The situation of the Church in Zambia had altered after the Federation ended. On January 16th 1965, less than three months after Independence, many of the churches and missions in Zambia came together as the United Church of Zambia. The Anglican Church and the African Reformed Church were not part of this union. The stumbling block for the Anglicans, particularly Africans, was the simple and 'Protestant' style of worship of the uniting churches. The U.C.Z ministers 'complain[ed] that the Anglican liturgy and outlook [was] too catholic.'[59] This situation hardly put the Railway Mission in a strong or bargaining position, being, as it was, part of a Church not caught up in the euphoria of national unity. It is not clear how Archbishop Green-Wilkinson expected the Railway Mission, which was increasingly starved of cash, to give much help to the Zambian Diocese with expenses. Not that Zambia was alone.

In Botswana, at the same time, the Mission reported:

> The church is thin on the ground ... and it is essential that a priest be established somewhere along the Mahalape [sic] line, which at present receives only a visiting-ministry from travelling missioners. The Diocese are unable to find the money or to provide a man, and appealed to the Railway Mission to fill the gap. Further, they would need money to establish a base from which the priest would work, and asked us to provide this too.[60]

The appeal from Zambia and Botswana did not fall entirely on deaf ears. The Standing Committee of the London Committee, when it met on November 27th, 1968, agreed to remit £1500 to Botswana (£1000 capital outlay and £500 towards stipend of a chaplain), with £500 for the following year also. For Zambia they agreed on a figure of 'up to £200 ... towards the Chaplain's travelling expenses for the year 1968-9.'[61]

On the railways, conditions did not improve:

> A "one-for-one" exchange of locomotives and rolling stock at Victoria Falls was imposed by the Rhodesian government to ensure a proper balance of stock, but, despite this, serious congestion of traffic ... occurred on ZR [Zambian Railways], resulting in periodic embargoes on goods from the south. In 1969 the through passenger service was discontinued and RR trains terminated at Victoria Falls, though goods traffic was worked through to Livingstone. The few rail passengers from Rhodesia to Zambia travelled by bus.[62]

A degree of co-operation was necessary between the two Railway authorities, for, 'In Africa railways transcend politics. If your enemy runs the railway which brings your maize, then you keep to his time-table.'[63] It may be noted that it was the coal of Wankie (Hwange) which, more than any other factor, sustained the fifteen years of UDI as far as the railways were concerned.

The rail congestion and embargoes had a 'knock-on' effect for the Railway Mission. In March/April 1970 it changed its name, for the last time, to that of 'The Railway Mission of Rhodesia and Botswana', realistically reflecting virtual cessation of its work in Zambia. In the May issue of *Partners* that year, Robert Chancellor, one of the three European missioners, reported: 'We are ... at a considerable disadvantage at present in our work along the line, because since the division of the Rhodesian .. and the Zambian Railways and the division of rolling stock, we have been left with only one Mission coach to operate the whole system ...'[64]

The guerrilla war in Rhodesia, the Second Chimurenga War, began in earnest on April 28th, 1966, when seven ZANLA guerrillas were killed at Sinoia. The course and history of the War is well documented and does not need substantial comment here. Briefly, the last phase of the conflict, following the firing on Altena Farm (Zambezi valley, north-east Zimbabwe) by ZANU guerrillas, just before Christmas 1972, escalated the disruptions within Rhodesia. This intensified after FRELIMO took control in Mocambique in 1974/5, with much of the guerrilla activity thence launched from Mocambique itself. The Rhodesian forces, in retaliation, launched furious offensives both within Rhodesia itself and across its borders. A passenger train was mined south of the Victoria Falls in

December 1976, and from that time until the end of the war passenger services ended at Thompson Junction, some five miles north of Wankie.

The chaplains of the Railway Mission could not but be affected by the War, particularly as they needed to move about the country travelling on vulnerable trains. The missioners who served in Rhodesia from 1970-1980 did make comments, usually in private letters, about the situation. Some were in agreement with Smith, following the majority of Whites in Rhodesia - 'against the world'. Most of these missioners are still alive and it would serve no purpose to reproduce their private views which were voiced in exceptional circumstances and under great pressure. It must suffice to illustrate their situation by referring to the few published letters and reports which were written during that period.

Bishop Mark Wood, when he left Rhodesia as Bishop of Matabeleland, in 1976, spoke of 'the increasing hazards and restrictions on travel on the railways in the insecurity caused by the guerrilla-war situation, apart from the ordinary ones inherent in any itinerant missionary's life (the extremes of cold and heat, the violence of storms, the discomforts of shunting, the irregularity of meals, etc.).'[65]

Earle and Ruth Hawkes, the only Canadian missioners in the history of the Railway Mission, found their time in Rhodesia rewarding, though stressful, particularly for Ruth Hawkes, on account of 'terrorist' activity. Their short (eighteen months) but intensive ministry was much appreciated by very many railway employees and families. George and Gertrude Deacon followed them, arriving in June 1977, becoming the last chaplains in the history of the Railway Mission.

The Deacons' first letter appeared in *Partners* in November 1977, written in September. George Deacon wondered how they could possibly minister to the various communities in Wankie, Gwanda, Colleen Bawn, West Nicholson and Beit Bridge, all of which he had pastoral care, let alone all the other places that the Railway Mission served. He continued:

> We worked out a pattern and we stuck to it faithfully in the first few months so that people know where we are and when to expect us. Many changes had to be made to our itinerary because of the tense situation, with lines blown up, trains cancelled and journey schedules changed ...
> We knew our work here entailed travel, travel and yet more travel, but we did not realize how long one can take to get from place to place in these troubled days. We are using our car far more than any previous Chaplain .. Dangerous? Very, but life is dangerous just now in Rhodesia and Botswana. We may have to appeal for a more powerful car soon ... people get more and more neglected unless we have the transport available ...[66]

The magazine *Partners,* in March 1979, reported that George and Gertrude Deacon 'had twice been in a train shot up by terrorists and... were at the Victoria Falls when it was shelled from Zambia.' The last 'ordinary' Meeting of the London Committee of the Mission took place on 23rd October, 1979. The main object of the Meeting was to report on a visit to Rhodesia made by the Chairman, Rev. Michael Fidgin, and to discuss the future and possible closure of the Mission. The Report stated:

> The situation out there [Rhodesia] is such that Railway Missioning as we knew it is no longer possible. Trains do not travel by night, and it was impossible for the Missioner to be shunted off at the more lonely places along the line. One Missioner had been bombed and shot at, and most of his travelling today was done by car, kindly provided by the Railway authorities ...[67]

The Rhodesian War of Independence made the last few years of the Mission difficult and dangerous. Yet there were many factors bringing about the final closure of the Railway Mission. To these we now look.

A decent and fitting funeral

> The Railway Mission gradually ceased to be an independent Mission and became more the mobile staff of each Diocese. This change was emphasised as the railways themselves changed ... With UDI a quite new situation developed - instead of being the pioneer church, we tended to become the dustbin church, trying to cope with those areas that could no longer support a priest of their own - so we ministered to the dying townships instead of the growing ones. And as the Dioceses ran short of money, they used African missioners in the railway townships and paid them from Mission funds although they seldom moved outside their fixed parish.[68]

As a former Missioner, last Chairman of the London Committee, photographer/film-maker for the Mission and the person delegated to visit and report on the Railway Mission during its final years, Michael Fidgin was in a unique and authoritative position in making the above comments to the former Rhodesian teacher-chaplain, Rev. Tony Grain, invited to 'bring the story up from the end of *God's Highwaymen* to the close of the Mission.' In this and other letters, some to the writer, Michael Fidgin was saying that basically the Mission changed and ended not as a matter of policy but because these were forced on it by the changing circumstances around it. It was no longer in a strong position to 'call the tune' but had, rather, to dance to a tempo given it and with fewer and fewer partners.

To the Bishop of Matabeleland, Kenneth Skelton, in 1970, Michael Fidgin wrote:

> I think that I must write ... to say that the London Committee is now nothing like what the constitution says it ought to be. No Missioner has come back to England for many years, and fewer and fewer go out from this country. The result is that our supporters get older and older, and most date back to the old days of South Africa. It is increasingly difficult to find committee members, and the support from churches and schools dwindles as little or no deputation work can be done. So we have had to limit our commitments, but can carry out all we have promised by careful use of our investment income - without which we would be in real trouble ...[69]

Since 1905, when the 'Scheme for closer co-operation between SACRM and the S.P.G' had been accepted, the Railway Mission and SPG/USPG had liased over recruitment and grants/finances. The degree of co-operation varied over a period of more than sixty years. Because of USPG's experience in recruiting and sending missionaries all over the world, and because of the smaller role played by the Railway Mission's London Committee once an Executive Committee had been formed in Rhodesia, after SACRM withdrew from South Africa, and for the reasons given above by Michael Fidgin, it had been agreed that USPG play a greater role in 'vetting' would-be railway missioners, particularly over suitability and health. It is not even necessary to read between the lines of correspondence from 1971 to 1975 to realise the rift that developed between the two bodies and to see that USPG played an (unwitting?) part in bringing the Railway Mission to an end. That, ultimately, USPG became both trustees for the residual funds and an uncertain depository for Railway Mission archives, does not lessen their earlier role.

Difficulties started in 1971 when USPG became critical of the Railway Mission, in London, not giving candidates 'full details of where they would be living and of their pay and allowances etc.'[70] As missioners were then receiving 'Diocesan scale' salaries in Rhodesia and were based at and sent to places as determined by the Rhodesian Executive Committee, these were unfair criticisms to make of the London Committee. Michael Fidgin pointed out to the Bishop of Matabeleland, to whom USPG had complained, that the new missioners were content with matters and 'it is just U.S.P.G. who are being very critical of the Mission in general and of me in particular.'

Some problems arose from the fact that, whereas 'in the old days' most of the men who went as missioners were single and fairly young, an increasing number of ordinands in the 70s were 'of a mature age, and ... often married.' Michael Fidgin pointed out to the Vicar-General of Matabeleland , in 1972, that 'a three year contract [had] very little appeal for them - it [was] neither a job overseas with prospects overseas, nor [did] it help when looking for a job [in England] on their return to the home church.' It was suggested that men be recruited for five years (normal for USPG candidates sent to Dioceses in Rhodesia) instead of the usual three years for Railway Missioners, but be accepted by both the diocese and the Mission. After three years working for the Railway Mission the man would then transfer to the diocese. The Rhodesian Anglican hierarchy did not, it would appear, take up this particular suggestion, which also had to have the approval of USPG. Soon after the suggestion had been made, a new missioner was recruited, sent to Rhodesia at a cost of £300 and, having signed a contract for three years, was moved to a parish after six months without any explanation offered to the London Committee. It was agreed, in London, that it made more sense if Railway Mission affairs were transferred to Rhodesia 'so that Rhodesia [ran] the whole affair.'[71]

Matters with USPG came to a head in 1974, shortly after a new Appointment and Training Secretary was in office in that Society and he started to interview would-be candidates for the Railway Mission. There was an almost unspoken fear among some in the Railway Mission that USPG might "pinch our men". This did happen, with applicants for the Railway Mission being treated as general applicants for USPG work anywhere in the world. In 1974 the Railway Mission spent £60 on two adverts for missioners. There were twenty enquiries, yet the Mission were 'more than surprised and disappointed' that USPG could not pass on even two candidates.[72]

The General Secretary of the USPG believed that Railway Mission priests should have 'associated missionary status' within the Society and, although accepting that there was confusion between different methods of appointment, did not accept the criticism by the Railway Mission. Michael Fidgin, in a letter to his Committee's Secretary, written after meeting the USPG Head, wrote:

> ... I was not over-happy after my interview with Canon Robertson at USPG. A summary of it could be that ... EITHER we work on our own, as we used to do, with USPG offering us personnel help (Doctors, bookings, etc.) on an unofficial level, OR letting USPG do the whole lot. We may not like the way they do it, but that is their problem and not ours. I can see his point of view, and approve of him

> standing up for his own staff against outside criticism, but it will not satisfy the Bishop in Rhodesia, and I fear our days are numbered.

The last decade of Railway Mission work was certainly a very difficult time for those involved, not least the members of the London Committee struggling to understand and to provide for the needs of the Mission in Rhodesia. It is quite clear from this correspondence, as well as from other USPG actions at that time, that USPG were not very flexible. They found it difficult to understand anyone not having, at the least, associated status within the Society. The smaller Railway Mission, with its tradition of itinerant and varied ministry, was by nature more flexible. Whereas it found benefit in any practical help given by the larger Society, it did not wish to be taken over or dictated to and was understandably aggrieved at blatant 'poaching'. A more helpful USPG almost certainly would have secured more missioners, which would have eased the problems faced by the one or two chaplains endeavouring to cover vast areas of work. Realistically, it must be said that the Mission would still have ended when it did, but it would have been a far less painful death.

Some of the, non-USPG, problems faced by the London Committee were outlined in a letter to the Bishop Wood of Matabeleland in November 1976:

> Wherever an African Government has taken over, the free travel facilities enjoyed by our Mission have been withdrawn, and the Mission has ceased to function in that country. It seems possible that a similar situation could occur in Rhodesia.
>
> I feel that the London Committee, growing older every day and having no new blood, should know what it ought to do with the capital it holds in this country. It's not a lot - about £4,500 I think, but it does bring in an income that has been useful to you and covers passages, pensions, outfit allowances, etc., and sends money out to you. If this work ceased, what should we do?[73]

Existing correspondence does not indicate whether or not the bishop replied. He retired as Bishop of Matabeleland the following year and Robert Mercer became the 4th Bishop of Matabeleland and the last titular President of the Railway Mission. In June 1978 he received a similar letter from Michael Fidgin to that of his predecessor, though the tone was more urgent. Crucially, he was informed:

> .... it looks from this distance as though the days of the London Committee are drawing to an end, and we think we ought to be making some decisions about the future, and particularly about the

money we administer at this end ... We hope the Railway Mission will not just "die out". Better that it close after doing a good job and while it enjoys a good reputation ... [The] London Committee will not last much longer .. and once we cease to send out staff, then the work here has no reason to continue.[74]

Three months prior to this letter Michael Fidgin had received an important letter from Bishop Skelton, who had left Rhodesia as Bishop of Matabeleland in 1970. He remained a valued member of the Railway Mission committee in England. His comments bear upon changes mentioned at the beginning of the chapter and upon African work detailed in Chapter 7:

> I can understand your feelings about the Rly. Mission, but even in my time the situation was changing, and frankly I thought it high time that the Diocese took most of the work over. Fewer and fewer white railwaymen were in fact living out of reach of the normal ministrations of the Church; CTC (centralised train control) had "automated" much of the line, and our "trek priest" was able to keep in touch with places on the Salisbury line. Raylton, Rugare and Lochinvar were, like ... Wankie, spoonfed by the Railway and ought to have been detached from the Mission years ago. The consequence - that Africans expect the Mission to build them new Churches - is only what one would expect as a result. In my time Kenneth Sims [Head of R. Mission] was the best-paid clergyman in the Province of Central Africa - not excluding the Bishops!
>
> [Some] preliminary thinking ought certainly to be done... on the understanding that the Rly. Mission will inevitably come to an end.[75]

Bishop Skelton's remarks about African expectations are a useful reminder of the role played by the African chaplains in the closing period of Railway Mission history. The final section of Chapter 7 outlined how the earlier work of Sigeca, Borerwe and Mhlabi petered out due to lack of funds and unsuitable appointments. At Rugare Lochinvar the main problem arose over a priest whose work was very unsatisfactory, yet who was receiving the same salary as the Head of the Mission, without any of the responsibilities or work load. It became necessary to suspend the work of the African priest at Lochinvar, not least because the Mission had no money to pay his stipend. The Diocese of Mashonaland was asked to take over responsibilities of the work, to which it did, eventually and reluctantly, agree.

The last missioner was not too happy with his predecessors who had 'by some means or other allowed the Africans to build their own Church buildings.'[76] By the time that he came onto the scene, all such buildings had to be licensed, and often the City and County Architects refused licenses because of the poor condition of the Churches. The African congregations called for the Railway Mission to pay for new buildings. One Church for an African congregation was built during the final phase of Mission work, that at Chinotimba, which 'beautiful and well-appointed church' was dedicated and consecrated on Easter Day, 1978.

Despite the fact that African priests served with the Railway Mission from 1959/60, the records show that not one of them ever attended a meeting of the Executive Committee of the Mission during those final twenty years. As they were not listed under 'Apologies for absence', we may assume that they were not invited. It is quite clear from the Minutes of the Meetings, from correspondence and from their own testimony during interview, that they were not involved in decision making. Their recollections are of the period prior to the last five or so years of the Mission, rather than of the last days themselves.

One African testimony as to the value of the Mission was given me during the field trip in 1993. We were on the weekly Bulawayo-Johannesburg 'No.6 Train', the modern version of the old 'Rhodesia Limited' Mail Train. The bedding attendant was an elderly Cape Coloured man who had worked on the route for most of his life. He spoke with great affection about the Railway 'padres' and how they had cared for and spoken to workers such as himself. He had, however, little experience of African missioners, which was not surprising, given his particular work and route. He did not understand why the Mission had ended. Willie Sigeca, when interviewed in Bulawayo two days before I left for Johannesburg, was similarly puzzled about the reasons for closure. Although he had worked faithfully for the Mission, his views had never been sought. Even in post-Independence Zimbabwe, I sensed a lukewarm hospitality for him as we met in one of the Meeting-Rooms in Bulawayo Cathedral. Yet he was proud of his service as a Railway Missioner and spoke warmly of many of the European staff. After the Mission closed, some missioners were frank enough to suggest, or admit, that the African priests and catechists had been added to the staff more for diocesan convenience and finances than for more noble reasons, though acknowledging the vital work done by them.

By November 1978 Michael Fidgin was informing the Missioners, George and Gertrude Deacon, that the Railway Mission business in London was moving to a private address, as the Transvaal and Rhodesia and Botswana Association (TRABA) office, which the Mission shared, was having to move from USPG house as that Society needed more room. He made clear that the London Committee could not go on much longer:

> ... if you are the last Missioner to go out from England - and it is our opinion that you should be; the Mission now needs to be staffed by local men with local knowledge and a grasp of the language - so we would like to make plans for the ending of this committee. We would prefer to close down than to just die out ...[77]

In March 1979 the last African priest employed by the Mission returned to diocesan work, and sadly therefore there was no black African presence at the end. Meetings were held in 1979 and the beginning of 1980 of both the London Committee and the Executive Committee in Bulawayo. All the meetings were concerned with the final arrangements for the closure of the Mission, the handing over and release of assets, the repatriation of the Deacons after their contract ended in April 1980, the preservation of archives and the appropriate use of remaining funds.

It was felt that some permanent record should be made of the pioneering work of the Ellison brothers. Their nephew, Gerald Ellison, was Bishop of London and, during his visit to South Africa in July 1979, dedicated a memorial plaque to his uncles. One of the two churches in Noupoort (Naauwpoort), the early railway centre from where much of SACRM's work had emanated, had been preserved as an 'ancient monument'. On July 19th 1979 the Bishop of Port Elizabeth opened the Church as Noupoort Museum. At the Dedication Service was George Deacon from Rhodesia. Bishop Ellison unveiled the plaque which had been sent out from England. The wording reads:

In thankful memory of

DOUGLAS and HARRY ELLISON

PRIESTS

who coming from England
pioneered the idea and work of the Railway Mission
and so founded many churches
in the Province of South Africa

1892-1911

They brought Light to the Line

The Executive Committee of the Railway Mission, in an Extraordinary General Meeting at the Railway Headquarters in Bulawayo, on April 1st 1980, agreed that the work of the Mission 'be terminated as from 1st May, 1980, from which date the Railway Mission in Zimbabwe-Rhodesia and Botswana will cease to exist as a body.'[78] The Railways agreed that the existing Railway Mission coach, a Railway asset, be preserved and displayed in the Bulawayo Railway Museum. Mission documents and photographs would be preserved in the Museum archives and in the coach. The plaque, which is now on the side of the preserved caboose, reads:

Railway Mission
1902-1980

This plaque is to commemorate the work of the
Railway Mission and the unselfish devotion
to duty of those willing to serve Railway People

'They brought Light to the Line'

Mission Coach 872, here on display, was
commissioned in November 1962 and is typical of
the type used by the Railway Missioners in their
journeys throughout the old Rhodesia Railways
System, which extended from Beira to Sakania
Border to the North and South from
Bulawayo to Vryburg

It is unfortunate that a starting date, for the Mission, of 1902 is given. Whereas this was the year in which the Grahamstown name was changed to 'The South African Church Railway Mission', Bulawayo was finally linked with Salisbury and, therefore, Beira, and the Railway School moved to Plumtree; the missioner Nelson Fogarty was first based in Bulawayo in 1897, the first train reaching the town on November 4th that year, and was officially given charge of the Bechuanaland Railway line (Vryburg to Bulawayo) in March 1898.

A more accurate starting date may be found on the walls of the cloisters of St. John's (Anglican) Cathedral in Bulawayo, where another plaque was placed. Surmounted by an engraving of a railway engine are the words: 'The Diocese of Matabeleland gives thanks for the work of the Railway Mission in this country from 1897 until 1980. In hoc signo vinces.' Sadly, nowhere is there a visible reminder of the originator of the Mission, Philip Barrington Simeon.

George Deacon conducted a final service for the Railway Mission in the chapel of the Victoria Falls Hotel on Easter Day, April 6th, 1980. 'He and his wife left the country on April 10th, the day of the expiry of his contract, but not before a farewell luncheon had been given in their honour by Mr. Trevor Wright [Former Manager, Rhodesia Railways], his wife and friends who had all rendered most warm-hearted personal support on the Bulawayo Committee for many years.'[79]

Just one week later, on the night of April 17th, Robert Mugabe was sworn in as Prime Minister of Zimbabwe. Ninety years after the British flag was first raised on the site which would become Salisbury / Harare, the Union flag came down for the last time. For over eighty years, most of Rhodesia's colonial history, the Railway Mission had served Rhodesia.

On October 2nd, 1980, a Thanksgiving Service (Eucharist) for the work and witness of this unique Mission was held in the USPG chapel, London, the preacher being the Rev. Michael Fidgin and the celebrant Bishop Gerald Ellison. About forty past members of the Mission were present.

One final scene remained to be played. It had been agreed, on April 16th 1980, that USPG be asked to become Trustees for the £14,000 capital left in Mission funds and for this to be used for the in-service training of African priests, thus remembering the original foundations of 'bringing light to more lonely places and building up the Church in Southern Africa.' Was it also, one might wonder, a kind of reparation for the paucity of 'African work' over the Mission's history? USPG accepted the Trusteeship. The Trust Deed, dated 24th July 1981, became the last official document of the former Railway Mission. Given the past uneasy relationship between the two Societies it was perhaps somewhat ironic that USPG be left with this responsibility, as well as that of preserving the archives. The latter task, fortunately and sensibly, they eventually passed over to Rhodes House Library, Oxford.

A Reader in those archives could do worse than remember the words quoted by Dorothy Ellison as she closed her account of the history (to 1938) of the Railway Mission:

> *Remember these men and women whose lives sanctify the iron roads of South[ern] Africa. The altar-rails of their Cathedral are of burnished steel, the pavement is of cinders and jarrah wood, the ceiling is the golden sky, the organ music is the Berg-wind on the telegraph wires, the chancel and the aisle are 15,000 miles long.*[80]

Conclusion

> I suppose that we met a need at a certain point in history, and tried our best to fill that need. But that special need passed, and with it the [Railway] Mission passed too.

So wrote Michael Fidgin in what became his final words on the Mission.

This work has charted the history of the South African Church Railway Mission and its successors. It has looked briefly at the development of the railway system in southern Africa, for the development and changes within the Railway Mission have been inextricably linked with those of the Railways themselves.

By using the diaries and letters written by the chaplains the account has examined the various practicalities of Mission work, such as the crucial issuing of free Passes, the use of railway cabooses and trolleys, and the reliance on food and hospitality along the lines. We have focussed on the life and work of the gangers and other railway workers and their families, noting the isolation and loneliness of many of these people. The work in education and nursing and the special contribution of the Women Workers have been identified and assessed. The record of the ministry of chaplains in 'far flung places', though questionable at times, basically stands scrutiny, and is a worthy and heroic record.

The central premise has been the problems, conflicts and tensions faced by the Railway Mission, and how these were or were not resolved. Now that the 'story is told' it is necessary to ask how far, if at all, these conflicts were implicit in the very nature of the Mission and its work. Or, rather, were problems caused by particular personnel? We must ask, also, whether it was all worthwhile.

In any situation some difficulties are going to be exacerbated by 'awkward' individuals. SACRM no doubt had some such. Indeed, in their letters home some chaplains admitted their failings. Yet, as a particular group of people, over 250 of them in the ninety-five years, they come across as remarkably tolerant and patient. In choosing to do the work they did, and to stick at it, they proved their exceptional qualities as human beings. The work, with its incredibly long and unpredictable hours, was no sinecure. I have not come across any occupation, in southern African history, that asked so much from its workers, or received so much. It is easy to see why the London Committee always recommended a maximum 'tour' of three years, as most missioners were worn out by then. Even so, some went back for further spells, often after a time serving elsewhere.

I would maintain that, if the Mission had not attracted and appointed the exceptional people that it did, then the various problems and difficulties encountered would have been far far worse. It is also clear why the bishops usually wanted to grab these highly skilled missioners for their own dioceses, even to the extent of 'poaching' them somewhat prematurely, in some cases before the ink on the contract was dry.

It would be wrong to pretend that all missioners were noble, hard-working and saintly. Inevitably, there were misfits, there were awkward individuals, there were a few who were quite intolerant of others' views, and there were some who had 'problems'. At least one was sent home at twenty-four hours' notice, for fondling / indecently assaulting an African youth in the Mission Coach. The speed of his return avoided arrest and scandal. He received help and understanding for his 'illness', as it was referred to. We may assume that the abused boy was given no such help. Another was known for his 'little weakness' regarding naked boys, although he kept to the right side of the law. In a less careful age one missioner could note in his letters that he had boys sleeping with him in the coach:- 'at Bush Tick [Mine] the other day I had three school boys sleeping on board ... two slept in my flea-bag which they were wildly excited to try, and which housed them quite well on a mattress on my stretcher-bed, and I shared the bunk bed with the third. It was a very tight fit and a case of "when father says 'turn' we all turn" '[81] This was, perhaps, more a case of innocent friendship than of impropriety. Yet, as one missioner stated, 'the caboose gave great privacy for folk to use as they wished.'[82]

Again, to view now photographs taken by some of the early missioners (not Hale), showing naked African boys and girls, raises queries which are perhaps unfair to those men. What do we make of such a photograph with the youth standing on his clothes, obviously removed for the shot? Paul Landau, among others, argues that photos not only reflect the ways that Westerners saw Africans, but helped create, and even subvert, those ways.[83] Some photographers refused to photograph Africans clothed, they were constructing an Africanness, which meant nakedness. ('European' meant 'civilised', 'modern' and 'clothed'. Africa was 'uncivilised' , 'primitive' and naked).

A few Railway Missioners certainly seemed guilty of treating some of their 'congregation' as specimens to be constructed and fixed in Western / White imagination. In this, of course, they were no different from many other missionaries, anthropologists and colonists!

It is known that at least one Woman Worker became involved in an 'improper relationship' and chose to return home at short notice. In spite of the strictures of the 'Vade Mecum' regarding drinking the Mission was known at one time as the 'Gin and It' mission! One Head, Ray White, was known as 'whisky Ray', as mentioned below; another Head, formerly an RAF chaplain, was an alcoholic and had an extremely bad temper. Some other Missioners, a minority, were partial to their 'sundowners' and certainly exceeded the 'one [drink]' recommended in the 'Vade Mecum'.

Conflicts were inevitable given the nature of such a Mission. The reading of any history of Missions shows tensions between the pioneering spirits and the settled church. There was no reason to suppose that the Railway Mission vis-à-vis Anglican parochialism would be different. It was not. Yet, some of the problems could have been avoided if the bishops had had a broader view of the Church. Sadly, many of them believed in transplanting the English parochial system to southern Africa which, in any case, could never have worked fully, there being no 'parson's freehold', and given the vast distances and racial intolerance that were prevalent. Until the 1950s each diocese in South Africa continued to be divided into parishes, which were in effect 'white' parishes, with a rector or (in Natal) vicar in charge. Other priests were licensed to look after the 'mission', ie African, churches within the parishes. Often the 'mission' church would be the daughter church of the white 'parish', and it was only in 1955 that missions and parishes were given equal status. The Railway Mission, with its wider remit, in both geographical and racial terms, did not fit easily into this pattern. Not everyone realised that SACRM was there to 'supplement not supplant the normal parochial agencies.'[84]

It is easy to be critical of the Church hierarchy, especially with hindsight. The Province of South Africa is a vast one. Most of the dioceses were and are predominantly rural, and their work consisted and consists 'almost entirely of attempts to reach scattered communities of Anglicans, black and white, in small country villages ...'[85] Itinerating work was necessary, and for this the Railway Mission was uniquely placed, if not always uniquely valued.

We have seen how the Chaplains frequently felt guilty that the ministrations of the church were not being brought to people of all races, and how SACRM work was often faced with racial prejudice. The missioners were basically powerless to change the way things were. Yet they challenged settler opinion, they showed the way forward by their own example, not always exemplary by today's criteria, yet ahead of most of their contemporaries, and they had occasional victories. However, the phrase 'too little and too late' may best sum up any conclusion with respect to 'African work'.

This book has outlined the way in which the Railway Mission workers constantly encountered people of other denominations and faiths. Given the background and high churchmanship of most of the missioners, it is unlikely that they went to Africa as convinced ecumenists or with expectations of accommodating those of the Jewish faith. To some extent the Mission workers were brought face to face with the inadequacies of their own beliefs. It is to their credit that most of the staff, ordained and lay, surmounted or at least acknowledged their inadequacies.

All the available correspondence indicates that those involved agreed that the time had come to end this particular ministry, though many had, quite naturally, feelings of sadness, mixed with satisfaction of a job well done. More than ten years on, Bishop Robert Mercer, the last President of the Mission, as Bishop of Matabeleland (now Bishop of the 'breakaway' Anglican Catholic Church of Canada), wonders whether the Mission ought to have closed:

> There simply wasn't enough support ... inside Zimbabwe, even though there was and still is plenty of work for the Mission to do. Nothing shakes the African Church of the conviction that the English or North Americans pay its way until the end of time.[86]

In response to being questioned about these remarks, the bishop admitted that much of the traditional work of the Railway Mission, particularly to gangers / isolated communities, had ended, with the changes that came to railway practice. He did, however, make the points:

> (1) People are still employed by the railways. The Missioners had right of access to them. I remember a station master saying to George Deacon, "Padre, I wish you could see Signalman X and his missus: their marriage is in danger of breaking up. Mind, I've no idea what church they belong to, if any." ... Missioners had the right to wander through workshops, up signalbox ladders, through booking offices, around staff houses ... Primary evangelism in non-parochial settings. What a pity to lose this access to non-believers! But of course the access has to be paid for. Dioceses in Africa can't normally afford anything other than the parochial ministry, and even that now is run largely by NSMs [Non-stipendiary ministers] ...
>
> (2) The parishes which the Mission helped found are disintegrating. There are not the clergy to serve them, not even NSMs, and if there were the clergy, there wouldn't be any money to pay them .. I know the Mission was founded for ministry largely to railwaymen, but it has always looked after African villages, schools, congregations, who lived relatively close to the tracks. There is still a need ...[But] there's no money from within Zim[babwe] to support the Mission ... But if the Mission did still exist, there's no doubt it could help save the four Zim dioceses, Botswana and Zambia too, from institutional collapse. But of course no blame attaches to Britain. You sent our personnel and money for close to 100 years. The church in Africa should learn what independence means ...[87]

We have noted, above, how Michael Fidgin and others had warned, in the period prior to 1980, that the Railway Mission ought to be staffed by 'local men with local knowledge.' Yet, even if this had happened, Bishop Mercer is right in stating that 'there [was] no money.' A few indigenous, black or white missioners may have kept the work going into Independence. But then the question would have arisen of free Passes from the Railways. Perhaps the missioners and Committee members were too pessimistic about the likely outcome of the change from Rhodesia Railways to Zimbabwe Railways.

The point about local recruitment, as opposed to British clergy, was emphasised by Hugh Palmer, former missioner, during interview. After discussing his work on the Mission (1956-60, plus subsequent part-time work when Rector of Que Que [Kwe Kwe]), he posed some questions:

> Why did the Railway Mission recruit green young curates from the UK for this most demanding work? Where were the Rhodesians who knew the country and the railway? Often, men were totally unsuitable, at first, and the first year was spent "learning to walk". If a young Rhodesian clergyman had been appointed, he would have said, "Based in Salisbury? - you're mad!"... Ray White - known as 'Ray Whisky'! - didn't know Rhodesia. I told him that the Mission was duplicating the work of Parishes - and he was cross [to be told]. I was given quarters in Salisbury - "You're forty years too late" I was told - there had never been a Railway Mission presence in Salisbury. But Ray White wouldn't listen to opinions. He was going on a Salisbury-Umtali train, so I booked on the same train in order to convince him they were duplicating the work of parishes. My section was down to Mahalapye, so I first had to travel from my base in Salisbury to Bulawayo - a "dead" journey for me, which I did for almost three years. All the major centres had by then Anglican parishes, so the Mission work just limped on. "What are you doing here?" I would be asked. Often I was the unofficial curate to parish clergy. Certainly the Railway Mission could have lasted longer if it had used locally recruited clergy ...[88]

In retrospect it appears that the Executive Committee in Bulawayo did not take enough responsibility, until it was too late, for managing their own affairs, recruiting Rhodesian staff, and giving more opportunities to African missioners. The London Committee were rather slow in letting go what had been their 'baby' for so long. Certainly there was inadequate communication between the two bodies. The roles of the bishops and of USPG have been outlined in detail. I do not believe that the Railway

Mission received the level of help or the understanding that it warranted. In the end it paid the price for being a small itinerant and unique organisation struggling for survival amidst a fairly monolithic and hierarchical Church.

In his *The Anglican Church in South Africa,* Hinchliff writes of 'two experiments' which the Church of the Province of South Africa undertook. One of these was the Order of Ethiopia, the other he gives as the Railway Mission. I would argue with his use of the term 'experiment' for something that lasted almost one hundred years and had become an official and recognised part of 'the Church'. Yet his comments and praise are generous, and I can do no better than to end (almost) with his conclusion, most of which can equally apply to the areas outside South Africa in which the Railway Mission worked:

> South Africa, particularly in the half-century between 1880 and 1930, lived by and along the railway line .. Until the coming of fast motor transport and the national roads system, towards the end of the 1930s, the railways were the only real binding link between one settled part of the country and another. It required Simeon's vision and Ellison's courage and ability to turn them into a means of solving one of the Church's most pressing problems .. - the need to care for scattered white Anglicans living in remote rural areas.[89]

At least one cathedral, Lusaka, and up to one hundred churches owe their beginnings to the visits of railway missioners to some lonely outpost beyond the reach of the normal parishes.

The final words must, rightly, go to a Railway Missioner, Canon Michael Fidgin. He had shown me the films that he had taken of the Mission, given me his many SACRM documents and letters, and then talked about what it was like to be a Railway Chaplain. He concluded:

> It was a very personal life, with a lot of waiting. When a train came in we walked down the train to see who we knew - there was sure to be someone. When we went to the outlying Stations - the first time, we just visited; the second time, we knew the family; the third time, we put the children to bed.[90]

And, as he ended his 'Epilogue' in *Mission Unaccomplished*,

> We have been privileged to play a small part in Church history, and we thank God for it. [91]

---

[1] Constable, DH, 'Proceedings', Institution of Railway Signal Engineers, 1969, 58
[2] Nock, 1971, 189
[3] Constable, 1969, 51
[4] Nock, 1971, 192
[5] QP 200, 1959 (No.2), 21
[6] Grain, 1985, 66
[7] Garnett, 1985, 17
[8] Fidgin/JMR. 1.8.1991
[9] QP 212, 1963, 3
[10] QP 205, 1961, 4
[11] Exactly the same point was made by Michael Fidgin in his last Railway Mission film, *The Church in a Changing World* (1968)
[12] QP 212, 1963, 3
[13] Croxton, 1973, 1982, 222
[14] Croxton, 1973, 1982, 224
[15] QP 187, 1954, 4/5
[16] *Partners*, XIX, 1, 16
[17] RM Newsletter, July 1965
[18] Ellison, 4.7.1914, X1441/1 f5 (Ellison Papers), RHL
[19] Grain, 1985, 20
[20] Ellison, 1930, 116
[21] QP 76, 1923, 13
[22] QP 76, 1923, 25/26
[23] Grain, 1985, 95
[24] SACRM 'Resolutions', 1935, JMR
[25] Wilkinson, 1992, 221
[26] AB940 WITS/CPSA
[27] AB940 WITS/CPSA, 17.7.1935
[28] AB940 WITS/CPSA, n.d.[Dec. 1936?]
[29] AB940 WITS/CPSA, n.d.[Dec. 1936?]
[30] AB940 WITS/CPSA, 1.2.1937
[31] AB940 WITS/CPSA, 7.2.1937
[32] AB940 WITS/CPSA, 8.10.1937
[33] AB940 WITS/CPSA, 18.11.1937
[34] AB940 WITS/CPSA, 18.11.1937
[35] de Gruchy, 1995, 29
[36] SACRM *Vade Mecum*, 16-23
[37] QP 59, 1918, 3
[38] Hale, 2.6.1905
[39] Hale, 15.6.1905
[40] Hale, 12.8.1905; 2.2.1906
[41] Hale, 26.11.1905
[42] Rusbridger, 7.7.1932
[43] Rusbridger, 1.11.1932
[44] Seacombe, 28.3.1916; 23.5.1916; 22.8.1916
[45] Rusbridger, 16.8.1932
[46] X1146, RHL
[47] QP 155, 1945, 13
[48] Hellig, 1995, 162
[49] HH 'Reminiscences'/JMR, 10

[50] Hale, 24.3.1906
[51] Stella, Sister Mary, CSP, letter to JMR, 4.1992
[52] QP 212, 1963, 2
[53] QP 214, 1964, 1/2
[54] Crane, 11.11.1965/JMR
[55] Croxton, 1973,1982, 238
[56] *Partners*, XIII,1,1967, 15
[57] Croxton, 1973,1982, 239
[58] *Partners*, XIII,4, 1968,14
[59] Bolink, 1967, 409
[60] *Partners*, XIII,4, 1968, 14
[61] X759, RHL, 27.11.1968
[62] Croxton, 1973,1982, 240
[63] Wood, "Zambezi Express", (BBC TV, 1979: 'Great Railway Journeys of the World':3))
[64] *Partners*, XV,2, 1970, 20
[65] Grain, 1985, 104
[66] Partners, XXII,3, 1977, 16
[67] X759, RHL, 23.10.1979
[68] Fidgin, 24.5.1984,/Grain/JMR
[69] Fidgin/JMR, 8.6.1970
[70] Fidgin to Bishop M Wood, 16.3.1971/JMR
[71] Fidgin to Rev J Mitchie, 3.5.1973/JMR
[72] Sec. to M Fidgin, 9.9.1974. Personal experience of dealing with USPG and their Appointment and Training Secretary at that period leads me to sympathise with the Railway Mission!
[73] Fidgin, 23.11.1976/JMR
[74] Fidgin, 15.6.1978/JMR
[75] Bishop Skelton, 22.3.1978/JMR
[76] Deacon to Fidgin, 13.3.1978
[77] Fidgin, 8.1.1978/JMR
[78] Bul.Cath., RM docs.
[79] Grain, 1985, 108
[80] Ellison, 1930,1938, quoting fr. "South Africa", 1928
[81] X1441/1 f10, RHL
[82] Monica James, Aug. 1995
[83] JSAS 20th Anniversary Conf., York, Sep.1994
[84] X1441/1, f5, 1, RHL
[85] Hinchliff, 1968, 210
[86] Bishop Mercer to JMR, 13.4.1992
[87] Bishop Mercer to JMR, 6.5.1992
[88] Palmer to JMR, 24.10.1994
[89] Hinchliff, 1968, 199/200
[90] Fidgin to JMR, 7.5.1991
[91] Grain, 1985, 128

Railway Mission (RM) Chronology

1885	Rev. Philip Barrington Simeon begins visits to railway workers and families (Grahamstown diocese).
	[Railway reaches Kimberley]
1886	Simeon's first official railway-visiting starts.
	('St. Paul's Railway Mission' - unofficial name.)
	[Railway reaches Ladysmith from Pietermaritzburg)
1888f	Revs. Ramsbottom and Freer briefly help Simeon.
1889	[Incorporation of BSA. Company (October)]
1890	[Railways reach Newcastle, Vryberg and Bloemfontein]
1891	Rev. Douglas Ellison arrives in Grahamstown as chaplain to Bishop Webb.
	School for 'railway girls' opens at St. Peter's Home, Grahamstown.
	[Anglo-Portuguese Treaty (Beira Railway)]
	[Founding of Mashonaland Diocese]
	[Founding of Lebombo Diocese (PEA)]
1892	Douglas Ellison takes over Simeon's railway work.
	[Likoma Diocese split from Zanzibar Diocese]
1893	[Railway reaches Mafeking]
1893/4	'Grahamstown Diocesan Railway Mission' title is used on a leaflet for the first time.
1896	GRAHAMSTOWN DIOCESAN RAILWAY MISSION (GDRM) comes into formal existence.
	First *Year Book, Monthly Letters* and *Light for the Line* are published.
	Douglas Ellison is appointed Head of the Mission.
	Appointment of Josiah Ngcambu, first 'Native catechist' (December).
	[Makeking-Bulawayo railway begun]
	[Full rail-service between Pretoria and Durban]
1897	Church Building Funds (Cookhouse and Naauwpoort) are begun by RM.
	Guild of the Good Shepherd is started (Grahamstown).
	[First train into Bulawayo]
1897/8	[Umtali moved 12 miles]
1898	N. Fogarty is given temporary charge of RM work on Bechuanaland Railway (across diocesan boundaries).
	[First train from Beira into Umtali]
	[Start of Anglican work in Damaraland]
1899	RM receives a 'pill-box' coach.
	London Committee (the 'Home Committee') is formed.
	Bishopsbourne Cottage is given as HQ House in South Africa.
	First RM-run school for 'railway children' is opened (Francistown).
	[Railway reaches Salisbury from Umtali]
	[Line north from Bulawayo starts]
	[Anglo-Boer War starts (November)]
1900	Grahamstown Sisters help RM with nursing.
	[Beira railway gauge widened]
1901	Harry B. ('HB') Ellison joins RM.

1902	The GDRM, crossing diocesan boundaries, becomes the SOUTH AFRICAN CHURCH RAILWAY MISSION (SACRM). *Quarterly Paper* (QP) ('Blue Quarterly') starts. RM School moves to Plumtree. First RM nurse arrives (Nurse Eardley). [Bulawayo reached by rail from Salisbury (line open from Cape Town to Beira: 2035 miles)] [End of South African War; Transvaal and OFS Railways become Central South African Railways (CSAR)] [Incorporation of Bas Congo-Katanga Railway Co.]
1903	RM commences work in the Transvaal. Local help (eg. Loyal Women's Guild) begins. St. Cyril's Cottage (Bulawayo) becomes northern HQ. CSAR gives free Passes and other concessions. Herbert Hale joins Railway Mission and goes to Rhodesia. [Start (?) of DRC Railway Mission]
1904	SACRM first Public Meeting (Johannesburg) is held. New large Mission coach (bogie-wheeled) is provided. Miss Nott-Bower, first 'lady-worker', arrives. First Confirmation Service is held in N-W Rhodesia.
1905	Head (D Ellison) visits UK (for recruitment etc.). Scheme adopted for closer co-operation with SPG. [Victoria Falls Bridge opened] [Kalomo, 94 miles NE of Falls, reached]
1906	Finance Council is formed. Nurse Pearn (first CNA nurse with Railway Mission) arrives. Herbert Hale ends his pioneering work. [Railway reaches Broken Hill (Kabwe)]
1907	SACRM work begins in Bloemfontein Diocese. First HQ house for women workers is opened. [Inauguration of Diocese of Northern Rhodesia]
1908	'HB' Ellison replaces Douglas Ellison as Head. ['Shire Highlands' Railway between Port Herald and Blantyre (Nyasaland) opened]
1909	RM work is extended northward. Exploratory visit is made to construction work in the Congo. 'Children of the Veld' (COV) is formed. [Railway crosses into the Congo]
1910	Plumtree School comes under control of the Government (SACRM chaplaincy remains until 1920). [Union of South Africa] [World Missionary Conference, Edinburgh]
1911	Rev. F. Rogers takes over as Head from 'HB'.
1912	Railway Mission work is undertaken in the Congo. SACRM Constitution is drawn up.
1913	Diocesan Synods agree to help fund missioners.
1914	Rogers, last of the original (Grahamstown Diocesan RM) staff, resigns. Archbishop of Cape Town (et al.) moots closing of Railway Mission. [Beginning of First World War]

1915	Arthur Hobson arrives (5 tours, 1915-55).
	Thornely Jones takes over as Head.
	The last CNA nurse is withdrawn from RM work.
	Annual Conference has its first woman speaker.
	[Lines in 'German S-W' linked with Union system]
1916	Initial Railway Mission work in S-W Africa commences.
	[South African Railways (Act)]
	[Railway reaches T'schilonga (Congo)]
1918	['Spanish influenza' pandemic]
	Agnes Burt and Ralph Seacombe die nursing Africans.
	[SAR Christian Union formed]
1919	RM is recognised as a Provincial Organisation.
	[White, then black, railway workers strike in Rhodesia]
1923	Harold Rolfe becomes the new RM Head and moves the HQ Office from Grahamstown to Johannesburg.
1925	First (?) visit to Beira is made by missioners.
	Astley House, Naauwpoort, is opened (for Women Workers).
1927	RM ends its involvement in S-W Africa (Namibia).
1929	Lawrence Hands replaces Rolfe as Head.
	Maude Agg-Large arrives as a Woman-worker (to 1948).
	[Railway unrest in Rhodesia (Strike by Whites; 'faction-fighting' by Africans)]
1930	*God's Highwaymen* is published.
1931	Bishop Paget of Mashonaland visits Sena Sugar Estates; asks the Mission to include SSE with Beira visits.
1932	Rev. Allen Rusbridger joins the Mission.
	Synge starts visits to Sena Sugar Estates.
	RM Chapel is dedicated in Victoria Falls Hotel.
1933	Hugh Wilson takes over SSE work.
1934	Lawrence Hands dies. Replaced as Head by Eustace Hill, C.R.
	Maude Agg-Large makes the first RM film.
1935	Visits start to Maun / Lake Ngami.
	Monica James joins RM as a Woman Worker.
	[Lower Zambezi bridge (Sena) completed]
1937	RM 'Native Hospital' is opened at Naauwpoort.
	[Amalgamation of Rhodesia Railways (RR) and Mashonaland Railway Co.]
1938	Maurice Lancaster becomes Head.
1939	[Start of Second World War]
1944	'Native Hospital' is handed over to diocese.
1945	Hobson visits Leopoldville (furthest Railway Mission work).
	[End of Second World War]
	[Railway strike by Africans (Rhodesia)]
1948	[National Party wins S. Africa elections]
1951	New RM Constitution is drawn up and agreed.
1952	Ray White replaces Lancaster as Head.
1953	Beryl House (RM) at Raylton (Bulawayo) is opened.
	[Federation of Rhodesias and Nyasaland]
	[Work begins on the 'South-east connection' - Bannockburn (SR) to Lourenco Marques (Mozambique)]

1954	Final RM visit to Elizabethville is undertaken.
	Filmstrip, 'The Travelling Church', is produced.
	8 mm. film, 'The Travelling Church', is produced.
1955	RM ends its work at Beira (port).
	[Inauguration of Province of Central Africa]
	['South-east Connection' opens for goods traffic]
1956	[Passenger service starts on line to Lourenco Marques]
1957	SACRM ends all work in South Africa. Becomes the RHODESIA & NYASALAND RAILWAY MISSION.
1958	[Full installation of C.T.C. starts on RR]
1960	Willie Sigeca and Noel Borerwe - first RM African priests.
	Kenneth Sims replaces Ray White as Head.
1961	RM visits to Sena Sugar Estates cease.
	New coach is especially built (by Rhodesia Railways) for RM.
	16 mm. film, 'The Travelling Church', is produced.
1962	Michael Fidgin becomes (last) Chairman of London Committee.
1963	[Break up of Central African Federation]
1964	RM becomes the RAILWAY MISSION OF THE CHURCH OF THE PROVINCE OF CENTRAL AFRICA.
	The 'Blue Quarterly' ceases with issue 215 (Dec.).
	Last mention of Maun/Ngamiland is made by RM.
	[Northern Rhodesia becomes Republic of Zambia]
	[Completion of Centralised Train Control on RR main lines]
1965	Sims resigns as Head and is replaced by Harold Crane, as 'Missioner-Secretary'.
	New RM Constitution is drawn up in Rhodesia.
	London Office is closed down (31 Dec.).
	[Southern Rhodesia declares U.D.I.]
	[Birth of United Church of Zambia (UCZ)]
1966	RM news begins to be included in *Partners* (TRABA).
	[Second Chimurenga War starts in earnest]
1967	[Rhodesia and Zambia railways split]
	RM is separated in Rhodesia/Botswana and Zambia.
1968	Rev. John Mhlabi replaces Willie Sigeca.
	New 16 mm film, 'The Church in a Changing World', is made for RM by M. Fidgin.
1969	[Passenger service terminates at Victoria Falls]
1970	The Railway Mission changes its name for the final time - THE RAILWAY MISSION OF RHODESIA & BOTSWANA.
1977	George and Gertrude Deacon arrive - the last missioners.
	[Last liner ('Windsor Castle') sails from Cape Town to UK (1857f.)]
1979	Bishop Ellison unveils RM plaque at Noupoort.
	African priests are moved from RM work.
1980	Final Service is held on Easter Day, 6 April.(Victoria Falls Hotel Chapel)
	Railway Mission closes as Deacons leave (10 April).
	[Zimbabwe achieves Independence (17 April)]
	Thanksgiving Service is held in USPG Chapel, London (2 October).
1981	USPG become Trustees for remaining RM capital.

Appendix A: Diary of a Woman Railway Missioner

In detailing the work of Women Missioners (Chapter 5) we noted the various accounts given by Monica James. She had worked in the Orange Free State from 1935 to 1944 and then returned in 1948 to work there and in the Transvaal. The following is her 'diary' of 'four typical days on the line':

Wednesday, April 12th [1950]. Left Bloemfontein in Coach 15065 at 4.11 a.m., after night spent in goods yard. Arrived De Brug station at 6 a.m., and was shunted up and down for quite a long time. Got up at 7.30, got breakfast, tidied coach and sallied forth to visit at 9.30. Went first to Mrs. "S.M."[Station Master], and found her [to be] an old friend of many years ago. Gossiped to her for nearly two hours and drank tea. Went next to pumper's wife who rejoined in the name of Malong and could not speak a word of English. Next to the ganger's wife, who had a wooden leg. She asked me to get her two and a half yards of net when next in Johannesburg, to make a meat safe. The next call to the labourers. In the first house a sick baby, teeth, and tummy upset with wrong food. It looked like a refugee, advised Oxo in barley water and dashed back to coach for Oxo cubes. Called on five more homes and went back to coach at 2 p.m. to get lunch. Was just about to put eggs on to boil when along came goods train and cattle truck behind, coach was shunted and they banged me up and down the station, so contented myself with bloater paste, bread and butter and raw apples. Next prepared for the S.M. to come to tea at four and prepared cool drinks, etc. for "Children's Hour" at 5.30. Mrs. "S.M." arrived at 3.30 and stayed till 5. Was just washing up tea things when at 5.10 first two children arrived, settled them, one with jig-saw of Good Shepherd, the other colouring in picture of Daniel in the Lion's Den, when thirteen more appeared. The next hour was a hectic scramble of snakes and ladders, dolls in cradles, winding up of Donald Duck and teaching two small boys (all in Afrikaans) to play dominoes. At 6.30 served orange drinks and biscuits, sang a hymn in Afrikaans, said the "Ons Vader" and packed them home at 7 p.m. Cleaned up complete chaos of a room, went to kitchen to boil eggs. Managed to boil them, was about to lay supper. A cry from outside, Mrs. and Mr. "S.M." come to sit with me till my train comes. In they come and we sit down to discuss Ruth Khama. Mr. "S.M." is a great nationalist and tells me the sjambok is the only remedy for the native. I am almost too far gone with hunger to disagree but manage a feeble squawk. At 9 p.m. I make coffee for the three of us, at 9.30 the train comes and I am shunted on behind the engine. I eat my cold eggs then and more bread and butter and bloater [cured herring or mackerel] paste. At 10 to 11 arrive at Immigrant [Station] and I am shunted off. I make cocoa, do a sketchy wash and tumble into bed.

Thursday, April 13th. Rise at 7 a.m., make breakfast. A cold grey morning, the Free State is having more rain than they want. Don my dungarees and get down on hands and knees to clean and polish floor. Realize yesterday meant no prayer time, so deliberately start meditation as I polish. This takes two hours, further half-hour to clean myself and set sail at 10 a.m. Large fat Mrs. "S.M." turned out to be another old friend. She speaks entirely in Afrikaans. I leave her and visit other houses. In a very poor labourer's house I discover an English family. Granny comes from Woking, Surrey. Daughter was brought up in Dutch Reformed Orphanage so was confirmed in the Dutch Reformed Church, but they are Church of England. On my enquiring if small boy of two has been Christened I am told he is not and Granny says thoughtfully, "I s'pose he ought to be. It's always the first question they ask in hospital." It leaves me musing on the teaching Mother Church gives her children! At 1.30 p.m., I go back to coach for lunch and manage to get some stockings washed before Mrs. "S.M." and her mother arrive for tea at 3.30. At 5 it is pouring with rain and fifteen muddy children pour in on my clean floor. The same programme follows and at 6.15 I begin to send them home. At 6.45 the last child disappears and I go out, in the rain, to visit the only person I have *not* visited on the station. It is an old Jewess who runs a native store and lives alone. Her house is indescribable in muddle and dirt and by the light of a guttering candle we discuss Newcastle-on-Tyne. At 7.45 I leave her, go back to the coach, clear up the chaos and get supper. It is now 8.30 and at 9.39 my train comes to pick me up, to take me to Paardeberg.

Friday, April 14th. I was woken at 6.30 a.m. by sounds of shunting and stuck my head out of the window to see my coach being bundled along towards Kimberley. I hastily put my head out at the first stop and on telling the guard I was going the wrong way I was put back to Paardeberg on the pick-up [train]... Got back to Paardeberg at 8.30 a.m. and got breakfast. Hastily tidied up coach and went to see very off-hand S.M., who is an Anglican. Went to see his wife who is an old friend of former days. She is English. I still puzzle over her husband's behaviour. Eventually she bursts out with the trouble - his politics have changed; now a nationalist, no English allowed in the home and he has been misbehaving with a lady clerk. She gets it all off her chest and I go off to visit the others. I do half the station and at 1.15 p.m. go back to coach for lunch. Fried eggs and Oxo! After lunch I discover the tanks are completely empty. The station is one where engines water and I go over to ask S.M. to fill tanks. He is extremely rude and refuses and I plough backwards and forwards with buckets. At 2.30 I am black with grime and an old farmer friend turns up and take[s] me out to their farm, five miles away. I go out and spend happy afternoon and evening with him and wife and small girl, Judith, who is a new arrival since my time. She is six. I arrange to send her my monthly Sunday School by Post for Church children. I stay to supper and at 8.30 they drive me back. The next problem is how to get washed with no water.

Saturday, April 15th. Arose at 7 a.m., breakfast and tidy coach. At 9 a.m. commence to visit the labourers, get two houses done and it is time to return to coach for first batch of children who arrive, fifteen strong at 10.25. We play games, sing hymns, I tell Easter story and at 12 p.m. they depart. I hastily make cup of tea, then dash out to finish visiting. I go to eight more houses and at 1.30 go back to coach for lunch. After lunch prepare for Mrs. "S.M." to come to tea and for second batch of children at 5 p.m. Mrs. "S.M." and two children arrive at 3.30 and we discuss her unhappy marriage from A to Z. I feel desperately sorry for her. At 5 she departs and ten children arrive. They leave at 6.15, I make a hasty supper and dash out to see the ganger's family as married daughters are home for the week-end who, years ago, were my Sunday School children. A great reunion follows in very hot kitchen by candle light. I inspect endless babies and toddlers and husbands. The kitchen is full. At 8 p.m., I plunge along pitch dark track and go in to say farewell to Mrs. "S.M." She is, by this time, rather tearful. I provide her with old copies of *Women and Home,* etc., tell her to keep smiling and leave her with, on my part, an aching heart. I promise to send her copies of my monthly Church Letter and to send S.S. by Post for her little girl. I return to coach at 9.15. I am moved at 8 a.m.

Reflections. This is the diary of four typical days on the Line. One wonders - has *any* good been done as you read back. But that is not for me to say. I am very tired. I have had no time to pray, let alone think, not much time to eat and no water to wash. No services have been taken, I leave them carrying the burden of their sorrows and worries in my heart and all I can do is to carry them to our Lord in my prayers. My mind goes back to a week ago, it was Good Friday and the Figure on the Cross seems to say, "Yes, it was for *them* I died". (QP 171, 1950, 8-10)

Appendix B: A trip to Sena Sugar Estates (John Oldham, 1950)

Without the Coach - to Portuguese East

We decide that we will travel on the train that leaves Umtali in the early morning, reaching Beira in the evening: this train only runs once a week [Thursday 'Mail Train, No.7', departing Umtali at 6.50 a.m.]: the other trains pass through this beautiful country during the night. We get on the train at 6.30 a.m., having packed everything we require for the remainder of the journey and left the coach to Bulawayo in charge of Nyambo, the African coach boy.

We have only been on the train for a few minutes when the Portuguese Immigration Officer comes into the compartment to see our passports and to stamp them. As soon as he has been round, we may go along to the restaurant car for breakfast. Here we have an excellent view of the lovely country through which we are passing. From Umtali the Railway makes a great bend, descending all the time to the bottom of the fertile valley where there are well-laid-out citrus farms. Already the climate seems to be getting hotter. We have now come down to below 3,000 feet, and are running into the ancient Portuguese town of Macequece [scheduled 8.08/8.23 arr./dep.], with its quaint old church perched on the top of a small hill, and the great Vumba mountains towering above ... Here the Portuguese officials board the train and go through the luggage. When this is over, the journey continues through the grand mountain scenery until about mid-day, when we arrive at the small town of Gondola [12.00/12.10], where there are a large number of farmers growing fruit and vegetables. Here the engine is changed, and we begin to drop down steeply into the Forest of Amatongas. The line twists and turns, first this way and then that; in one place it is possible to see the track far below. The mountains have now been left far behind, and instead, we are in the heart of a dense tropical jungle; along the sides of the track there are huge trees... and, beyond, impenetrable forest, infested by lion and elephant. Now it is getting uncomfortably hot - a foretaste of the humid heat of the coast. Clothing which one had to put on in the chill morning at Umtali is now discarded for cooler attire. In the middle of the afternoon [14.48/15.00] we reach the bottom of the escarpment, and arrive at a station [Vila Machado] which is 180 feet above sea level. From here it is still sixty miles to Beira. We travel across the hot swampy flats and over the Pungwe River, spanned by a huge steel bridge. This is typical jungle country with rice fields and palm and paw-paw trees. We arrive at Beira at 5.30 p.m., if the train is punctual.

To the Sena Sugar Estates

We are not going to stay in Beira at the moment, but are going straight to the Estates. We cross the platform on Beira station, and get into the Trans-Zambesi Railway train which is already waiting [dep. 6.30 p.m.]. We are probably struck by the ancient and primitive carriages and by the friendly atmosphere of the little dining car at the back, where already there are a number of people sitting and chatting. A few British residents have come on board to see friends, or to have a few words with "Mac" the Scotch steward in the restaurant car. We find our berth on the train, put in our luggage, and then go to the dining car to greet our Beira friends, and as soon as the train starts we take our places for dinner. This train only runs twice a week [Mondays and Thursdays], and it is usually full between Beira and Blantyre. There always seem to be interesting people travelling on this route - a government official from Zomba, a young man going up to join the Forestry Department, or a Missionary going back to the U.M.C.A. after furlough. After an excellent dinner, we return to our compartment where the beds are made up, together with the essential mosquito nets. We shall have to be in bed early tonight, as we have to get out of the train at 3 a.m. At about 2.30 we are called by the guard who informs us that the train is approaching Caia where we have to get off. We dress and pack our belongings, and before long the train draws up at the station. There we are met by one of the officials of the Sena Sugar Estates, a Swiss, who takes us up to the guest house, where we get a hot bath and a shave and a cup of coffee, and have time to say Mattins. Then at about 6 a.m. we are taken to the private railway of the Estates, and here we are put on a motor trolley which will take us seventy miles down the Zambesi to Marromeu the first of the Sena Sugar Estates. It is a thrilling journey, with frequent views of the great river flowing down towards the ocean; we feel that we are really in the wilds of Africa, and here one may get a glimpse, if one is lucky, of some of the wild life, monkeys of all sorts and sizes, perhaps a pair of vultures or even an elephant. About half way to Marromeu we stop for a few moments at Chipanga [Chupanga/Shupanga]. There is a Mission here once run by some Swiss Protestants, but now Roman Catholic. It was at this place that Mrs. Livingstone, sailing up the Zambesi to join her husband, developed Blackwater Fever and died: here she was laid, and we cross to the Churchyard to see her tomb, and to pay tribute to the bravery which brought her here, and to the many other pioneers of the Gospel who died of that dreadful scourge.

The work to be done - a cosmopolitan Parish!
We arrive at Marromeu, and are met by the estate manager, once a choir boy in Cape Town Cathedral: he and his wife are both South Africans and are keen church people. We are to stay with them for three days to visit the people in the village. I wonder if anywhere else there is a more mixed community! There are Britishers, South Africans, Portuguese, Dutch, Danes, Demararas, Mauritians, Africans, Coloureds, and Natives of St. Helena. We spend 2or 3 days visiting - there is a Chinese baby to be baptized, two coloured men are being prepared for Confirmation, and one has not seen them for three months; most of their preparation has to consist of a series of instructions sent to them by post week by week - now we have one of the occasional opportunities of seeing them and of discussing the papers that have arrived in the last three months: then we have to visit an African family where we find the father in bed with fever.

A Verandah serves as a Church for all
The Services take place on the large verandah of the Manager's house, and a great majority of the English-speaking community, or I should say those who have a knowledge of English turn up. One often has eight or nine different nationalities at Evensong. The next morning we have Mass, again at the Manager's house, and eight or ten will be present there to receive the Bread of Life. Here indeed is a testimony to the Universality of the Church and the Gospel: this isolated cell of the Christian community. We see men and women of different colours and races, kneeling side by side at the Altar of God: here all are one in Christ Jesus.... Here is a cross section of that great multitude, of all nations and kindreds and people and tongues who ever lift up holy hands unto God. There is no more wonderful experience than to say Mass for this tiny congregation so far from anywhere, and so representative of the peoples of the whole world. After Mass, Communion has to be taken to our sick African and his wife who has had to stay behind to look after him. The Hosts [consecrated wafers] have been reserved from the Mass, and on arriving at the hut we find the family waiting, with father in bed in the corner, mother kneeling by his side, and the children around in a circle - no one could wish for a more devout congregation.

By River Steamer to Luabo

After lunch we have to be on our way again, for now we have to visit the larger of the two estates, Luabo, twenty miles down the river. We travel on the river steamer which is a very quaint double-decked affair. On each side is attached a barge of sugar being taken down to Chinde, the port at the river's mouth, where it will be shipped to Europe. These barges are stacked on top with wood logs, which are fuel for the engine, and besides these, there is room for a number of African passengers who sit on top of the barge, with all their belongings and animals round them, a dog tied to the side and perhaps a few hens or even a goat. We get to the top deck of the steamer, where there is a comfortable lounge, and, if we feel like a siesta, there is a cabin with a bed in it. More probably we shall want to sit at the front of the steamer and watch for the crocodiles lying out in the sandbanks, and the hippo which suddenly surface for air, as they do so, blowing out a spout of water. The journey to Luabo takes about two hours, but if the river is very low it may take longer: on one occasion the steamer got stuck on a sandbank and we spent all night on board. If we left Marromeu in the late afternoon, we would be rewarded by one of the most magnificent sights I have ever seen - the African sunset reflected in the waters of the Zambesi. The sun sinks in a glory of flame, lighting up the whole sky, and this in turn is reflected in the water: then by way of contrast, the darkness swiftly gathers, and the palm trees at the water's edge are silhouetted in the fading light, and the silence of the African night falls, broken only by the sound of the water and the "chug chug" of the steamer's engine. It is quite dark when we arrive at the "gombi" or wharf at Luabo. There is great activity on the bank, and a group of people carrying torches and lanterns. The boat brings the bi-weekly mail, and there is always someone to be met. We recognise the General Manager on the bank, and with him the Field Manager and his wife, with whom we are to stay; they are both out from England where both their fathers were clergy.

We stay for another three days at Luabo, and here again there is visiting to be done, and services are held. On our return journey we may go up the side of the river by car, and then cross to Marromeu by "dug out" ...

Back to Beira

The train leaves Caia at 10 p.m. [Sun.10.45 p.m. dep.(10.10 a.m. from Blantyre)] and we arrive in Beira at about 8.30 [sched. 8.35 a.m.], having had breakfast on the train. Here we stay in the Hotel over the week-end, when we shall be having services in the ..war memorial Church of S.George. There are about 200 British residents in Beira, and the port is always full of British ships, so there is plenty to do visiting the residents and the ships, going round to the offices and houses, and making contacts with as many people as one can. In the intense heat the majority .. go to bed at mid-day .. so it is not tactful to go visiting before 3.30. We may be able to get a little relaxation in the evenings, perhaps dinner on a ship or at a house of a British resident. On Sunday we have a full round of services in the Church, the only one on the Section at the moment.

The end of a six weeks' tour

The train leaves Beira on Monday evening for Bulawayo [Mail Train No.6, dep. 7.15 p.m.], and we have now been all round the section. We have thirty -six hours in the train, and arrive in Bulawayo on the Wednesday morning ['Rhodesia Limited' from Salisbury, arr, 7.00 a.m.], after a trip lasting almost exactly six weeks. There is much to be done in Bulawayo, registers have to be made up, letters read and written, perhaps some very essential shopping to be done, and a whole host of other jobs, for we must be out again on Friday. (QP 172, July 1950, 3-7).

Appendix C: 'Welcome to South Africa' Letter

The following is a typical example of the letter which Heads of SACRM wrote to new staff, 'to reach them on board [ship], c/o the Union-Castle people in Cape Town':

'South African Church Railway Mission
(Church of the Province of South Africa)
(Anglican)
Zuid Afrikaanse Kerk Spoorwegsending
(Kerk van die Provinsie van Suid Afrika)
(Anglikaans)

P.O.Box }
Posbus } 1131
JOHANNESBURG

6. ii. 51

Dear Millins [The next letter started 'My dear Leslie'!]

I am just off out on the Line, so shall write now, a word of welcome to S.A. Glad you've arrived, & I hope you'll like the work. Enclosed are your rail pass, First Class, & forms for your luggage: book all the luggage you don't want with you in the next week while you are on the trains & in Johannesburg direct to Bulawayo. Don't use an agent, just get a porter after you've been through the Customs & get him to take your stuff along to the S.A.R. luggage office on the docks. You book it there, & that's the last you see of it till you pick it up in Bulawayo.

Keep with you a suitcase or so for the train, etc.

Your seat is booked on the train leaving Cape Town at 8.0 p.m. on the day you arrive, for Johannesburg. You'll arrive in Johannesburg on the morning of Saturday, 10th., where I shall hope to meet you.

If anything goes wrong there, & I wasn't there, all you'd do would be to give your stuff to one of the Victoria Hotel porters, not an S.A.R. porter, & follow him to the Hotel, book a room there for two nights.

Our office is about 50 yds. from the hotel door, just past Mappin & Webb's shop, & opposite their side window, & on the 1st. floor.

But I shall almost certainly be there: I'd better wear a dog-collar to help you pick me out, as you'll be a bit hard to discover.

Monday night, the 12th., you'll be leaving for Bulawayo, where you'll arrive early on Wednesday, 14th.

Mrs. Cowling, of Bryngowan, Romney Rd., Green Point, Cape Town, will entertain you for the day. If you did miss her at the docks, take a taxi & go & see her.

From the time you land onwards everything you spend is refunded: tips, taxis, extra luggage charges, bedding on the trains, meals, etc. But not of course clothing.

Good trip. Yours [signed] Maurice Lancaster.'

(Millins/JMR)

Appendix D: Railway Mission Staff

No definitive list exists of men and women who have served the Railway Mission, under its various titles, down its ninety-five years. The following list is based on information contained in copies of the *Quarterly Paper,* the *Light for the Line,* the GDRM *Letters* and various SACRM Reports and publications. Careful use has been made of the 'incomplete and inexact' list in *Mission Unaccomplished.*

Most missioners undertook 'tours' of three years. Where the termination date is unknown, it is.reasonable to assume such a time-span. At least eighty per cent of the men were clergy. Some of the laymen became ordained during their time on the Mission, or between 'tours'. Names in capitals refer to people who played a crucial part in the history of the Railway Mission and/or whose letters and reports are used extensively in this work. The term 'Missioner-Secretary' was used, instead of 'Head', after 1965, following a drastic reduction in staff. Inevitably (and sadly) fewer details are known about the African catechists, evangelists and readers, not least because they were not recruited in London and did not 'sail home' at the end of their contract. They are signified below by 'A', with 'AP' noting those (post-1959) who were priests. In all cases first names are given where known.

1929 - 1945, 1951-52	Maude AGG-LARGE
1937 -	Sister Ethel Agnes, CR.
1963 -	Peter Aikman
1940 - 1945	John Alliston
1919 -	Elsie Andrewartha
1911 - 1920 (?)	Mary Attlee
1913 -	Arthur Austin
1911 -	Wentworth Austin
1923 - 1932	Christine Barker
1908 - 1911, 1924-25	Percy Barnes
1933?-	Nina Barrow
1920 - 1927	Julienne Batcham
1903 - 1905	Gladwyn Batty
1925 (6 months)	Harold Beardmore
1907 - 1910, -1920?	Miss Beckwith
1927 - 1928	Richard Beer
1927?-	Lionel Bell
1943 -	Sister Myra Belleas
1903 -	Walter Belu (A)
1914 -	William Benya (A)
1923 - 1924	Paul Beresford
1910 -	A. Bickerdike
1934 - 1941, 1957-64	Gwen(doline) Bliss
1909 - 1911	Ira Boon
1960 - 1971	Noel BORERWE (AP)
1911 - 1912	Nurse Borradaile
1931 - 1932	Howard Bostock
1911	Miss Bridge
1902 - 1904	J. Brocklebank
1927 - 1930	Charles Brown
1911 - 1914	Nurse Brownlow
1916 -	Miss Burt
1931 - 1932	R. Causewick

1969 - 1971	Robert Chancellor
1912 -	Miss Chapman
1937 - 1942, 1963	Denis Charlton
1970? -	Solomon Chipfupa (AP)
1931 - 1934	Maurice Clack
1931 - 1934	Winifred Clack
1947 - 1949	Elsie Clarke (= Sister Mary Stella CSP)
1911 -	H. Coles
1937 -	Kathleen Coles
1927 - 1930	Helen Collier
1934 - 1937	Thomas Colman
1909 - 1914	John Coombs
1963 - 1969	Harold CRANE (Missioner-Sec., 1965-9)
1911 -	Alexander Crossfield
1967 -	Matthias Damasane (A)
1917 -	Moses David (A)
1957 - 1960	Rachel Davies
1930 (9 months)	P. Langston Day
1977 - 1980	{ George DEACON (Missioner - Secretary)
1977 - 1980	{ Gertrude Deacon (last missioners)
1915 -	Nurse Deeks
1911 - 1914	T. de Laune Faunce
1957 -	Evelyn d'Lepu
1902	A. de Rougemont
1933 - 1936	Esther Disney
1911 -	Geoffrey Douglas
1925 - 1928	Hamilton Douglas
1943 - 1945	Nesta Dowlman (= Winkley)
1902 - 1903	Nurse Joyce EARDLEY (First GDRM nurse)
1953 - 1956	Stephen EASTER
1903 - 1907	John Ellis
1927- 1928	Wilfrid Ellis
1892 - 1908	Douglas ELLISON (Founder / First Head)
1901 - 1912	Harry ('HB') ELLISON (Head, 1908-12)
1910 -	Sister Emily, CR.
1913 - 1916, - 1919?	Everard Esdaile
1928 - 1934	Norman Faull
1952 - 1955	Michael FIDGIN (last Chairman)
1897 - 1904	Henry Forshaw
1896 - 1900	Nelson FOGARTY
1938 - 1942	Theodore Franklin
1889 (briefly)	S. Freer (helping Simeon)
1961 -	B. French
1904 - 1911	Nurse FULLER (First SACRM nurse)
1927 - 1930	Violet Gabb
1938 -	Solomon Galane (A)
1920 - 1923	Kathleen Gardner
1920 - 1923?	Reginald Gardner
1955 - 1958	Peter GARNETT
1920?-	Solomon Gitywa (A)
1912 - 1915	Pearl Glassier
1931 -1938, 1941 - 1949	Violet Godfrey

1907 - 1908	Clive Goldring
1903 (briefly)	Wilfrid Gore-Browne
1949 (6 months)	Nancy Green
1911 - 1914	Sidney Griggs
1943 - 1947, 1950 -1952	Charles ('Bill') Gunter
1971 - 1978	Cyprian Gwatidzo (AP)
1973 - 1976	Ernest Gwetu (AP)
1903 - 1906	Herbert HALE
1935 - 1938	Valerie Hall
1899 - 1901	John Hallward (co-founder, Plumtree School)
1955 - 1958	Dorothy Handcock
1903 - 1911, 1925-34	Laurence HANDS (Head, 1930-34)
1929 - 1932	Capt. A. Harding, C.A. (seconded)
1916 -	Martyn Harries
1910?-	Gilbert Harris
1932 -	Miss W. Harris
1976 - 1977	Earle HAWKES (Missioner-Secretary)
1976 - 1977	Ruth Hawkes
1913 - 1916	Maude Heddy
1934 - 1937	John Henwood
1927 - 1929	Charles Hepworth
1920 - 1924	Edward Herbert
1899 - 1901	W. Hewett
1909 (6 months)	Mr. Hewitt
1914 -	Priscilla Hewu (A)
1907 -	H. Heyu (A)
1900 - 1904, 1935-38	Eustace HILL, C.R. (Head, 1935-38)
1916 - 1919, 1922-25,	Arthur HOBSON (also 1940-46, 1954-55)
1912 - 1914	E. Holden
1932 - 1934	Richard Holderness
1946 - 1949, 1950-53	Philip Holland (also 1959-60)
1910 -	Eirene Holmes
1932 - 1935	Muriel Hooper
1898 - 1899	A. Hopkins
1910 -	Thomas Hopkyns
1934 - 1937	Llewellyn Hughes
1953 - 1956	Richard Hughes
1937 - 1942	Harold Insley
1969 - 1972	James ISHERWOOD (Missioner-Secretary)
1936 - 1943, 1949-51	Monica JAMES
1966 - 1967	Albert Jenkins (last missioner in Zambia)
1915 - 1923	Canon R. Thornely JONES (Head, 1915-23)
1902 -	Benjamin Kaba (A)
1947 - 1950	Anthony Karney
1949 - 1950	Alexander Kesseck
1907 - 1908	Frederick Kinch
1961 - 1964	Richard Kirkham
1908?- 1909	Mr. Knapp-Fisher
1911 -	Samuel Kula (A)
1903 -	James Kutshwayo (A)
1928 -	John (Samuel) Kuze (A)
1936 -	Robert Kwaza (A)

1931 -	Peter Kynaston
1911 -	Walter Lack
1949 -	Stanley Lakaje (A)
1936 - 1951	Maurice LANCASTER (Head, 1938-51)
1935 - 1948	Winifred Lea
1896?-	James Leary
1934 - 1937	Donald Leavey
1937 - 1940	Arthur Lee
1897 - 1900	Ambrose Leefe
1914 -	Mr. Lejeune
1914 -	Mrs. Lejeune
1905 - 1908	Henry Lewis
1899 - 1902?	Edgar Lloyd (co-founder, Plumtree School)
1925 -	David Lolwana
1897 - 1904	Alfred Long
1952 - 1953	Samuel Long
1967 - 1970?	Eli Magava (A)
1911 - 1934 -?	Johannes Magxaka (A)
1943?- 1947?	Ben Mahanyele (A)
1911 -	James Makambi (A)
1967 -	Eli Magava (AP)
1939 -	Enos Makgana (A)
1897 - 1898	John Malton
1938 - 1944?	Nurse Violet Mama (A)
1949 -	Francis Marishane (A)
1909 - 1912	Nurse Marlande
1901 -	Kenneth Mather
1902 -	G. May
1914 -	Archibald Mbolikwa (A)
1939 - 1943	Douglas Mbopa (A) (Deacon)
1896/7 (briefly)	Jonas Mcangangwa (A) (First catechist)
1897?-	Hector McKenzie
1917 -	Miriam Mderka (A)
1931 - 1934	Frederick Mervyn
1917 -	David Mgeni (A)
1967 - 1973	John MHLABI (AP)
1971 - 1974, 1975 - 1976	John MICHIE (Missioner-Secr. 1972-74, 1975-6)
1971 - 1974, 1975 - 1976	Sally Michie
1941 - 1947	William Middleton
1951 - 1952	Leslie Millins
1924 -	David Mjezu (A)
1898 - 1899	Leonard Moxon
1920 -	David Mozeni (A)
1941 - 1944?	Nurse Mvula (A)
1920?-	Miriam Mdjesha(?) (A)
1933 - 1936	Everil Nash
1941 - 1950	Fred(erick) NAYLOR
1898 - 1907	Josiah NGCAMBU (A) (pioneer catechist)
1904 - 1908	Miss Nott-Bower
1907 -	Felix Nquka (A)
1941 -	Joseph Nuntsu (A)
1949 - 1952	John OLDHAM

1908 -	Miss Orwin
1957 - 1960	Hugh Palmer
1903 -	E. Parker
1938 - 1941	Helen Paterson
1924 - 1925	Mr. Paterson
1906 - 1909	Nurse PEARN (First CNA/SACRM nurse)
1921 - 1923	John Peppercorn
1927 - 1929	Arnold Pierce-Jones
1919 - 1927, 1930-?	Millicent Porter
1937 (9? months)	Charles Potts
1904 -	P. Preston-Thomas
1923 - 1929	Gladys Raikes
1926 - 1930	Humphrey Ram
1888 (briefly)	W. Ramsbottom (helping Simeon)
1908 - 1913	Kathleen Ramadge (=Sister Janet, SSJD)
1947 -	Molly Rand
1908 - 1911	Mark Rice
1900 - 1903	L. Richards
1927 - 1930	Mabel Richards
1931 - 1932	Mark Risdon
1954 - 1955	Lavinia Roberts (= Fidgin)
1909 -	Nurse Roberts
1925 - 1928	Reginald Robinson
1899 - 1915	Fred(erick) ROGERS (Head, 1912-15)
1947 - 1949	Rose Rogers
1923 - 1929	Harold ROLFE (Head, 1923-29)
1907 -	Nurse Ross
1915 - 1917 (-1919?)	Vernon Rossborough
1931 - 1938	Allen RUSBRIDGER
1905 -	Mr. Russell
1949 - 1956	Constance (Connie) Saunders (= Piers)
1928 - 1931	Tom Savage
1916 - 1918	Ralphe SEACOMBE
1930 - 1934	Edward Shennan
1921 - 1923, 1924 - 1929	Norah Short
1959 - 1967	William SIGECA (AP)
1885- 1892	Philip B. SIMEON (Originator of RM)
1960 - 1965	Constance Sims
1960 - 1965	Kenneth SIMS (Head, 1960-65)
1935 - 1938	Roy Sinker
1939 - 1942	Stephen Skemp
1898 - 1903, 1905 - 1912	Lawrence (Laurie) SKEY (+ Vice-Head)
1943 -	John Skomalo (A)
1928 - 1935	Barbara Smith
1920 - 1926	Edmund D. Smith
1924 - 1928	Edwin Smith
1931 -	E.R. Smith
1920 - 1926	Lucy Smith
1907 - 1911	Lionel Sparks
1920 - 1923, 1928 - 1931	Charles Stenson-Stenson
1928 - 1931	Jeanne Stenson-Stenson
1920 - 1923	Olive Stenson-Stenson

1937 - 1938	Frederika Stoker
1936 - 1938	Leslie Stoker
1947 - 1950	Gwen(doline) Stone (= Naylor)
1911 -	Samuel Susela (A)
1952 - 1955	Charles Sutton
1903 -	John Sutton
1917?-	F. Swithinbank
1930 - 1933	Francis Synge
1968 -	Johnson Tswatswa (A)
1939 - 1950	Paul Tembo (A)
1911 - 1912	R. Thomas
1914 - 1923?	George Thorne
1911 -	Jonathan Thukani (A)
1909 - 1912	Arthur Thurlow
1904 - 1908	Cecil Tomlinson
1906 -	James Toy
1929 - 1935, 1936-?	Clarice Trentham
1907 -	Abraham Tulwana (A)
1907 -	Henry Tyokom (A)
1909?-	Bernard Tyrwhitt-Drake
1905 - 1911	Robert Urquhart
1938 - 1946	Hilda Venables
1941 -	Sister Vermark
1930 - 1931	Magdalen Vickers
1956 - 1960	Derek Waldron
1956 - 1960	Dr. Jean Waldron
1895 - 1896?	William Wallace
1933 - 1936	Ernest Walls
1911 - 1914, 1924 - 1927	Nurse Wardale
1927 -	Louise Wardale
1907 - 1908	Miss Waring
1904 - 1905	John Warner
1901 -	Reginald Wathen
1910 - 1916	Miss Watson
1914 -	Edward Winnington-Ingram
1927 -	C. Wheeler
1931 -	Miss Wheeler
1930 - 1931	H. White
1947 - 1960	Lilah White
1934 - 1938, 1947 - 1960	Ray WHITE (Head, 1952 - 1960)
1949 - 1950	Percival Williams
1947 - 1949	W. Williams
1917 -	E. Willmott
1933 - 1936	Hugh Wilson
1941 - 1945	Edward Winckley
1928 - 1931	Frederick Wintle
1972 - 1973?	Ronald Woods
1904?	Herbert Wright
1904 -	William Xesi (A)

Appendix E: Anglicans on the sections

From time to time the Railway Mission staff would submit numbers of Anglicans or Anglican families who lived on their Sections and who were seen by the Mission. They did not include any Anglicans in places worked by parish clergy. Inevitably, given the frequent moving of railway employees, these numbers constantly changed, although not usually in any dramatic way. By 1957, when the Mission withdrew from South Africa, the numbers of Anglicans to whom it ministered in that country had fallen considerably. It has not been possible to discover, in archives or among former staff, any copy of the actual Returns given by the SACRM missioners. The account which follows was, fortunately, printed in the *Quarterly* in 1950, the only time (?) such a list was published. The numbers almost certainly refer to adult confirmed Anglicans, ie. excluding children:

'THE SOUTH AFRICAN CHURCH RAILWAY MISSION

Addenda to 1949-50 Report

Anglicans on the Sections

1. CAPE EASTERN SECTION

Naauwpoort, 40; Indwe, 50; Viedgesville, 5; Bityi, 4; Amabele, 20;
Debe Nek, 1; Sherborne, 6; Rosmead, 10; Bowkers Park, 1; Ida, 5; Halseton, 3;
Blaney, 4; Munyu, 5; Ryno, 2; Middeldrift, 4; Arundel, 2; Dohne, 8;
Kroomie, 10; Stormber, 2; Willmerton, 7; Tidburg's Toll, 5;
Lower Adamson, 4; Bailey, 5; Cookhouse, 20.

Showing a total of 221 Anglicans found in 43 places on a Section containing approximately 200 small stations and sidings, not counting places worked by parish clergy.

2. ORANGE FREE STATE AND WEST TRANSVAAL AND CAPE NORTHERN.
(Numbers here are of *families*.)

Sepani, 2; van Tonder, 1; Kerelaw, 1; Klip River, 1; Redan, 1; Marseilles, 2;
Vinies, 1; Kilmarnock, 1; Modderport, 2; Gumtree, 2; Kommandonek, 1;
Kransfontein, 1; Africa's Kop, 2; Aberfeldy, 3; Meets, 1; Kaalagte, 3.

Showing a total of 25 Anglican families at 24 places visited in the Orange Free State out of an approximate total of 190 sidings and stations, not counting those worked by parishes.

Coligny, 2; Lucerne, 3; Afrikaner, 5; Boons, 8; Vlakdrift, 1; Buckingham, 2;
Dronfield, 1; Goot Maciro, 7; Border, 1; Bank, 5; Wolmaransstad, 10.

Showing a total of 45 Anglican families at 24 places visited on the West Transvaal and Cape Northern Section out of a total of 145 sidings and stations not visited by the parish clergy.

3. MASHONALAND SECTION

Beira, 100; Ruwa and Melfort, 75; Marromeu, 25; Luabo, 25; Sherwood, 2; Umniati, 9; Imbizo, 3; Inhminga, 2; Odzi, 5; Marabada, 1; Makwiro, 3; Daisyfield, 4; Bembesi, 4; Heany, 26; Insiza, 8; Somabula, 13; Ntabazinduna,1

Showing a total of 306 Anglicans in 37 places visited on a Section containing approximately 83 sidings and stations, not counting those worked by parish clergy, and not counting the sidings and stations in P.E.A.

4. BECHUANALAND SECTION

Mahalapye, 65; Gaberones, 27; Lobatsi, 52; Serowe, 40; Notwani, 8; Ootsi, 3; Hildavale, 1; Khlale, 13; Palla Road, 4; Nata, 2; Maun, 12; Sehitwa, 1; Nockaneng, 7; Palapye, 8; Kazengula, 5; Kasane, 1; Serondellas, 1; Katima Mulilo, 7; Sesheke, 3; Mokoro, 4; Artesia, 4; Pisani, 2; Batoen, 3; Tsessebe, 8; Moeng, 6; Ratholo, 6.

Showing a total of 293 Anglicans in 40 places visited on this Section, not counting those worked by the parish clergy.

5. MATABELELAND SECTION

Wankie, 50; Entuba, 5; Tshontanda, 5; Thompson, 7; Victoria Falls, 40; Dett, 12; Kennedy, 2; Gwaai, 6; Matetsi, 4; Sawmills, 2; Malindi, 4; Mambanje, 6; Dibangombie, 8; Masuie, 3; Jafuta, 6; Igusi, 4; Ngamo, 8; Umgusa, 3; Zanguja, 6; Bushtick, 20; Essexvale, 45; Balla Balla, 4; Gwanda, 70; Colleen Bawn, 15; West Nicholson, 30.

Showing a total of 368 Anglicans at 30 places on a Section containing approximately 55 sidings and stations, not counting those worked by the parish clergy.

6. CAPE MIDLAND SECTION.

Coerney, 5; Bluecliff, 1; Glenconnor, 1; Middleton, 1; Commadagga, 4; Coega, 3; Alicedale, 17; Trappes Valley, 8; Eagles Crag, 15; Dassie Deur, 2; Cookhouse, 30; Barkly Bridge, 11; Zuurberg, 5; Doornkom, 7; Bushmans River, 6; Bethesda Road, 2; Gamtoos, 4; Assegailbosch, 3; Karreeview, 4; Joubetina, 16.

Total number of Anglicans 145, not counting those worked by the parish clergy.

7. NORTHERN RHODESIA SECTION

The figures for this Section are not to hand.

[Other evidence points to a figure of approximately 70-80 *families*, at 20-25 places visited on a Section containing 71sidings and stations.)

8. EASTERN TRANSVAAL SECTION

The figures for this Section are not to hand, and there is at present no Chaplain on this Section.'

(QP 171, 1950, 21-22)

Appendix F: Railway Mission Churches

In the same way that no definitive list exists for Railway Mission staff, there is none in existence for churches founded or built by the Mission. The nearest we have is a list in a letter sent by the Secretary of SACRM in South Africa, Mr. J.L. Durant, to his counterpart in London. The letter, dated 24th October, 1934, furnished Miss Brooks with names of churches 'under the charge' of the Mission. This of course is not identical with churches physically built by SACRM, although, in most cases cited in the letter, this had happened. The details below are based on information gleaned from the same sources used for the list of Mission staff, with a slightly greater use of letters written by individual missioners. There are very few copies of *Light for the Line* available in this country. A careful and exhaustive scrutiny of all the issues scattered in archives throughout southern Africa would, no doubt, furnish more names. The list below suggests that a possible total of between eighty and one hundred churches were actually built by the Mission.

Partners, in February 1971, stated that, 'one hundred and seventy parishes have been founded by the Railway Mission'. This seems a high total, but it could well be true. Certainly, the number of churches (ie. 'congregations') founded by the Mission is likely to be far greater than the number of church buildings they constructed. Frequently, parishes were handed over by SACRM to a diocese in advance of a building being erected and without a mention by name in the Mission's publications. Inevitably, after a number of years, the names of these places were forgotten in the collective memory of the Railway Mission. There is no doubt that very many Anglican churches throughout southern Africa, including one cathedral (Lusaka), owe a tremendous debt to the founding work of the Railway Mission.

(Where a church was listed as 'Native church' this is indicated by 'A' [African]. Some of the other churches, particularly where two are noted under the same name, may have been founded for African use).

Place	Dedication	Date of dedication (where known)
Addo	St. Luke	1895
Addo	?	1953?
Alicedale	St. Barnabas	1900?
Baddeley	St. Elizabeth	1960s
Balla Balla	?	1953
Bloemhof	St. Catherine	1917
Braamfontein Railway Camp	?	1927
Brits	St. Matthew	1933
Bronkhorstspruit	Holy Name of Jesus	1934
Cookhouse	?	1904 (A)
Cookhouse	St. Paul the Traveller	1905
Christiana	St Philip & St. James	1907
Darwendale	St. Cyprian	1960s
Delmas	St. John the Evangelist	1930
Dett	St. Christopher	1961
Esigodini	St. Mary	1951?
Essexvale	St. Michael and All Angels	1922 (A)?
Essexvale	St. Mary the Virgin	1923
Essexvale	?	1953

Figtree	St. Nathaniel	1927
Francistown	St. Patrick	1923?
Gaberones	?	1953?
Gatooma	?	1960s
Gwanda	St. Martin	1949
Gwelo	?	1960s
Hartley	?	1960s
Jansenville	St. Saviour	1899
Jansenville	St. Margaret	1902 (A)
Jumbo	?	1960s
Kafue	?	1962
Kalomo	St. Aidan	1959
Kamativi	?	1960s
Kliplaat	St. James	1910
Lobatsi	St. Mark	1936
Lochinvar	Christ the King	1953
Lusaka	All Saints [Later, cathedral]	1932
Lusaka	?	1936 (A)
Maryland	St. Luke	1960s
Mazabuka	?	1927?
Mazabuka	St. Anne	1959
Mazoe Mine	St. Cecilia	1960s
Monze	?	1958
Mount Hampden	St. Catherine	1960s
Naauwpoort	All Souls	1901
Naauwpoort	St. Agnes	1904 (A)
Norvals Pont	?	1899
Odzi	St. Philip	1960s
Paunseley	St. Mark	1960s
Raylton	St. Christopher	1961?
Rosmead	St. Luke	1926 (A)
Rosmead	St. Mark	1927
Rugare	St. Christopher	1960s
Sabie	St. Peter	post -1913
Sabie	St. Peter	1924 (A)
Sandflats	All Saints	1902
Schweizer Reneke	St. Ninian	1923
Silverton	All Saints	1925
Sterkstroom	?	1900
Steytlerville	St. Paul	1900
Summerville	?	1953?
Umferesi	?	1960s
Vereeniging	?	1904
Victoria Falls Hotel	(chapel)	1932
Vlakfontein	?	1904
Volksrust	?	1920s?
Wakkerstroom	?	1920s?
Wankie	?	1954
Warrenton	?	1938
Waterval Boven	All Saints	1905?
Waterval Boven	St. Bede	1933 (A)
Waterval Onder	?	?
West Nicholson	?	1945
Witbank	?	1904

Appendix G: Chaplains' Service Contract

The Chaplains and Women Workers signed a contract before they started as Railway Missioners. The Agreements, or Contracts, changed but slightly over the years. These changes were chiefly regarding 'stipend', 'initial allowance' and 'holidays'. The following is a typical example, from the 1920s:

1. <u>PERIOD OF SERVICE</u>	Three years from date of landing in South Africa to date of leaving.
2. <u>WORK</u>	Every chaplain is pledged to work wherever the Head of the Mission shall direct.
3. <u>STIPEND</u>	£96 per annum paid monthly and beginning from the date of arrival in South Africa. [£72 for Women Workers!]
4. <u>EXPENSES</u>	The Mission pays all expenses for travelling, Board, lodging, washing, Medical Expenses (Doctors' fees) and Dentistry (up to £5 in any one year); and any other expenses actually incurred in the work whilst in South Africa. Chaplains pay their own board and lodging while on holiday.
5. <u>INITIAL ALLOWANCE</u>	A sum of £50 is payable by the Mission on behalf of each new chaplain, to cover outfit allowance, cost of passage, rail fares, and incidental expenses on the voyage.
6. <u>BONUS</u>	At the completion of three years' service a chaplain is entitled to a bonus of £15 on his arrival in England. This does not apply if he is taking the furlough under Section 11.
7. <u>HOLIDAYS</u>	Two annual holidays of 34 days in each cycle of three years, to include not more than four Sundays. The first holiday to be arranged in consultation with the Head and not to be taken until after a full year's service. A free pass is available to any place on the railway in South Africa or Rhodesia so long as this privilege is granted by the authorities.
8. <u>RETURN PASSAGE</u>	On the completion of a full three years' service a chaplain is entitled to a return passage from Capetown to London at the rate of Third Class on the Mail.
9. <u>TERMINATION OF AGREEMENT</u>	Three months' notice on either side is required to break this agreement.
10. <u>RESIGNATION</u>	Should a chaplain leave the Mission (except on account of illness or a reason satisfactory to the Head) before completing eighteen months' service, he shall refund to the Mission a proportion of the initial allowance; and should he not complete three years' service he has no claim on the Mission for return passage money.
11. <u>FURLOUGH</u>	Should a chaplain on completion of the three years' service undertake to rejoin the Mission for a further three years he is entitled to a six months furlough. During his furlough he will be paid at the rate of £15 a month [£12.10s for Women] on condition that he returns to South Africa, and provided he is willing to do deputation work if called upon. Should he, however, fail to return after drawing furlough pay, the amount of deputation work undertaken by him on behalf of the Mission will be considered in arriving at the amount repayable by him. ....(signed.......)

BIBLIOGRAPHY

MANUSCRIPT SOURCES

Archives

(i) Rhodes House Library, Oxford
a) USPG 'X' Series:

X1441/1 Grahamstown Diocesan Railway Mission (various 'Ellison' papers; Quarterly Letters)
X1441/1 f4 Thornley-Jones [Thornely Jones] correspondence
X1441/1 f5 Ellison Papers
X1441/1 f10 (RS) Seacombe Letters, (1916-18)
X1146 (AR) Rusbridger Diaries (1932-4, 1937)

b) Colonial Nursing Association (Overseas Nursing Association)
MSS. Brit. Emp. s 400: Letters, Papers and Articles. (ONA Box 120, etc)

(ii) Cory Library for Historical Research (Archives of the Diocese of Grahamstown), Rhodes University Library, Grahamstown

Berning, J.M. 'Local History: taking the documents to the people.' *SA. Archives Journal*, 29 (1987): 23-31
Cory Library MS 14 886: Registers of Baptisms performed by SACRM missioners in the Diocese of Grahamstown, 8.11.1885 - 18.9.1955 (5 vols)
Cory Library MS 14 887/1: Registers of Burials performed by SACRM missioners in the Diocese of Grahamstown, 10.4.1901 - 3.4.1937(1 vol)
Cory Library MS 14 887/1-3: Registers of Marriages performed by SACRM missioners in the Diocese of Grahamstown, 25.12.1901- 11.6.1940 (3 vols)
Cory Library MS 16811: SACRM Letters and Papers

iii) Appleton Roebuck (York Diocese)
Parish Registers 1853-1994

(iv) Census Returns 1871 Hawes

(v) Plumtree School Archives, Zimbabwe: Documents, Letters, photos

(vi) University of the Witwatersrand, Johannesburg (CPSA Archives)
AB 940 WITS/CPSA: SACRM correspondence etc. (1935-1949)

(vii) Bulawayo Railway Museum, Zimbabwe: Railway Mission Archives.

(viii) Bulawayo Cathedral (Diocesan Office), Zimbabwe:
Anglican Church Archives (Ref. GMP:Railway Mission).

Private (Originals with author, except where indicated otherwise)

Agg-Large, M. Letter re. her work with SACRM, plus family correspondence.Letter (1995)
Barrow, J. Letter (1995) re. SAR&H CU Railway Mission. [D. Littley]
Charlton, D. Letters to author.

Crane, H. Letters to and from him as Missioner/Secretary
Letters to author.
Deacon, G Account re the final years of the Mission.
Easter, S. Many letters to author re SACRM work.
Fidgin, L. Letters to author.
Fidgin, M. Letters to and from him as Chairman of London Committee.
Letters to author.
Garnett, P. 'Some Recollections of a Railway Missioner'. (19 pp., 1984)
'African work on the Railway Mission'.
Letters to author.
Hale, H.P. 'Letters from South Africa': Bound letters of Herbert Hale (1903-06). [Mrs. F.Folliott]
'South African Reminiscences'. [Mrs. F. Folliott]
Hawkes, E. Part (70 pp) of draft MMS of biography, relating to 1976/7 - his work on the Railway Mission.; autobiob. 'The Wonder of Divine Influence', 1995
Letters to author.
Holderness, R. Letter (1985) re. his time with SACRM.
Account to author, 1995.
Holland, P. Letters (1946) [Rev. Dr. I.R. Phelps]
Hughes, R. 'SACRM June 1953 - July 1956'. (Account to author, 1994)
Isherwood, J. 'One memorable afternoon and evening'. (Letter, 1971)
James, M. Letters re. her work on SACRM.
'Livingstone Parish Log Book' [D. Whitehead]
Mercer, Bishop R. Correspondence with author.
Millins, L. Letters to and from (1950s).
Correspondence with author.
Simms, K. Last letter as Head (July 1965).
Sinker, R. 'SACRM Jan. 1935 - Jan. 1938'. (Full account, 1984)
Skemp, S.R. 'SACRM - 50 years ago'. (Account to author, 1992)
Stella, Sister Mary, CSP. Letters (1992/3) re. her SACRM work
White, R. 'Memoirs of the last Head of the original South African Church Railway Mission and the first Head of the Rhodesia and Nyasaland Railway Mission'. (20 pp. account, 1980)

PRINTED SOURCES

Primary Sources

(i) Reports

Cape Town Railway Mission (CTRM) 'Notice', March, 1942
Rhodesia & Nyasaland Royal Commission Report (Bledisloe Commission), (London, 1939)
Rhodesia: Report of the Commission on Rhodesian Opinion (Pearce Commission), (London, 1972)

(ii) Periodicals and Newspapers

Central Africa U.M.C.A periodicals (various)
Morning Post (June 1915)
Grahamstown Diocesan Railway Mission (various), 1894f
Partners (The Journal of the Transvaal, Zimbabwe and Botswana Association) (various)
Rhodesian Railway Review (various)

Sitima (Rhodesia Railways (African) Newspaper) (various)
South African Church Railway Mission. *Quarterly Paper* (various) (= *QP*.)(and successors to SACRM)
South African Church Railway Mission. *Light for the Line* (various) (= *LL* .)
S.A. Railways & Harbours Magazine 1918, 1924, 1926, 1927, 1967.
Transvaal & Southern Rhodesia Missions (T&SRM) *Partners* (various)

(iii) Railway Mission Publications

a) **Books and leaflets** (chronological order)

1918 *A Short History of the South African Church Railway Mission* (11 pp.)
n.d.(1920s?)(2nd. revn. 1941) *Manual of Prayers* (29 pp.)
1925? *The Need* (4 pp.)
1925? *The Purpose* (4 pp.)
1925 *In Journeyings Often* (32 pp.) (Brief impressions from the letters of SACRM workers 1885-1925)
1929 *Simple Lessons in Preparation for Confirmation* (L. Hands) (35 pp.) (Based on the Church Catechism)
1930 *God's Highwaymen* (Dorothy Ellison) (159 pp.) (Story of SACRM) (2nd edn. 1931; 3rd edn. 1938)
1931 *Along the Line* (R.F. Beer) (SACRM Play) (Cyclostyled)
1934 *He that Seeketh Findeth*: 'A Railway Mission ABC' (16 pp.) (In the form of a catechism)
1935 *Up the Line with the Railway Mission* (28 pp.) (The work of SACRM)
1938-42 Series of six 4 pp. leaflets about SACRM work:-
No.1 [title unknown)
No.2 'The Mission in PEA and Eastern S. Rhodesia'
No.3 'And what about the Money?'
No.4 'Up in the North'
No.5 'A Woman Worker's Job'
No.6 'The Mission in the E. Transvaal'
1939 [Cookery Book]
1941 (and revns.) *The Line Book* (127 pp.) (Order for Matins, Evensong, Holy Communion, etc., + Hymns + Alternative Liturgy)
1954 (revn. 1955) *The Happy Travellers* (24 pp.) (Brief history + stories of missioners in 1950s) Compiled by Monica James
n.d. *The Romance of Train Travel in Southern Africa* (Folded leaflet)
1959 *Your Travelling Church* (R&NRM) (Folded leaflet)

b) Periodicals and Miscellaneous

Annual Reports (GDRM and SACRM)
GDRM *Children's Letter*
GDRM *Monthly Letter*
GDRM *Quarterly*
Letters from the Line (Children's Quarterly)
Light for the Line [= *LL*]
Prayer Leaflet (Loose, inside *QP*)
Quarterly Paper ('The Blue Quarterly') [= *QP*]
[The News Sheet] (GDRM)
(Plus occasional leaflets)

Secondary Sources

(i) Books and Articles

Anstey, R. *Britain and the Congo in the Nineteenth Century* (Oxford, 1962)
Baeta, C.G. (ed.) *Christianity in Tropical Africa* (Oxford, 1968)
Baeta, C.G. 'Missionary and humanitarian interests, 1914-1960', in Duigan, & Gann, L.H. (eds) *Colonialism in Africa 1870-1960* , Vol.2, (Cambridge, 1970, 422-49)
Bailey, J.R.A *Zimbabwe: The Search for Common Ground* (Drum; Harare, 1992)
Barnes, J.C. 'The Beira-Mashonaland Railway', *Rhodesiana*, Vol. XXXVII, pt.5, (1977)
Baxter, E.C. 'The Church's Missions amongst white settlers in South Africa', *Pan-Anglican Papers*, SE. 1(c) (London, 1908)
Baynes, A.H. *Handbooks of English Church Expansion: South Africa* (London, 1908)
Beer, Rev.R.F. *Along the Line* (SACRM Play (unpub.), 1930)
Beidelman, T.O. *Colonial Evangelism: A Socio-Historical Study of an East African Mission at the Grassroots* (Bloomington, 1982)
Berger, F. *Silozi-English Dictionary* (3rd editn. Jalla, A) (Sefula, Zambia, 1970)
Blood, A.G. *The History of the Universities' Mission to Central Africa*, Vols.II, III (UMCA, London, 1957, 1962)
Bolink, *Towards Church Union in Zambia* (Sneek, 1967)
(The) *Book of Common Prayer* (BCP 1662/1922), (London, 1926)
Botswana-Zambia Transportation Survey (URS Research Co. for US/AID, San Mateo, 1970)
Brook, D. *The Railway Navvy* (Newton Abbot, 1983)
Butler, J. 'Review Article: Cecil Rhodes', *The International Journal of African Historical Studies*, x, 2 (1977), 259-281
Carter, D.J. 'The Railway Mission - Regina', *Journal of the Canadian Historical Society*, X, No.4 (Dec. 1968), 202-216
Carter, D.J. 'The Archbishops' Western Canada Fund and the Railway Mission', *Saskatchewan History*, XXII, No.1, (Winter 1969), 13-28
Chadwick, O. *The Victorian Church*, Part II (London 1972)
Charles, J.L. 'Zambia Rail Situation', *Canadian Geographical Journal* , Vol.75, 1967, 207-17
(The) *Churchman's Missionary Atlas* (SPG, London, 1908)
Clarke, M. *The Plumtree Papers* (Bulawayo, 1983)
Colclough, C. & McCarthy S. *The Political Economy of Botswana* (Oxford, 1980)
Coleman, T. *The Railway Navvies* (London, 1965)
Collin, B.M. *J. Hornung: A family portrait* (Orpington, 1970)
Comaroff, J. & J. 'Through the Looking-glass: Colonial Encounters of the First Kind.' *Journal of Historical Sociology,* Vol. 1, No. 1 (March 1989)
Comaroff, J. & J. 'The Colonization of Consciousness in South Africa.' *Economy and Society*, Vol. 18, No. 3 (Aug. 1989)
Crockford ('Crockford's Clerical Directory') (London, 1924, and various)
Croxton, A.H. *Railways of Zimbabwe* (Newton Abbot, 1973/1982)
Curtis, S.J. & Boultwood, M.F.A. *An Introductory History of English Education since 1800* (London, 1962)
Dachs, A. *The Road to the North - The Origin and Force of a Slogan* (Central Africa Historical Association, Local Series 23, 1969)
Dachs, A. 'Missionary Imperialism - The Case of Bechuanaland.' *JAH*, 13 (4), (1972)
Dalrymple Hay, M.E. 'The Colonial Association Nurse', *The Nursing Times*, (Nov.5, 1910), 919
Davies, R.H. *Capital, State & White Labour in South Africa 1900-1960* (Brighton, 1979)
Day, J.R. *Railways of Southern Africa* (London, 1963).
de Gruchy, J.W. *The Church Struggle in South Africa* (Grand Rapids, 1986)

Delius, P. 'From Refuge to Resistance: Botshabelo, Mafolofolo and Johannes Dinkwanyane: Missionaries and Converts under the authority of the Zuid-Afrikaansche Republiek, 1860-1876.' *Working Papers in Southern African Studies*, Vol.III (ed. Hindson, D.C.) (1983)

Dictionary of South African Biography (4 vols) (Pretoria, 1968-81)

Donaldson, M. 'The Voluntary Principle in the Colonial Situation: Theory and Practice.' *Studies in Church History*, Vol. 23 (ed. Sheils & Wood) (1986)

du Plessis, J. *History of Christian Missions in South Africa* (London, 1911)

Elliot-Binns, L.E. *Religion in the Victorian Era* (London, 1946)

Ellison, D.F. *God's Highwaymen: The Story of the South African Church Railway Mission* (London, 1930)

Ellison, Douglas. *The Pioneer work of the Church* (SPCK Tract, Pan-Anglican Congress, 1908) (London, 1909)

Enklaar, I.H. *Life and Work of Dr. J.Th. Van der Kemp 1747-1811* (Cape Town, 1988)

Fairbridge, K. *The Story of Kingsley Fairbridge* (Oxford, 1927)

Fields, K. 'Christian Missionaries as Anticolonial Militants.' *Theory & Society* (II) (1982)

Freeman-Grenville, G.S. *Chronology of African History* (Oxford, 1973)

Gilbert, A.D. *Religion and Society in Industrial England* (London, 1976)

Goldblatt, I. *History of South West Africa* (Cape Town, 1971)

Goodwin, H. *Memoir of Bishop Mackenzie* (London, 1864)

Grain, A.E. *Mission Unaccomplished* (Lingfield, 1985)

Gray, C.N. *Life of Robert Gray* (London, 1883)

Gray, R. *The Two Nations* (London, 1960)

Gray, R. *Black Christians and White Missionaries* (London, 1990)

Groves, C. *The Planting of Christianity in Africa*, vols I- III(London, 1948-1955)

Hansen, K.T. *Distant Companions: Servants and employers in Zambia*, 1900-1985 (Ithaca, 1989)

Hastings, A. *A History of African Christianity, 1950-1975* (Cambridge, 1979)

Head, J. 'Sena Sugar Estates and migrant labour', *Mozambique* (Edinburgh, Seminar, 1978; 47-77)

Hellig, J. 'The Jewish Community in South Africa', in Prozesky, M. & de Gruchy, J. (eds) *Living Faiths in South Africa* (London, 1995, 155-76)

Henkel, R. *Christian Missions in Africa* (Geographica Religionum. Band 3) (Berlin, 1989)

Heydenrych, D.H. 'Indian Railway Labour in Natal, 1876-1895', *Historia* Vol.31, 1986, 11-20

Hinchliff, *The Anglican Church in South Africa* (London, 1963)

Hinchliff, *John William Colenso* (London, 1964)

Hinchliff, 'Voluntary Absolutism: British Missionary Societies in the Nineteenth Century.' *Studies in Church History* Vol. 23 (ed. Sheils & Wood) (1986)

Holland, F. *The Steam Locomotives of the South African Railways, 1859-1910* (Cape Town, 1971)

Holland, H. Scott. *A Bundle of Memories* (London, 1915)

Hotel and Boarding House Guide, South African Railways (Johannesburg, 1921)

Huddleston, Father T, C.R. *Naught for your comfort* (London, 1956)

Inglis, B. *Roger Casement* (London, 1973)

Isaacman, A.F. & Isaacman, B. *The Tradition of Resistance in Mozambique* (London, 1976)

Isaacman, A.F. & Isaacman, B. *Mozambique: from Colonialism to Revolution, 1900-1982* (Boulder, 1983)

Isichei, F. *A History of Christianity in Africa* (London, 1995)

Jeal T. *Baden-Powell* (London, 1989)

Jeffries, R. *Class, Power and Ideology in Ghana: The Railwaymen of Sekondi* (Cambridge, 1978)

Kanduza, A.M. *The Political Economy of Underdevelopment in Northern Rhodesia, 1918-1960* (New York, n.d.)

Kapenzi, G.Z. *The Clash of Cultures: Christian Missionaries and the Shona of Rhodesia* (Washington, 1979)
Katzenellenbogen, S.F. *Railways and the Copper Mines of Katanga* (Oxford, 1973)
Keller, J.W. 'The Progress of the R.R.W.U. : Reminiscences', *Rhodesian Railway Review* (Jan. 1929, 18-21)
Kennedy, D. *Islands of White: settler society and culture in Kenya and Southern Rhodesia* (Durham, 1987)
Kingsford, W. *Victorian Railwaymen* (London, 1970)
Kruger, B. *The Pear Tree Blossoms*: A History of the Moravian Mission Stations in South Africa 1737-1869 (Genadendal, 1966)
Latourette, K.S. *A History of the Expansion of Christianity:* Vol.V. 'The Great Century' (New York, 1943)
Lewis, C. & Edwards, G.E. (eds.), *Historical Records of the Church of the Province of South Africa* (London, 1934)
Lloyd, R. *The Church of England* 1900-1965 (London, 1966)
Lovett, R. *The History of the London Missionary Society, 1795-1895* (Vol.I) (London, 1899)
MacGill, *Children of the Dead End* (1914, & London, 1983)
Maclaren, I.(ed) *Some Renowned Rhodesian Senior Schools, 1892-1979*. (Plumtree School, 211-225) (Bulawayo, 1981)
Macmillan, W.M. *Bantu, Boer, and Briton* (Oxford, 1963)
Mansfield, C. *Via Rhodesia* (London, 1910?)
Martelli, G. *Leopold to Lumumba: A History of the Belgian Congo 1877-1960* (London, 1962)
Maylam, R. 'The Making of the Kimberley-Bulawayo Railway:a Study in the Operations of the British South Africa Company', *Rhodesian History* (1977), 8, 13-33
McCracken, J. *Politics and Christianity in Malawi* (Cambridge, 1977)
McKenna, F. *The Railway Workers 1840-1970* (London, 1980)
Michell, Hon.Sir Lewis, 'The Cape to Cairo Railway', *Journal of the Society of Arts*, No.2822, Vol.LV, (Dec.21, 1906)
Mother Cecile in South Africa (By a Member of the Community of the Resurrection of our Lord, Grahamstown), (London, 1930)
'NZASM 100' (ed. De Jong, et al) *The Buildings, Steam Engines and Structures of the Netherlands South African Railway Company* (Pretoria, 1988)
Nock, O.S. *Railways of Southern Africa* (London, 1971)
Oliver, R. *The Missionary Factor in East Africa* (London, 1965)
Page, B.T. *The Harvest of Good Hope* (London, 1947)
Pakenham, T. *The Scramble for Africa* (London, 1991)
Palmer, M. *The History of the Indians in Natal* (Cape Town, 1957)
Parker, J. *Rhodesia: Little White Island* (London, 1972)
Parsons, N. & Crowder,M. (eds.) *Monarch of all I Survey* (Bechuanaland Diaries 1929-37 of Sir Charles Rey) (Gaborone, 1988)
Paul, J. 'Revolution and quietism: the Anglican experience in Mozambique', *Mozambique* (Edinburgh, Seminar, 1978, 32-45)
Pauling, G. *The Chronicles of a Contractor* (Bulawayo, 1926/1969)
Pavey, A.E. *The Story of the Growth of Nursing* (London, 1951)
Perkin, H. *The Age of the Railway* (London, 1970)
Phimister, I.R. 'The Shamva Mine Strike of 1927: An African Proletariat', *Rhodesian History*, 11 (1971), 65-88
Phimister, I.R. 'Towards a History of Zimbabwe's Railways', *Zimbabwean History* (1981), XII. 71-99
Phimister, I.R. *An Economic and Social History of Zimbabwe, 1890-1948* (London, 1988)
Pirie, G.H. *Aspects of the Political-Economy of Railways in Southern Africa* (Johannesburg, 1982)

Pirie, G.H. 'Towards an Historical Geography of Missions in Nineteenth Century South Africa', *South African Geographical Journal* Vol.67, No.1, 1985
Pirie, G.H. 'White Railway labour in South Africa, 1873-1924', in Morrell, R (ed.), *White but Poor* (Pretoria, 1992), 101-114
Pirie, G.H. 'Railway ganging in southern Africa, c.1900-37', *Journal of Transport History* vol.14(1), 1993, 64-76
Pollock, N.H. *Nyasaland and Northern Rhodesia: Corridor to the North* (Pittsburgh, 1971)
Ranger, T.O. *The African Churches of Tanzania* (Nairobi , [1967?], 3)
Ranger, T.O. 'Protestant Mission in Africa', in Blakely, T.D., van Beek, W.E.A. & Thomson, D.L. (eds) *Religion in Africa* (London, 1994, 275-313)
Ransford, O. *Bulawayo: Historic Battleground of Rhodesia* (Cape Town, 1968)
Rotberg, R.I. *Christian Missionaries and the Creation of Northern Rhodesia, 1880-1924* (Princeton, 1965 a.)
Rotberg, R.I. *The Rise of Nationalism in Central Africa:The Making of Malawi & Zambia, 1973-1964* (Harvard, 1965 b.)
(SACRM) *A Staff Vade Mecum* (London, 1949)
Sanneh, L. 'The Yogi and the Commissar: Christian Missions and the African Response.' *International Bulletin of Missionary Research*, Vol. 15, No. 1 (Jan. 1991)
Schapera, I. (ed.) *David Livingstone. Family Letters 1841-56* Vol.1 (1841-48) (London, 1959)
Searle, C. *The History of the Development of Nursing in South Africa, 1652-1960* (Cape Town, 1965)
Sibley, J.R. *Tanganyika guerilla: East African campaign 1914-18* (Pan/Ballantine History of First World War: Book 4, London, 1973 ed/n)
Simeon, P.B. 'Reminiscences', *Light for the Line*, (SACRM) (Johannesburg, April, 1925)
Smit, P. 'Botswana Railway Line', *Bulletin of the Africa Institute of South Africa*, Vol.8, 1970, 273-81
Smith, A.K. 'Antonio Salazaar and the Reversal of Portuguese Colonial Policy.' *JAH*, XV, 4 (1974), 653-667
Sundkler, B. *The Christian Ministry in Africa* (London, 1960)
Swaisland, C. 'Nineteeth-Century Recruitment of Single Women to Protestant Missions' in Bowie, F., Kirkwood, D. & Ardener, S. (eds), *Women and Missions: Past and Present* (Oxford, 1993), 70-84
Taylor, J. *Christianity & the Natives of South Africa: A Year Book of South African Missions* (Lovedale, 1928)
Tennant, Sir D. 'The Railway System of South Africa', *Proceedings of the Royal Colonial Institute*, 1898, Vol.29. 3-30
Tooley, S.A. *The History of Nursing in the British Empire* (London, 1906)
Turner, A, 'The Growth of Railway Unionism in the Rhodesias, 1944-1955' in Sandbrook, R, & Cohen, R. (eds), *The Development of an African Working Class* (London, 1975, 73-98)
Vail, L. 'The Making of an Imperial Slum: Nyasaland and its Railways, 1895-1935', *JAH*, XVI, 1 (1975), 89-112
Vail, L. 'Mozambique's Chartered Companies: The Rule of the Feeble', *JAH*, XVII, 3 (1976), 389-416
Vail, L. (ed.) *The Creation of Tribalism in Southern Africa* (London, 1989)
Vail, L. & White, L. *Capitalism and Colonialism in Mozambique: A Study of Quelimane District* (London, 1980)
Van Onselen, C. 'The 1912 Wankie Colliery Strike', *JAH*, XV, 2 (1974), 275-289
Van Velsen, J. (Forward to) *The Life of a Zambian Evangelist* (Lusaka, 1973)
Varian, H.F. *Some African Milestones* (Bulawayo, 1953, 1973)
Vaughan, M. *Curing their Ills: Colonial Power and African Illness* (Oxford, 1991)

Verstraelen-Gilhuis, G. *From Dutch Mission Church to Reformed Church in Zambia* (Franeker, 1982)
Verstraelen-Gilhuis, G. *A New look at Christianity in Africa* (Gweru, 1992)
Vickery, 'The Railway Mission', *Heritage* (Zimbabwe), Vol.I, 1981, 25-31
Vickery, K.P. 'The Rhodesia Railways African Strike of 1945, I, II', *JSAS*, 24, 3 (1998), 545-560; 25, 1 (1999), 49-71
Villa-Vicencio, C. *Trapped in Apartheid* (New York, 1988)
Villa-Vicencio, C. 'Mission Christianity', in Prozesky, M. & de Gruchy, J. (eds) *Living Faiths in South Africa* (London, 1995, 45-71)
Webb, A.B. *Sisterhood Life and Women's Work* (London, 1883)
Weinthal, L.(ed)., *The Story of the Cape to Cairo Railway & River Route. 1887-1922* Vol 2 (London, 1922)
Weller, J.C. *The Priest from the Lakeside* (Blantyre, 1971)
White, L. *Magomero: Portrait of an African Village* (Cambridge, 1987)
White, L. *Bridging the Zambesi* (Basingstoke, 1993)
Wilkinson, A. *The Community of the Resurrection: A Centenary History* (London, 1992)
William, G. & Hackland, B. *The Dictionary of Contemporary Politics of Southern Africa* (London, 1988)
Wilson, M. 'Missionaries: Conquerors or Servants of God?' *South African Outlook* (March, 1976)
Working Timetable, No. 43, The Rhodesia Railways, Limited, (Bulawayo, Sept. 1943)

(ii) Theses

Lunn, J.R. *Capital and Labour on the Rhodesian Railway System* (unpubl. Ph.D Thesis, Oxford University, 1986)
Purkiss, A.J. *The Politics, Capital and Labour of Railway Building in the Cape Colony, 1870-1885* (unpubl. Ph.D Dissertation, Oxford University, 1978)

AUDIO-VISUAL SOURCES

Railway Mission A-V (In chronological order)

1902 [Railway Mission Map of South Africa]
1902f [(Annual) Wall Almanack]
1903? a) Set of official SACRM Postcards (some reprinted in 1940s) -
- 'Chaplain visiting isolated station and lonely gangers' cottages in Mission Coach [the first one, No. 404] attached to goods train'
- 'Altar of railway sleeper, the ganger the one communicant in the "bush" alongside Line, Rhodesia'
- 'The New Mission Coach' [CGR No.404, plus three chaplains]
- ?} (Number and subjects of other cards is
- ?} not known)

b) Set of South African Postcards, stamped 'S.A.C.R.M' -
- 'Mail Cart'
- 'A Railway Baby'
- 'Wild Arums'
- (possible other cards)

c) Set of '25 Picture Postcards' [noted in QP37, 1912] possibly same as (b)

1905? [Slides from H. Hale's photographs]

1934	[8 mm. SACRM film] (Maude Agg-Large) (3 - 4 mins.)
1954	Filmstrip, *The Travelling Church* (B/W) (M. Fidgin)
1954	8 mm. Film, *The Travelling Church* (Col.) Silent +Script [alt.tape-recording] 29 mins. (M. Fidgin) (Filmed in 1953); (Later) Another copy with sound (Zonastripe) (R&NRM, ie. post-1957)
1961	16 mm. Film, *The Travelling Church* (Col.) Silent, 28 mins. (A different film from the 1954 film with same title) (M. Fidgin); (Copy II) (1967) Sound added
1968	16 mm. Film, *The Church in a Changing World* (Col.) Sound, 25 mins. (M. Fidgin)

(Items in square brackets - not seen by writer; not known if still existent. Other items - held by writer)

Oral Sources

Fidgin, Michael	May 1991	Interview
Folliott, Mrs. F.	March 1992	Interview
Garnett, Peter	Feb. 1992	Interview/Recording
James, Monica	Mar. 1992,	Aug. 1995 Interviews
Naylor, Fred	Jan. 1992	Interview/Recording
Nyenhuis, Dick	}	
Thompson, Murray	}Apr. 1992	Interviews/Recording
Palmer, Hugh	Oct. 1994	Interview
Piers, Constance	Sept. 1992	Interview
Sigeca, Willie	Aug. 1993	Interview/Recording

Other Audio-Visual

[(Associated Television) Film of RM work in Rhodesia, Dec. 1962 (Shown in UK)]
'Cape Town to the Lost City': *Great Railway Journeys*, BBC TV film, 1994 (Rian Malan)
[*In Town Tonight* BBC Broadcast July/Aug. 1953 (Ray White)]
Missionaries: No. 2 (Africa). BBC TV film, 1990 (Julian Pettifer)
The Civilisation of Africa, B/W Film, (1929 trip from Cape Town to Cairo)
'The Congo': *River Journeys*, No.1. BBC TV film, 1984 (Michael Wood)
'The Idea of Empire': *Arena*. BBC TV film, 1992 (Edward Said) (Includes 1905 Pathe newsreel of railway navvying in Southern Africa)
'Zambezi Express'; *Great Railway Journeys of the World*, No.3. BBC TV film, 1979 (Michael Wood)

Index

The index relates only to the general text, and not to the Appendices.
Clergy titles are those used for the bulk of an individual's time connected with the Railway Mission.